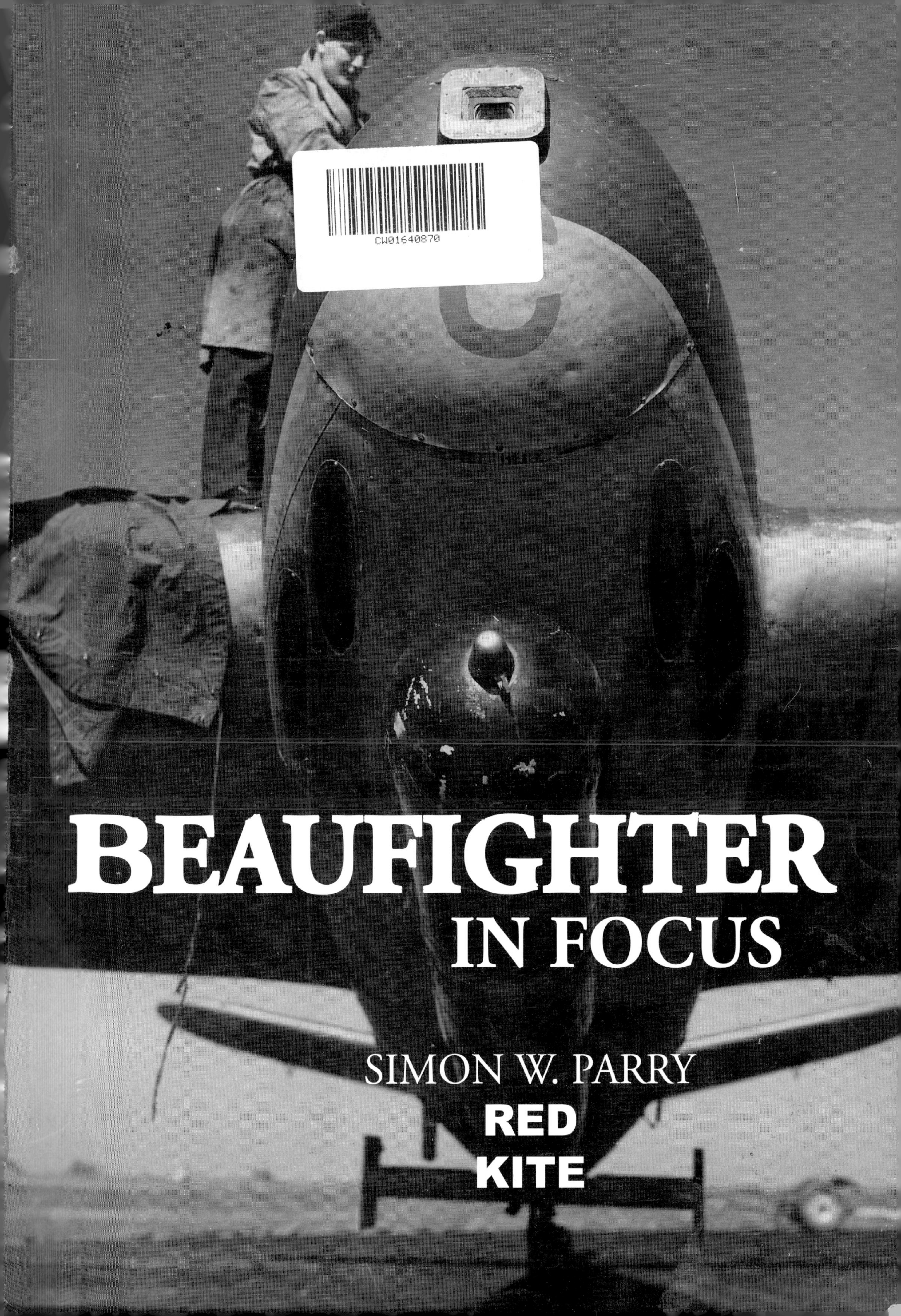

BEAUFIGHTER
IN FOCUS

SIMON W. PARRY

RED KITE

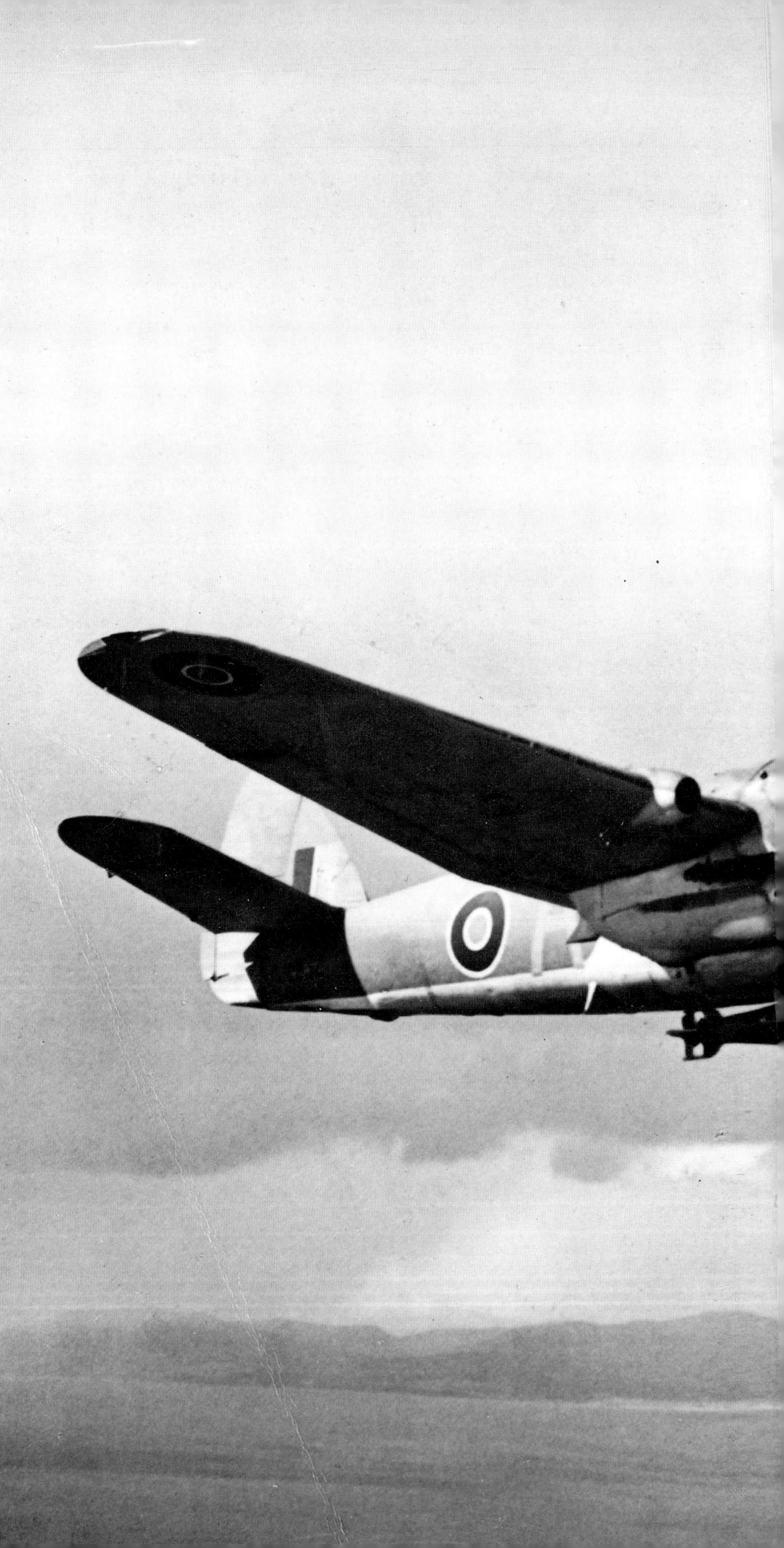

First published 2002 by
Red Kite
PO Box 223,
Walton on Thames
Surrey, KT12 3YQ

Printed in Malta by
Interprint.

ISBN 0-9538061-2-X

Contents

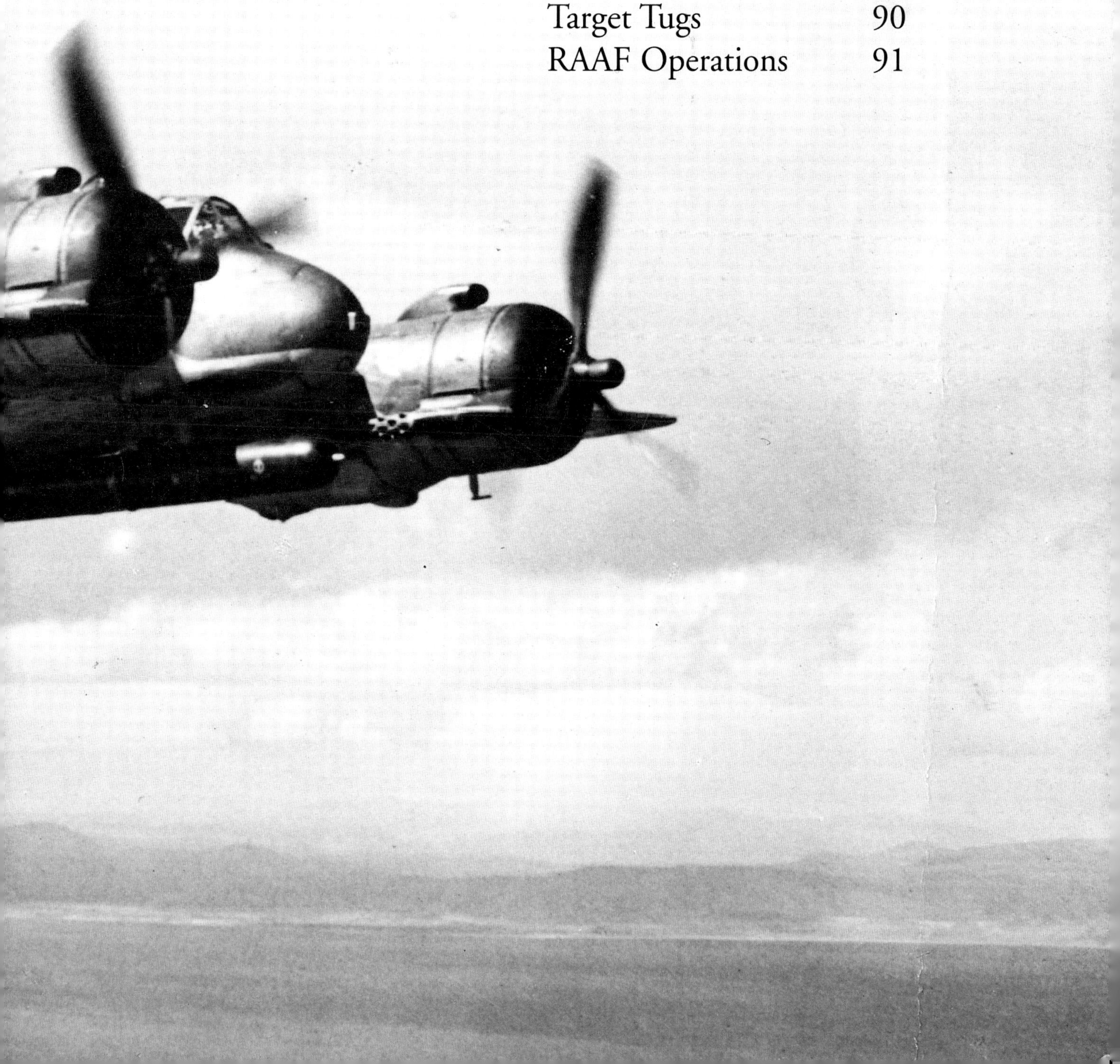

[illegible]graphy

Aces High - C Shores & C Williams
Beaufighter at War - Chaz Bowyer
Beaufighters over Burma - David J Innes
The Blitz - Then and Now - Winston Ramsey (Ed.)
Bristol Aircraft since 1910 - C H Barnes
Bristol Beaufighter - Victor Bingham
Bristol Beaufighter Profile - Philip J R Moyes
British Military Aircraft Serials - Bruce Robertson
Camouflage & Markings - Philip J R Moyes
Famous Fighter Aces - Bryan Philpott
Fighter Command Losses - Norman Franks
Intruders over Britain - Simon W Parry
RAF Aircraft Serial logs - Air Britain
RAF Squadrons - W/Cdr C G Jefford MBE
Squadron Codes 1937-56 - M J F Bowyer & J D R Rawlings
The Squadrons of the Royal Air Force - J J Halley
The Strike Wings - Roy C Nesbit
Twenty-one Squadrons - Leslie Hunt

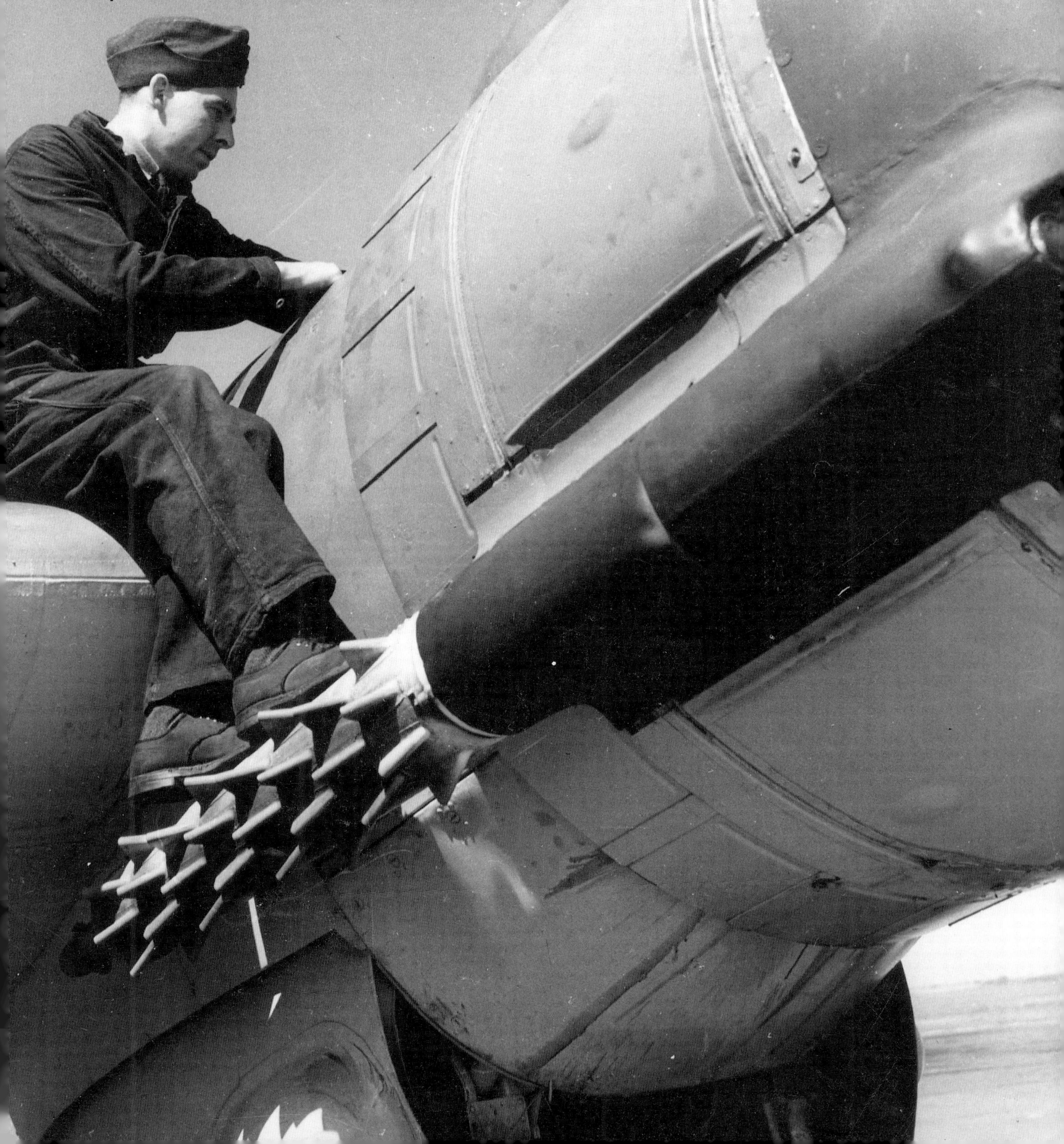

Production Batches

R2052 - R2055 (4 prototypes)
R2056 - R2057 (2 Mk.If)
R2058 (1 Mk.IIf prototype)
R2059 - R2060 (2 Mk.If)
R2061 - R2062 (2 Mk.IIf prototypes)
R2063 - R2269 (139 Mk.If)
R2274 Mk.V prototype
R2270 - R2479 (15 Mk.IIf)

T3009 - T3227 (150 Mk.IIf)
T3228 - T3355 (82 Mk.Ic)
T3356 - T3389 (72 Mk.IIf)
T4623 - T4647 (25 Mk.If)
T4648 - T5099 (300 Mk.Ic)
T5100 - T5352 (175 Mk.VIc)

V8131 - V8218 (75 Mk.IIf)
V8219 - V8385 (125 Mk.If)
V8386 - V8901 (400 Mk.VIf)

X7540 - X7541 (2 Mk.If)
X7542 - X7543 (2 Mk.VI Prototypes)
X7544 - X7879 (236 Mk.I)
X7880 - X7924 (25 Mk.VIf)
X7925 (1 Mk.VIc)
X7926 - X7936 (14 Mk.VIf)
X7937 - X7939 (3 Mk.VIc)
X7940 - X8029 (50 Mk.VIf)
X8030 - X8099 (80 Mk.VIc)
X8100 - X8269 (110 Mk.VIf)

BT286 - BT303 (18 Mk.VIf)

EL145 - EL218 (53 Mk.VIf)
EL219 - EL534 (246 Mk.VIc)

JL421 - JL875 (98 Mk.VIc)
JL876 - JL948 (52 Mk.XI)
JL949 - JM104 (8 Mk.VIc)
JM105 - JM267 (100 Mk.XI
JM268 - JM417 (160 Mk.X)

KV896 - KV203 (150 Mk.VIf)
KW277 - KW416 (110 Mk.X)

LX779 - LZ544 (480 TF Mk.X)

MM838 - MM948 (100 Mk.VIf)

ND139 - ND322 (156 Mk.VIf)
NE193 - NE832 (500 TF Mk.X)
NT888 - NV632 (500 TF Mk.X)

RD130 - RD867 (500 TF Mk.X)

SR910 - SR919 (10 TF Mk.X)

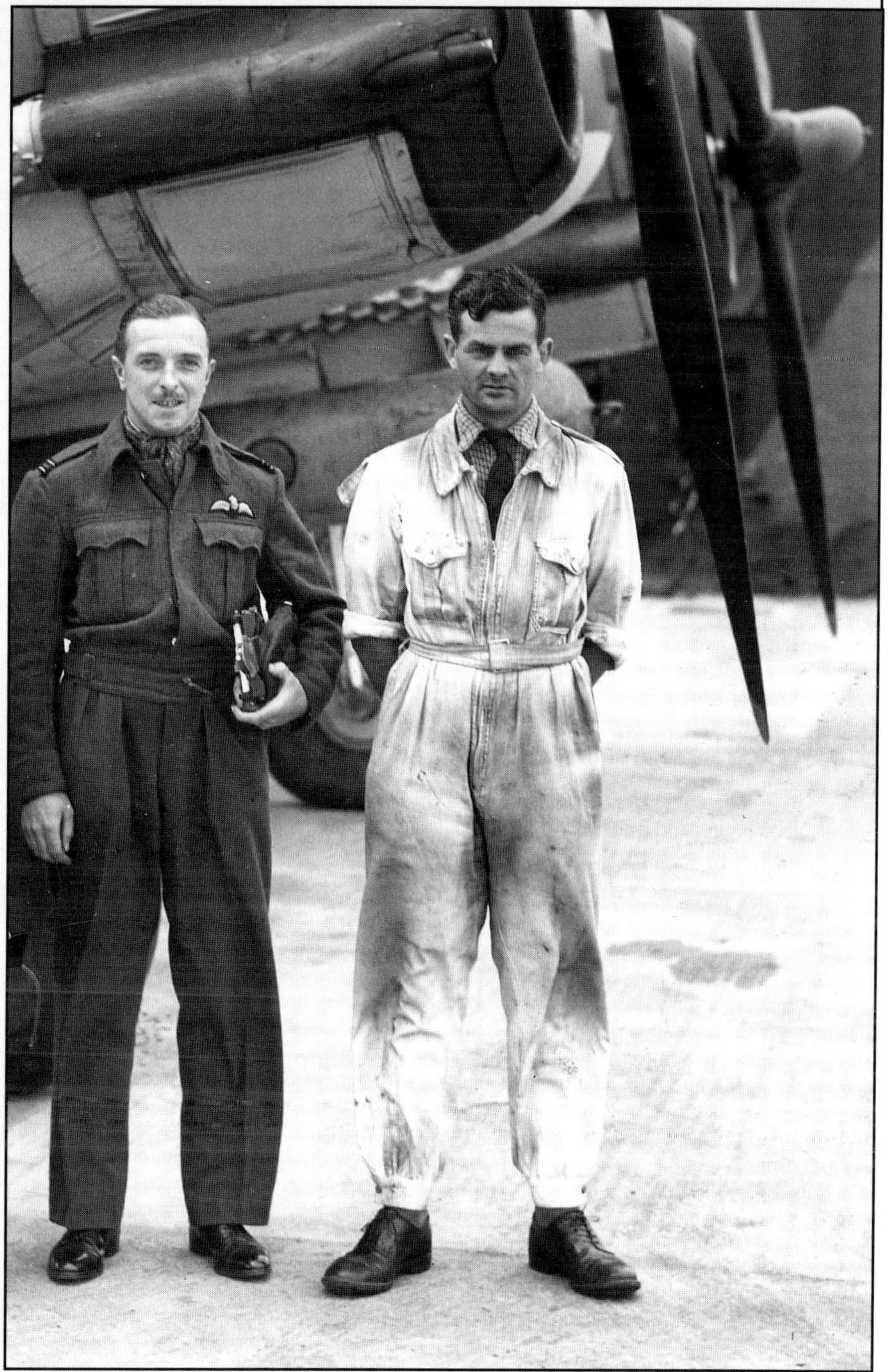

The following TF Mk.Xs were converted to TT10s

RD515, RD545, RD546, RD548, RD564, RD566, RD573, RD577, RD688, RD693, RD694, RD708, RD710, RD747, RD751, RD752, RD754, RD758, RD759, RD761, RD763, RD764, RD767, RD771, RD778-781, RD783, RD788, RD802, RD806, RD807, RD809, RD811, RD812, RD814, RD815, RD821, RD828, RD831, RD832, RD849, RD850, RD851, RD854, RD855, RD859, RD860, RD862, RD864, RD867, SR911 - SR914, SR916, SR917, SR919

Note:
Cancelled batches are not included.
Each batch of serials included gaps, thus the difference in numbers does not represent the number of aircraft produced.

Bristol's Beaufort - Fighter

In March 1935 the Air Staff's Operational Requirements Committee sat to lay out their requirement for a new generation of heavily armed fighter aircraft. Since the First World War the standard guns fitted to RAF aircraft were 0.303 inch, 'rifle' calibre guns such as the Vickers and Lewis, but it was known that on the Continent experiments were being made with 20mm cannon and in America with 0.5 inch heavy machine guns. Not wanting to be left behind, the Air Staff wanted a two-seat day/night fighter (specification F9/35) and a single seat day/night fighter (specification F10/35). As the pre-war years ticked by Westland took on the single seat project which eventually materialised as the highly original Whirlwind. At the Bristol Aeroplane Company the design team looked toward converting one of their existing designs, the Blenheim or Beaufort to a fighter. In October 1938 Leslie Frise, Chief Designer at Bristol, submitted a proposal to meet the revised Air Ministry specification F11/37. The original proposal was to utilise the wings, tail, and rear fuselage of a Beaufort with more powerful Bristol Hercules engines and a new cockpit/nose arrangement to house four 20mm cannon. The apparent simplicity of this idea appealed to the Air Ministry as many of the Beaufort jigs could be used, and the project came to be called the 'Beaufort - Fighter', sometimes shortened to Beau' Fighter. Turning the theory of converting a Beaufort bomber into the practice of a high performance fighter was not as simple as Frise first believed and the two designs came to be viewed as separate projects, so much so that the Resident Technical Officer of the Ministry of Aircraft Production submitted a request to the Air Ministry in July 1939 that the aircraft previously known as the Fighter conversion of the Beaufort, be formally known as the Beaufighter Mk.I

In February 1939 a contract had been placed for 300 aircraft to the specification F.17/39, a specification that the Air Ministry had written specifically for the Beaufighter because it fell outside all previous specifications. Four handmade prototypes were already under construction and Bristol's Chief Test Pilot, Cyril Unwins, made the first flight (in R2052) on 17 July 1939. Both R2052 and the second prototype, R2053, had Hercules HE1-SM engines and no operational equipment, but the third, R2054, had the Hercules III engines, had full operational equipment. The fourth prototype, R2055, had Hercules II engines, was fully equipped, and became a test-bed for armament development. So began the legend of the Beaufighter, almost 6,000 of which served the RAF operationally in all theatres for the next ten years.

The prototype Beaufighter Mk.Is, R2052 and R2053, were based on components from the 71st and 72nd Beauforts. The first flight was made on 17 July 1939 from Bristol's airfield at Filton, on the northern outskirts of the City of Bristol. The prototypes were fitted with Hercules HE1SM engines as the Mk.III engines envisaged at the early design stage were not available. R2052 was sent to A&AEE for performance trials, while R2053 was set aside for engine development. These first two prototypes were delivered without operational equipment.

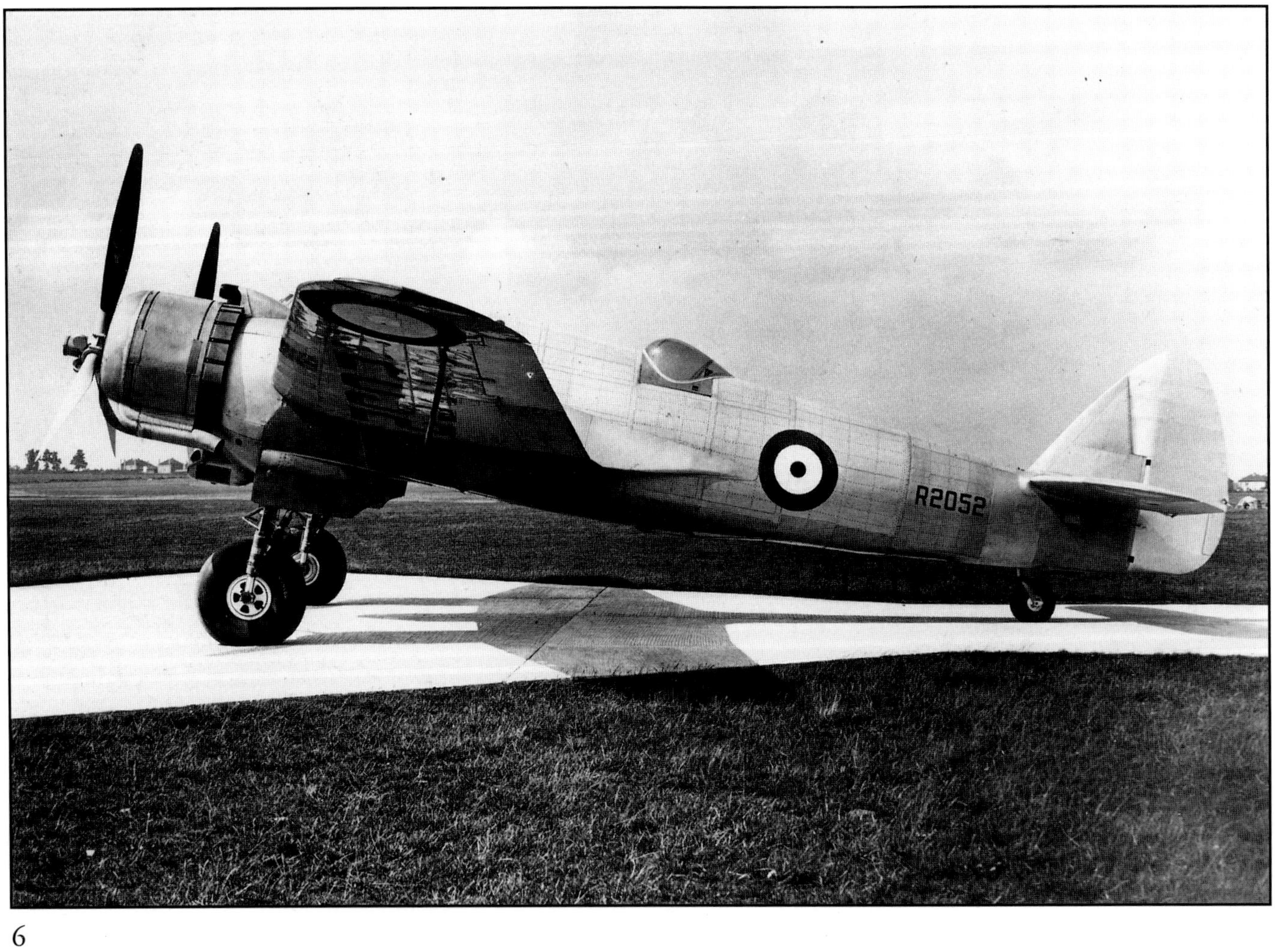

Airborne Interception

The difficulty of intercepting enemy aircraft at night was already appreciated before the war, but Britain had a lead in Radio Direction Finding technology. This early work resulted in the creation of the Chain Home series of ground based RDF stations around England's south-east coast that were so vital in the Battle of Britain. In parallel to a ground based network it was appreciated that and system that could be mounted in an aircraft would be vital. This concept of Airborne Interception was eagerly supported by the Air Officer Commanding in Chief, Fighter Command, Hugh Dowding. In July 1939 Dowding flew in a Fairey Battle fitted with Airborne Interception (AI) equipment and reached the conclusion that an ideal mount for the new device would be a twin-engine machine. This would afford safety at night, and have room for a separate compartment for the AI operator to work in. Initial installations in Bristol Blenheim Mk.1fs with AI Mk.III were less than successful, largely because the Blenheim was so slow that Luftwaffe bombers could out pace them. The new Beaufighter seemed to be just the machine Dowding needed and, as the air assault on Britain progressed through the daylight raids the Battle of Britain to the Night Blitz, the need for the aircraft to become operational became desperate.

Four squadrons were to re-equip with Beaufighters as soon as possible and were allocated one aircraft each on 2 September 1940. The squadrons were No. 25 Squadron, based at North Weald; No. 29 Squadron, based at Digby; No. 219 Squadron, based at Catterick; and No. 604 Squadron, based at Middle Wallop. No. 600 at Hornchurch got its first machine on 8 September. Unlike later aircraft the first fifty aircraft were not fitted with the proposed six machine guns in the wings, but had only the four cannon. The original proposal had been for eight Brownings in the wings, but the wing-gun installation would slow production still further. Chief designer, Frise, also noted that in order to put four guns in the port wing the landing light would have to be re-positioned, thus a compromise was reached of four guns in the starboard and two in port wing.

AI Mk.IV, with its arrow-head aerials on the nose, was the standard installation. This was fitted after delivery at No. 32 MU, St. Athan, from September 1940 and was not fitted at the factory. The first operational sortie was flown on 17 September and the first 'kill' (without AI) on 25 October. On 19 November Flight Lieutenant John Cunningham made the first successful AI assisted interception in a Beaufighter, the first of many for the man who became known as 'Cat's Eyes'.

R2052 achieved its estimated maximum speed of 335 mph at 16,800 feet during early tests without any equipment. Many minor modifications were made including the removal of the oil coolers from below the engines, improved elevator control runs, new oleo legs to allow greater weight, and new propellers. By June 1940 R2052 (below) and R2053 were required to be armed and fully operational. Fully operational, like R2054, performance dropped alarmingly to 309 mph.

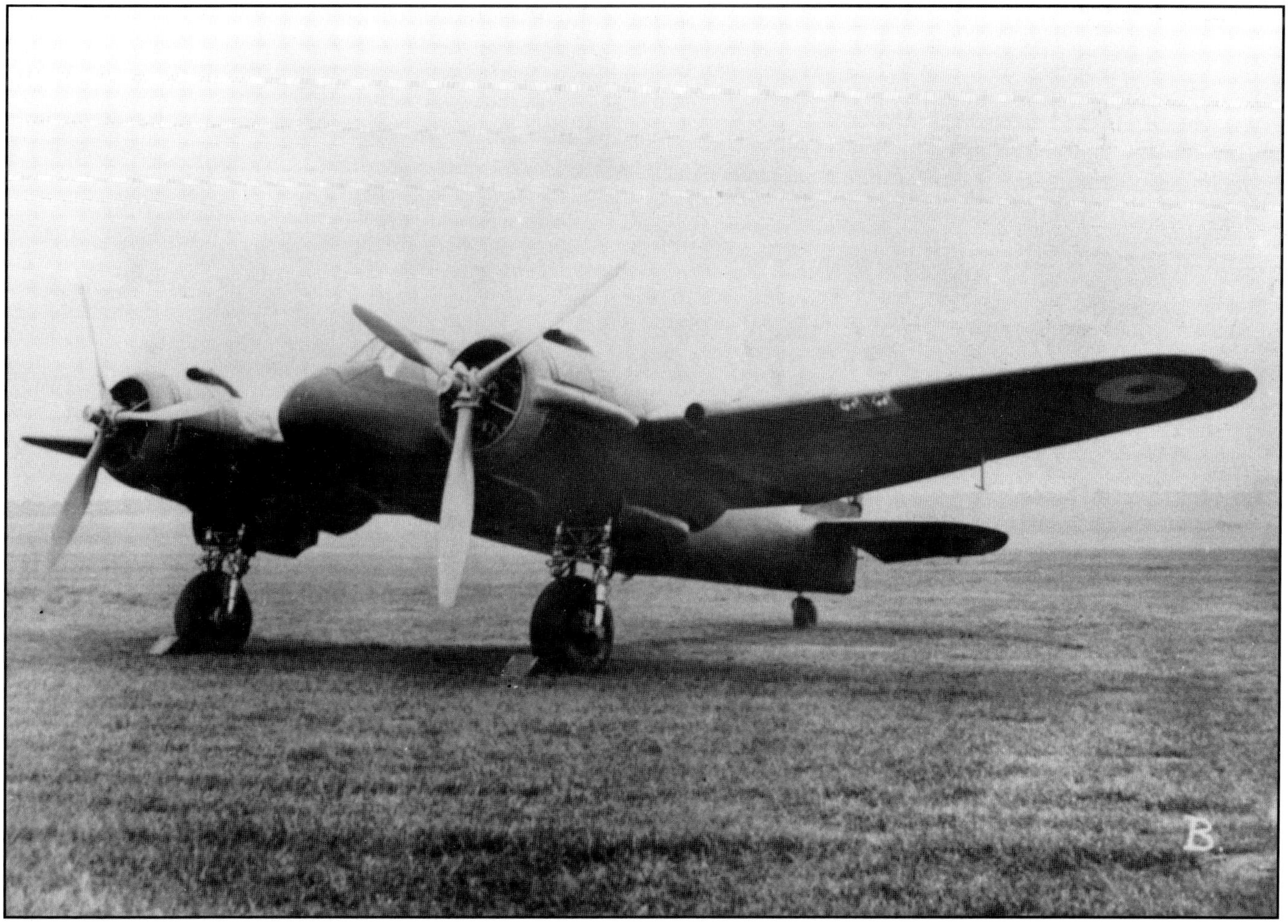

Mk.If

BEAUFIGHTER

Dimensions:
Span 57' 10"
Length 41' 4"
Height 15' 10"
Engines:
Bristol Hercules III. 1,400hp, fourteen cylinder sleeve-valve radial air cooled.
Armament:
Four 20mm Hispano cannon in nose. Six 0.303 inch machine guns in wings.
Number Built:
557

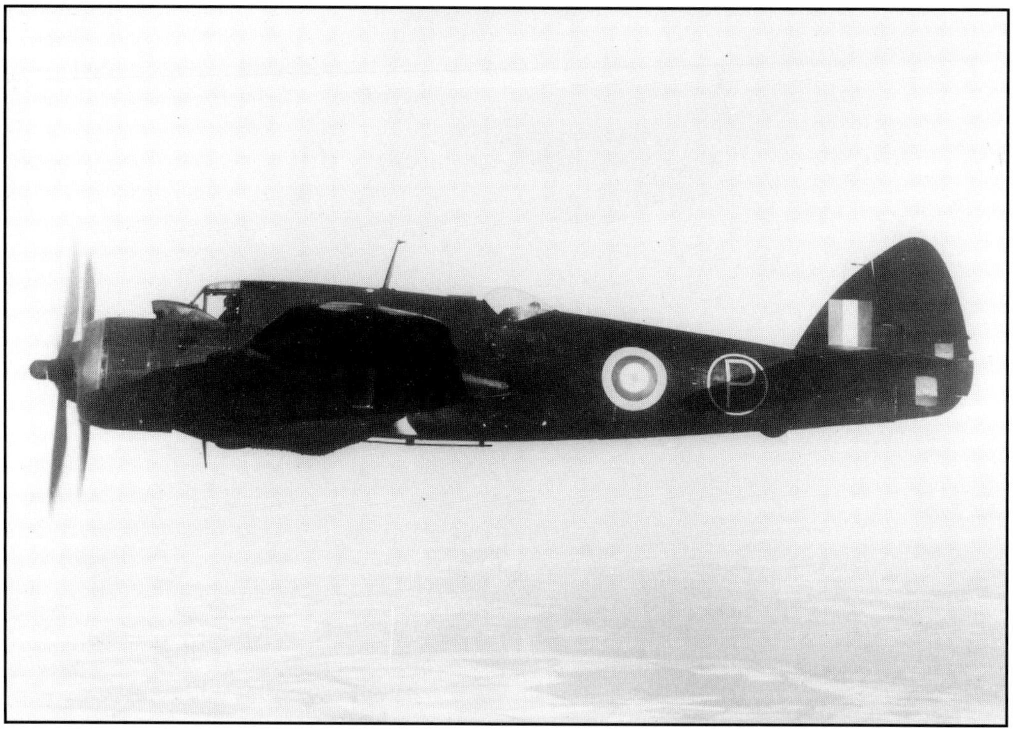

Above right: **Beaufighter Mk.If, X7579, built at Weston was allocated to A&AEE for trials of the 10cm AI Mk.VIII, and carries the yellow 'P' in a circle indicating a prototype. The AI Mk. VIII was the first of the new generation AI sets made possible by the invention of the Magnetron Valve that permitted centimetric wavelengths compared to wavelengths measured in metres of the Chain Home stations. Development was carried out at the Telecommunication Research Establishment (Hurn) where up to eight Mk.Is were used in trials.**

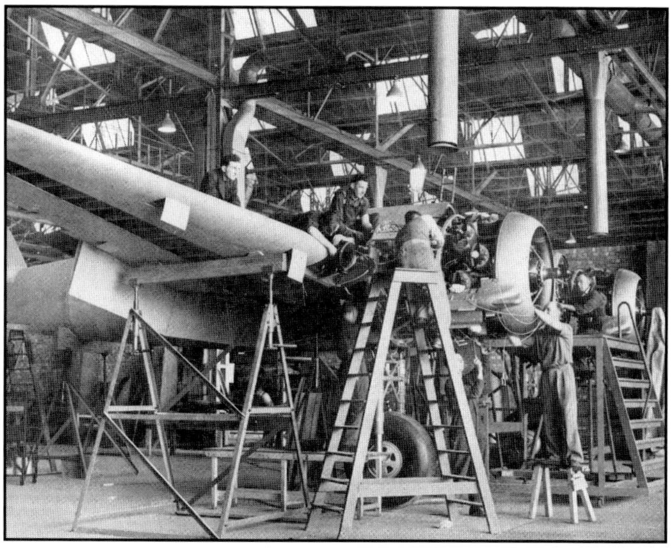

Right: **A Beaufighter being assembled. Great emphasis was placed on the sectional constructional methods which allowed production in many shadow factories. This, the Ministry of Aircraft Production hoped, would frustrate any enemy attempt to halt production by bombing the factories. The fuselage was made in three sections and at final assembly were married with wings, engines and smaller components.**

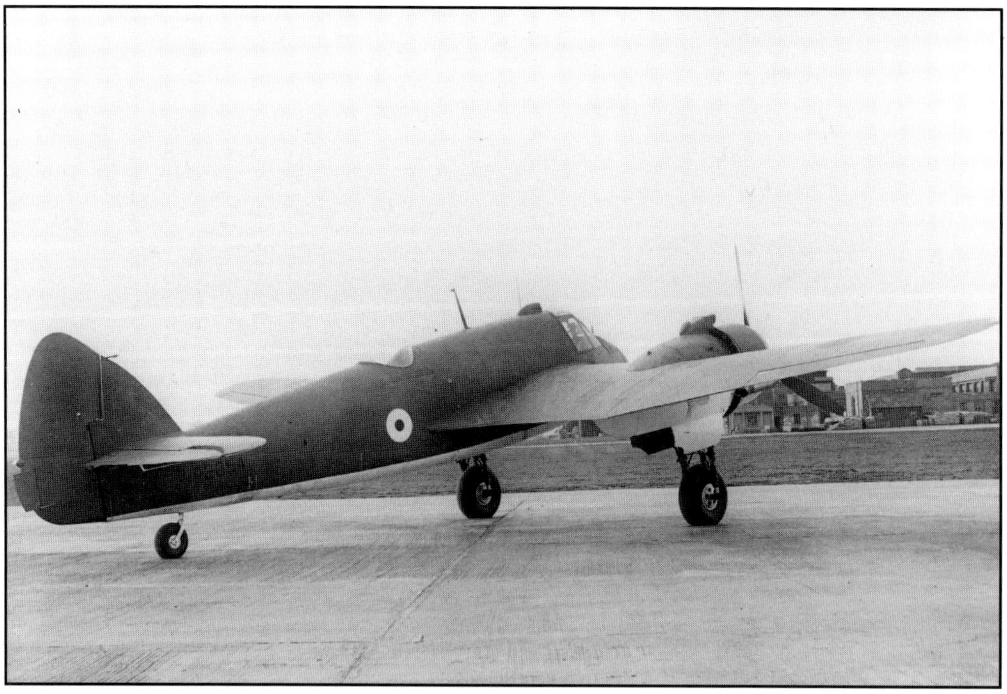

Left: **R2054, the third prototype, was fitted with four 20mm Hispano cannon fed by 60 round drums. After the 60 rounds from each gun had been exhausted it was the job of the AI operator to change them, a difficult and lengthy task. Bristol had developed a servo-fed mechanism of 240 round capacity, but the Ministry of Aircraft Production favoured a French Chatellerault recoil-operated system that had been brought to England by escaping Free-French officers. It took until September of 1941, and the 401st Beaufighter, for a the new feed mechanism to replace the 60 round drums.**

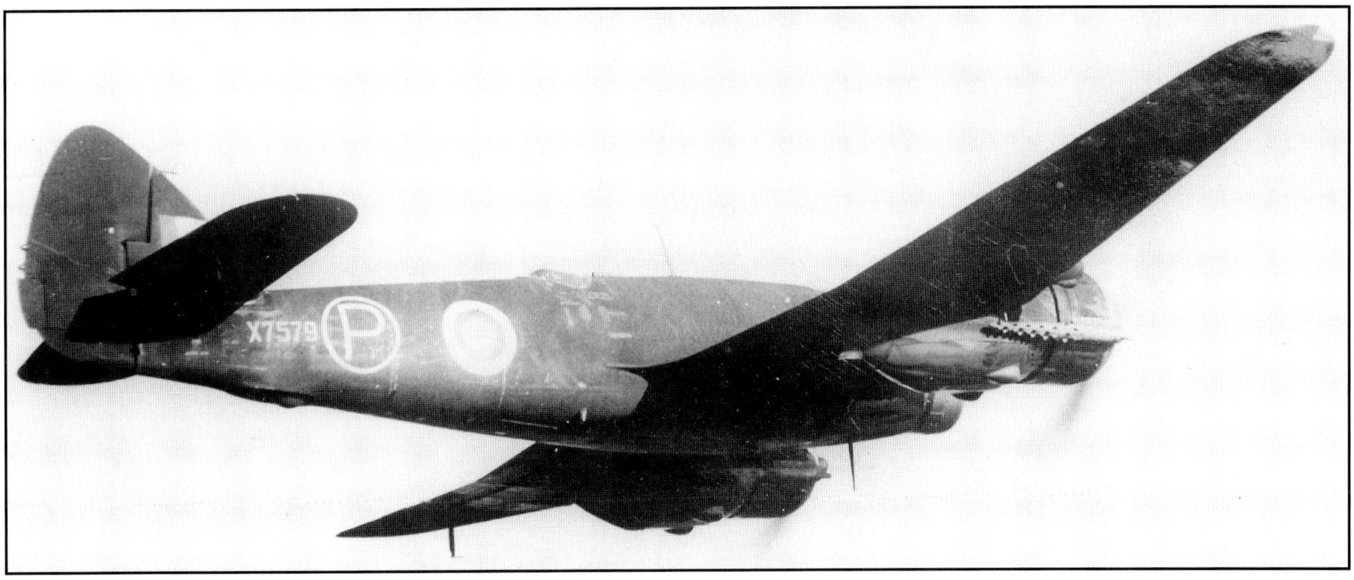

Above: **Beaufighter Mk.If, X7579 again in October 1941 when modified at TRE for radar trials. As well as developing AI Mk. VII and Mk.VIII, the TRE experimented with interception techniques, jamming, IFF Mk.III, and an early form of head-up display for AI and artificial horizon. X7579 survived the war in operational and training units, only to be broken up in 1945.**

Right: **R2268, a Mk.I with the experimental twin tail at Filton in 1940. Early trials showed longitudinal instability below 190 mph and a series of modifications were devised to cure the fault. The wide-span tailplane with endplate fins and rudders was fitted to R2268, but tests showed that the tail failed to fix the problem and reduced the performance. The problem was not cured until a 12 degree dihedral was incorporated in the Mk.II, but some Mk.Is were also modified.**

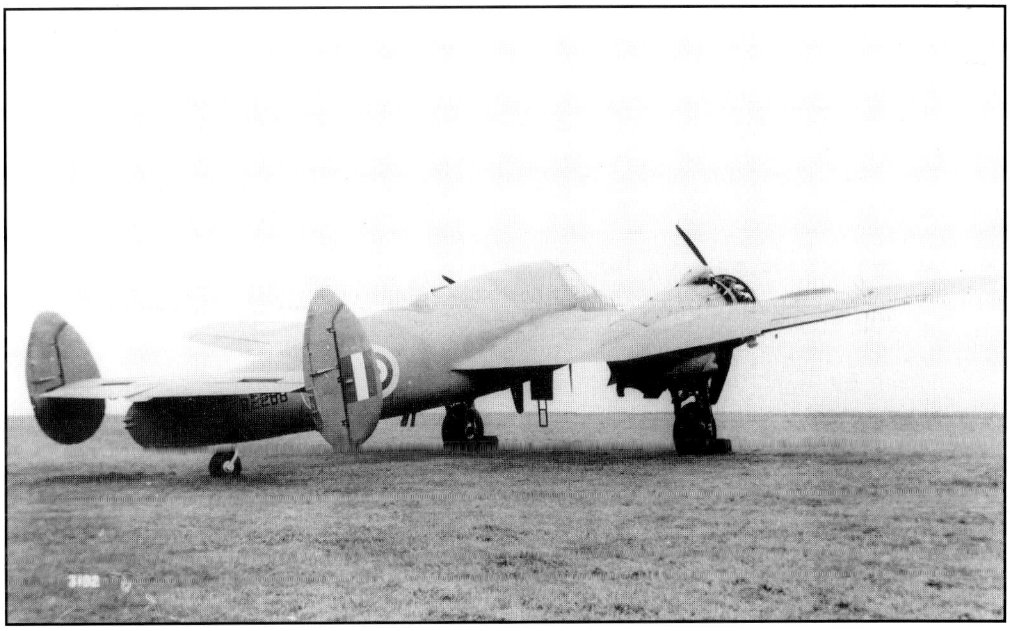

Right: **The early 1940 Night and White scheme shown to good effect in another photograph of R2054. The aircraft was finished in the standard fighter scheme of Dark Earth and Dark Green upper surfaces with Night and White undersurfaces. When tested at A&AEE, Boscombe Down, in June 1940 R2054 achieved a speed of 309 mph at 15,000 feet in fully equipped trim. R2054 went into service with No. 604 Squadron and was lost of 6 February 1941 when it crashed on approach to Middle Wallop.**

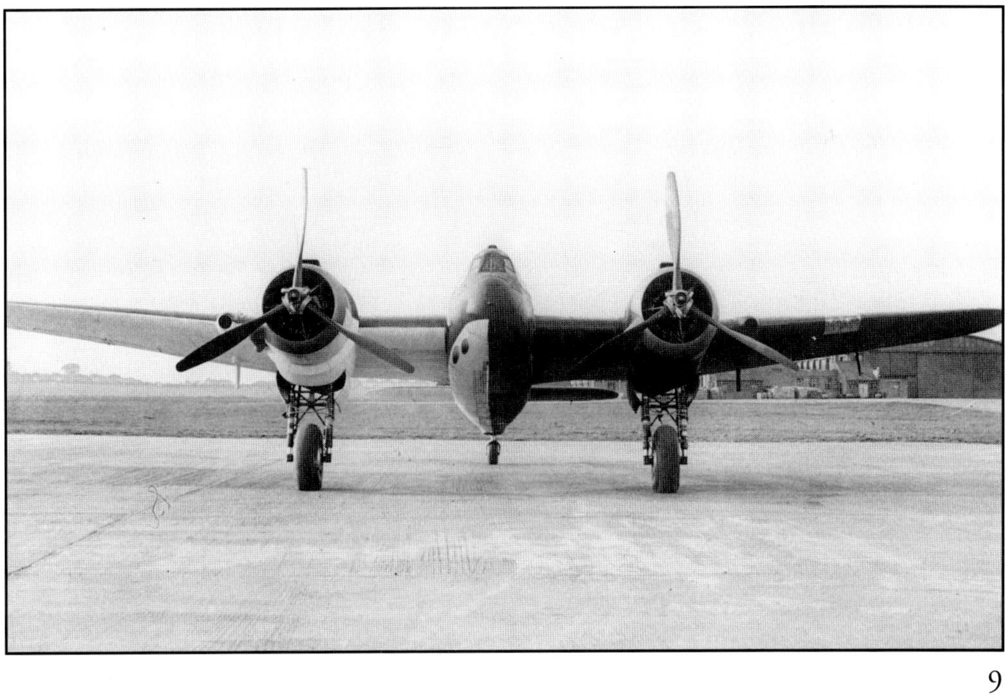

Mk.Ic

BEAUFIGHTER

Dimensions:
Span 57' 10"
Length 41' 4"
Height 15' 10"
Engines:
Bristol Hercules III. 1,400hp, fourteen cylinder sleeve-valve radial air cooled.
Armament:
Four 20mm Hispano cannon in nose.
Number Built:
397

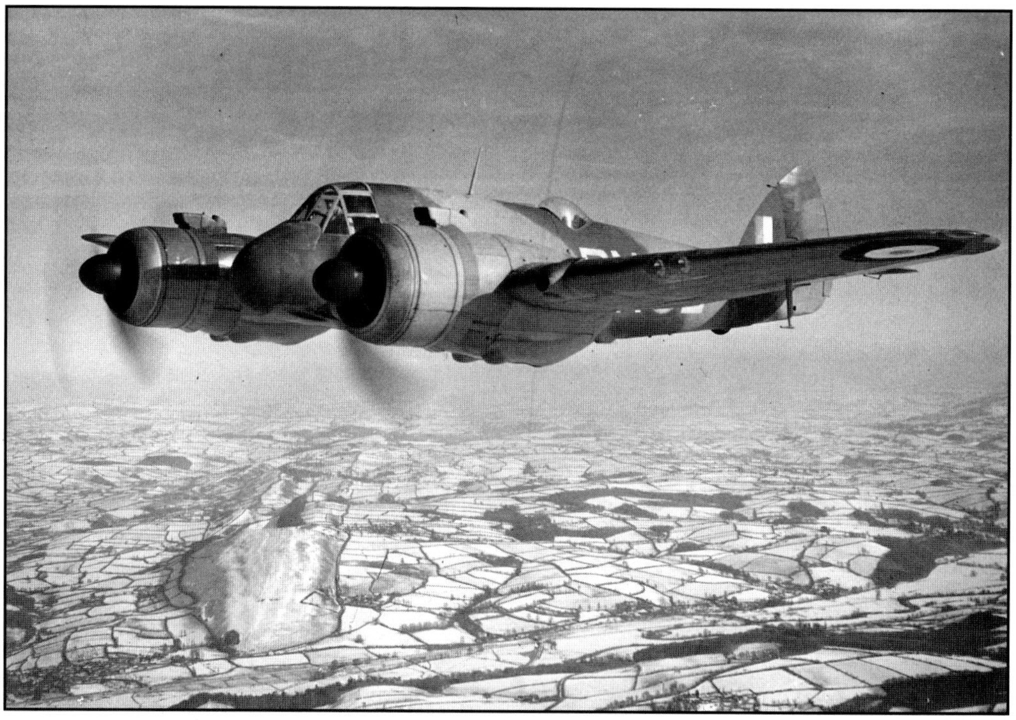

Right: **Beaufighter Mk.Ic of No. 252 Squadron coded PN-B.**

Mk.Ic - Coastal Command

In December 1941 a decision was made to separate the Fighter and Coastal Command versions of the Beaufighter Mk.I on the production line. The first production Mk.Ic was the 217th aircraft, delivered in February 1941. The first aircraft were modified only after they had come off the production line so as not to disrupt night fighter production. The first coastal Beaufighter was R2152, which was modified by removing the wing guns and fitting fifty gallon fuel tanks in their place. A navigation table was fitted in the fuselage and the camera-gun replaced with a DF loop.

252 Squadron was the first Coastal Command squadron to receive Beaufighters to use in the strike-fighter / long-range escort role. The aircraft arrived in March 1941, but the extra tanks had yet to be made and, as an interim measure, Wellington fifty gallon tanks were fitted on the floor between the cannon bays.

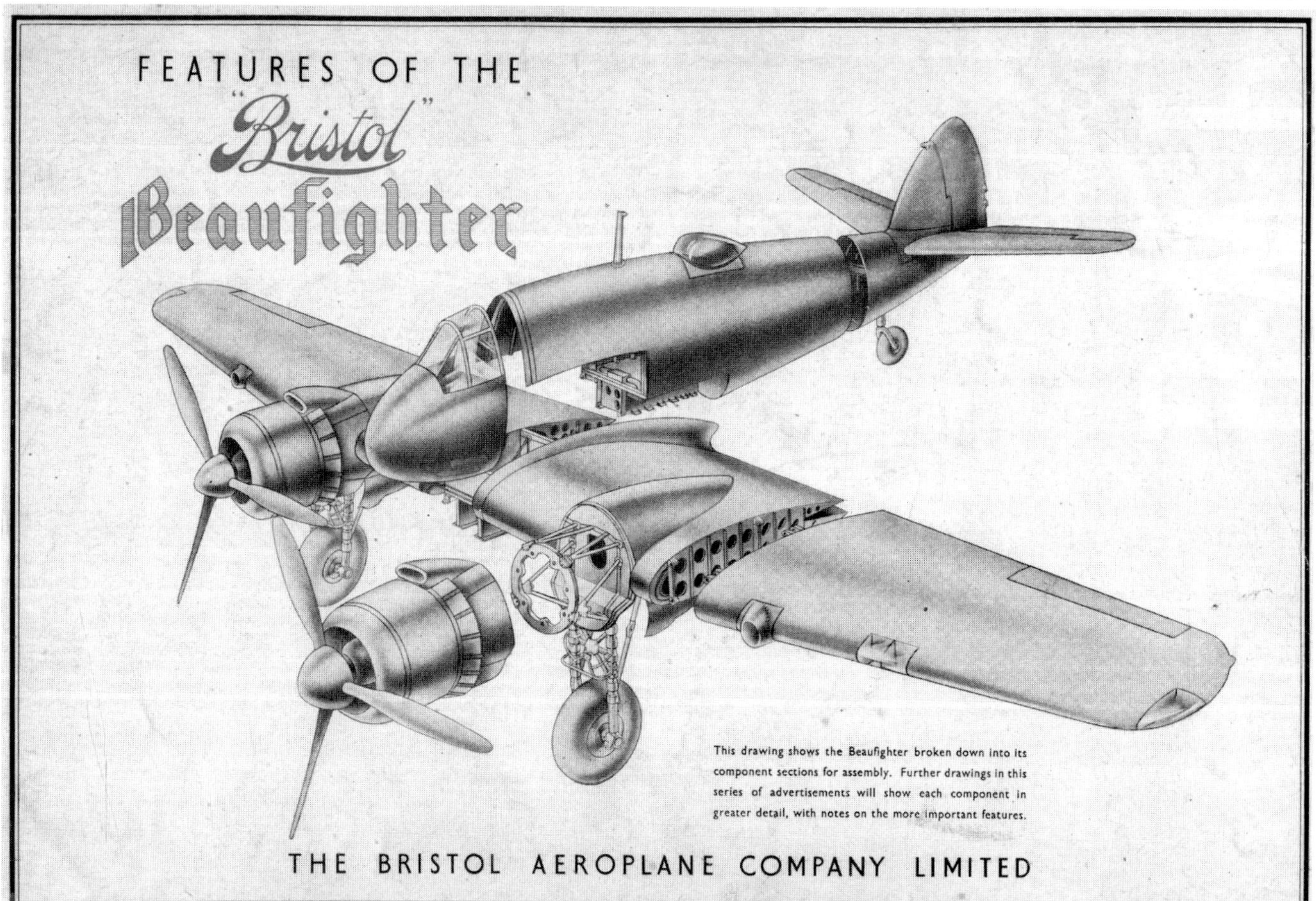

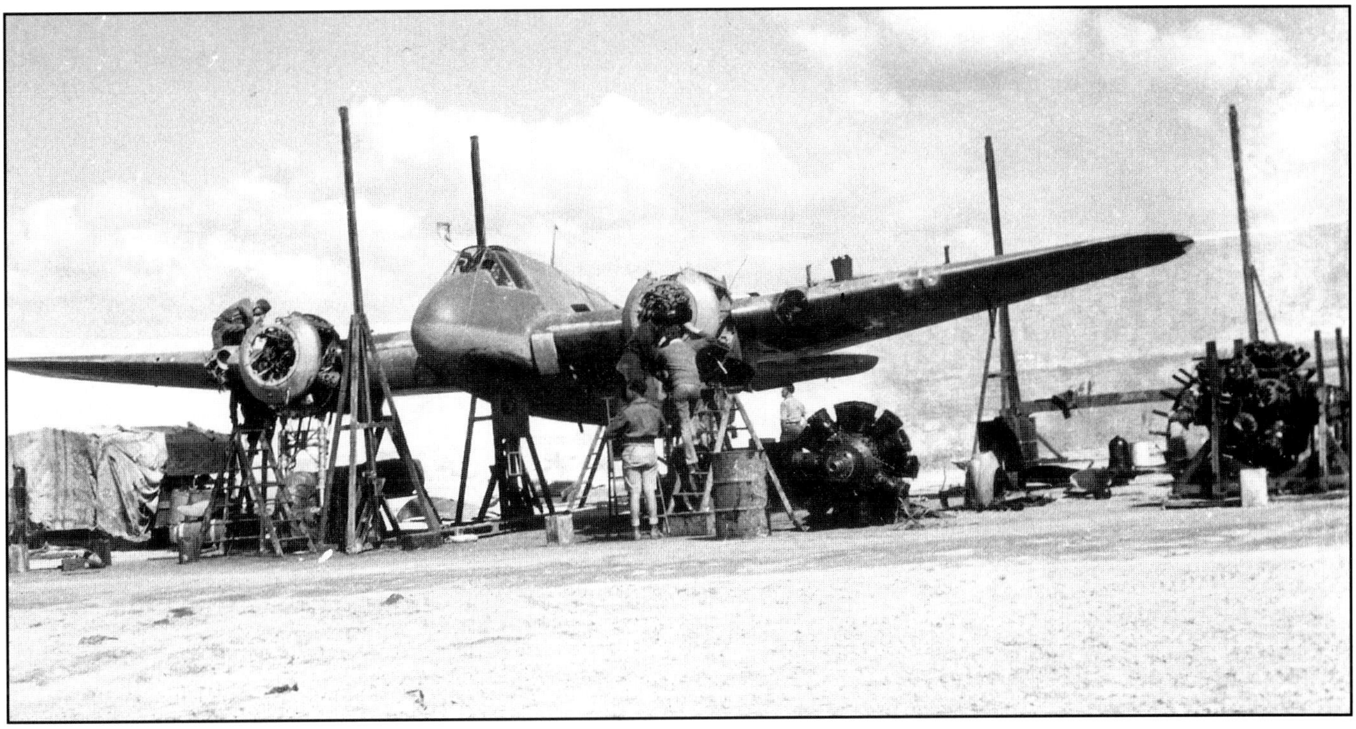

A major inspection at Idku, one of the dusty Middle Eastern airfields where Beaufighter squadrons were based in March 1943.

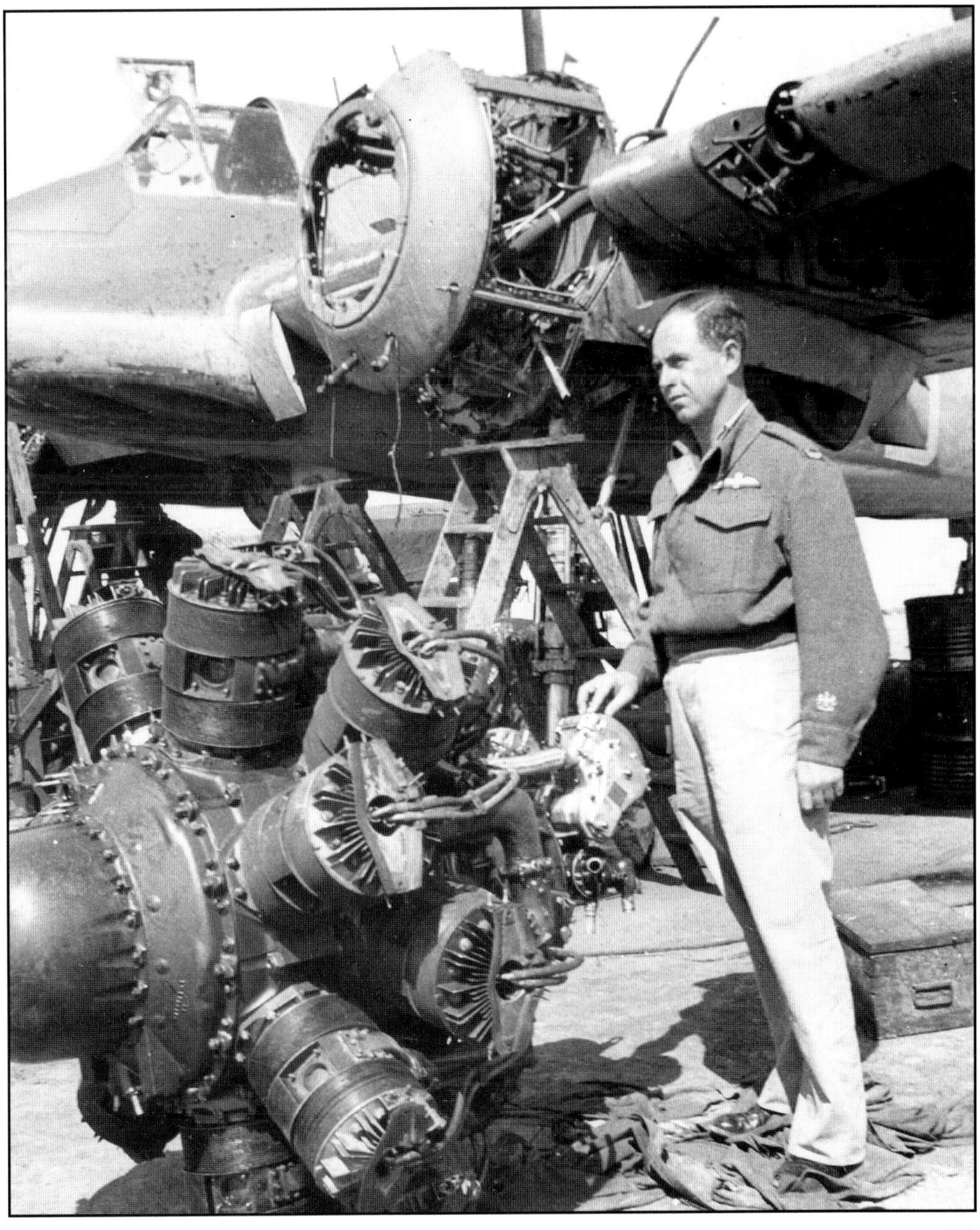

The Hercules

The standard Bristol Hercules Mk.III was of huge capacity, 2,360 cubic inches compared to a Rolls-Royce Merlin's 1,649. Under the leadership of Alfred Feddin and his team Bristol spent £2,000,000 developing the Hercules. The fourteen cylinder, air cooled engine was based on a totally different principle to the normal push-rod and valve system used on other radial and in-line engines of the time. In Feddin's engine the sleeve valve surrounded the piston and moved during the engine cycle to open and close the intake and exhaust ports in the cylinder itself. The spark plugs were sited ideally in the cylinder heads as there were no head valves or rocker gear to obstruct them.

Mk.IIf
BEAUFIGHTER

Dimensions:
Span 57' 10"
Length 42' 9"
Height 15' 10"
Engines:
Rolls-Royce Merlin XX 1,250 hp, twelve cylinder liquid cooled.
Armament:
Four 20mm Hispano cannon in nose. Six 0.303" Browning machine guns in wings.
Number Built:
477

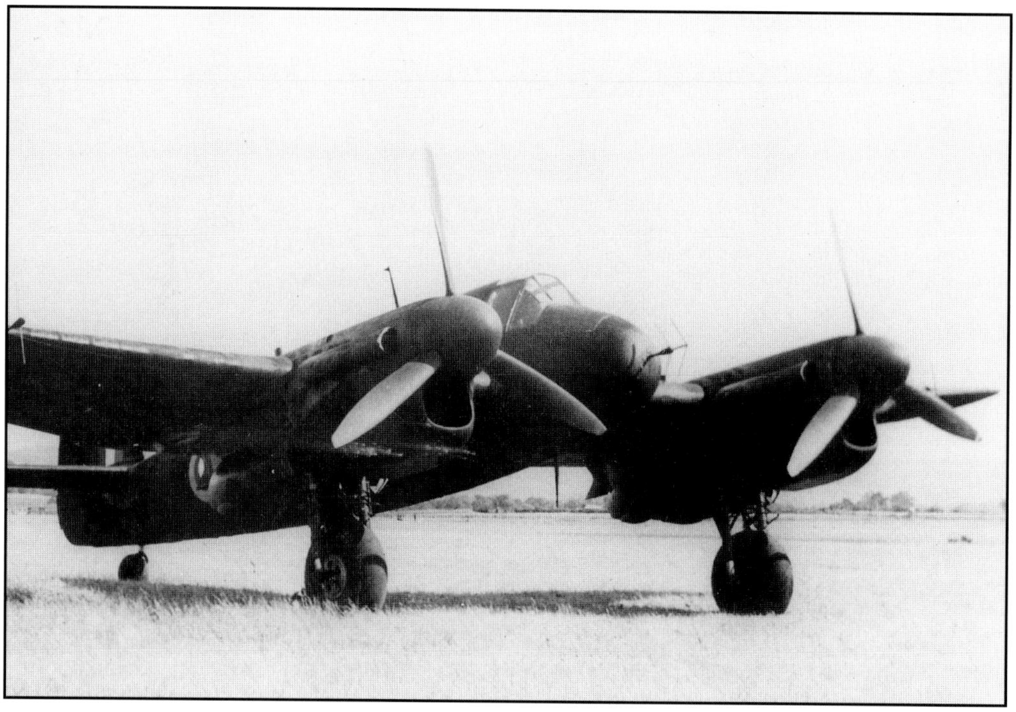

Above Right: **T3144, a Mk.II that later went to the Fleet Air Arm for trials.**

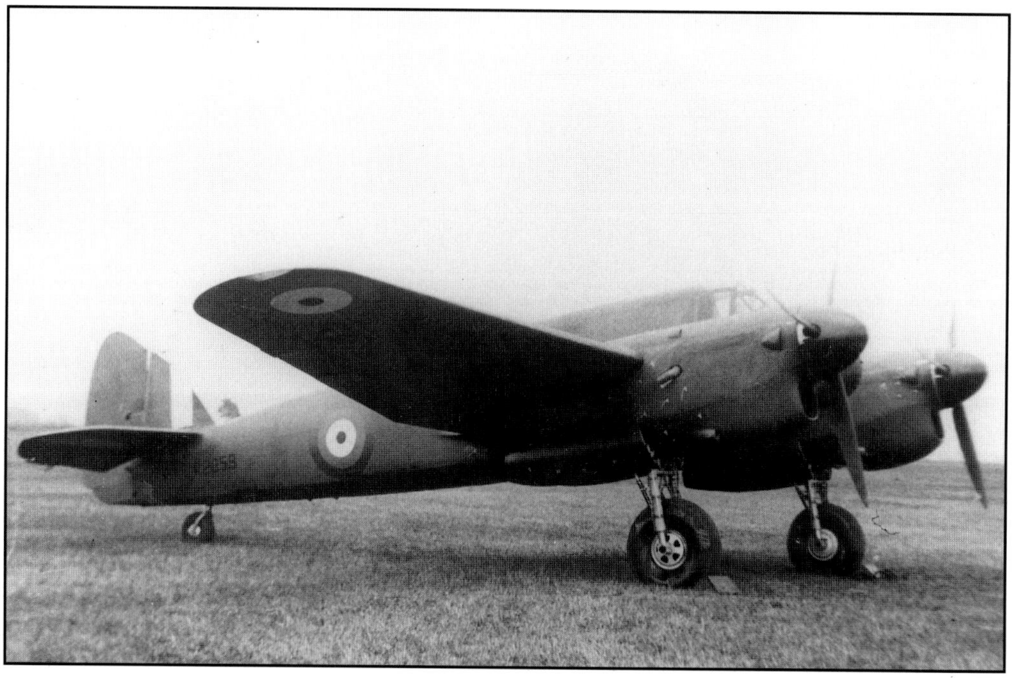

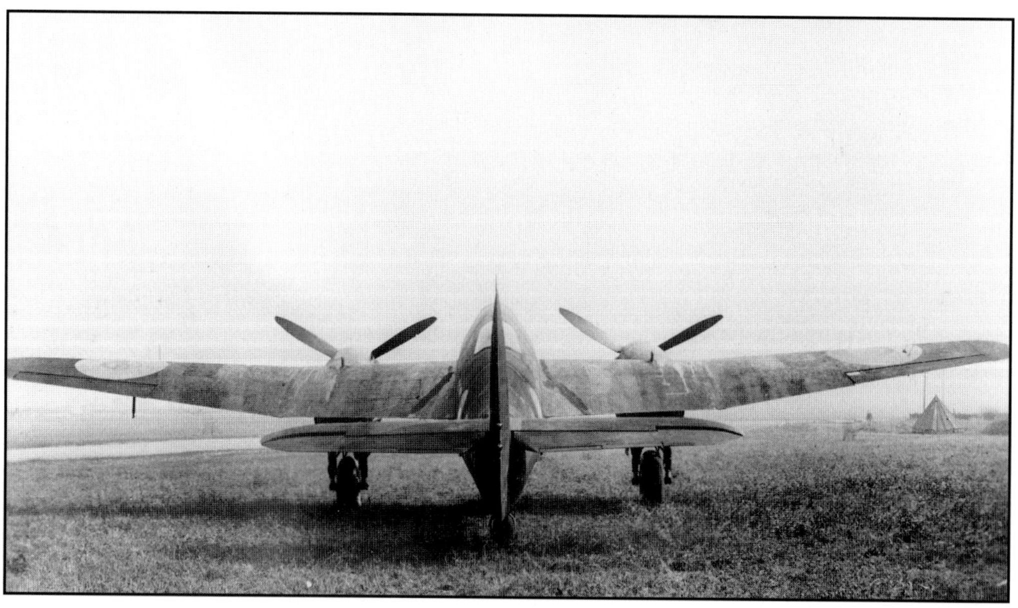

Right and below: **R2058, the prototype Mk.II, which first flew in July 1940 with Merlin Mk.X engines. All 477 aircraft were built at Filton and featured a modified engine mounting designed by Rolls Royce and made by Morris Motors at Cowley.**

Merlin Shortage

R2058 and R2062 were assigned to Rolls-Royce at Hucknall in 1940 for development of a Merlin XX installation. All the Merlin engined Beaufighters were fighters (Mk.IIf) but were not popular with the squadrons, such as 600 Squadron, that were allocated them. The take-off run was longer than the Hercules variant, but the Mk.II was slightly faster at altitude. The shortage of Merlin XXs, also used on Lancasters, lead to many Mk.IIs being shipped from Filton to Whitchurch and Colerne by road to await engines.

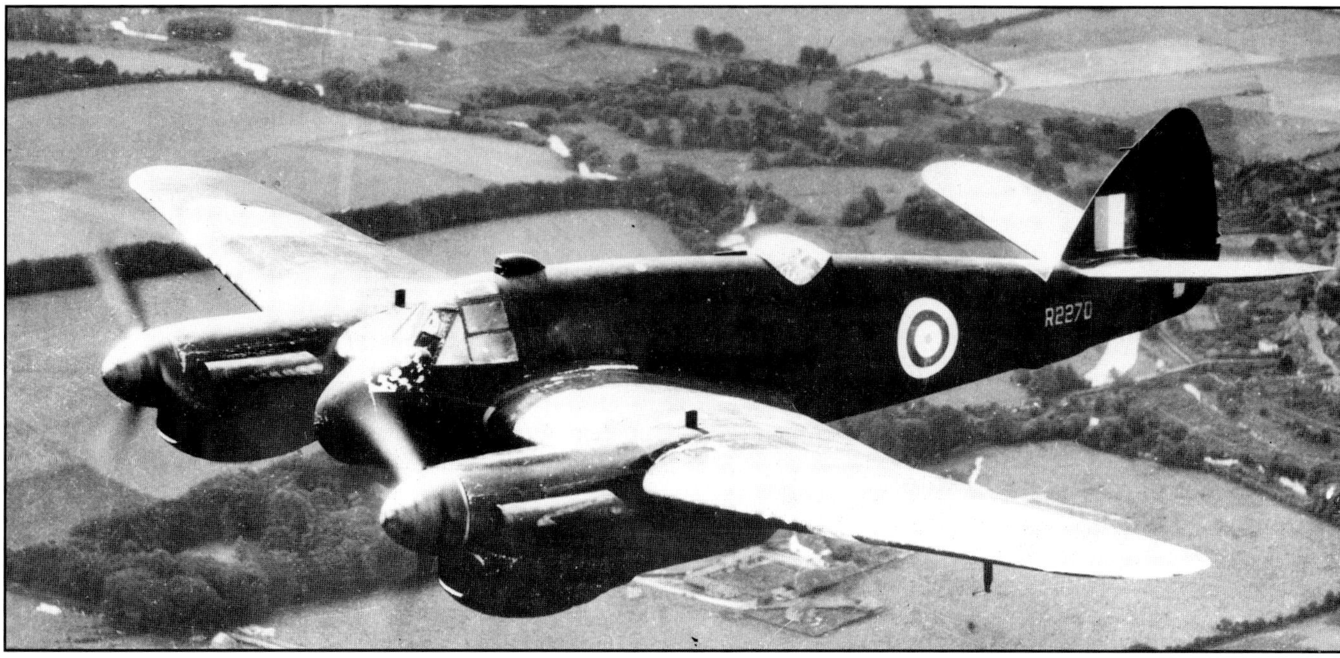

Above: **R2270, the first of a batch of 150 delivered between March and October 1941, with the dihedral added to the tailplane. After extensive trials at Boscombe Down and Farnborough the aircraft went to Nos. 604 and 406 Squadrons.**

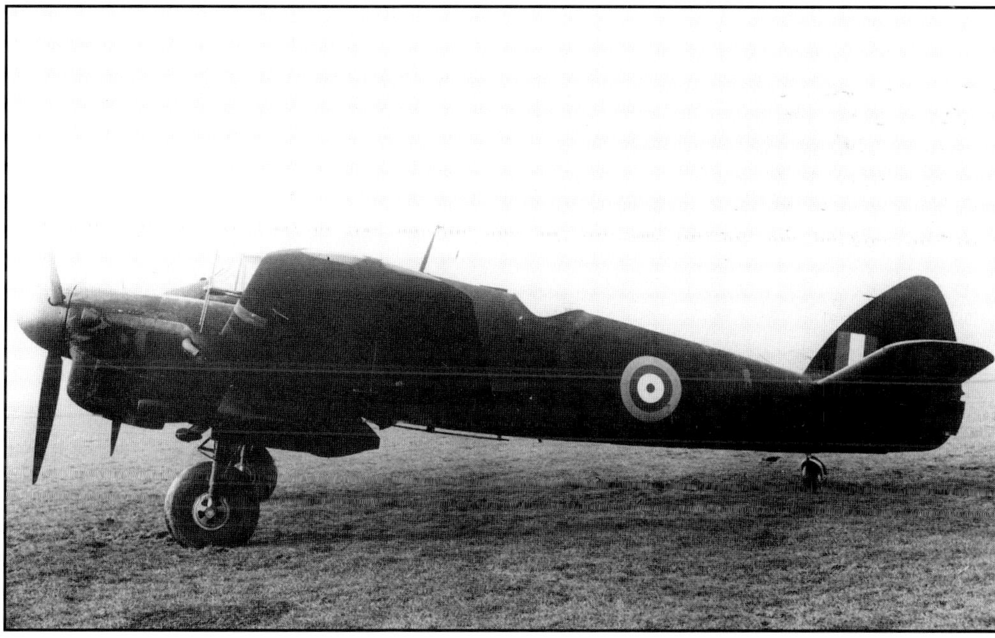

Right: **T3032 photographed in January 1943 with Radar aerials visible and a dihedral tail. This machine never reached an operational unit, but spent the entire war as a test vehicle with RAE, A&AEE, and FIU (Fighter Interception Unit) at Ford. The AI equipment evaluated with the FIU for early Beaufighters was the AI Mk.IV.**

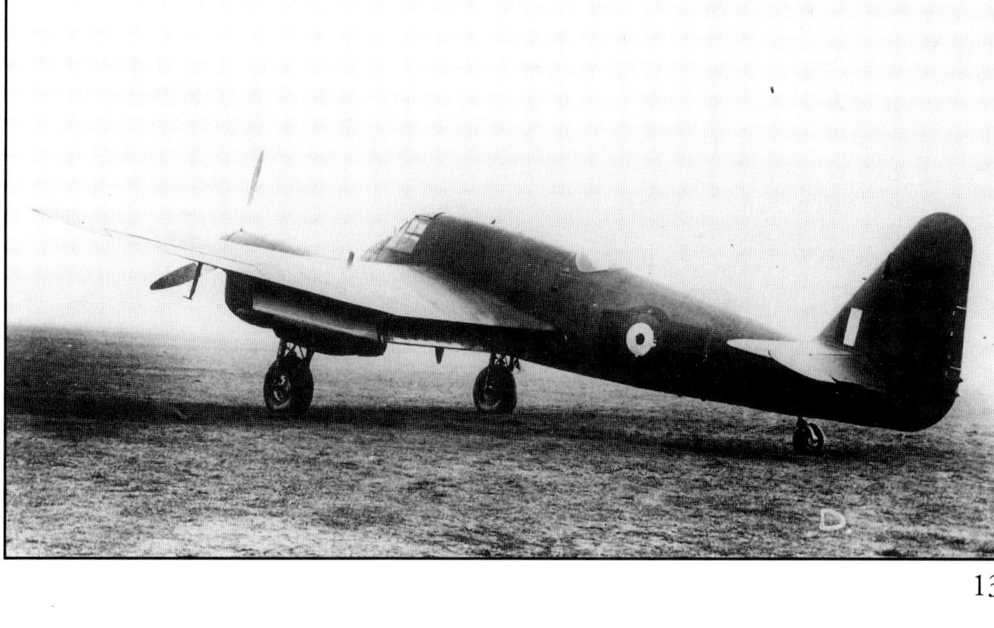

Right: **R2058, once more, now fitted with an experimental taller fin and rudder but with no dihedral. This was yet another experiment to reduce the take off swing of the Mk.II that failed to improve the situation. The Merlin XXs were fitted with Rotol airscrews and Schwartz wooden blades.**

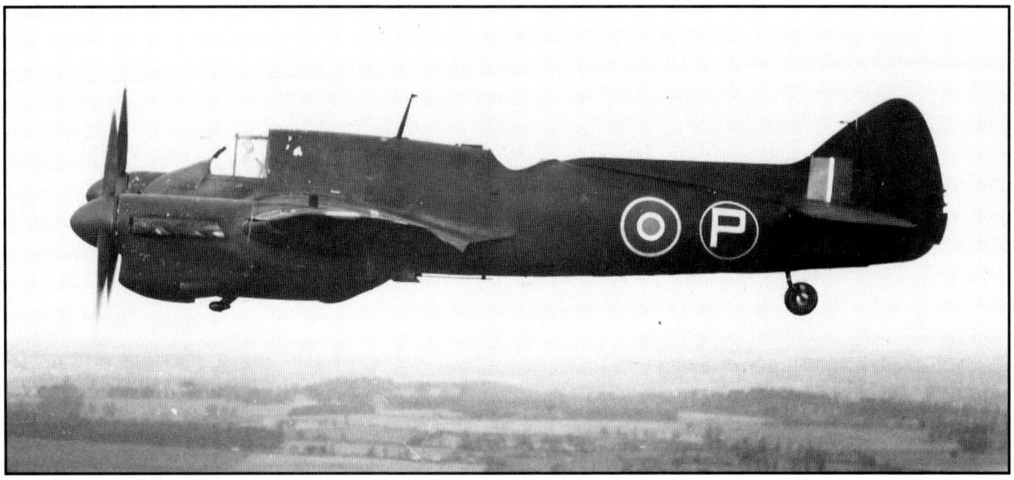

T3032, testing the long dorsal fin and Rotol RS/5/5 propellers and spinners. In an attempt to improve directional stability, and a pronounced swing on take-off, the fin was tried and increased the vertical area by 13.1 square feet. The modification was later incorporated on the Mk.X and some Mk.IVcs when the torpedo and other equipment moved the centre of gravity too far aft.

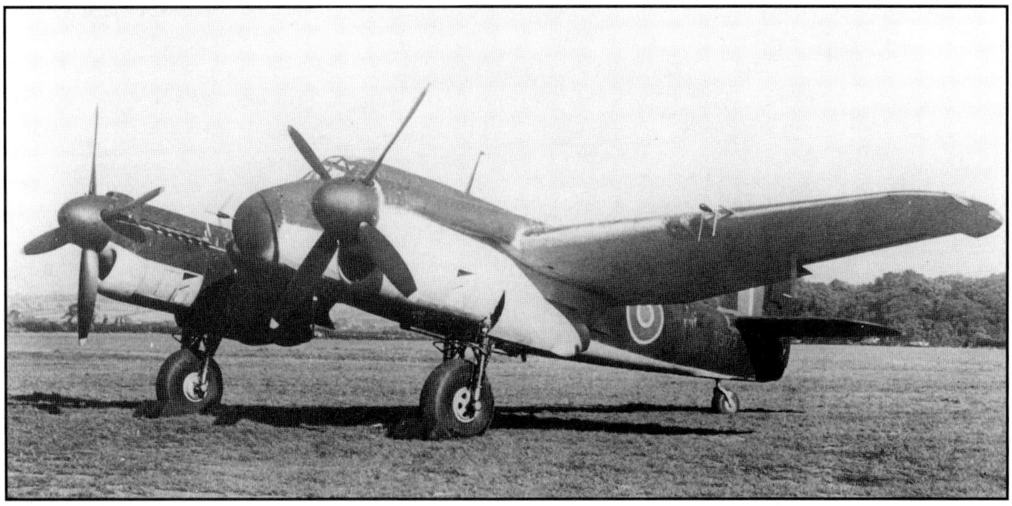

T3177, was fitted with Rolls-Royce Griffon IIB engines and four bladed propellers as an experiment. The modifications were made at Hucknall in 1941, but the performance was found to be inferior to the Merlin engined Mosquito at altitude and the idea was abandoned. T3177 survived into 1943 when it was destroyed in a crash at Driffield on April 2nd.

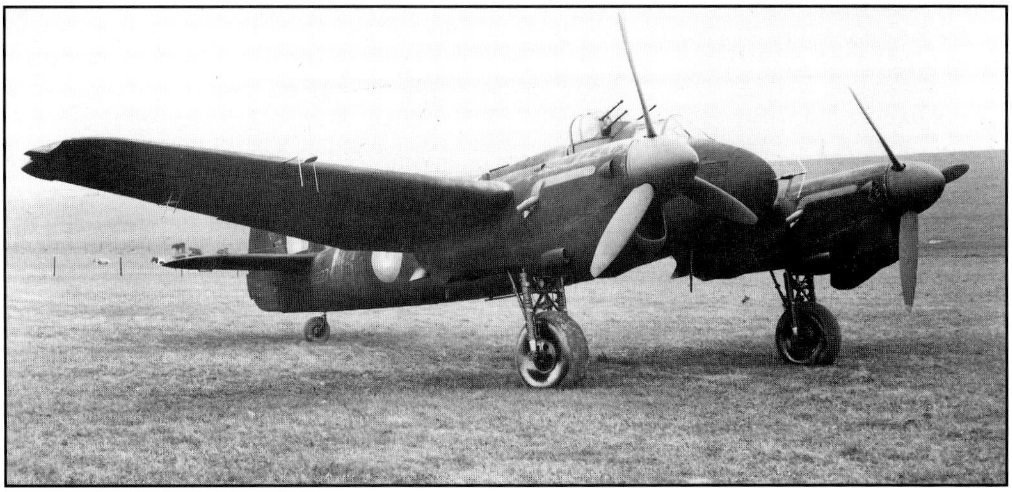

R2274, Beaufighter Mk.V. Two Beaufighters (R2274 and R2306) were converted to carry a four-gun Boulton Paul BPA.1, similar to the Defiant turret, behind the cockpit. R2274 served with No. 406 Squadron (RCAF). R2306 was flown by No. 29 Squadron and coded RO-O. The six wing-mounted machine guns and two outboard cannons were removed.

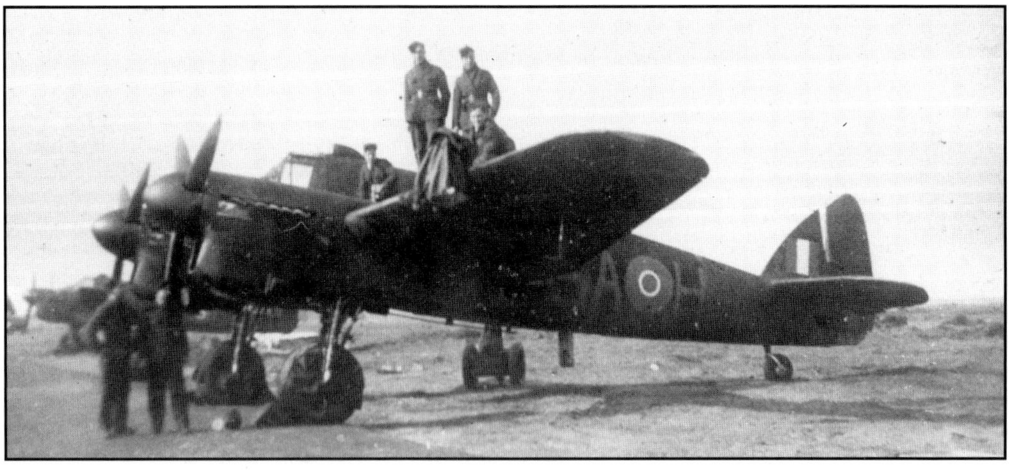

A Mk.II in service. This veteran served with No. 456 Squadron (RCAF) at RAF Valley, which used Mk.IIs from September 1941 until it replaced them with Mk.VIfs in January 1943. In service it was found the radiators were easily damaged in combat.

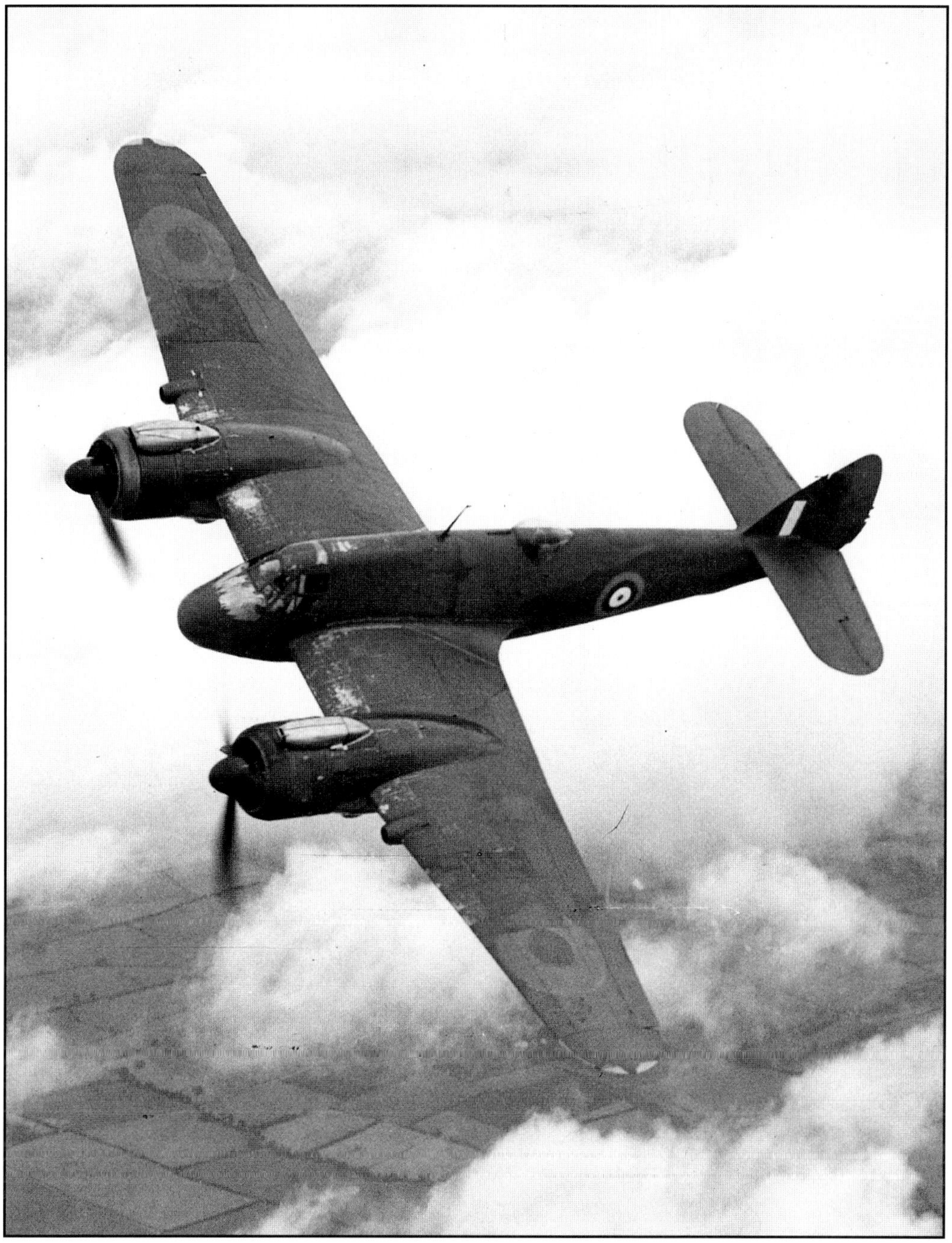

Mk.VIf

BEAUFIGHTER

Dimensions:
Span 57' 10"
Length 41'
Height 15' 10"
Engines:
Bristol Hercules VI or XVI. 1,670hp, fourteen cylinder sleeve-valve radial air cooled.
Armament:
Four 20mm Hispano cannon in nose. Six 0.303" Browning machine guns in wings.
Number Built:
1078

Left: **X7543, built as a Mk. I, but became the prototype for the Mk.VI. Note the amount of paint that has worn off and the 'flat' tail.**

New Engines

X7542 and X7543 were sent from the Weston production line with Hercules Mk.VI engines and became the prototypes for the Beaufighter Mk.VI. The new engines gave a greater high altitude performance, but there were no significant airframe modifications.

Below: **V8442, a Mk.VIf fitted with a dihedral tail, saw service with No. 409 Squadron.**

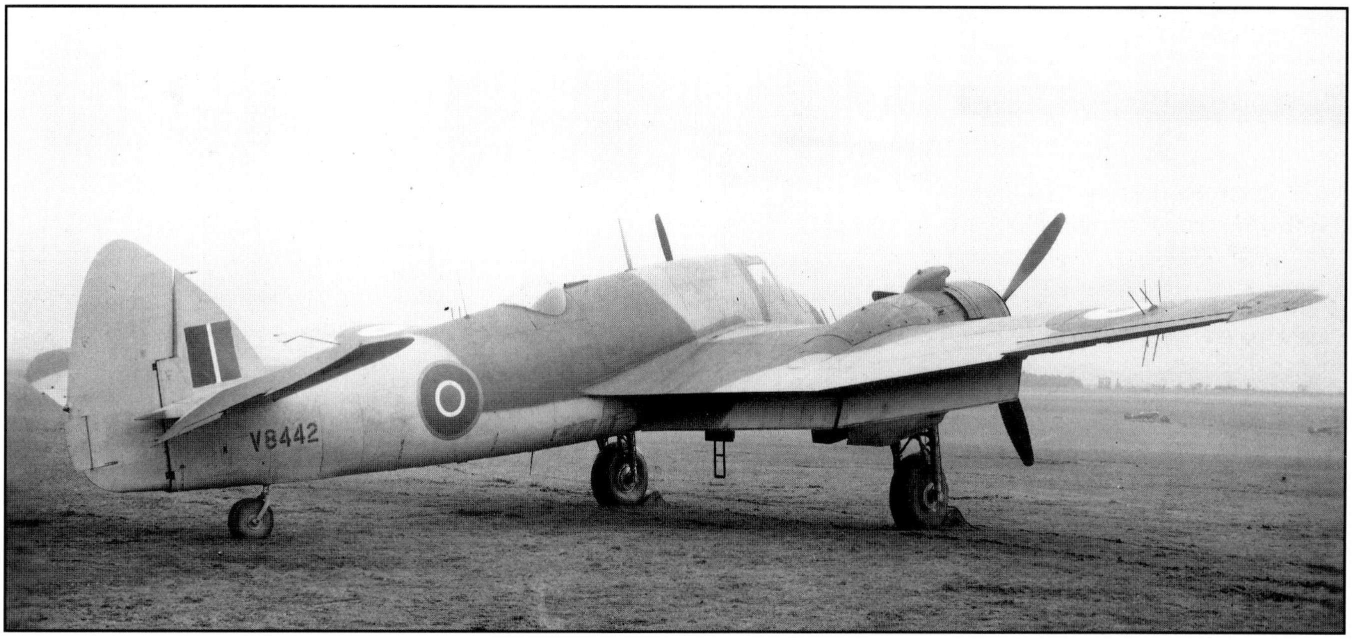

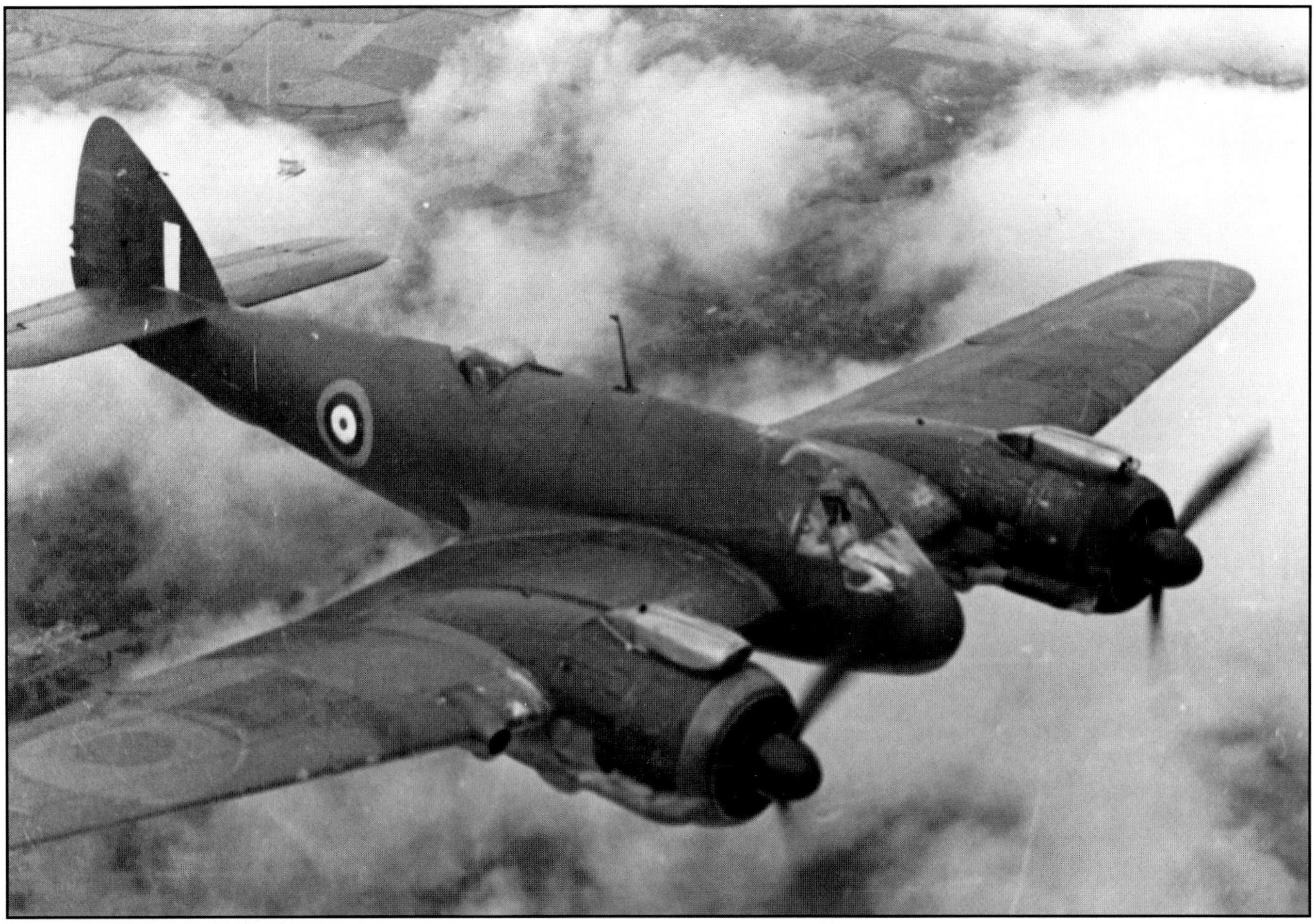

Above: **The Beaufighter Mk.VI with its Hercules Mk.VI engines had a slightly improved performance at altitude and eventually equipped 22 squadrons. The range was 1,480 miles at the most economic speed of 243mph. Later Mk.VI Beaufighters were fitted with Hercules Mk.XVI engines which differed only in the operation of the carburetter. Standard production Mk.VIfs were fitted with the 12 degree dihedral tail plane. When AI Mk.VIII was available, a radome was fitted to the nose and the arrow shaped aerials vanished.**

Right: **Detail of the port undercarriage of a Mk.VI from the Canadian No. 406 Squadron. The original all-up weight of an operational machine was 19,600 lb, but by the time the Mk.X became operational the weight had risen to 25,400 lb. To take this increase the basic undercarriage was modified by strengthening the top mountings and fitting stronger Lockheed shock absorbers.**

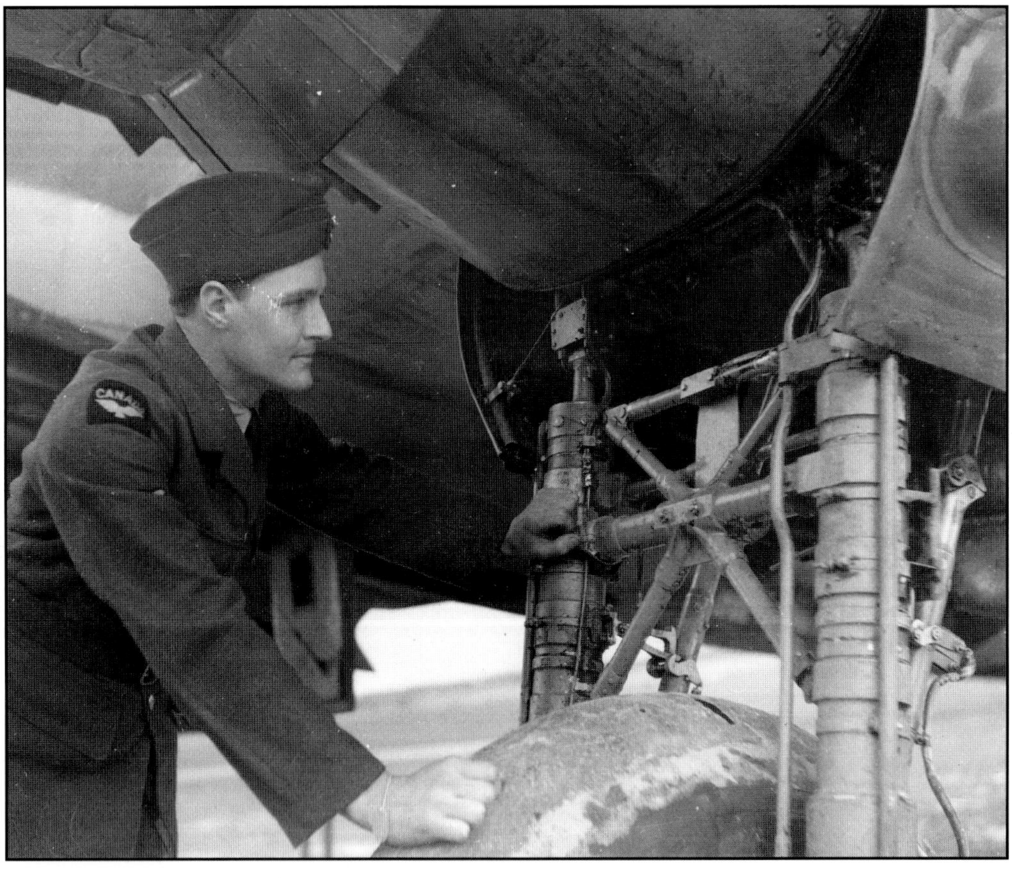

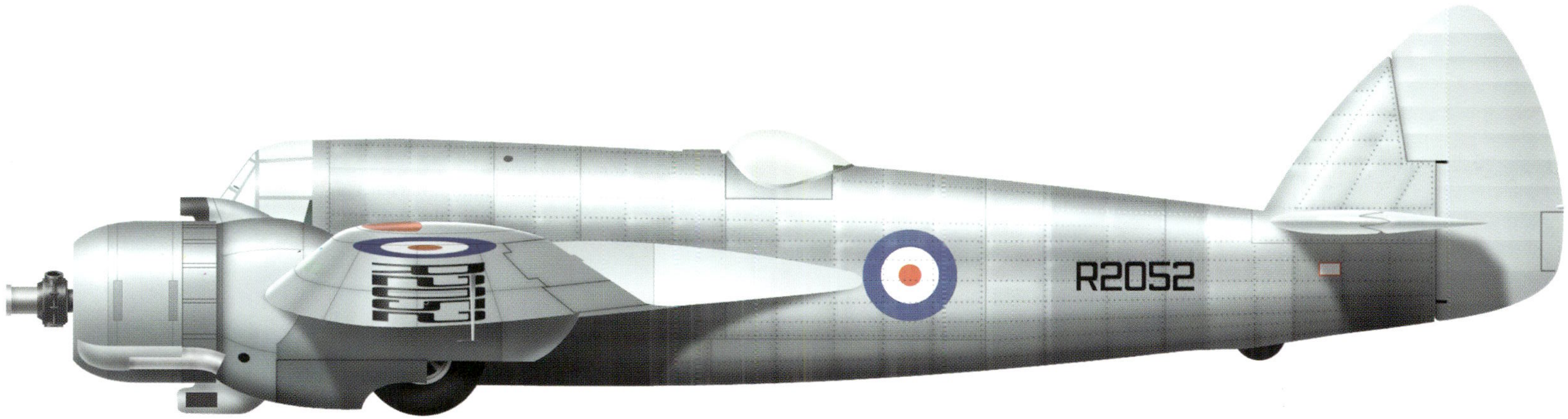

R2052, the prototype Beaufighter, at the Bristol factory in Filton. For initial trials the aircraft was left in it's natural metal finish. Photo reference page 6.

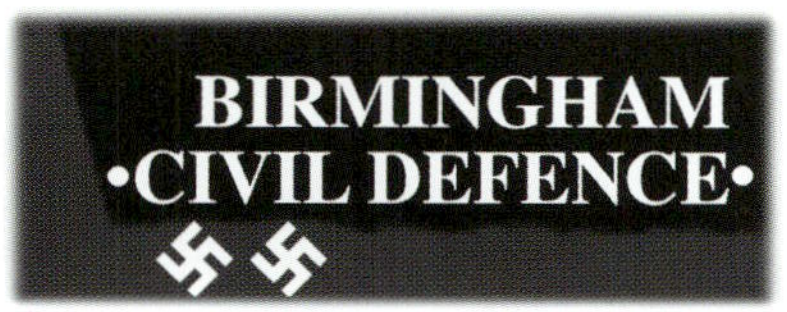

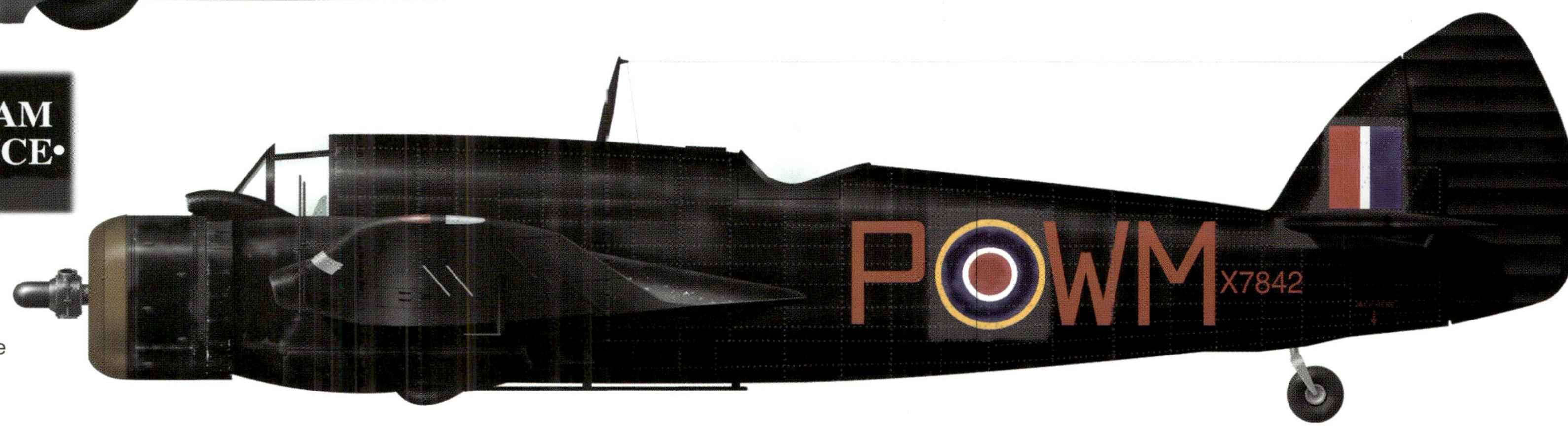

X7842 P-WM, of No.68 Squadron, in the classic 'Night' night-fighter finish. This aircraft carried the name 'Birmingham Civil Defence' on it's nose. Photo reference page 39.

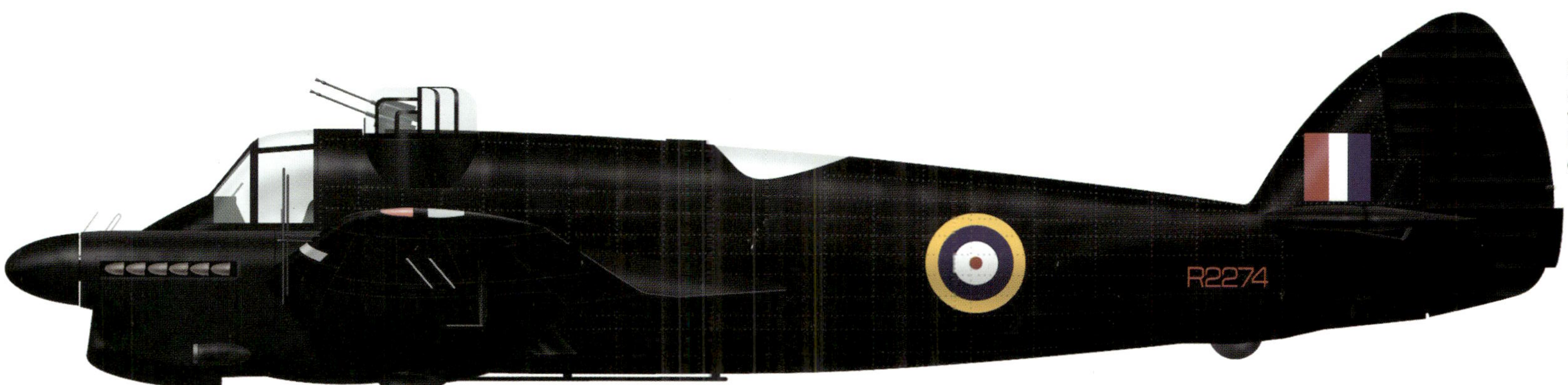

R2274, one of the two turret equipped and Merlin-engined Mk.V's built. Both were used operationally, R2274 with No.406 (RCAF) Squadron. Photo reference page 14.

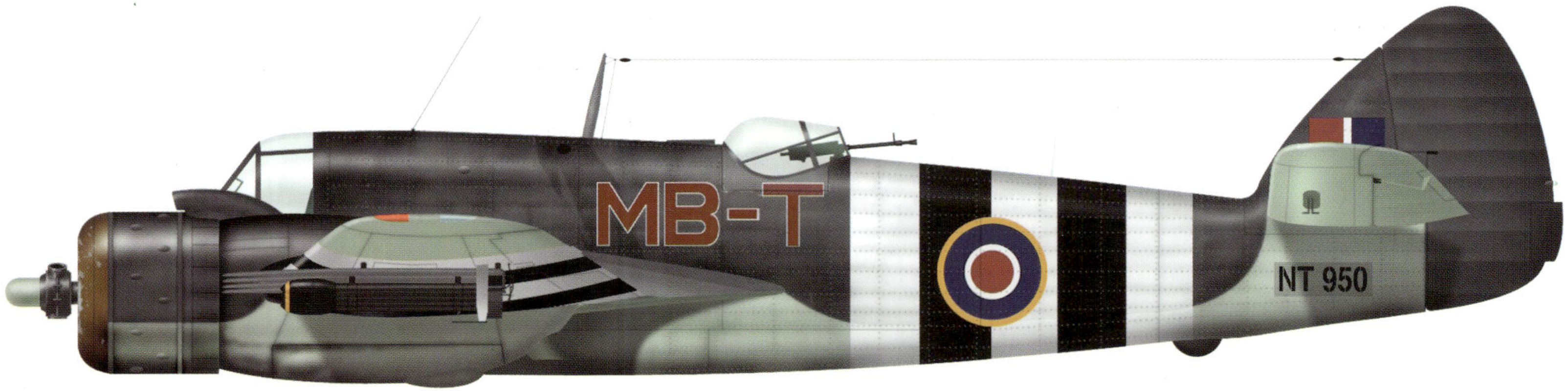

NT950, a TF Mk.X, in service with No.236 Squadron wearing the codes MB-T and D-Day invasion stripes. Dark grey and sky finish. Photo reference page 57.

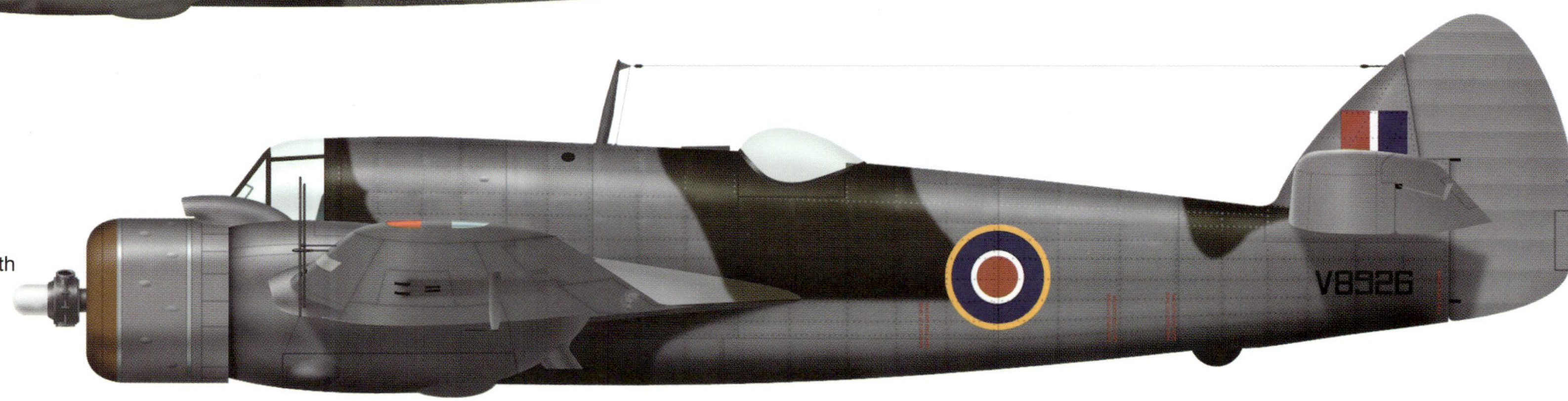

V8926, a Mk.VIf as delivered in the standard grey/green finish. The aircraft went on to serve with Nos. 153 and 96 Squadrons. Photo reference page 53.

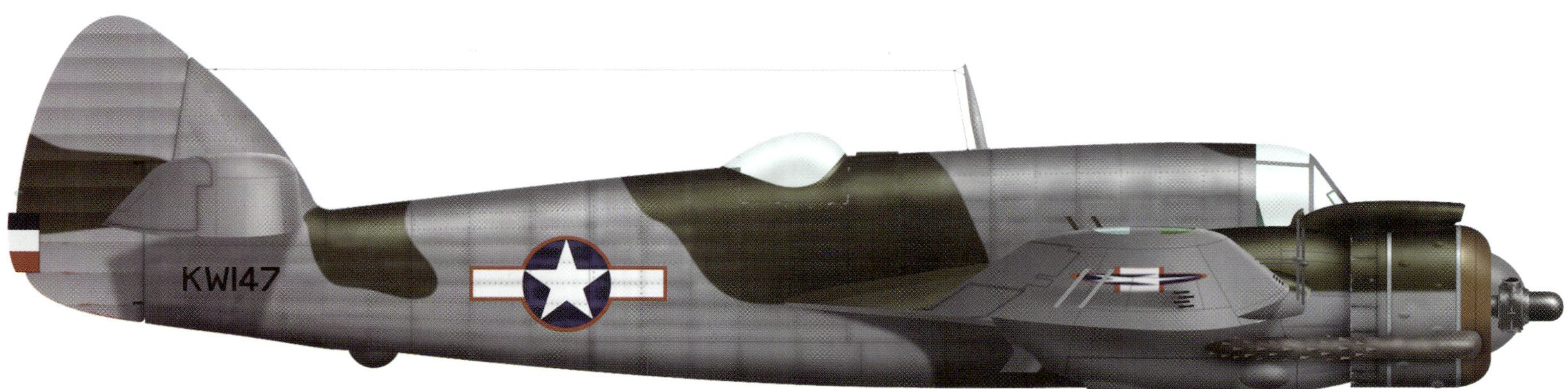

KW147, one of the Mk.VIfs delivered to the USAAF for service in Italy, carried the standard RAF colours with American markings applied. Photo reference page 86.

Mk.VIc BEAUFIGHTER

Dimensions:
Span 57' 10"
Length 41'
Height 15' 10"
Engines:
Bristol Hercules VI or XVI. 1,670hp, fourteen cylinder sleeve-valve radial air cooled.
Armament:
Four 20mm Hispano cannon in nose. Two 250 lb bombs or eight rockets.
Number Built:
753

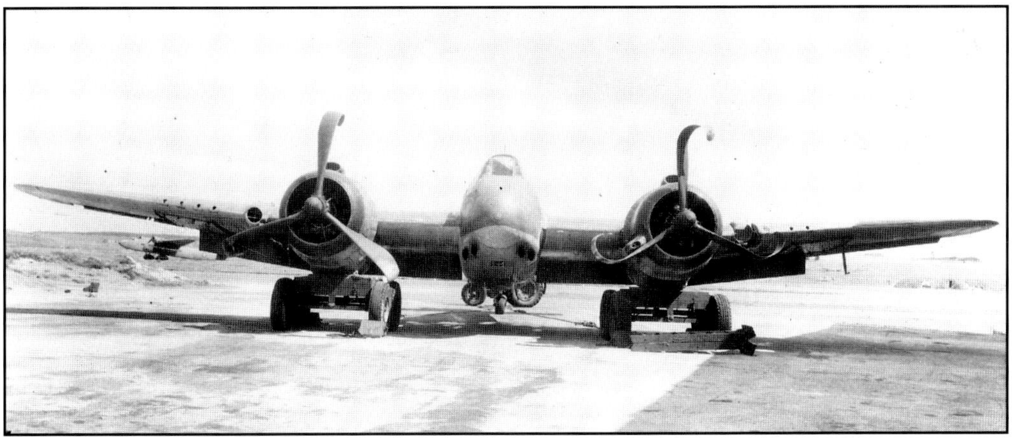

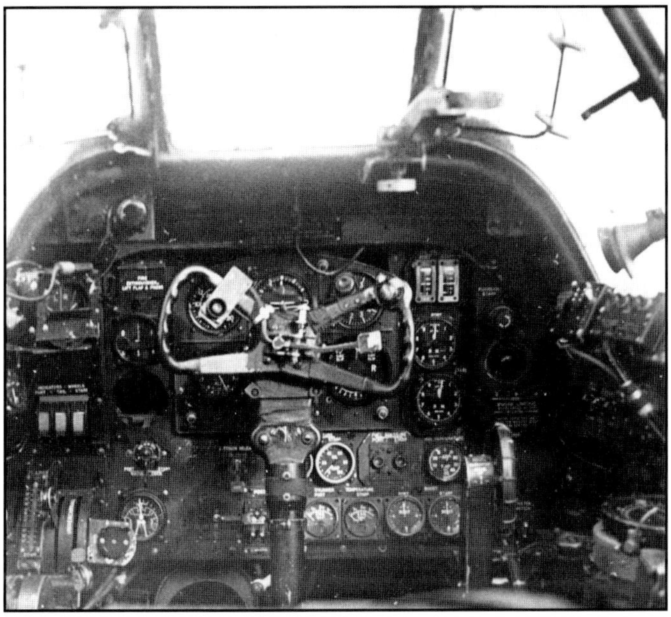

Above: **JL725 'T-Tommy' crash landed after combat with two Me109s. The pilot was Flying Officer H J Thomas.**

Left: **The cockpit of a Mk.VI.**
The pilot's view from the cockpit was considered to be the best of any RAF aircraft in World War II, giving an uninterrupted panorama from wingtip to wingtip.

Below: **A new Hercules Mk.VI for No. 406 RCAF Squadron based at Valley, in Wales gets a look over before installation in one of 'Lynx' Squadron's Mk.VIs. The standard engine was not liked by Coastal Command squadrons because it sacrificed low level performance for high level. A modification to the impellers and locking the blowers in 'M' gear improved performance, the engine then became a Mk.XVII.**

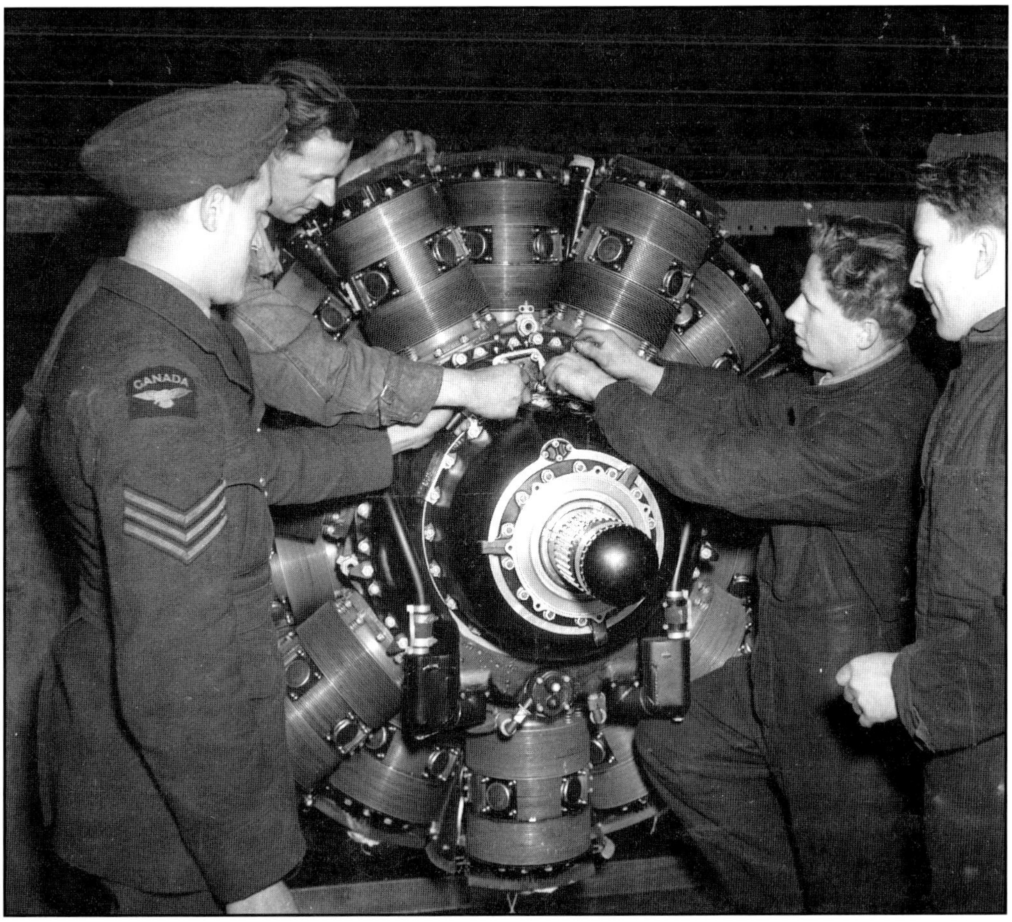

Hercules Mk.VI Specification:

Capacity:
2366 cu in.
Weight:
1930 lb.
Fuel:
100/130 Octane.
Carburettor:
Hobson AIT
Compression ratio:
7.0 : 1
Bore:
5.75 in.
Stroke:
6.5 in.
Maximum power:
1615 bhp

TFMk.X
BEAUFIGHTER

Dimensions:
Span 57' 10"
Length 41' 4"
Height 15' 10"
Engines:
Bristol Hercules XVII. 1,670hp, fourteen cylinder sleeve-valve radial air cooled.
Armament:
Four 20mm Hispano cannon in nose. Two 250 lb bombs or eight rockets. One torpedo.
Number Built:
2205

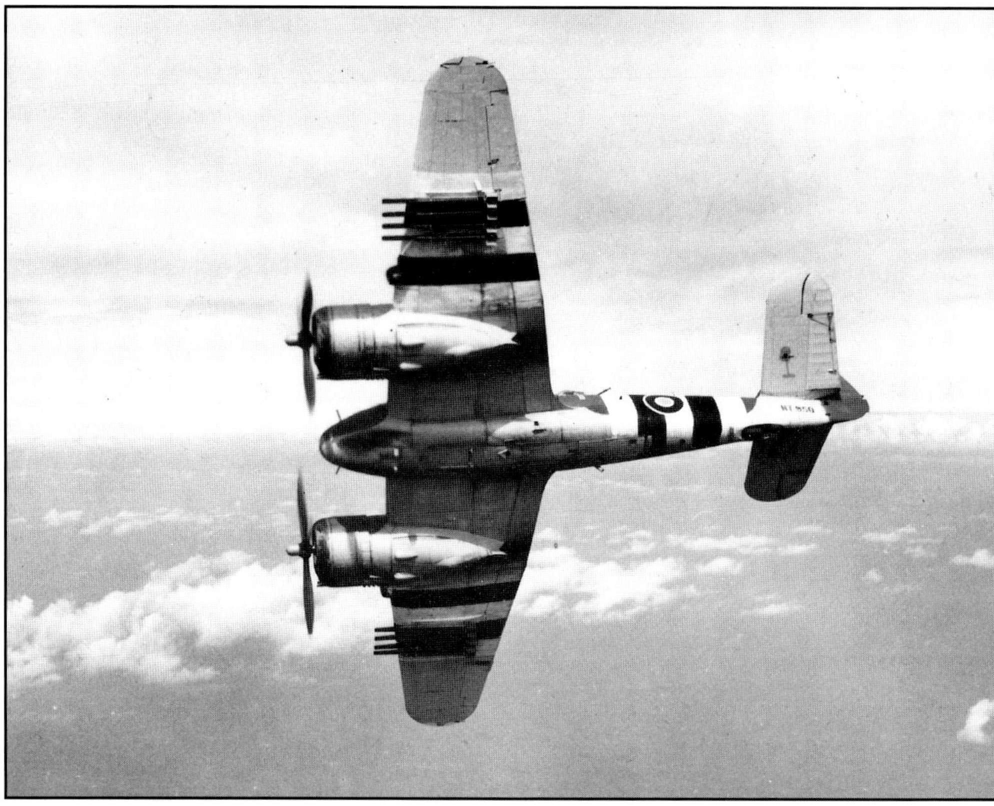

Above: **NT850, a Mk TF Mk.X belonging to No. 236 Squadron. The Mk.X became the standard equipment of the Coastal Command Strike Wings, being variously fitted with a torpedo or rockets. The Strike Wings encompassed Nos. 143,144, 235, 236 and 254 Squadrons from the RAF. The Canadian No. 404 Squadron, the Australian No. 455, and New Zealand No. 489 Squadrons made a total of eight squadrons which were originally based in Scotland for operations across the North Sea. Following the D-Day landings the Strike Wings moved south to support the invasion.**
A total of 2,205 Mk.Xs were built, mostly at the Weston factory, with a further 110 aircraft finished at Stoke-on-Trent.

Heavyweight Beaus

The Mk.X with torpedo gear began to replace the Beaufort in Coastal Command service from 1942. All production aircraft were fitted with a 0.303 Browning machine gun in the observer's position for rearward defence. AI Mk.VIII was installed in a nose radome for ASV work, the torpedo gear with gyro-angling, radio and navigation equipment moved the centre of gravity and increased instability problems. To cure this the elevator area and fin area were increased on later aircraft.

Right and Below: **Three inch RPs (Rocket Projectiles) on the under-wing racks. These are fitted with 25lb semi-armour-piercing heads. When used in large numbers by Strike Wings it was quite possible to sink a sizable ship with rockets alone.**

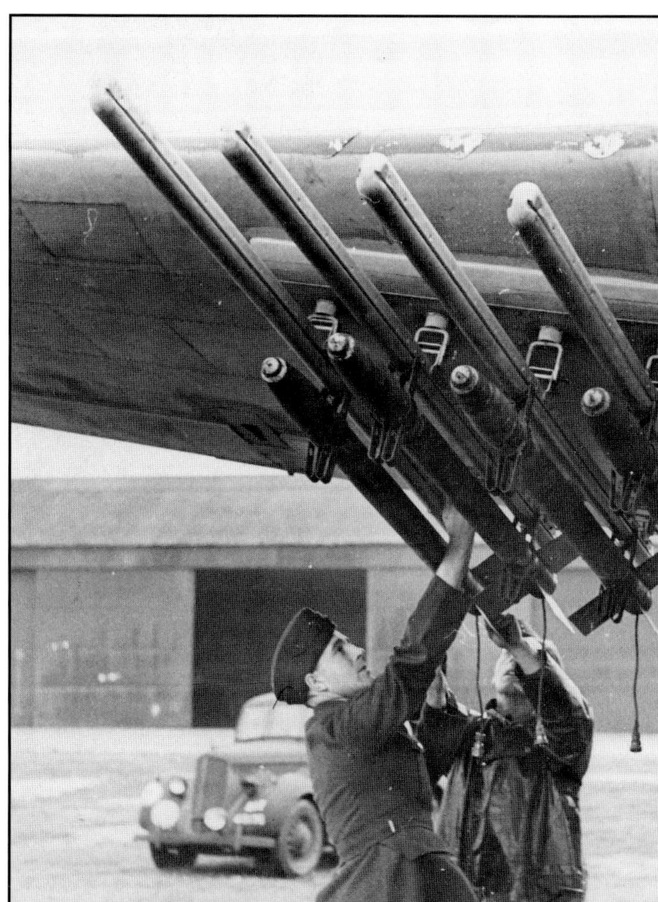

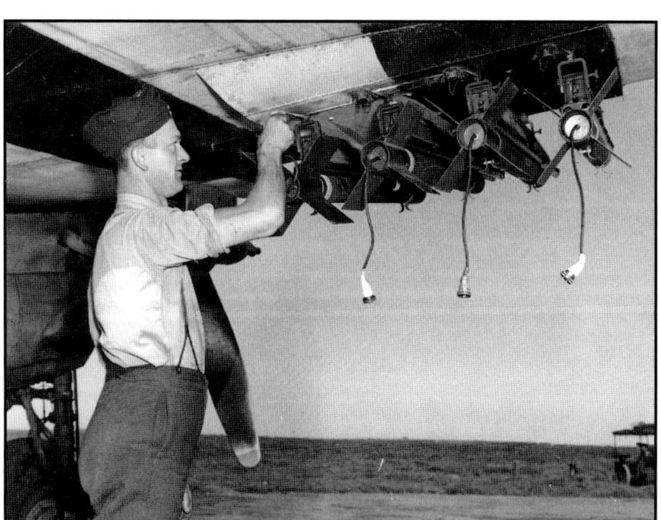

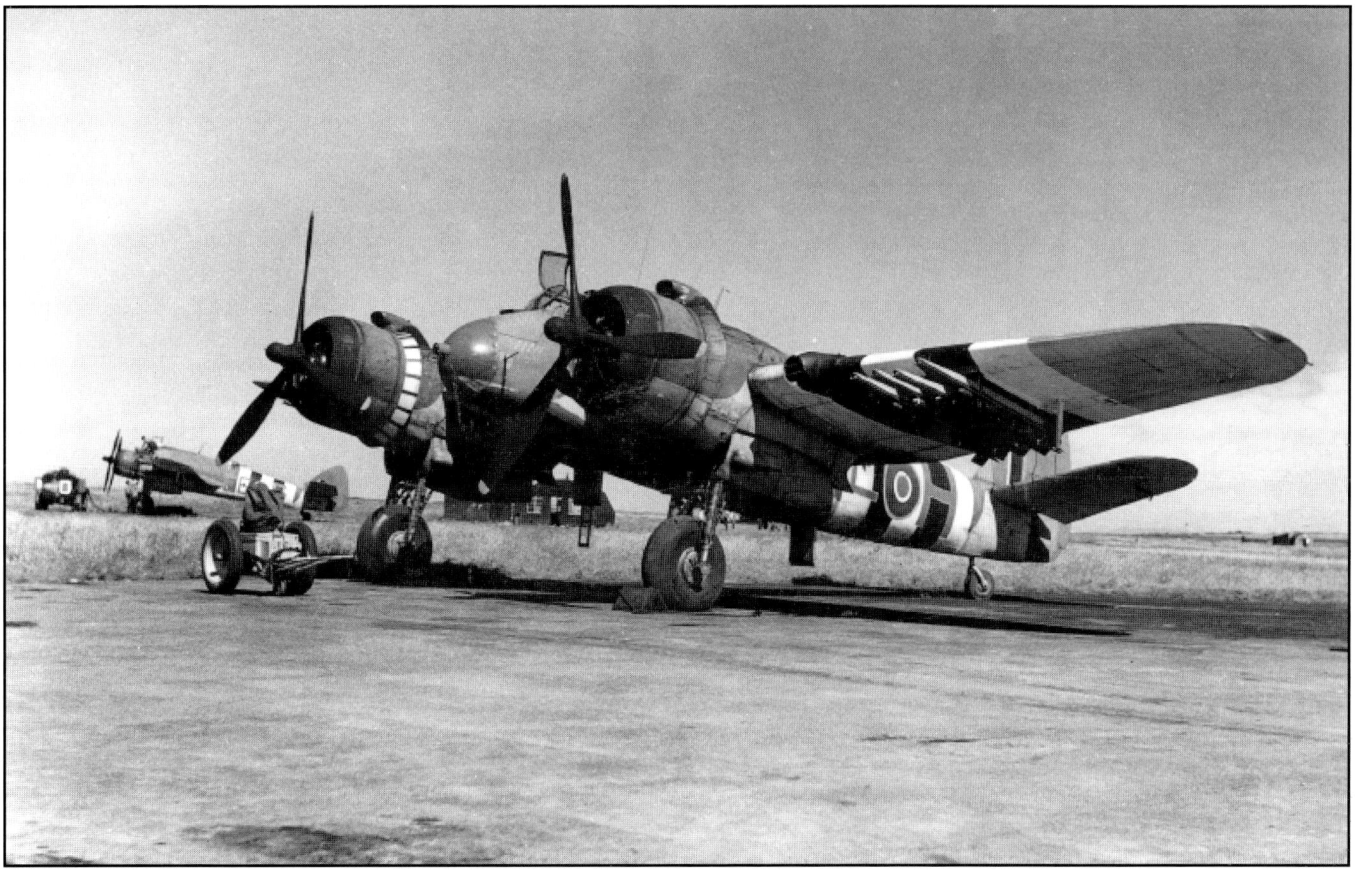

Above: **TF Mk.X NE355 of No. 404 Squadron, based at Davidstow Moor, Cornwall, in August 1944. This Beaufighter has a Fairchild camera mounted in the nose to enable the attack to be photographed for later assessment.**

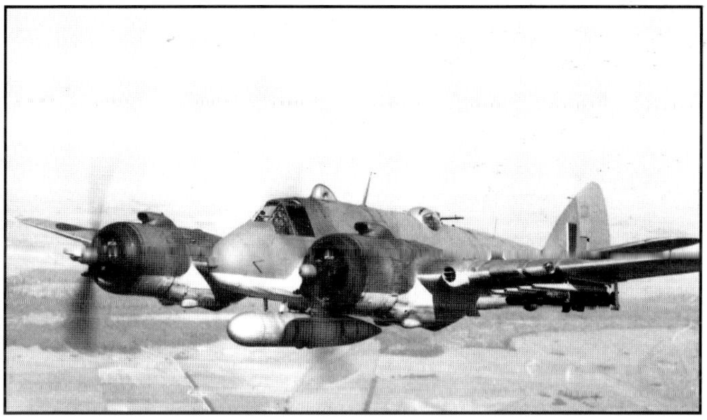

Right: **This TF Mk.X displays its 1770 hp Hercules engines and a 200 gallon long-range fuel tank mounted on the torpedo carrier under the fuselage centre line. This tank was often used for ferry flights to the Far East which became common place as operations switched from Europe in the later stages of the war. This aircraft also shows the Vickers K gun in the dorsal turret.**

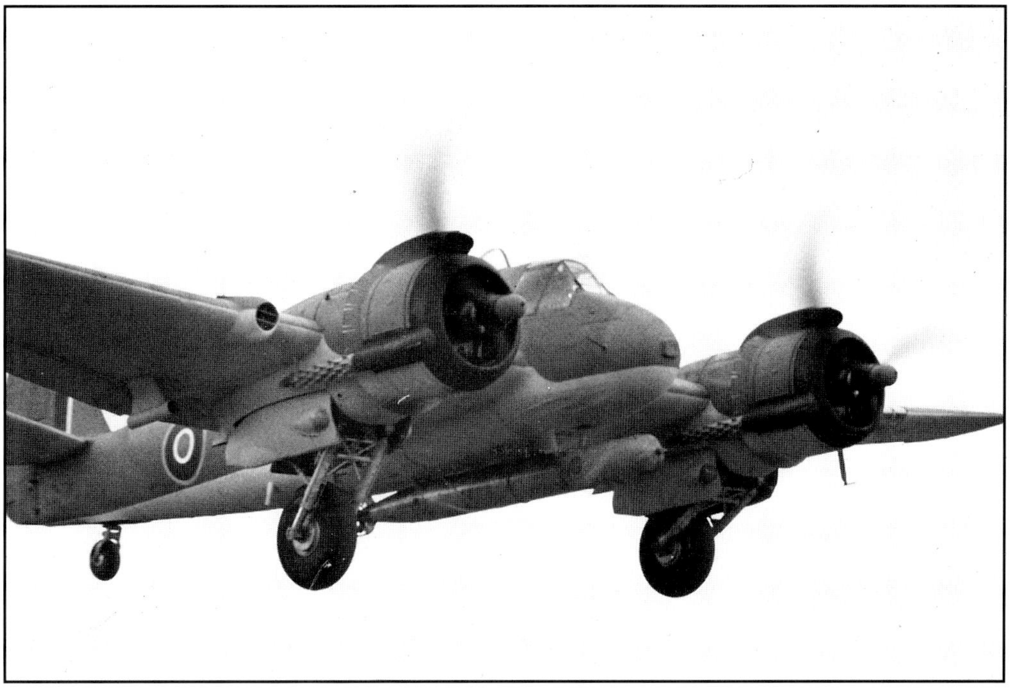

Right: **LZ414, a TFX prior to delivery to a squadron carrying a torpedo. Trials with torpedoes under Beaufighters began in 1942 and led to the development of a torpedo capable of being dropped at high speed. The Monoplane Air Tail (MAT) torpedo had a gyro controlled tail fin that held it stable after release. The MAT Mk.IV equipped torpedo could be dropped from between 60 and 1,000 feet at speeds of up to 300 knots. The standard drop was from 250 feet at 250 knots.**

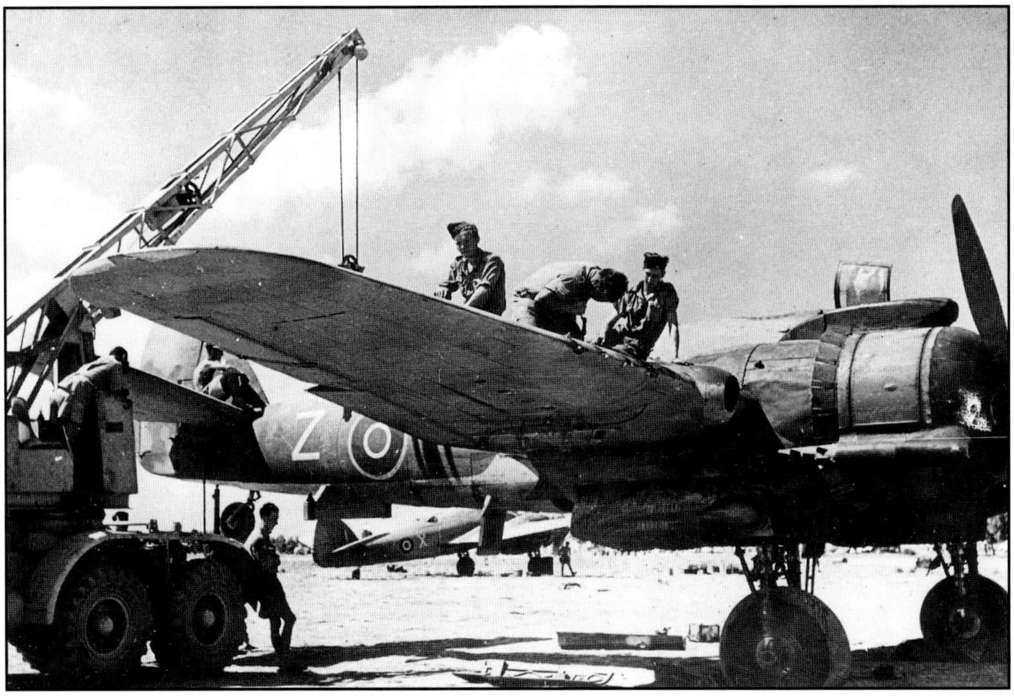

Left: **JL899 was one of 163 Mk.XI Beaufighters built. In this photograph a new starboard wing is lifted into place during a major service on Malta.**
The Mk.XI was similar to a TF Mk.X, but had no torpedo rack under the fuselage. All the Mk.XIs were made at the Weston factory.
Difficult to identify, the Mk.XIs fell into the serial ranges JL876 to 915, JL937 to 948, JM105 to 136, JM158 to 185, JM206 to 250, and JM 262 to 267.

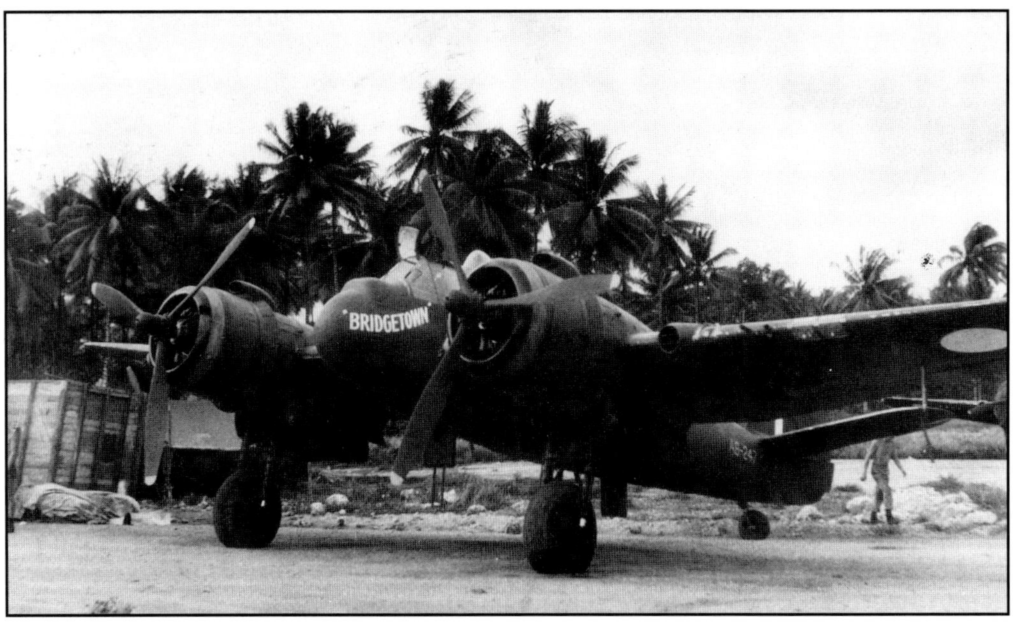

Left: **The Australian Mk.21, A8-247 from No. 30 Squadron at Los Negros in the Admiralty Islands during 1945. The aircraft was painted in a darker than usual black-green and carried the name 'Bridgetown' after a town in Western Australia.**
364 Beaufighters were made at the Fishermen's Bend factory. Based on the Mk.X, the Mk.21 carried two 0.5 inch machine guns in each wing and an obvious bulge on the nose housing a Sperry autopilot.

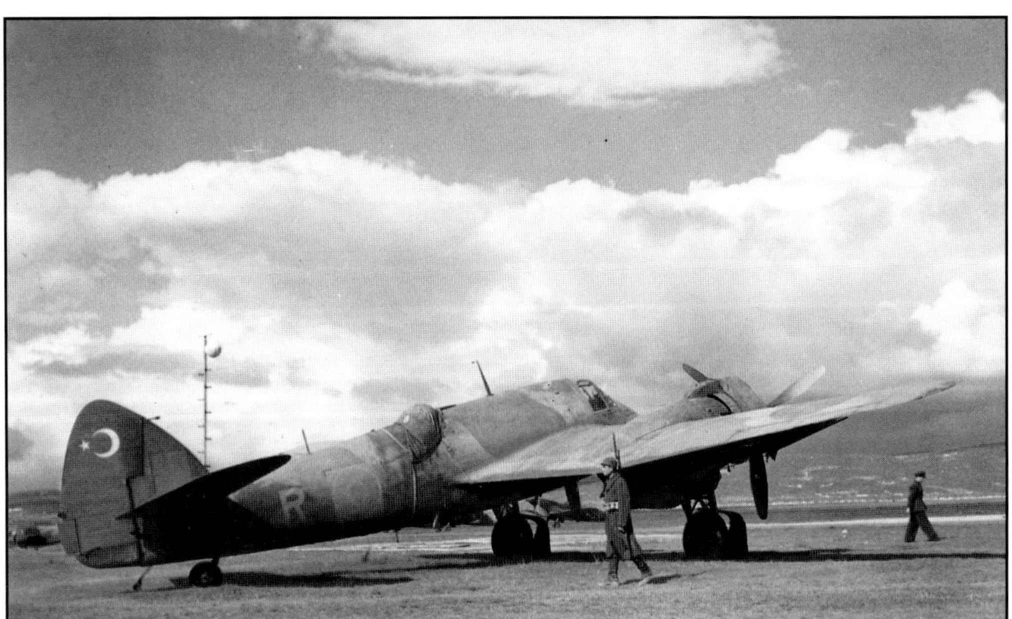

Left: **NV215, a TFX, was transferred to the Turkish Air Force in 1944. The white star and crescent national emblem has been painted on the all red tail, but the RAF markings still show through under a thin coat of paint.**
After the war, in 1946, a further 20 refurbished Beaufighters were supplied to Turkey. Portugal used a total of 18 aircraft, and ten went to the Dominican Air Force. Four Mk.Xs were purchased under cover for use by the Israeli Air Force.

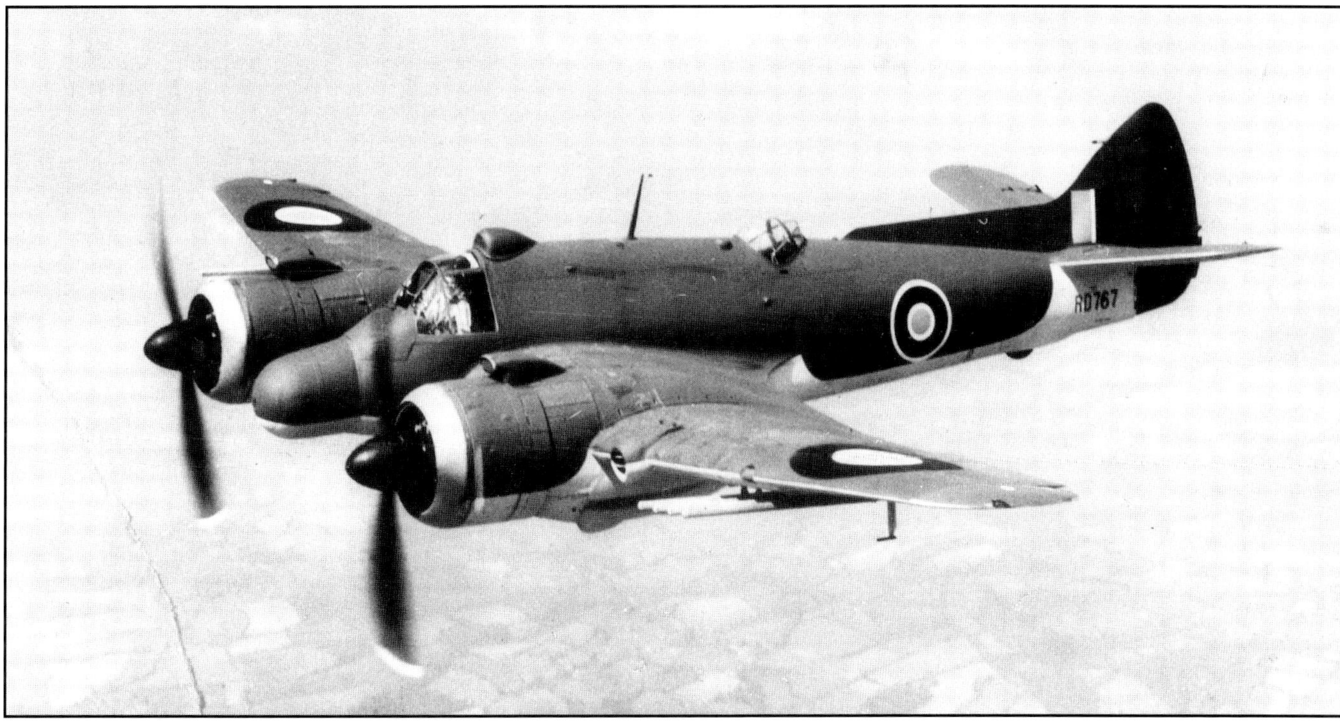

Above **RD767** and Below **SR919 represent the ultimate Beaufighters. Both are TF Mk.Xs with radome nose for AI Mk.VIII, dorsal fin, rocket rails and centre line torpedo rack.**

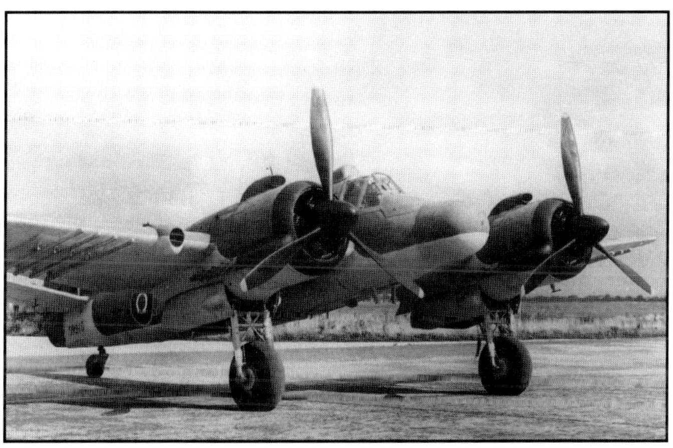

Below: **The cockpit of a TT10 at Seletar Base Flight in 1955 (RF Chandler)**

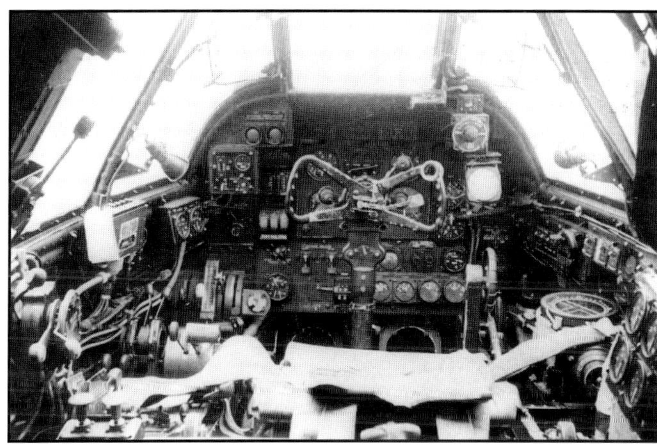

Right: **The TT10 target tugs were the last operational RAF Beaufighters. This, RD859, served with Seletar Base Flight which made the very last sortie on 16 May 1960. (R F Chandler)**
Work on the TT Mk.10 began in November 1947 and the conversion involved fitting a windmill winch and removing all Radar and armament. The prototype flew in May 1948 and was followed by 35 more aircraft converted at Filton.

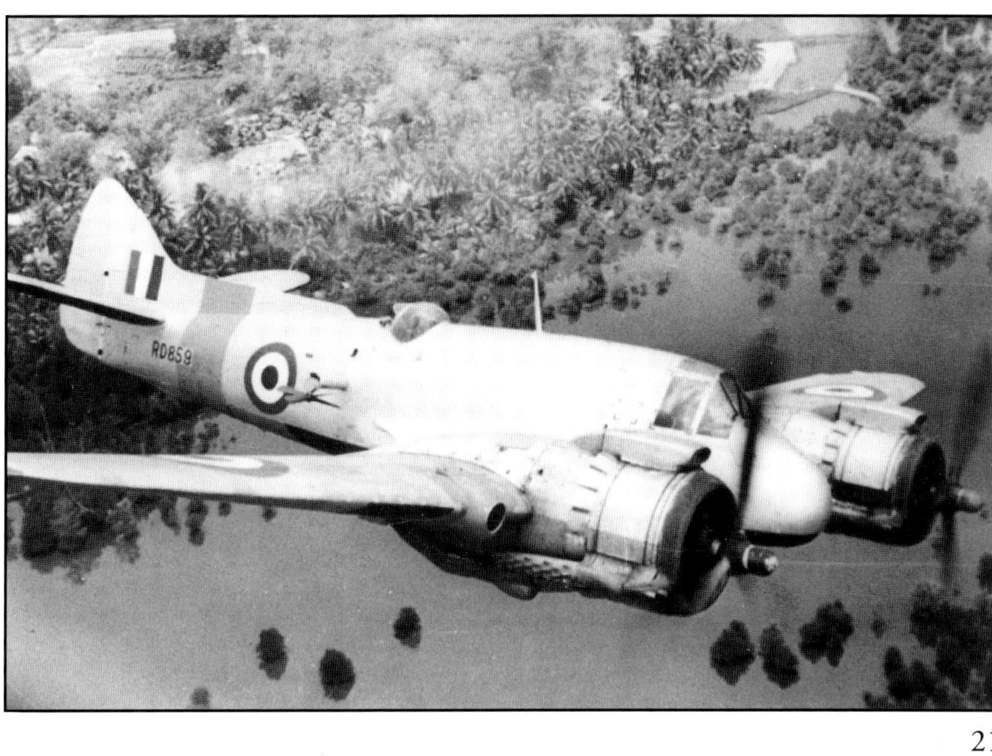

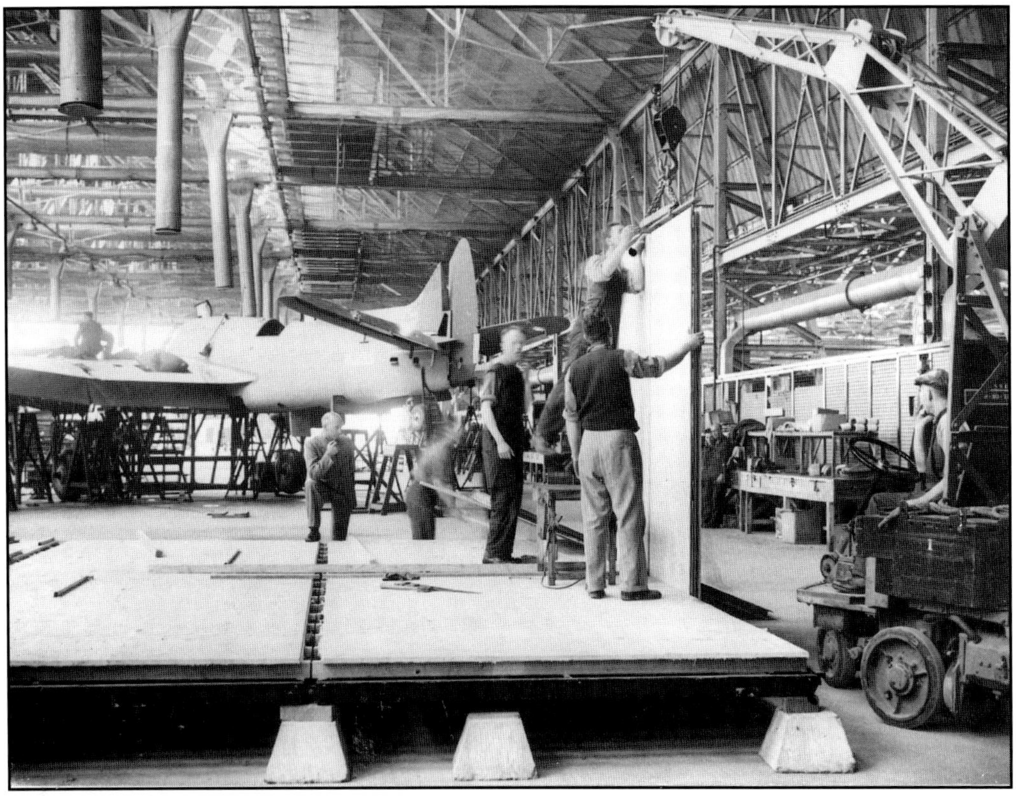

Left: **In July 1945 the Bristol factory at Weston-Super-Mare changed from producing Beaufighters to prefabricated houses. This had the double benefit of easing the housing crisis caused by German bombing and providing jobs for the otherwise redundant workers. The houses were made from aluminium sheet and were prefabricated in four units to be assembled on site. Each bungalow had two-bedrooms, a kitchen, bathroom, hall and lounge. It was planned that production would reach 1,200 houses a month at the Weston factory.**

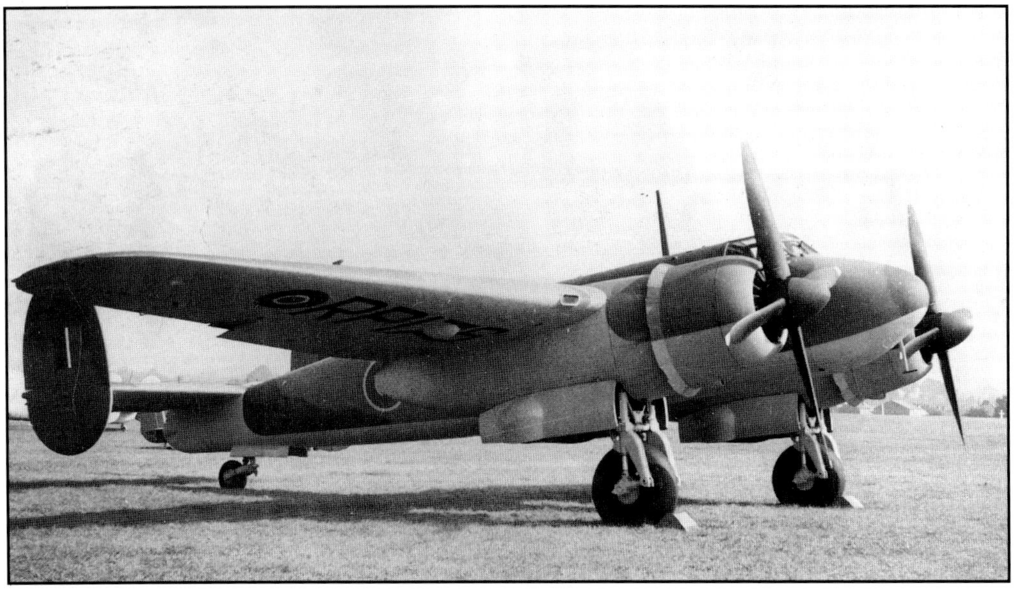

Left: **Loosely based on the Beaufighter, was the Buckmaster Mk.I, RP175, seen in October 1945. Throughout the war many specifications were issued. One resulted in the Buckingham, a fast, heavily armed day bomber with a three man crew, but the performance asked for was not achievable. In the immediate post war years a dual-control version of the Brigand was called for, so 110 unfinished and unwanted Buckingham airframes were converted to become Buckmasters.**

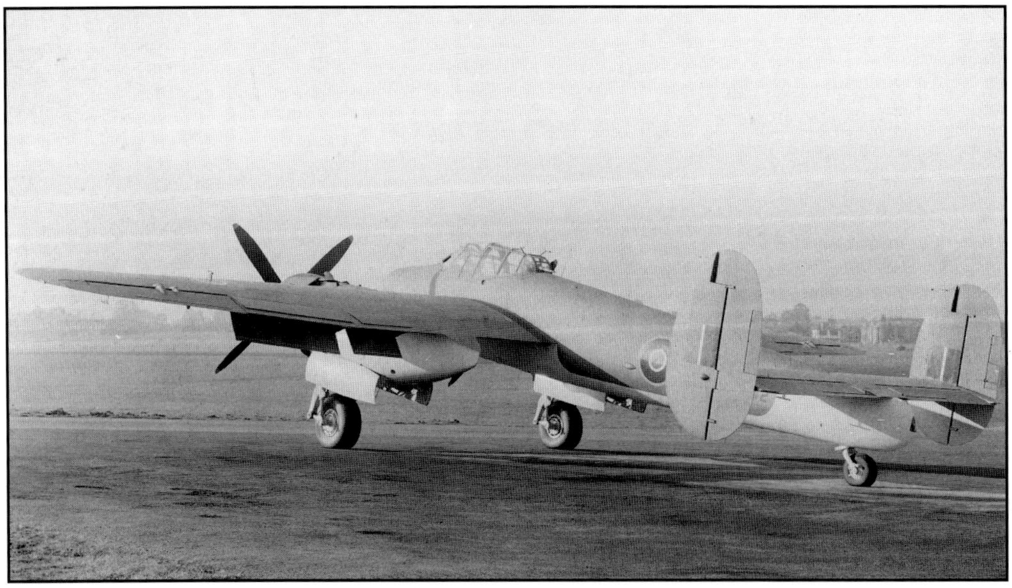

Left: **Designed to replace the Beaufighter in RAF service, the Bristol Brigand. The first eleven Brigands were delivered in 1946, by which time there was no need for a new coastal strike aircraft. They were then modified for use in the Far East as light bombers, finally entering service in 1949 with No. 8 Squadron in Aden. In 1950, No. 45 Squadron replaced its Beaufighters with Brigands for operations over the Malayan jungle, thus ending ten years of Beaufighter operations.**

THE SQUADRONS

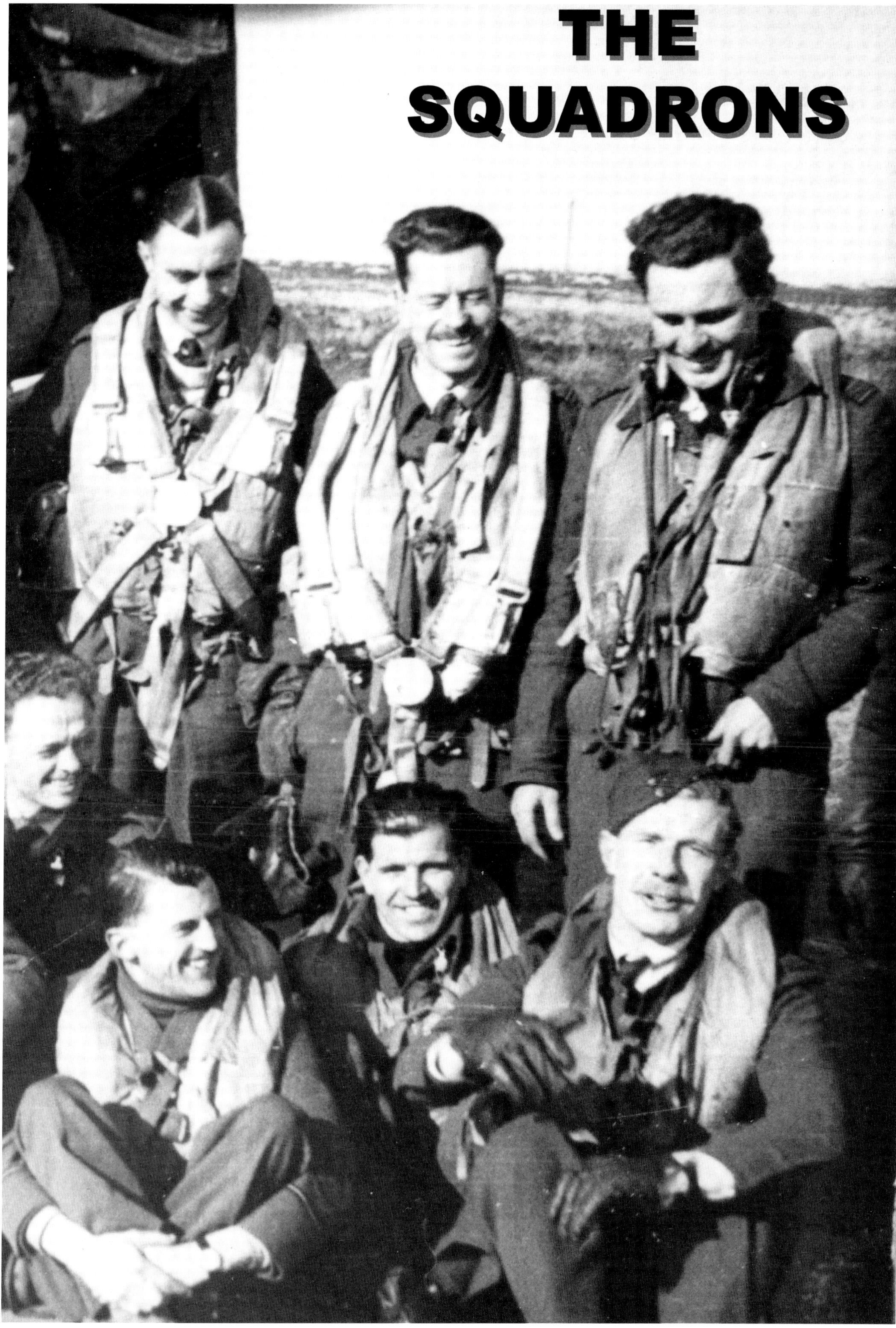

22 SQUADRON

Preux et audacieux
(Valiant and Brave)
Code Letters:
OA
Usage:
Mk.X
June 44 to Sept 45
Rôle:
Attacking Japanese shipping from Ceylon and Burma
Bases:
Ratmalana. 6/44 - 7/44
Vavuniya. 7/44 - 12/44
Kumbhirgram. 12/44 - 1/45
Joari. 1/45 - 4/45
Chiringa. 4/45 - 6/45
Gannavaram. 6/45 - 9/45

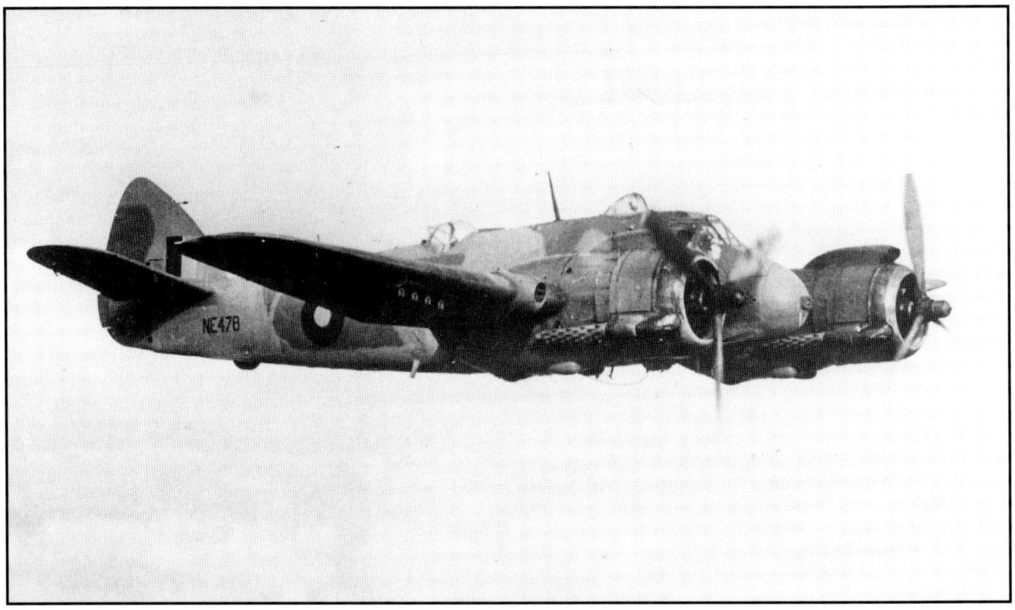

Above: **No. 22 Squadron replaced their Beauforts with Beaufighter TF Mk.Xs, in June 1944. Rockets and torpedoes were carried for anti-shipping duties, but their main role changed in December 1944 to ground attack on the Burma front. Above is NE478, 'V' of No. 22 Squadron, operating from Ratmalana in June 1944. (A Thomas)**

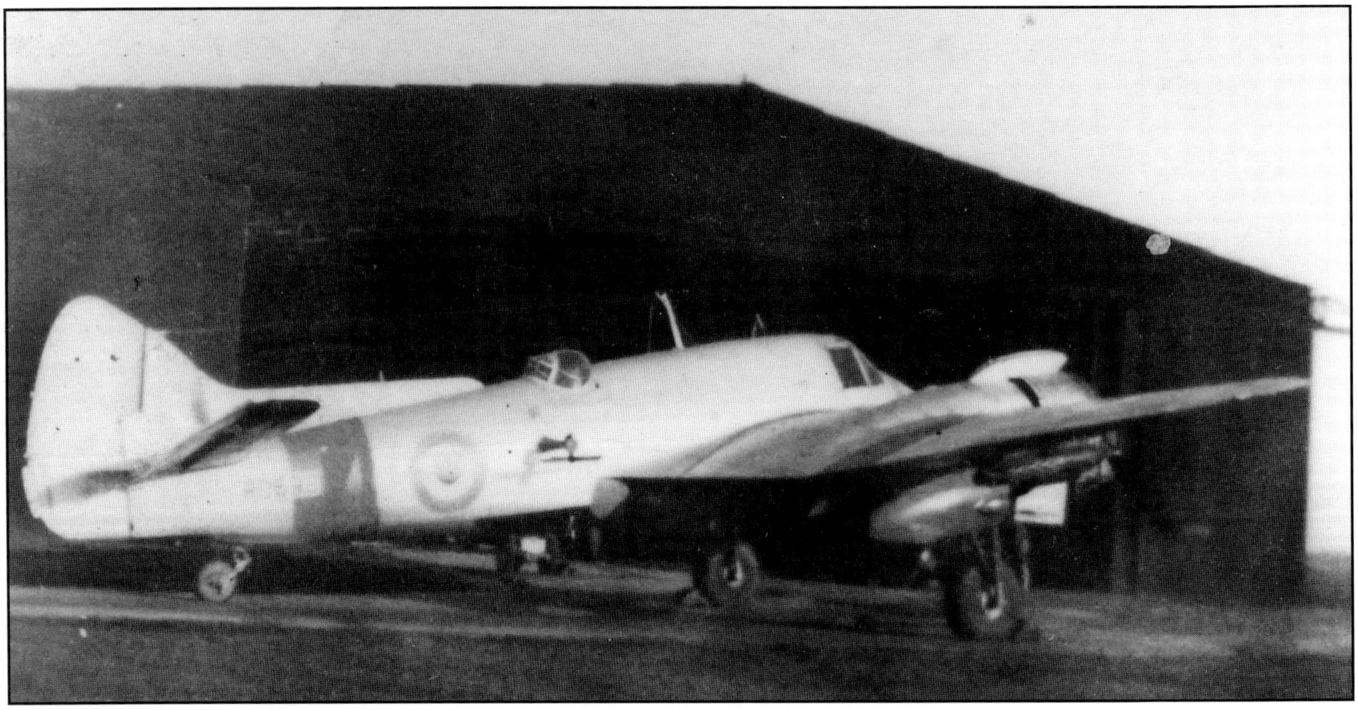

Above: **In 1947 thirty-five Mk.X airframes were allocated for conversion to TT10s at Filton. The TT10 had no armour or armament and was fitted with Hercules Mk.XVIII engines. The target was launched from the lower rear escape hatch. The wind driven winch is clearly visible on the starboard side.**

5 SQUADRON

Usage:
TT10
Jan 50 to Sept 51
Rôle:
Anti-aircraft target towing duties
Base:
Pembrey, Wales

17 SQUADRON

Usage:
TT10
May 49 to May 51
Rôle:
Anti-aircraft target towing duties
Base:
Chivenor

20 SQUADRON

Usage:
TT10
Feb 49 to Oct 51
Rôle:
Anti-aircraft target towing duties
Base:
Llanbedr and Valley, Wales

25 SQUADRON

Ferines tego
(Striking I defend)
Code Letters:
ZK
Usage:
Mk.1F
Oct 40 to Jan 43
Rôle:
Night fighters
in defence of Britain
Bases:
Debden 10/40 - 11/40
Wittering 11/40 - 1/42
Ballyhalbert 1/42 - 5/42
Church Fenton 4/42 - 1/43

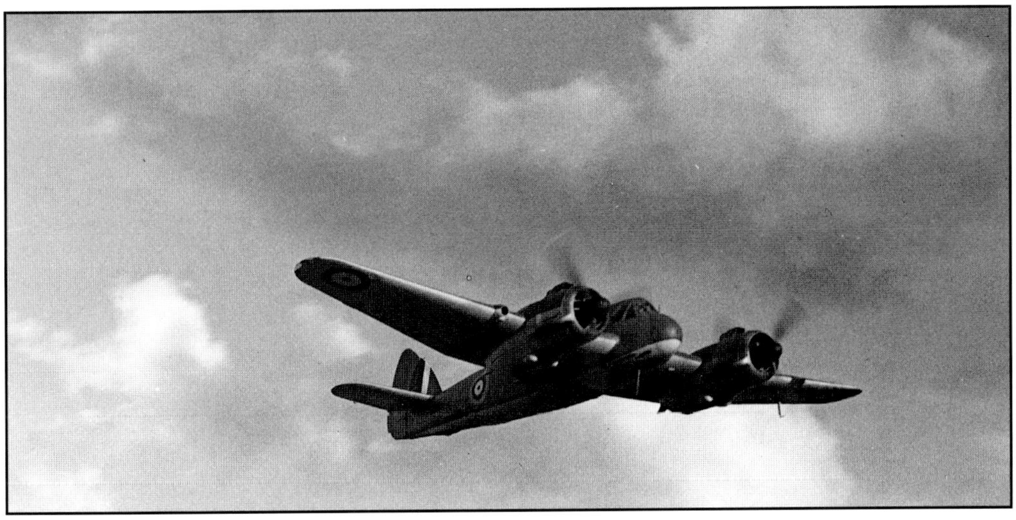

Above: **One of No. 25 Squadron's first Beaufighters, with no wing guns or AI equipment.**
Below: **R2081 in a blast pen at Debden.**

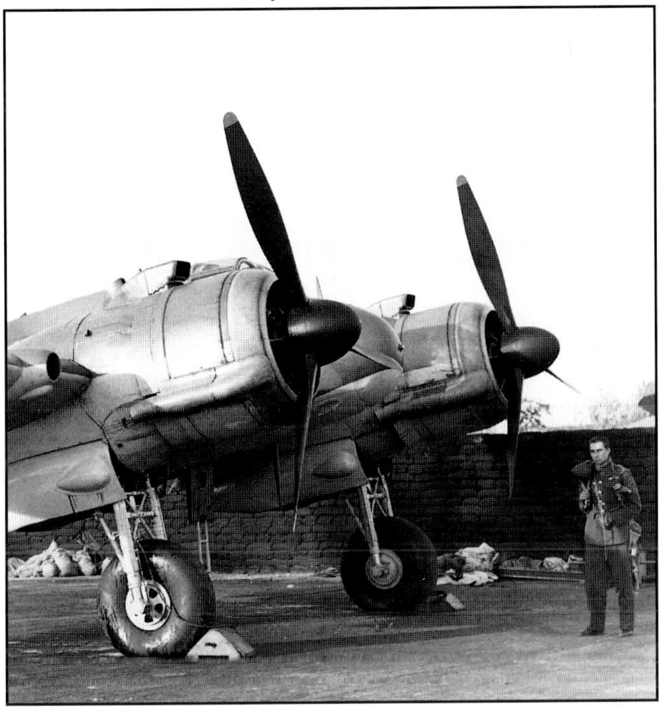

Squadron Leader Mike Herrick

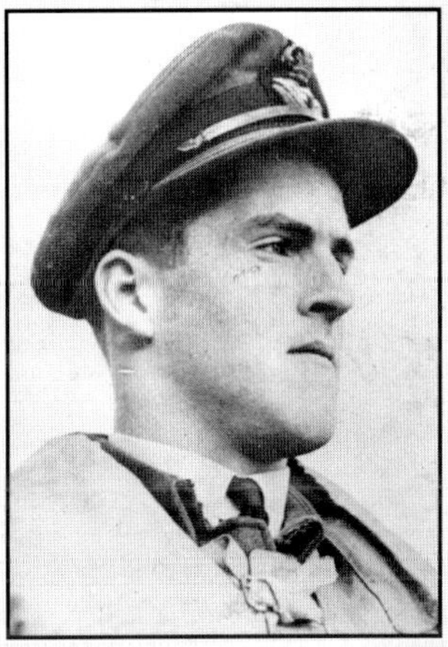

Michael James (Mike) Herrick was a New Zealander flying with No. 25 Squadron in 1940 when he claimed an He111 and Do17 on the night of 4/5 September. For this he was awarded a DFC. On 22 June 1941 he, with AI Operator Pilot Officer Yeomans, shot down a Ju88 in R2277. His victim was a Luftwaffe night intruder of 1./NJG2 coded R4+JH that crashed at Deeping St. James, near Peterborough. Herrick then flew with RNZAF in the Pacific and returned to Europe to fly Mosquitos with No. 305 Squadron in 1944, but was killed after being shot down off Denmark on 16 June.

Below: **R2069 was one of the first three Beaufighters to arrive at Debden and No. 25 Squadron, the others being R2067 and R2068. In the background are the Blenheim Mk.Ifs that the Beaufighter was replacing. Wearing an early camouflage scheme of Dark Green and Dark Earth upper surfaces with Sky undersides this can be seen as one of the very first production aircraft as it has a 'full-height' fin flash. This aircraft had an eventful career and served with No. 68 Squadron, No. 256 Squadron and finally No. 51 OTU. It was with the OTU that the aircraft was lost when its pilot lost control during a practice attack on a B-17. It crashed at Easton Maudit, Northants, on 24 March, 1943.**

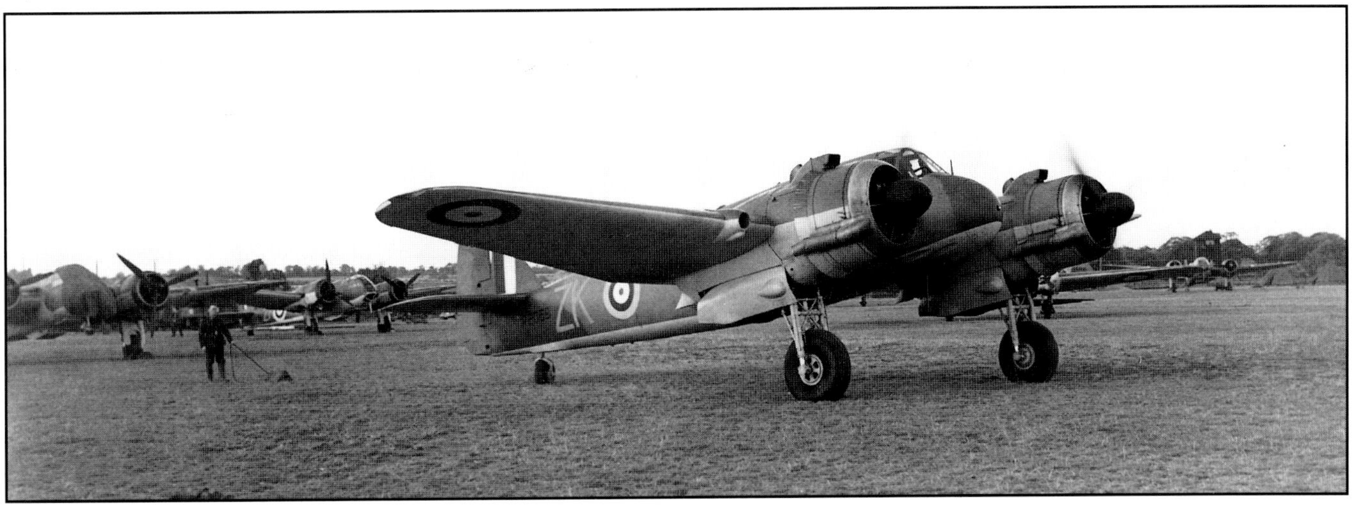

27 SQUADRON

Quam celerrime ad astra
(With all speed to the stars)

Usage:
Mk.VIf Nov 42 to Mar 44
TF Mk.X Mar 44 - Feb 46

Rôle:
General attacks on Japanese supply lines in Burma and India.

Bases:
Kanchrapara 1/43-2/43
Agartala 2/43-2/44
Parashuram 2/44-3/44
Cholavaram 3/44-9/44
Ranchi 9/44 - 10/44
Agartala 10/44
Dohazari 10/44-11/44
Chiringa 11/44-6/45
Akyab 6/45-10/45
Mingaladon 10/45-2/46

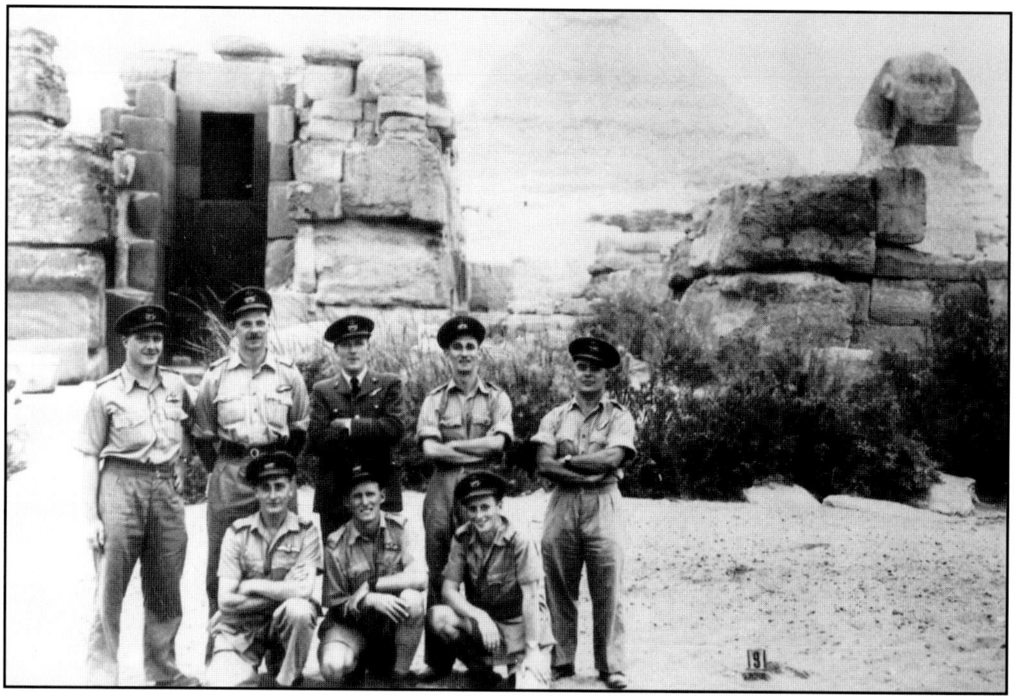

Above: **No. 27 Squadron was re-formed on Beaufighters in September 1942. Crews came from the Middle East as well as some posted straight from No. 2 (C) OTU Catfoss. These men, posing in front of the Sphinx in November 1942, were posted from Nos. 227, 252 and 272 Squadrons.** Back row L-R: **P/O Hassell (+14/11/43), P/O Goodman, P/O Welch, P/O Dinwoodie, P/O Herbert (shot down 18/11/43 and died in captivity).** Front Row L-R: **F/O Williams (died with Herbert above), P/O Innes, P/O Sterling.**

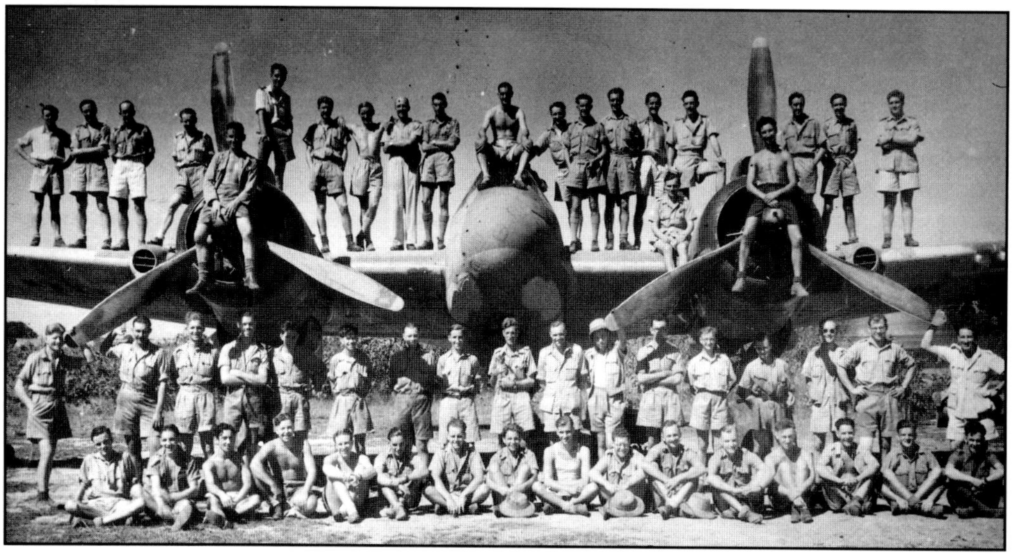

Left: **'B' Flight, No. 27 Squadron assemble for the photographer at Agartala in 1943.**

No. 27 Squadron had been flying Blenheims in Malaya for most of 1941. As Pearl Harbor came under attack, other Japanese forces attacked Malaya and in the course of several attacks wiped out the squadron as an effective unit. The squadron began re-forming in September 1942, to become one of the first three Beaufighter squadrons in the Far East. It was not until February 1943 that it became operational from Agartala, East Bengal. Operations in the early months were in support of Wingate's *Phantom Army*, and the task was to interfere with enemy rail and road transport behind the front lines.

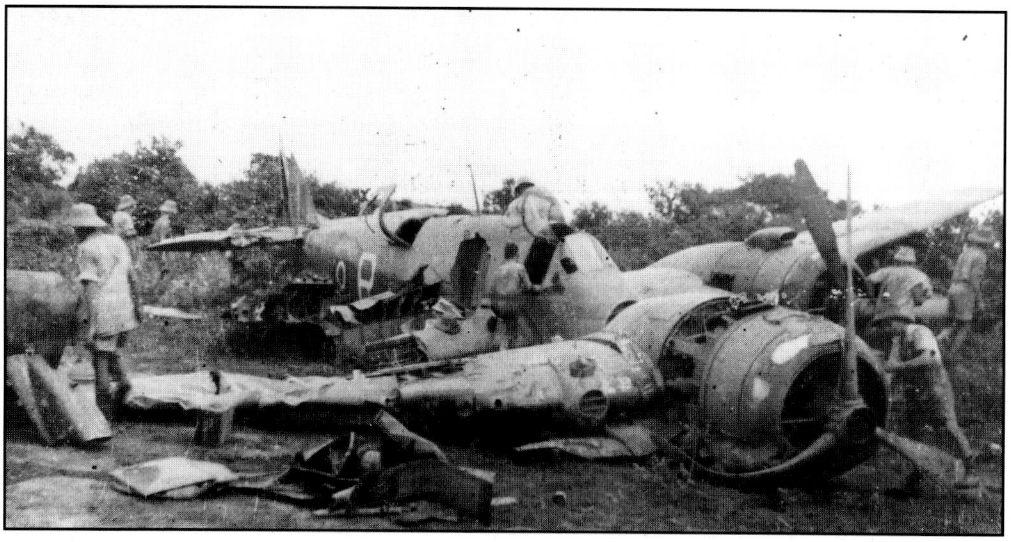

Left: **Beaufighter Mk.VIf 'R' of No. 27 Squadron which crashed in 1943. The squadron did not use any two letter code.**

Right: **On 16 December 1943 Flight Sergeant Ron Thorogood and his observer Flying Officer Edgar Welch were flying with Pilot Officer David Innes as a pair of Beaufighters when they spotted new defences on Ramree Island. They got a hot reception and small arms fire hit both aircraft. Thorogood's was worst hit and the hydraulics failed, necessitating a wheels up landing at Kanchrapara Maintenance Unit.**

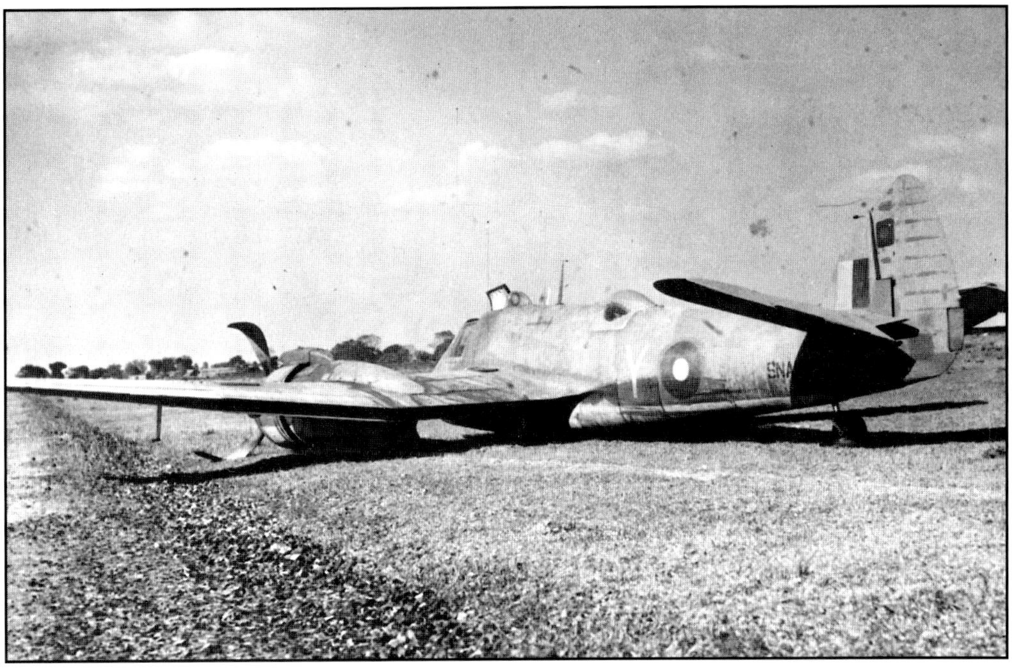

Right: **Thorogood and Welch again in another incident. This time Beaufighter Mk.VI, EL439, hit the air traffic control hut at Agartala on 4 July 1943 after the brakes failed. Again both walked away.**

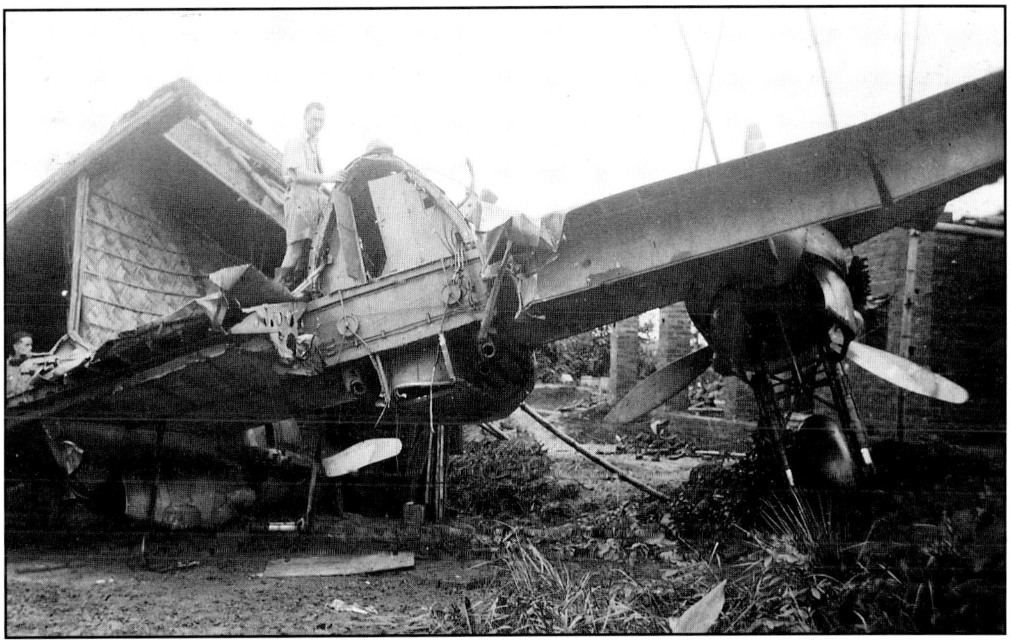

Right: **On 19 October, 1943, Thorogood (right) and Welch (centre) set off with Wing Commander Nicholson VC and his observer Lieutenant Franklin to strafe enemy communications. Between them they damaged five locomotives, bringing the squadron's total to 100 in the eight months they had been operating.**

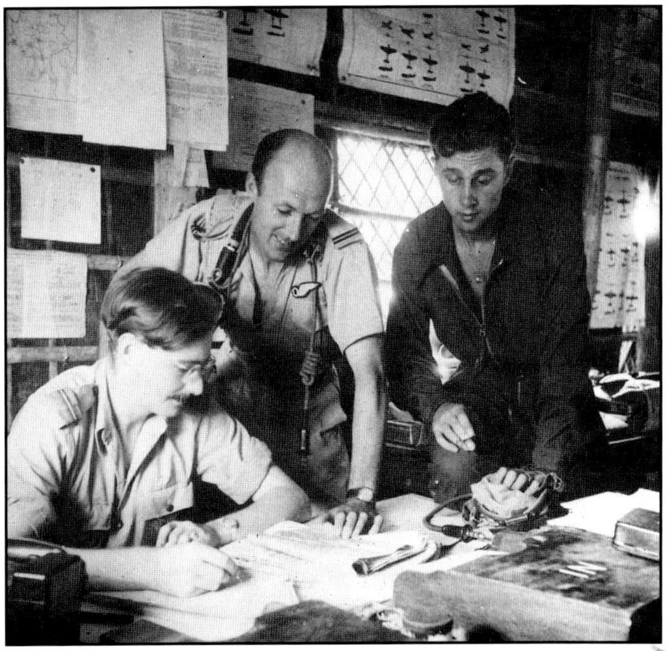

Below: **a typical train-busting attack.**

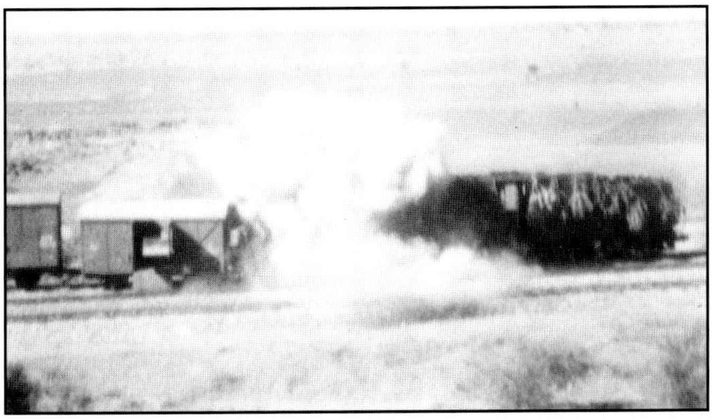

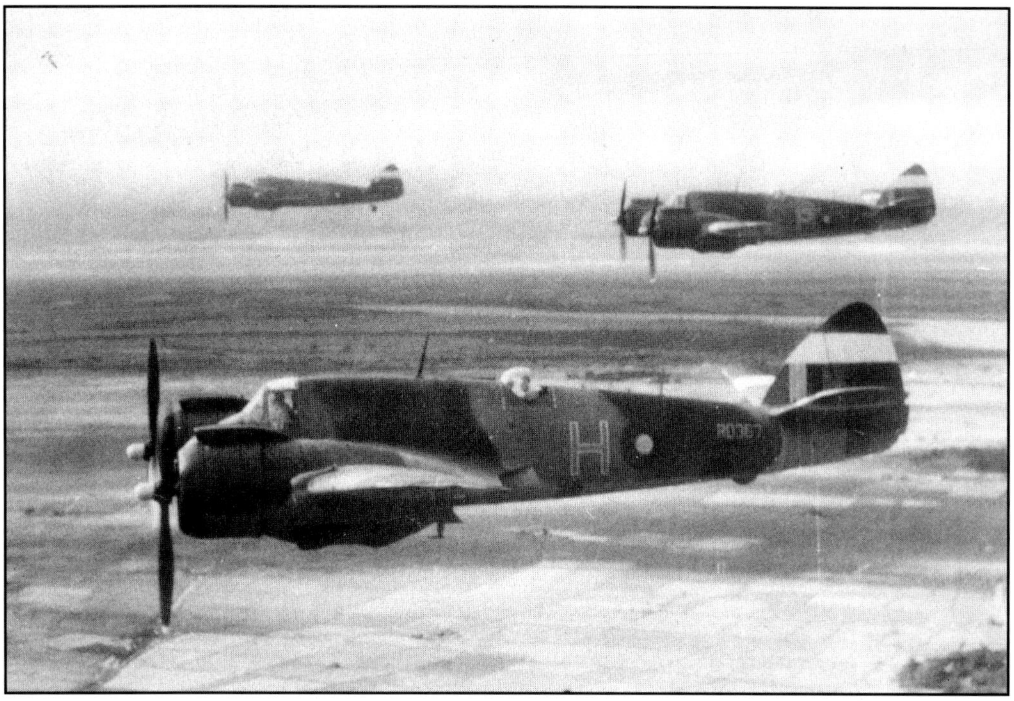

Left: **Mk.Xs of No. 27 Squadron in 1945. Note how the SEAC markings have changed and now include conspicuous white flashes on the tail. The nearest aircraft is RD367 'H'.**
The squadron took on its first rocket firing Mk.Xs in October 1943, gradually replacing their Mk.VIs. They then joined with No. 47 Squadron to form an anti-shipping strike wing, but they returned to ground attack duties in Burma in November 1944. Later they flew search and rescue missions over the jungles until disbanded in 1946.

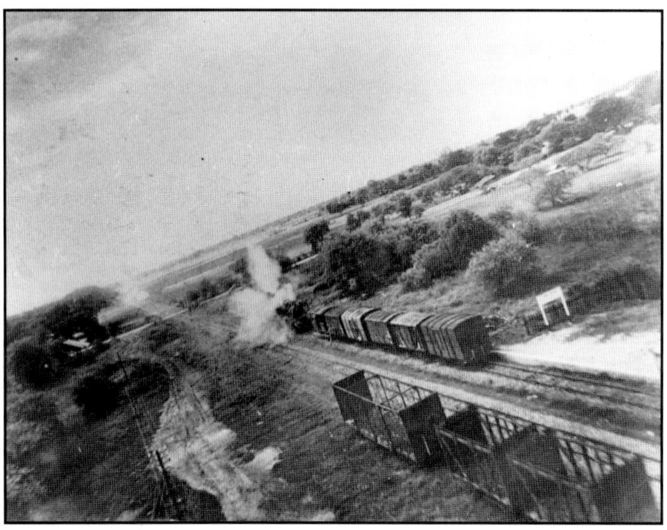

Train busting with Flight Lieutenant Williams along the Kume Road, 23 September 1943.

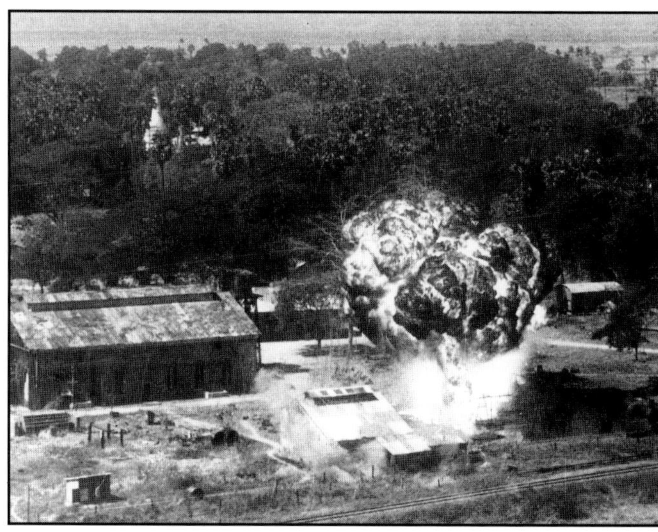

The Thegon oil pumping station ablaze near the mouth of the Sittang River, Burma, 1944.

A river steamer at Pakokku under attack with 20mm and .303 machine-gun fire on 10 December 1943. The areas of Pakokku and Paul were regular hunting grounds for the Beaufighters.

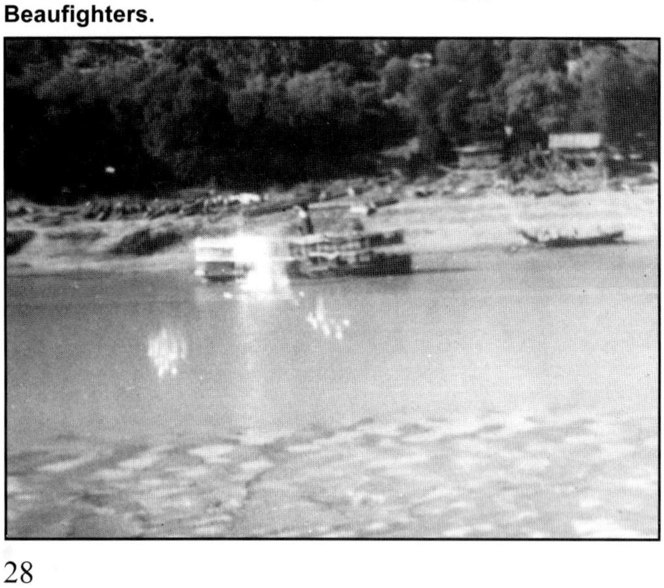

No. 27 Squadron's photographic officer, David Innes, had a 14 inch camera mounted in the nose of his Beaufighter to get better results. The camera was known as *Chota Beau Dekko*, in English, *Little Bo Peep!*

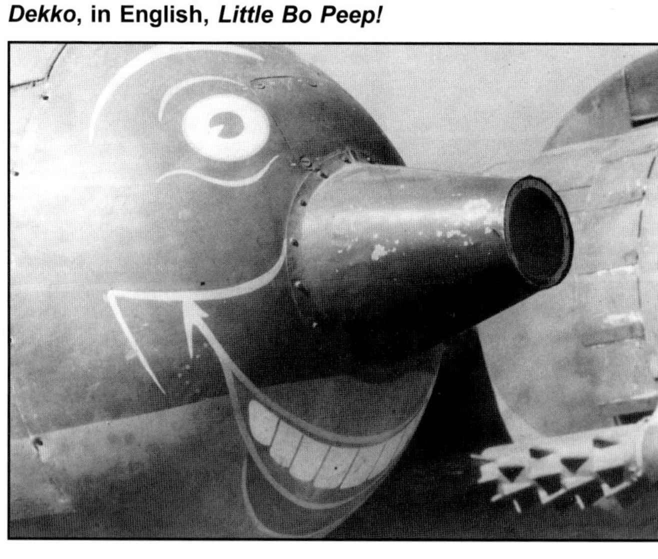

29 SQUADRON

Impiger at acer
(Energetic and keen)

Code Letters:
RO

Usage:
Mk.1F
Nov 40 to May 43
Mk.VIf
Mar - May 43

Rôle:
Night fighters
in defence of Britain

Bases:
Wellingore 11/40 - 4/41
West Malling 4/41 - 5/43

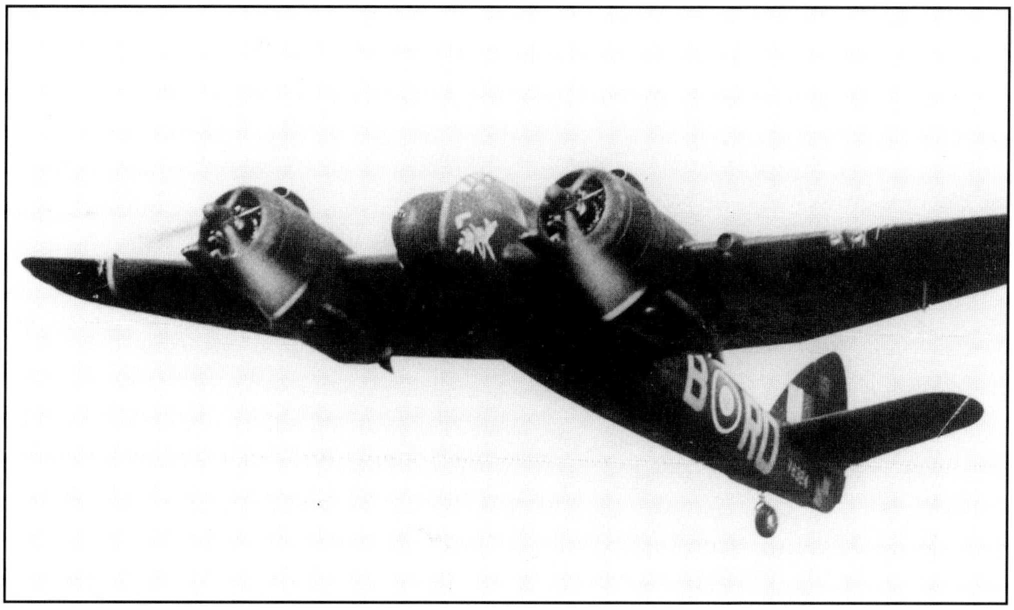

V8324, RO-B, a Mk. IF with a dihedral tailplane and AI Mk.IV was named 'Bambi'. It went on to serve with No. 51 OTU and dived into the ground at Barton-in-the-Clay, Bedfordshire, on 17 June 1944. The squadron was one of the first three to get Beaufighters and flew the first recorded operational sortie on 17 September 1940.

J R D 'Bob' Braham

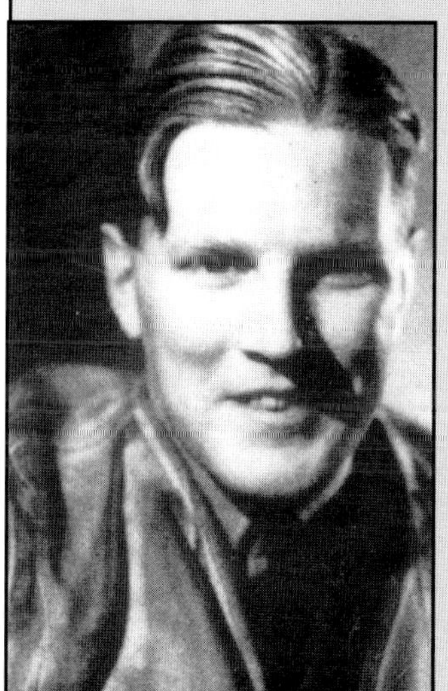

Somerset born 'Bob' Braham Joined No. 29 Squadron in December 1938 when it was flying Hawker Demons. In September 1939 the squadron was designated a night fighter squadron and was fully equipped with Blenheims. He claimed his first enemy aircraft destroyed on the night of 24 August 1940 when he shot down an He111 over the Humber estuary.

His next 'kill' did not come until 13 March 1941, when he claimed a Do17, after that he submitted a further seven claims before spending a short period helping No. 141 Squadron convert from Defiants in November 1941. In January 1942 he was posted to No. 51 OTU as an instructor, and also received promotion to Squadron Leader on 1 June. With a 48 hour leave pass Braham visited No. 29 Squadron on 6 June and took a Beaufighter on a patrol during which he claimed a Do217 shot down over the Channel. He was back at No. 29 Squadron by the end of July as 'A' Flight commander and claimed four more aircraft destroyed, a probable, and three damaged before being posted again to No. 141 Squadron in December 1942. As Commanding Officer of the squadron he made a further seven claims for aircraft destroyed, six of them during sorties over Europe using 'Serrate' homing equipment to locate *Lichtenstein* radar equipped German night fighters in support of Bomber Command operations.

Following another 'rest' at the Army Staff College, he was made Wing Commander Night Operations 2 Group and 2nd TAF. Still intent on flying operations he changed to Mosquitos, one of which he was forced to ditch. On 25 June, 1944, he was shot down over Denmark and spent the remainder of the war in captivity.

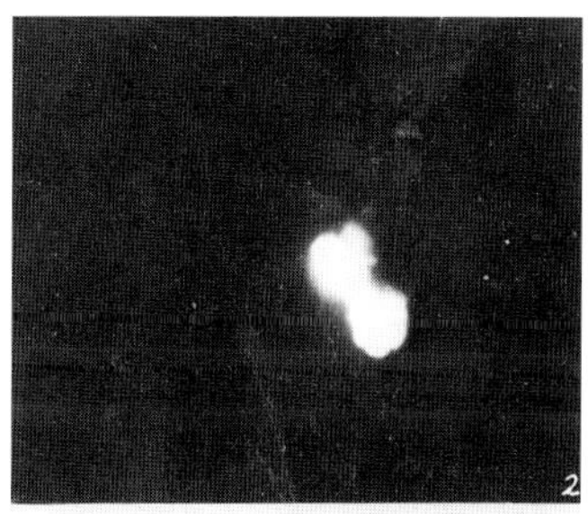

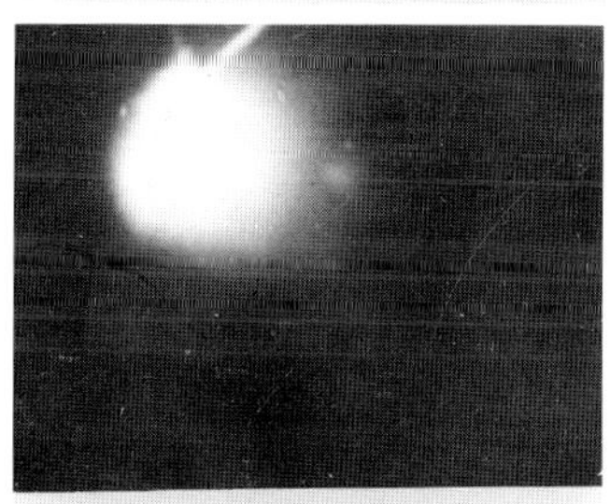

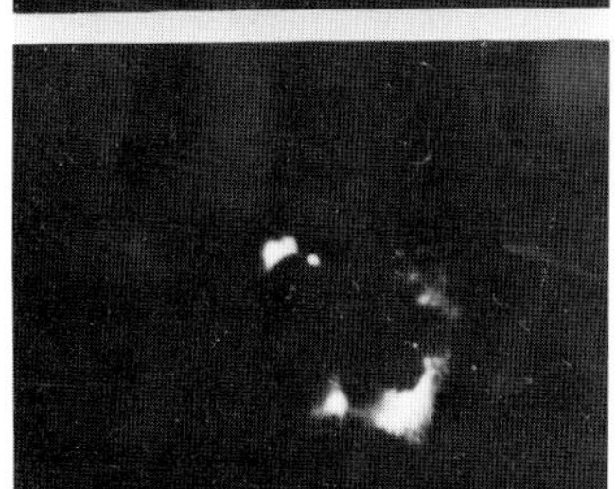

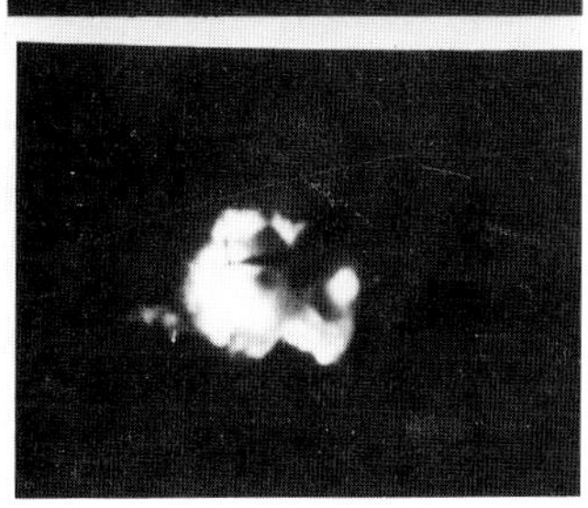

George Pepper DFC and Bar

The destruction of a Do217 of I/KG2 captured by Flying Officer George Pepper on the night of 31 October/1 November 1942, when flying V8233.

Canadian born Pepper had teamed up with his operator Joseph Toone in December 1941. He claimed three enemy aircraft destroyed and one probable in 1942: an He111 on 26 June; a probable Ju88 on 15 July; an unknown bomber on 8 August; He177 (Sic) on 20 August.

On the night of 31 October 1942 he claimed three Do217s in a single night. The three Dorniers were part of a force from KG2 attacking Canterbury. For this exploit Pepper was awarded a Bar to his DFC and Toone won a DFC. However, before these awards were gazetted the pair, known in the squadron as 'Salt and Pepper', were killed in a day-time flying accident near Detling on 17 November, 1942.

The Wing Commander's Night Out

On 16 January 1943, 201 aircraft of Bomber Command raided Berlin. A pathfinder force of 12 Lancasters and 5 Halifaxes led a further 178 Lancasters and 6 Halifaxes. Of the main force, 146 aircraft found their target and dropped 143 tons of high explosive bombs together with 224 tons of incendiaries on the city. A single Lancaster of 61 Squadron, brought down near the target was the only casualty. This was the first time since 8 November 1941 that a raid of any size had been aimed at Berlin. Hitler and the German High Command were stirred into action as the population demanded retribution for the increasing tempo of the RAF attacks.

Luftwaffe's Revenge Attack

The following morning bomber crews of Luftflotte 3 were ordered to stand by for operations that night. Ground staff began to black up the aircraft with distemper and bomb loads were prepared. At 18.00 hours on 17 January 1943 the crews gathered for briefing. That night, they were told, they would attack London in strength for the first time since July 1941. To make the operation more effective crews were expected to fly two consecutive sorties, pausing only to refuel and re-arm. For experienced crews targets were specified as the King George V and West India Docks, or railways in the area of the Isle of Dogs. The many new and inexperienced crews received less specific instructions. They would fly towards the greatest concentration of searchlights or anti-aircraft fire and release their loads there, this it was assumed would be London.

The Luftwaffe's preparations had not gone unnoticed in Britain for the 'Y' service, a radio monitoring organisation had been listening in to the increased level of radio traffic. At West Mailing in Kent, Wing Commander Wight-Boycott, the Commanding Officer of 29 Squadron, had been informed of the expected raid. Since taking over the squadron in September 1942, there had been few night raids over the Wing Commander's sector. Only the occasional reconnaissance aircraft or mine layer approached the coast. Flying singly or very low over the sea, these were notoriously difficult to intercept. The prospect of some real action was greeted with excitement by the Beaufighter crews.

Michael Wight-Boycott from Somerset, then aged thirty-two, had joined the RAFVR before the war and was on the staff of the Commissioner of Police of the Metropolis when called up at the outbreak of the war. His first posting was to No 219 Squadron at Tangmere. Having taken command of No 29 Squadron he met Flying Officer E. A. (Tony) Sanders who was to remain his Radio Observer until promoted to Squadron Leader in April 1944. On the evening of 17 January, Wing Commander Wight-Boycott was well down the list of those flying.

'Being the unit's Commanding Officer still didn't mean that I could jump the queue,' Michael recalls. 'I had, however, arranged for a non-operational flight in co-operation with the Navy. The local RAF Liaison Officer had asked us to fly along the Channel coast to see if it was possible to observe the fall of shells from coastal artillery batteries. For this purpose I was to carry Flying Officer John McAlister in addition to Tony Sanders as an observer. Unfortunately there was no accommodation in our Beaufighter for a third person and McAlister would have to stand on the escape hatch behind me. This, we thought, would be safe enough for the planned flight.'

As 29 Squadron's Commanding Officer left West Mailing heading out to Dungeness, the German crews were already on their way. Amongst the units operating were *Kampfgeschwadern* 2, 3, 6, 40, 53, 76 and 77. A large number of aircraft came from the *Geschwader IV Gruppen* which consisted mainly of *Ergansenstaffeln* with crews in training. By 19.45 hours two separate raids had been plotted. The first raid, a diversion by ten of IV./KG 40's Ju88c night fighters, was heading towards Portland. A second raid of about thirty-five aircraft was in the Somme and Boulogne area and these flew on steadily towards the English coast between Dungeness and Beachy Head.

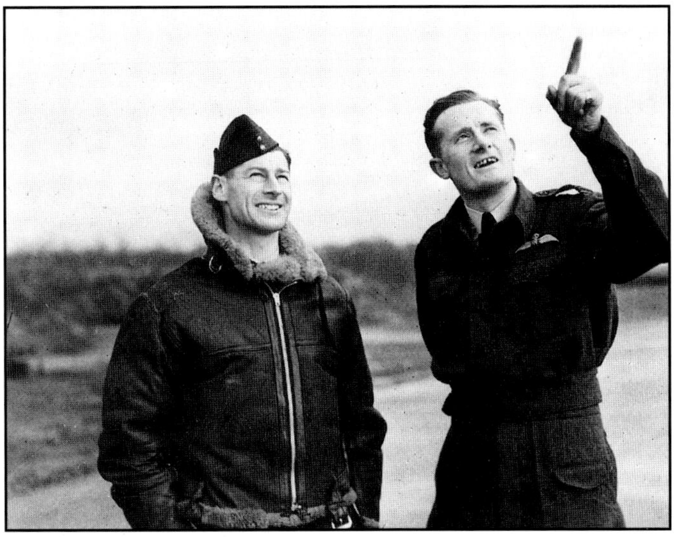

Above: **After the hat trick, the press descended on West Malling where Tony Sanders (left) and Wight-Boycott posed for this photograph.**

Fighter Command began to order up their night fighters in defence but Wing Commander Wight-Boycott was already in an ideal position.

'At a position some twenty miles off Dungeness we waited for the coastal batteries to open fire. It was perfectly easy to see the flash from the shells as they hit the sea. We then flew eastwards along the Channel to another battery firing but we were called by the local GCI station before reaching the shelling area. The Group Controller asked us to take over the interception of a 'bogey' from another 29 Squadron crew.

'Our luck was really in'

'Our luck was really in. We were given several vectors by the Controller before two contacts appeared at about three miles range on the AI set. Both were heading north and weaving violently. Our aircraft was equipped with the first centimetric Mk VII AI and Tony Saunders had no difficulty in guiding me into a visual at 1,000ft range. Although it was a dark night I was able to see what I took to be the twin fins of a Do217. A positive identification was usually difficult and most pilots, like myself, had little experience of recognising hostile aircraft at night and under operational conditions. Having found my target it was not too difficult to manoeuvre the Beaufighter dead astern and a little below, getting the enemy aircraft on the dot in the middle of the reflector sight. I made sure that we were not skidding, that is the rudder central, and prepared to open fire with four 20mm cannons and six .303 Brownings. At 13,000 feet and 220mph IAS the aircraft ghosted along, blissfully unconscious. I pressed the gun button on the control column and fired two short bursts. A flash came from behind the cockpit followed immediately by an explosion and the aircraft went into a dive. I began to follow but my RO had another contact. He gave me directions which enabled me to get a visual on a second aircraft apparently spiralling to port and below me. I was in a very poor position to attack, and could only fire two or three bursts with maximum deflection but thought I saw one strike on it.'

At that moment there was a violent explosion on the ground below. Flying Officer McAlister had been hanging on grimly to the armour plating as the Wing Commander threw the Beaufighter around the sky and was able to confirm that the aircraft had fallen near the coast. It was to prove to be a Ju88 which fell near Brenzett in Kent. The second aircraft had slipped away into the night.

At West Malling an early night-flying breakfast with an extra egg was waiting, the custom in night fighter squadrons after a successful sortie. Two hours later Wing Commander Wight-Boycott and Flying Officer Sanders were up again, patrolling for two hours without undue excitement. Back at their bases the German bombers were refuelling and bombing up for the night's second raid.

‘At 03.45 hours the same night, or rather the next morning, we were airborne again. We were being controlled by Squadron Leader Igo at Biggin Hill who told us to patrol out to sea off Manston at 12,000ft. Shortly after getting there we were ordered to return and orbit searchlight beacon “K” on land. It seemed that sector had decided to put as many fighters as possible into the bomber stream and allow them to operate on a freelance system. The Germans looked as if they had taken a leaf out of Bomber Command’s book and concentrated their aircraft into a single wave. The usual system of ground controlled interception controlled two fighters at a time, which was all right as long as the enemy was well dispersed but it seems that the first wave had swamped the system. On the second raid the freelance system would allow far more fighters to be fed into the stream.

The Beaufighter was out of control

‘We orbited beacon ‘K’ for five minutes before the light ‘smacked’. The searchlight beam lowered in the direction of an intersection of beams which were, in theory, illuminating an enemy aircraft but on this occasion we were unable to see any intersection. It did not matter as almost immediately we obtained a contact on the AI set, five miles ahead, coming head on at 11,000ft. This led to a sighting on another Dornier. The aircraft spiralled up, turning right and left but not taking any real evasive action. I closed in to between three and four hundred yards firing a two second burst from astern. The Dornier immediately caught fire. I began to close on it very rapidly and throttled back violently to avoid a collision. The next thing I knew the Beaufighter was out of control. I had the impression that we were upside down. Instinctively I tried to find the lever operating the escape hatch with my left hand but hit the oxygen supply valve with my elbow. Just then the ground was lit up by the explosion of the Dornier. It had dived into a chalk pit which I recognised as one close to Westerham.

‘As soon as I had regained control I saw another 217 but eventually lost it and began to return to the beacon. My ever vigilant RO then picked up an AI contact one and a half miles away at 12,000ft. The contact jinked violently as I followed it, but I was having more and more difficulty manoeuvring the Beaufighter. I felt tired and frustrated by my ineptitude. Eventually I got a visual at 1,000ft and fired a two second burst. The aircraft appeared to be hit on the starboard side behind the cockpit and the engine seemed to be on fire as well. It dived away steeply firing twin streams of tracer as it went. At the time we were convinced that we had shot the aircraft down.

‘By this time I was feeling very tired and was not coping at all well. I was about to ask control to return me to base when I noticed that my oxygen supply had been turned off. This must have happened when I hit the butterfly valve with my elbow, I turned it back on and immediately regained my zest for combat. A navigational fix told us that we had moved to the Kenley area and almost immediately we had an AI contact on a violently jinking target. After a long chase to 14,000ft I saw a Ju88, clearly identified by its exhaust pattern. One long burst from practically minimum range set the aircraft on fire from end to end. As I drew level I could see the swastika painted on its tail. The aircraft started to dive and pieces fell away. I took them to be the crew baling out. The Junkers went down in flames and exploded in a heavily built-up area on what appeared to be a playing field, buildings and streets were lit up clearly by the flames. Later I learnt that another 29 Squadron pilot had been getting into position to fire on this aircraft when, to his disgust, it went down in flames before his eyes.

‘Shortly after this control ordered us to return to West Malling. As soon as we had landed we began to taxi towards our dispersal which lay on lower ground. A dense fog had settled here and, as there were no perimeter tracks to follow we were forced to abandon the Beaufighter on the grass. Our return to the dispersal was eventually made on foot.’

Other 29 Squadron crews included F/O Musgrove and Sgt Petrie who thought that a Ju88 they had attacked went down in flames south east of Maidstone and F/Sgt Wood with Pilot Officer Slaughter attacked an ’88 over Tonbridge. Both of these claims were later down graded to ‘damaged’ due to a lack of evidence. From 85 Sqn Wg Cdr G. L. Raphael, DFC and Bar, with F/O Addison, DFM, and his RO claimed a Ju88 in the sea off Bradwell Bay. The only other crew to have an aircraft confirmed as destroyed was that of Sqn Ldr I. G. Esplin, an Australian with 29 Squadron, and his RO Flying Officer A. H. J. Palmer. Flying on a freelance sortie their AI set had gone ‘US’ but they continued on a ‘cat’s eye’ patrol. Shortly after 05.30 hours when near Ashford, an aircraft held in searchlight beams was spotted. Turning steeply the Beaufighter chased after the Ju88 at full throttle, catching it still held by the lights and taking violent evasive action. Sqn Ldr Esplin closed in to 300 yards and fired a three or four second burst which set the starboard wing and engine on fire. Illuminated by the lights and already burning, a second burst from dead astern tore pieces off the Ju88 which began a vertical dive into the ground south west of Ashford.

Leg broken when putting the cat out

Whilst high drama was being enacted thousands of feet above south east England by very few men, those on the ground were having a traumatic time as the Luftwaffe’s bombs fell. Forty-two London Boroughs were affected, with Woolwich, Lewisham and Wandsworth bearing the brunt of the attack. There were 124 high explosive bombs reported, 38 of these being unexploded. In the City incendiaries caused a ten pump fire at the Smith and Bull Wharf. Twenty-five casualties were caused by ‘HEs’ in the Briar Road and Cheveney Road area of Norwood, thirty were injured and more trapped around Peckham High Street. By morning the death toll had risen to 74 with 233 seriously injured. Some of the casualties were caused by British AA shells. The anti-aircraft fire was described by the press, as ‘probably the most intensive screen of fire that has ever been unleashed in the protection of a city.’ Even experienced Luftwaffe aircrew admitted that this was the worst AA fire they had ever seen and many Londoners stood in the streets to watch the enormous firework display overhead. On Victoria Embankment a soldier and a girl were killed when an anti-aircraft shell exploded near them. In a pub in Dagenham four people were killed when shell splinters penetrated a four inch wooden wall. The caretaker of Thessaly Road flats, Battersea, was killed on firewatching duty and Fred Moir had a leg broken when he went to put the cat out and a shell fell near him.

Between seventy and eighty aircraft had attacked London that night. At the same time, 120 Lancasters and Halifaxes were on their way to Berlin for the second night in succession. A fearsome tonnage of ordnance was dropped, 117 tons of high explosive and 213 tons of incendiaries. This included four 8,000lb HEs, fifty-four 4,000lb HCs, nearly four thousand 4lb explosive incendiaries and four 2501b target indicators for the Path Finder Force. Nineteen Lancasters and three Halifaxes failed to return and the crew of one Lancaster baled out near Bridlington on their return.

Below: **Ju88 A14 Wn.144349 3E+BB of Stab KG6 fell in Town End Recreation Ground at Caterham on the Hill, Surrey. Fw Karl Heinz Schulz baled out, but Oblt Bernd, OGefr Schieweck and Gefr Prophet were killed.**

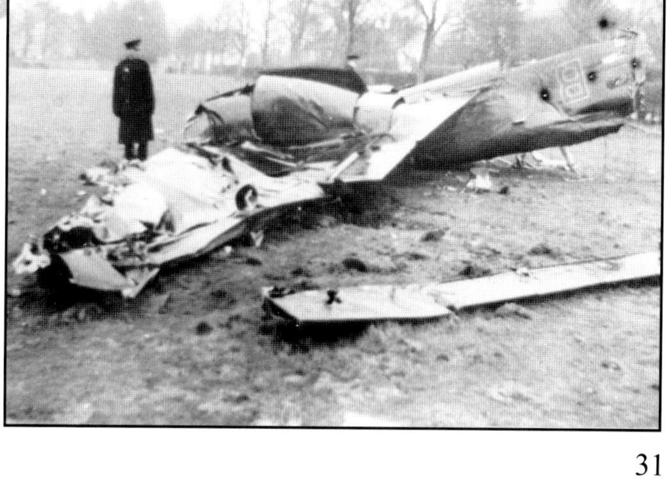

The following morning officers from RAF intelligence departments were at work. Four enemy aircraft were to be found and five aircrew captured. The first aircraft down was the victim of Wing Commander Wight-Boycott's 'spotting' sortie, Ju88 A14 Wn.4356 coded 3E+CH from 1/KG6. This, the only raider destroyed over the UK in the early attack, hit the ground in a diving turn near King Street Crossing, Brenzett. The engines embedded themselves deeply in the ground leaving a water filled crater whilst the remainder of the airframe was scattered across a field. Its four crew, Uffz Sailer, OGefr Funk, Uffz Fleischmann, and Uffz Binder were all killed.

A Ju88 A5 of IV./KG3 was in trouble on its return from London. At 21.17 hours a distress signal was sent, 'Engine failure — Landing in sea'. Its control called on radio for half an hour but there was no reply. All four of its crew died when their aircraft fell into the sea off Boulogne. The locations given by Wg Cdr Wight-Boycott for his combats proved to be very accurate. At 04.30 hours Dornier 217 E4 Wn.5591 U5+MR of 7./KG2 dived vertically into a chalk pit near the Pilgrim's Way at Westerham. The aircraft was totally destroyed and the wreckage was still burning twelve hours later. Once again all the crew were killed, Uffz Schnabel, Gefr Schafer, Gefr Raab and Uffz Hargenberger were all interred at Sevenoaks. Much of the wreckage was left in the chalk and many enthusiasts recovered pieces until, in 1981, an Army Bomb Disposal Unit brought mechanical plant to search for suspected bombs. None was found, only the two propeller hubs and parts of the engines.

The Wing Commander's final victim had fallen on a playing field as he had described. In fact it was the Town End Recreation Ground at Caterham on the Hill. Ju88 A14 Wn.144349 3E+BB of Stab KG6 caught fire in the air and fell largely in one piece although some parts had fallen in the surrounding area. An undercarriage leg together with its wheel fell through the roof of Lewis's Garage and smashed a Wolseley car. Only one of the Junker's crew had been able to escape. Fw Karl Heinz Schulz baled out but Oblt Bernd, OGefr Schieweck and Gefr Prophet were all killed.

The final aircraft to fall that night was Squadron Leader Esplin's victim; After their controls had been damaged the crew baled out of Ju88 A14 Wn.4347 3E+GK from 2./KG6. Fw Muller's parachute failed and he fell to his death, but ObFw Diecke, Uffz Fenger and Uffz Lüsch all survived their descent. Their aircraft dived vertically into soft ground at the edge of a pond near Bethesden. There was one other victim that night. Uffz Erich Lingnau baled out of his Ju88 near Ashford after it was attacked by a fighter. The remaining three crew members nursed their damaged aircraft back to France and baled out near St Just, north-west of Paris.

'Flying Policeman caught four in one night'

The following day the newspapers carried the story of the night's events and Wg Cdr Wight-Boycott became a national hero overnight with headlines such as 'Flying Policeman caught four in one night'. Forty years later he recalled the publicity.

'There was considerable excitement at West Mailing about the claim for four aircraft destroyed in a single night. That morning the Sector Commander at Biggin Hill, Group Captain 'Sailor' Malan appeared in person to tell me that I was to be awarded the DSO. Normally it was the Station Commander's responsibility to write the citation to go with this, but I was the Station Commander.

'I refused to have the embarrassment of writing it myself and eventually 'Sailor' Malan wrote the citation. There was also instant publicity in the national press, mainly to mollify the inhabitants of South London who had suffered severe casualties in the raids. The press were told by the Air Ministry's public relations organisation that in civilian life I had been a civil servant on the staff of the Commissioner of Police. This was enough to earn me the sobriquet of the 'Flying Policeman'. My personal history was published with interviews with everyone I had ever spoken to, including the parson who christened me. My parents received my fan mail by the sack load and I was ordered to Broadcasting House to describe my adventures. It was embarrassing for me that, when my claim was assessed, the aircraft I claimed when suffering from anoxia was, quite rightly, downgraded to damaged. Very few people knew that the claim had been downgraded, and those that did know did not hold it against me although some were envious of my luck. Success as a night fighter pilot was always a matter of luck in being in the right place at the right time, and it was equally important to have a good Radio Observer. Without their RO's skill, none of the aces, not John Cunningham, nor Bob Braham, nor Burbridge of 100 Group fame, would have got their DSOs and DFCs and they would be the first to admit it, as do I. Unfortunately Airborne Interception was the subject of intense security and in my broadcast the only thing I was allowed to say about Tony Sanders was that he complained about the hardness of his seat after flying for six hours. In fact it was entirely due to Tony that on my night out he had provided me with seven visuals of which only three were properly despatched by me. For this his reward was only a DFC and no personal publicity, whereas I got the DSO and was treated as though I had won an Oscar.'

Below: **Ju88 A14 Wn.4347 3E+GK from 2./KG6 dived vertically into soft ground near Bethesden, Kent. Fw Muller's parachute failed and he fell to his death, but ObFw Diecke, Uffz Fenger and Uffz Lüsch all survived their descent.**

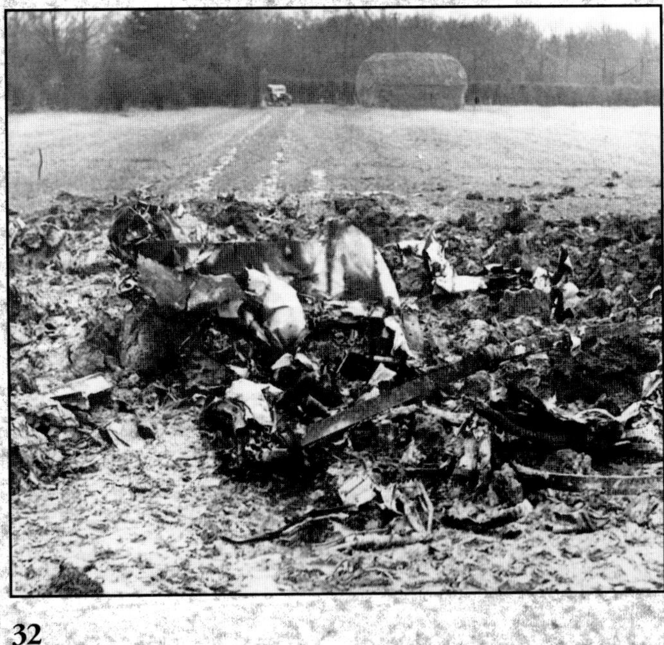

Below: **Dornier 217 E4 Wn.5591 U5+MR of 7./KG2 dived vertically into a chalk pit near the Pilgrim's Way at Westerham, Kent. Uffz Schnabel, Gefr Schafer, Gefr Raab and Uffz Hargenberger were all killed.**

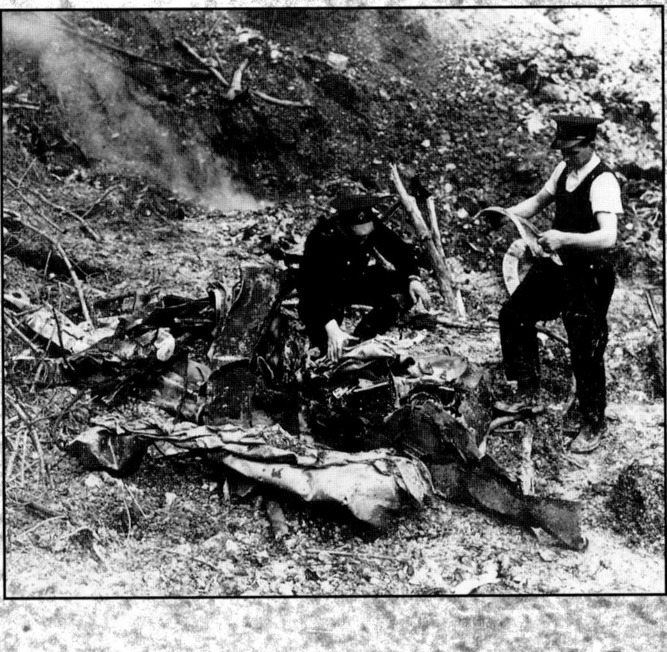

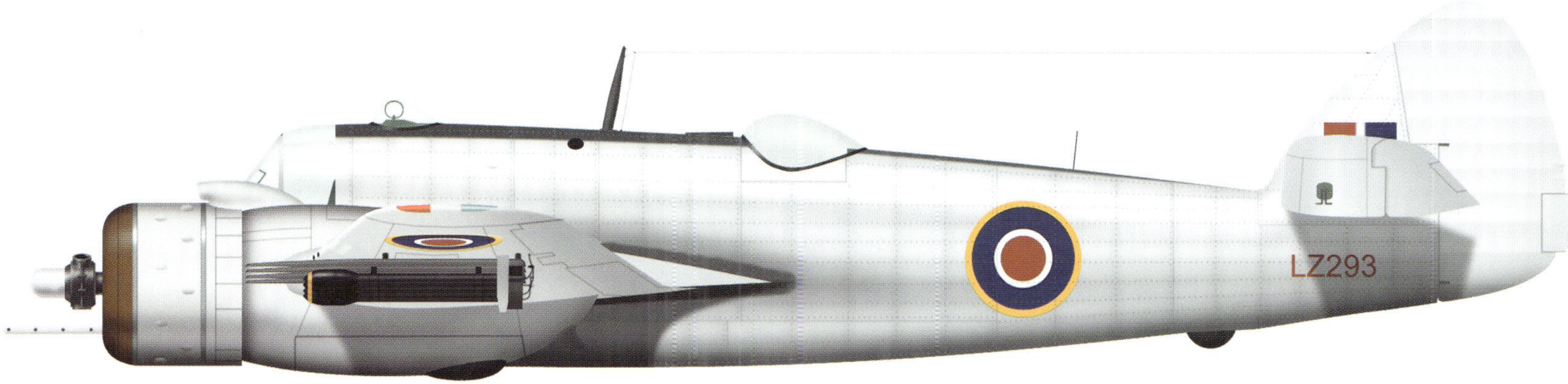

LZ293, a TF Mk.X, wore a Coastal Command finish, of dark sea grey on white. Serving with No.236 Squadron, it was equipped with ASV radar. Photo reference page 57.

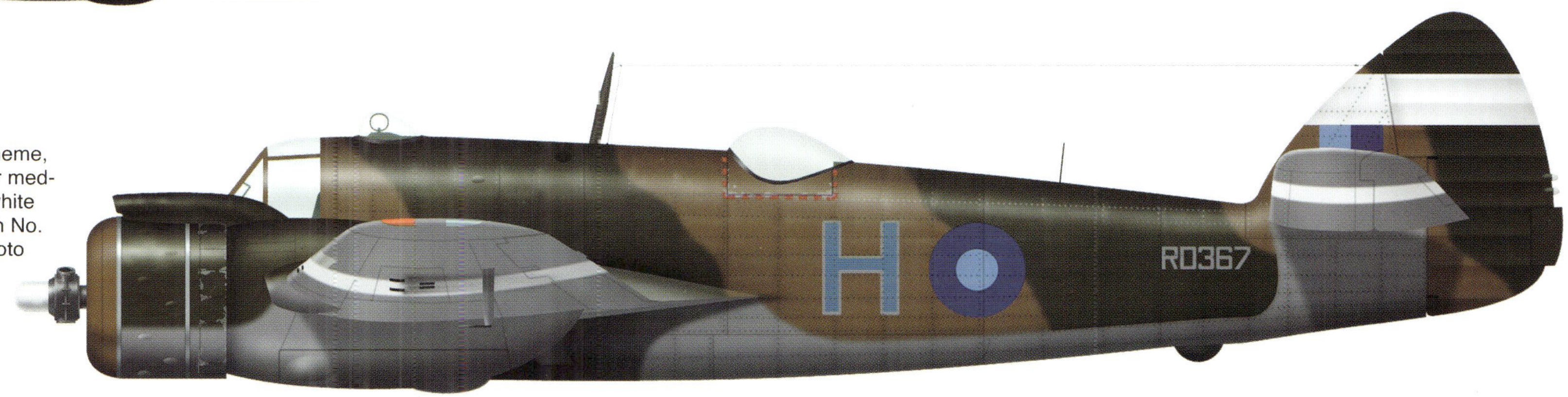

RD367 in the standard SEAC scheme, of dark green and dark earth over medium sea grey, with conspicuous white flashes. This machine served with No. 27 Squadron, in the Far East. Photo reference page 28.

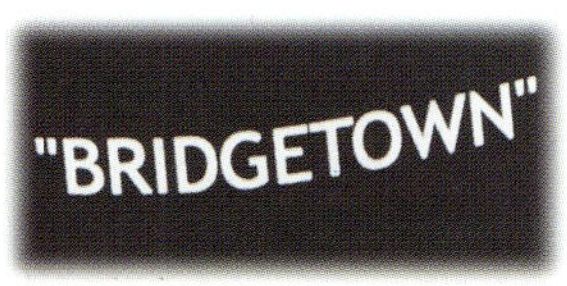

Nose art as applied to A8-247.

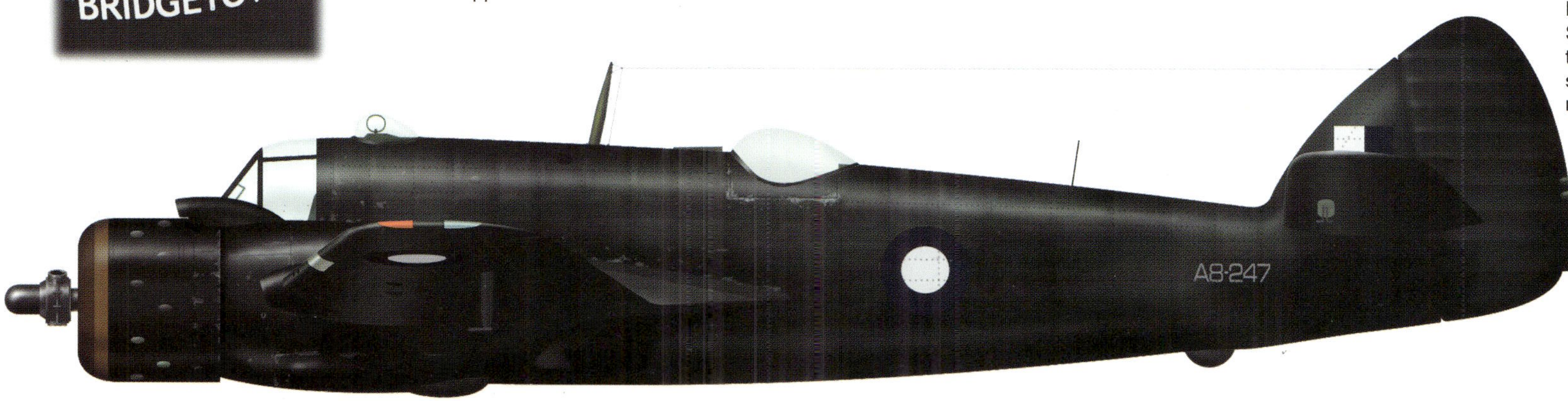

A8-247, an Australian-built Beaufighter Mk.21, serving with No.30 (RAAF) Squadron, at Los Negros in the Admiralty Islands. Aicraft is finished in an overall scheme, of dark foliage green. Photo reference page 20.

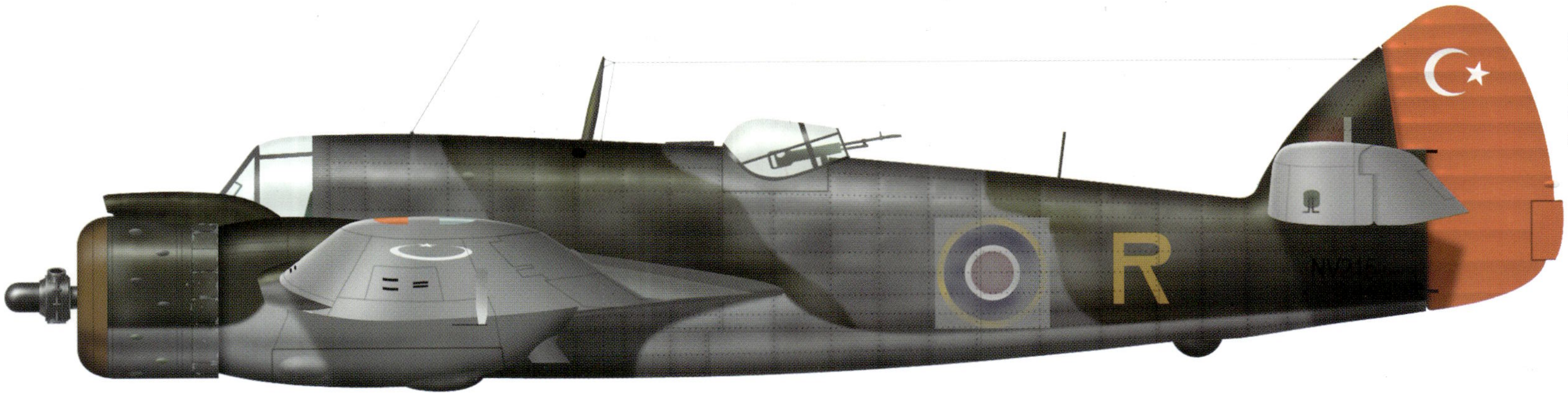

NV215, a TF Mk.X transferred to the Turkish Air Force in 1944. The aircraft wears a rather faded RAF dark green, dark sea grey, and medium sea grey scheme. Photo reference page 20.

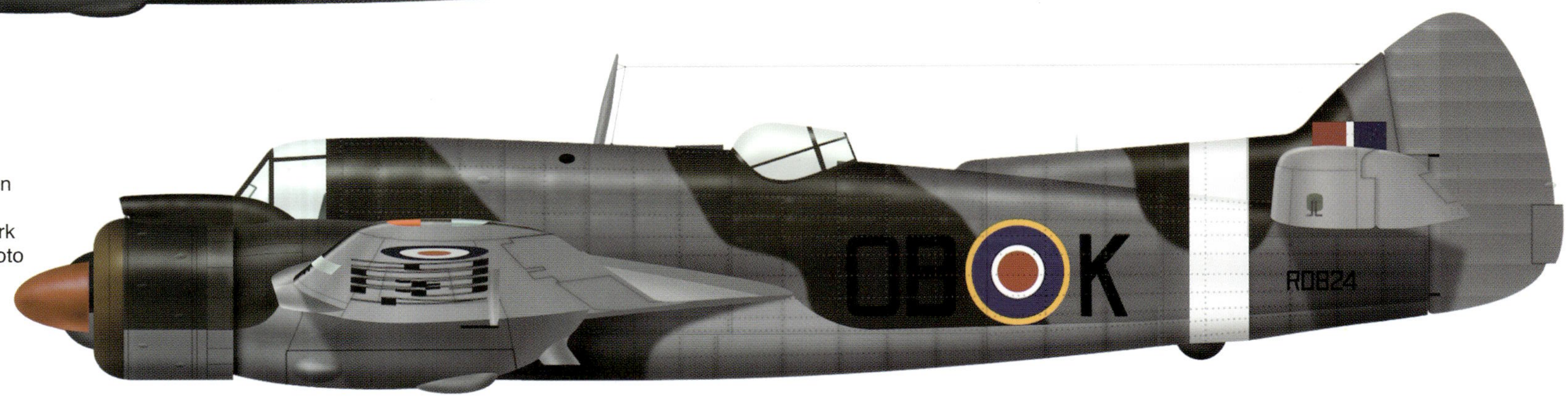

RD824 serving with No.45 Squadron in Ceylon, in February 1947. The aircraft is finished in dark green, dark sea grey and medium sea grey. Photo reference page 35.

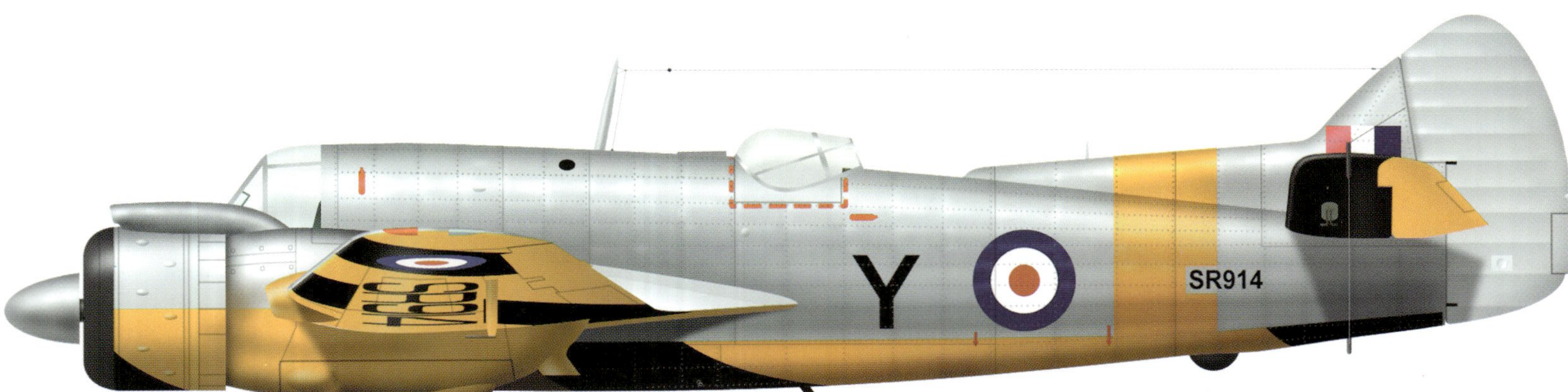

SR914, a TT10 target tug conversion from a TF Mk.X, finished in overall metal, with black and yellow striped undersides. photo reference page 90.

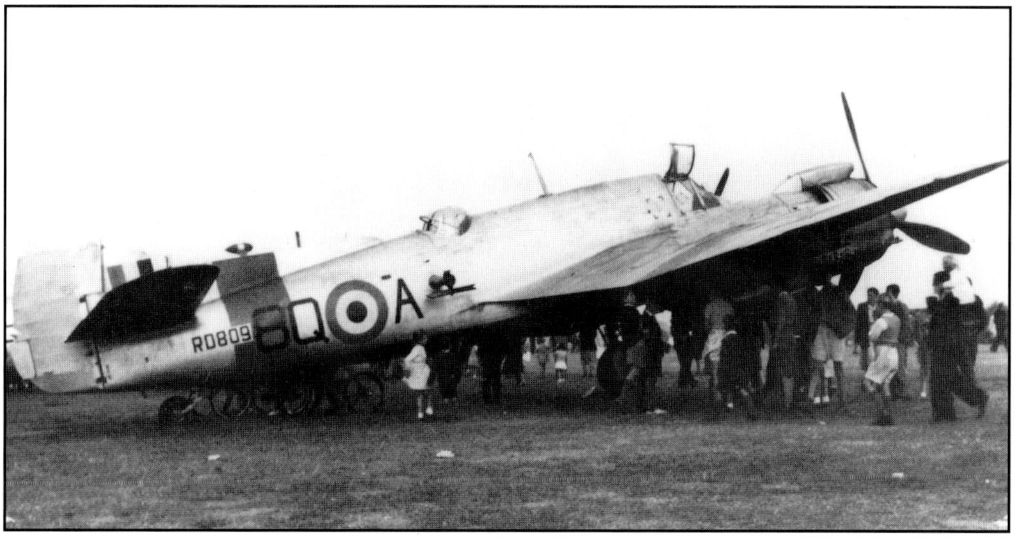

Above: **Snapped at North Weald in September 1949, this is RD809, a TT10 coded 8Q-A of No. 34 Squadron.**

34 SQUADRON

Lupus vult, lupus volat
(Wolf wishes, wolf flies)
Code Letters:
8Q
Usage: TT10
Feb 49 to July 51
Rôle:
Anti-aircraft target towing duties
Base:
Horsham St Faith

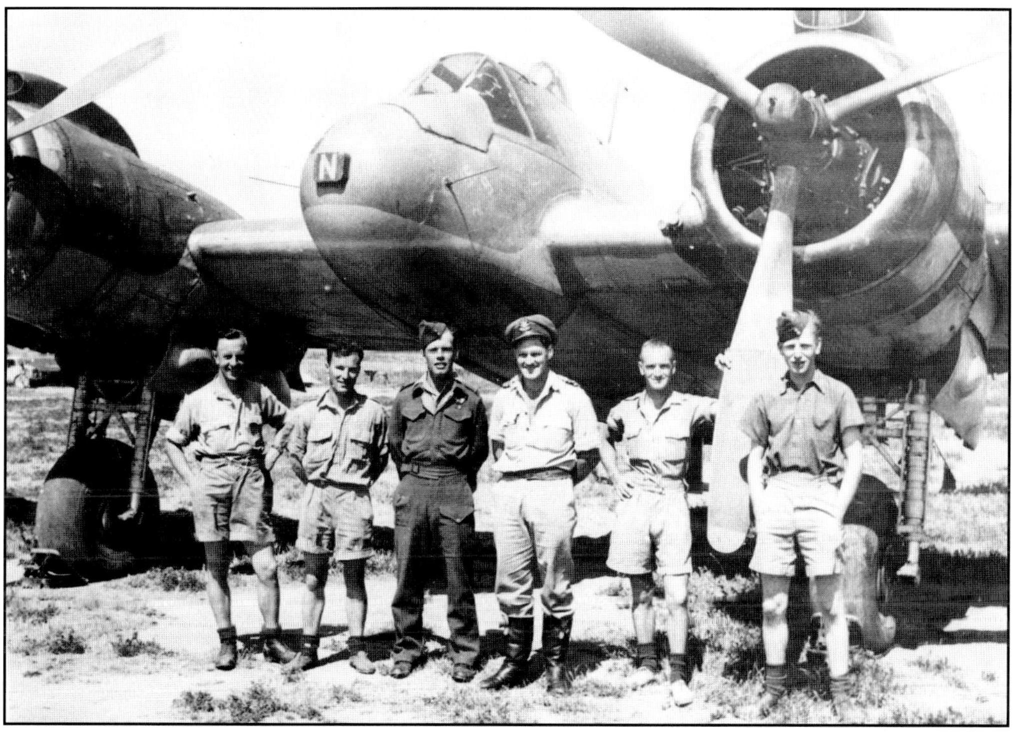

Above: **Members of No. 39 Squadron in front of one of their Beaufighter Mk.Xs at Alghero, Sardinia in 1944. Note the two swastikas marked on the nose. The squadron operated in the Central Mediterranean area, performing shipping strikes from bases in North Africa and Sardinia. They also flew night intruder sorties to northern Italy, and attacked shipping off the French and Italian coasts. Finally the squadron operated over the Balkans before converting to Marauders in December 1944. (T C Hellier)**

39 SQUADRON

Die noctuque
(By day and by night)
Usage:
TF Mk.X
June 43 to Dec 44
Rôle:
Shipping strikes
Bases:
Protville II 6/43 - 10/43
Sidi Amor 10/43
Reghaia 11/43 - 2/44
Alghero 2/44 - 7/44
Biferno 7/44 - 12/44

Below: **Four of No. 39 Squadron's TT Mk.Xs line up on the runway at Biferno in 1945. The closest aircraft is NV150 'I'.**

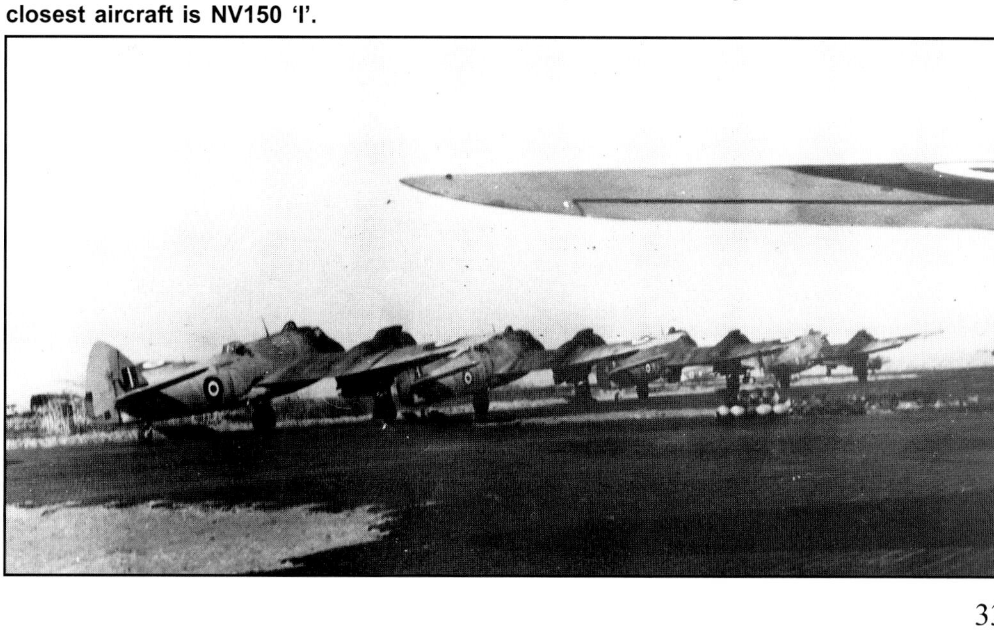

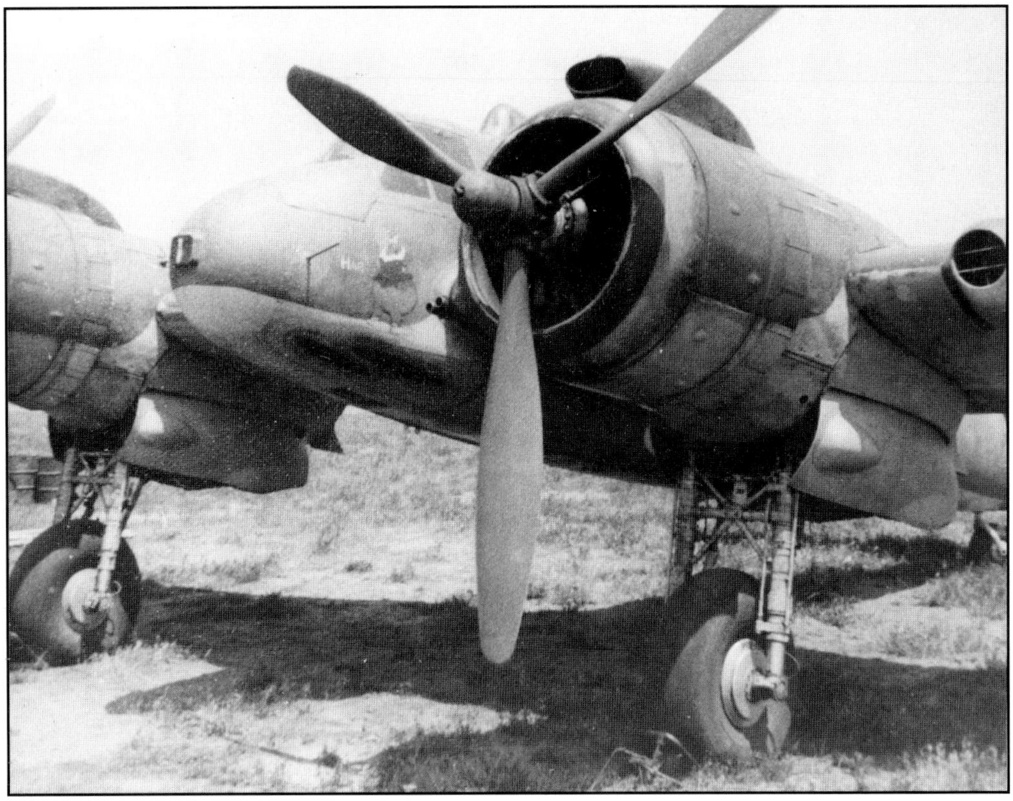

Left: **'Happy' the Walt Disney character adorned the nose of another of No. 39 Squadron's Beaufighter TF Mk.Xs. The squadron formed part of No. 328 Wing at Protville II from June to October 1943 with No. 47 and part of No. 144 Squadron under the command of Wing Commander Nelson B. Harvey. In October 1943, following the German withdrawal from Corsica, the squadron began operations over the Adriatic and changed from a torpedo to rocket attacks. In 1944 the squadron flew escort to Allied convoys ferrying in supplies and troops in support of the push through Italy.**

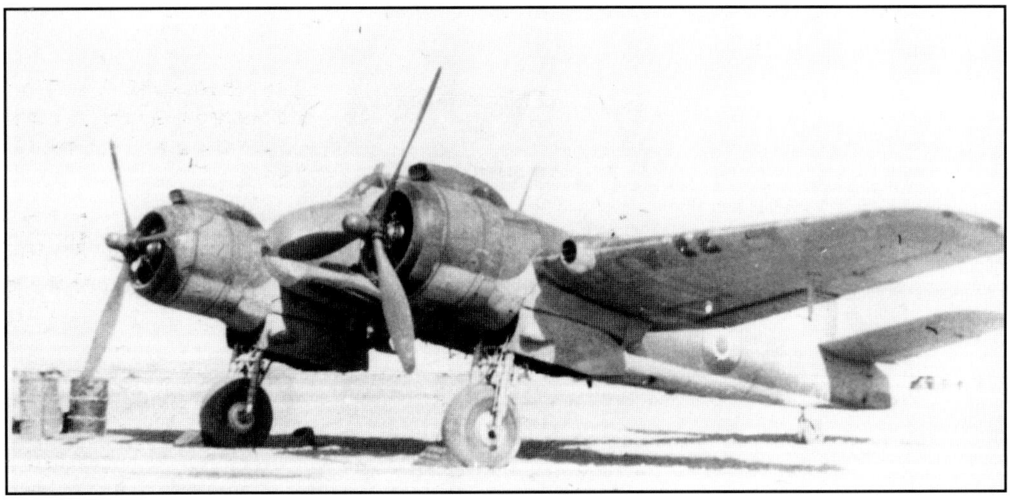

Left: **A Mk.X on a dusty Protville II airfield, Tunisia, in 1943, shortly after the squadron converted from Beauforts. The squadron moved to Alghero in February 1944 with No. 272 Squadron and formed a Strike Wing charged with attacking a variety of targets including. Radar installations.**

Below: **Two Beaufighter TF. Mk.Xs of No. 39 Squadron over the Mediterranean. Both have rocket projectile rails, but only the machine on the right carries the aerials for ASV Radar.**

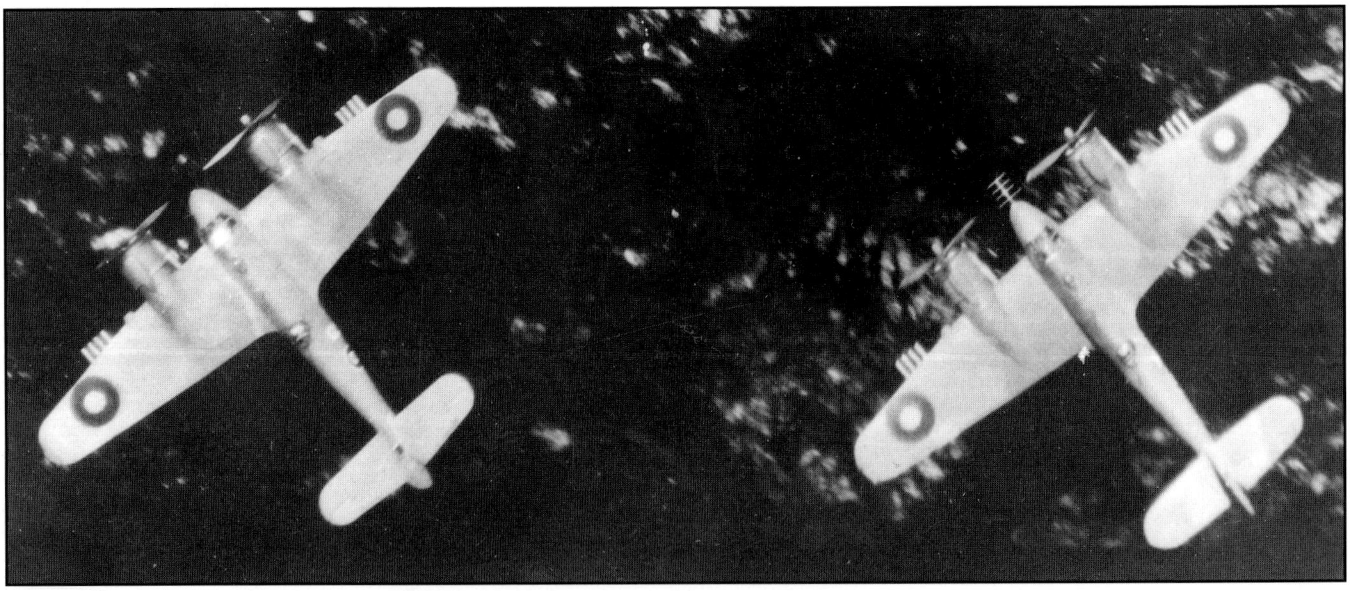

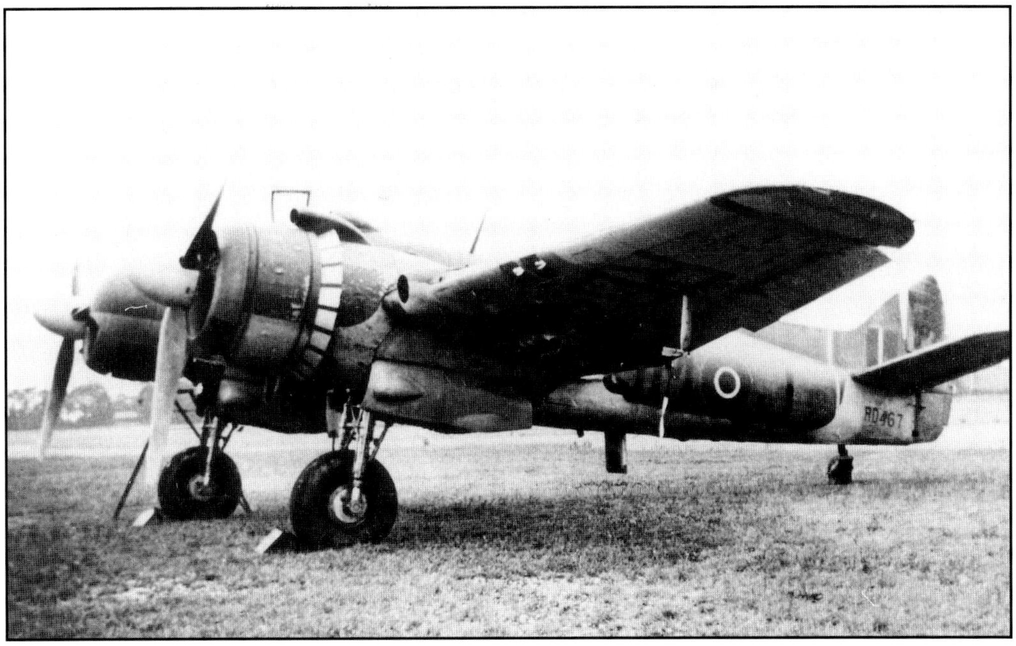

Above: **TF Mk.X RD467, coded QM-J, with No. 42 Squadron based at Thorney Island in 1946. This aircraft has been fitted with the dorsal fin enlargement. The squadron had been formed as a result of re-numbering No. 254 Squadron.**

42 SQUADRON

Foriter in re
(Bravely in action)
Code Letters:
QM
Usage:
TFMk.X
Oct 46 to Oct 47
Rôle:
Coastal Command strike duties
Base:
Thorney Island

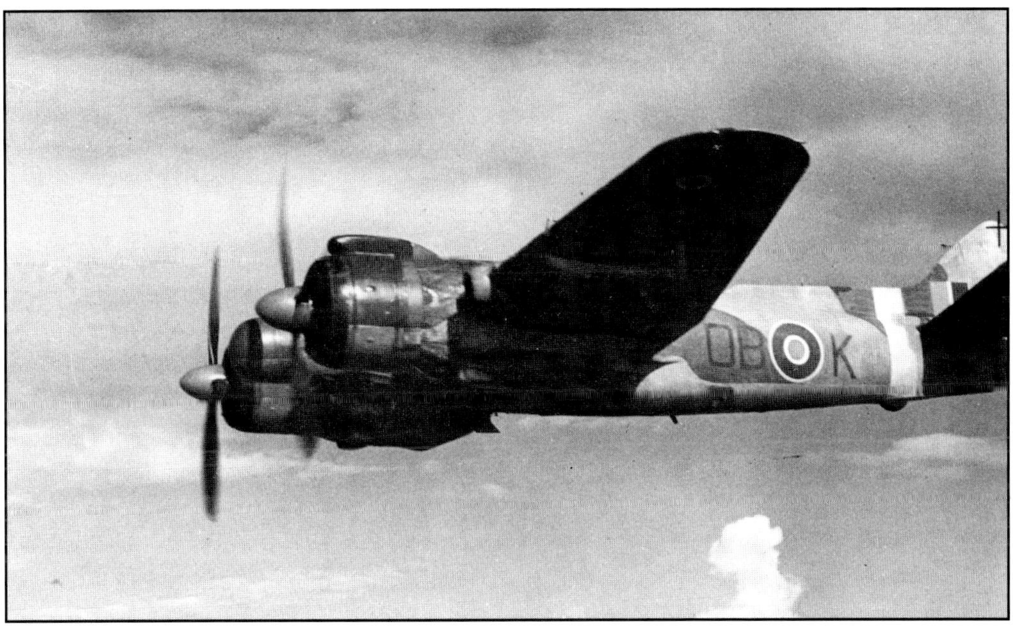

Left: **RD824, OB-K with tail band marking at Ceylon in February 1947.**

Below: **RD819, OB-F, of No. 45 Squadron displaying the thimble nose in September 1948.**

45 SQUADRON

Per ardue surge
(Through difficulties I arise)
Code Letters:
OB
Usage:
TFMk.X
Dec 46 to Feb 50
Rôle:
Strike duties from Ceylon
Base:
Negombo

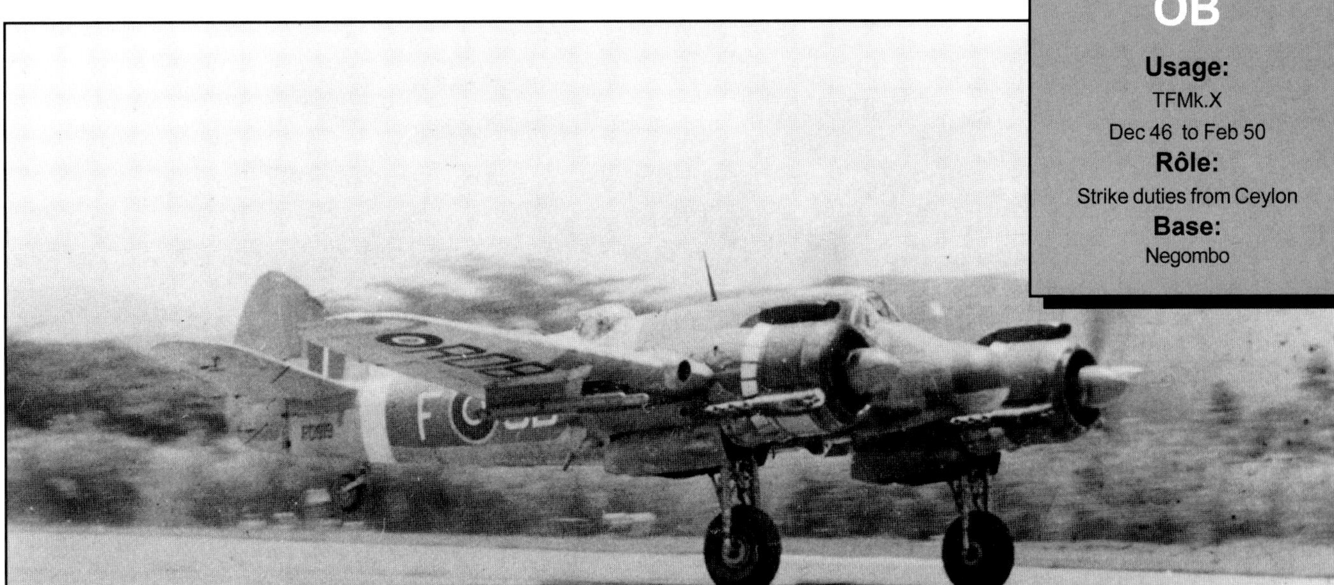

46 SQUADRON

(We rise to conquer)

Usage:
Mk.1F
May 42 to July 42
Mk.VIF
May 42 to Dec 44
TF Mk.X
Apr 44 to Jul 44

Rôle:
Night fighters over the Mediterranean. From August 43 intruder ops over the Greek Island and eastern Mediterranean.

Bases:
Idku 7/42 - 7/44
With detachments around North Africa as required.

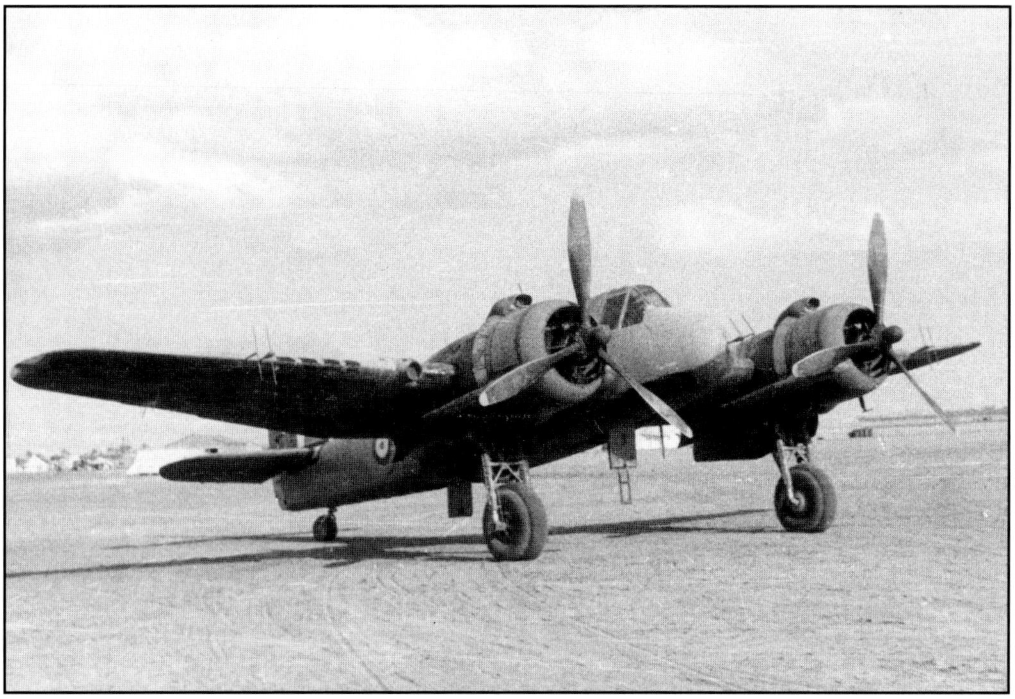

Above: **V8310, a Mk.If in Egypt during 1942. This aircraft overshot on landing at St. Jean on 25 April 1943 and was written off. On arrival at Idku in May 1942 the squadron absorbed a detachment of No. 89 Squadron that was already equipped with Beaufighters.**

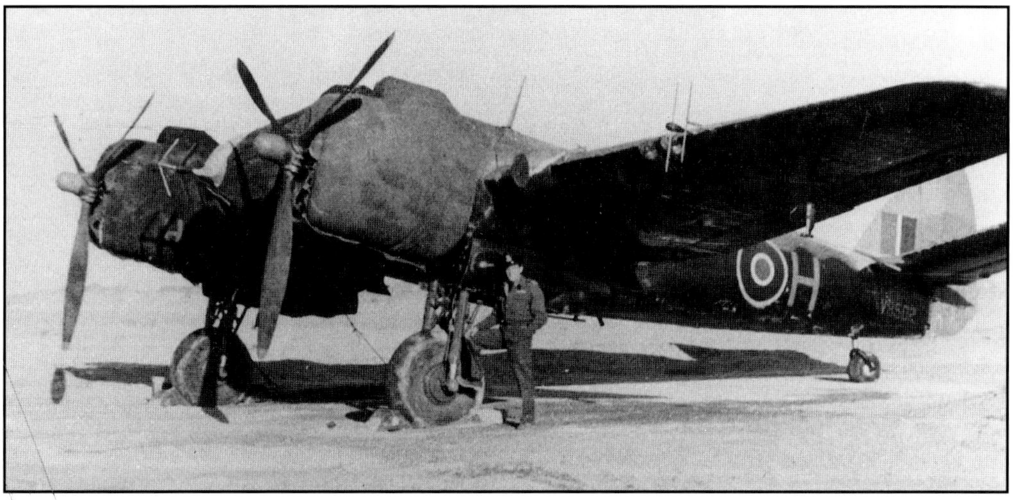

Right: **Mk.VIf V8502 at Mersa in 1943. The main task of No. 46 Squadron on arrival in North Africa was the night defence of Egypt, as the black undersides and fuselage sides of this aircraft indicate. The tell-tale aerials of the AI Mk.IV are also apparent.**

Below: **Idku, March 1943. This Beaufighter's starboard undercarriage collapsed after failing to lock down. This unusual view shows the AI aerials and canvas gun patches well.**

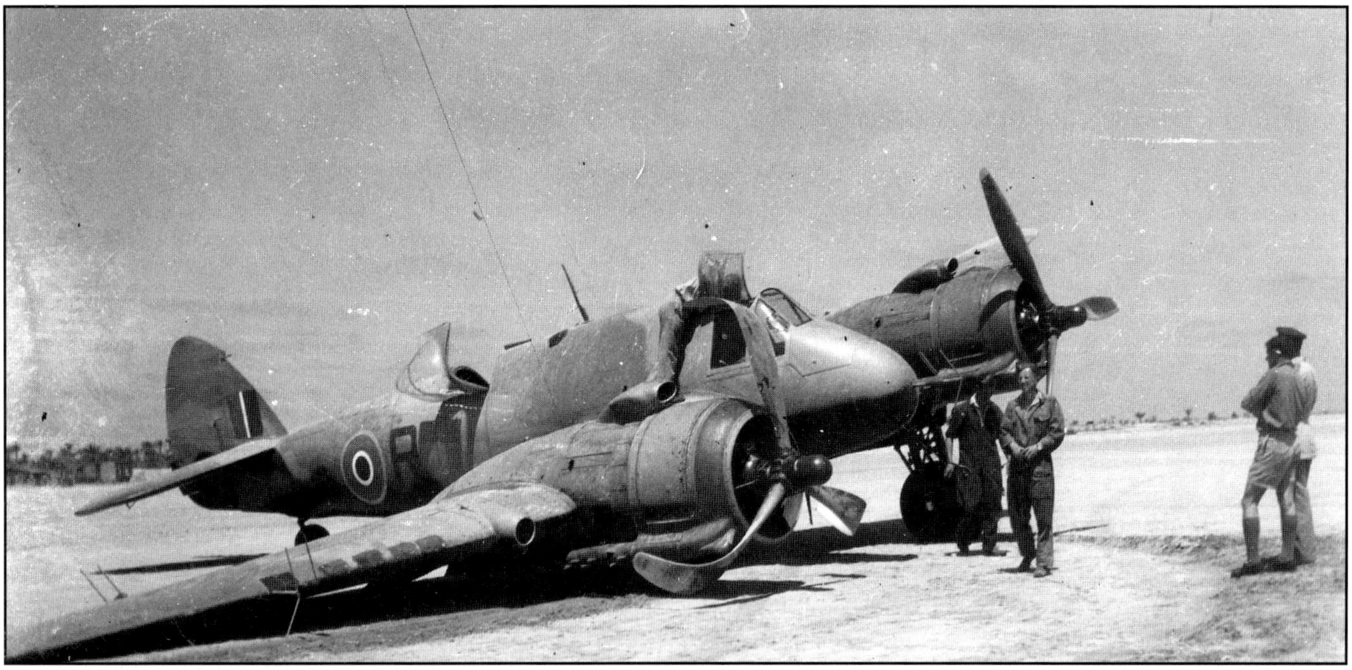

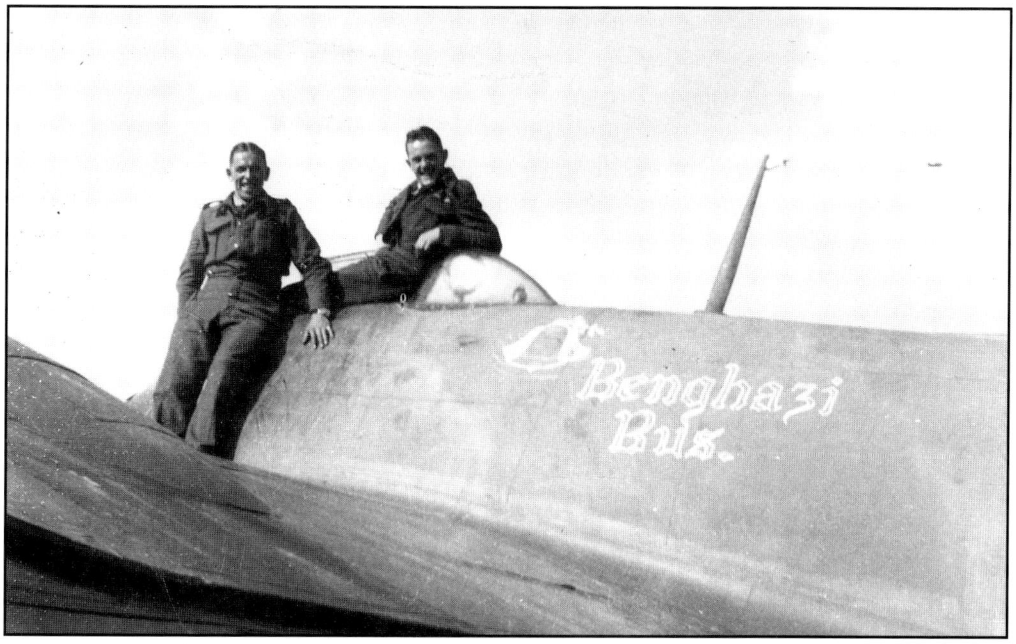

Left: **Flight Lieutenant E J Ledwidge and his navigator pose with T5273 of No. 46 Squadron at Edku on 24 December 1942. The aircraft had been given this name when being used to deliver Christmas food parcels.**

No. 46 Squadron's heaviest losses occurred on 3 October 1943. With Nos. 89, 252 and 272 Squadrons they attacked the German invasion fleet landing on the island of Cos, in the Aegean Sea. Wing Commander Reid, No. 46 Squadron's commanding officer was lost when his Beaufighter was hit over the target at 1,500 feet and span into the sea. Four other Beaufighters were also lost. One of them was being flown by Flight Lieutenant Ledwidge who ditched and then managed to reach mainland Turkey.

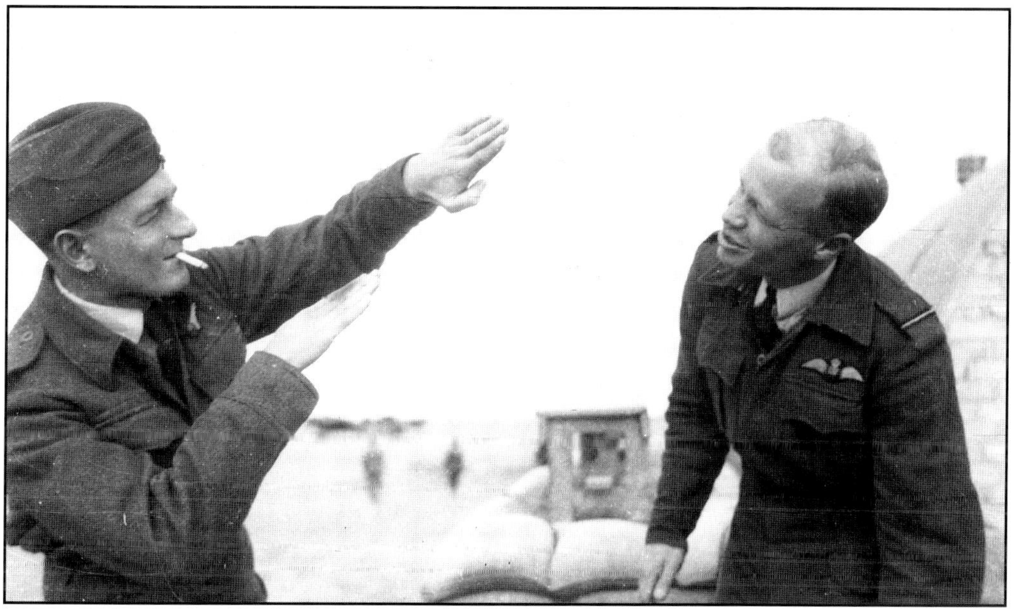

Left: **Flying Officer Alec Craig shooting a line to Flying Officer Pete Babury at Abu Sueir.**

Below: **Flight Lieutenant E J Ledwidge's T5273 again showing the 'H' code over Benghazi in December 1942.**

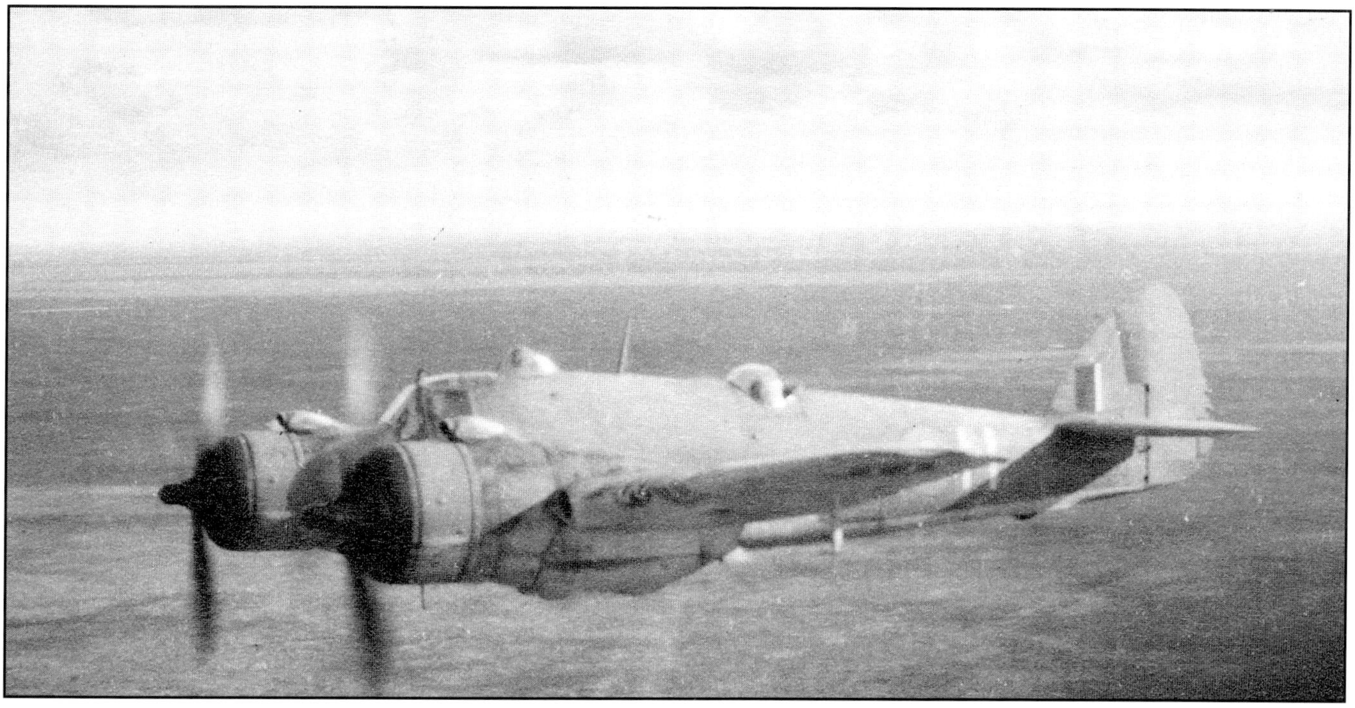

47 SQUADRON

Nili nomen roboris omen
(The name of the Nile is an omen of our strength)

Usage:
TF Mk.X
June 43 to Apr 45

Rôle:
Shipping strikes over the Mediterranean.
From March 1944 moved to India for operations.

Bases:
Protville II 6/43 - 10/43
El Aden 11/43
Gambut 11/43 - 3/44
Amiriya 3/44 -
Cholavaram 4/44 - 10/44
Yelahanka 10/44
Ranchi 11/44
Kumbhirgram 1/45 - 4/45

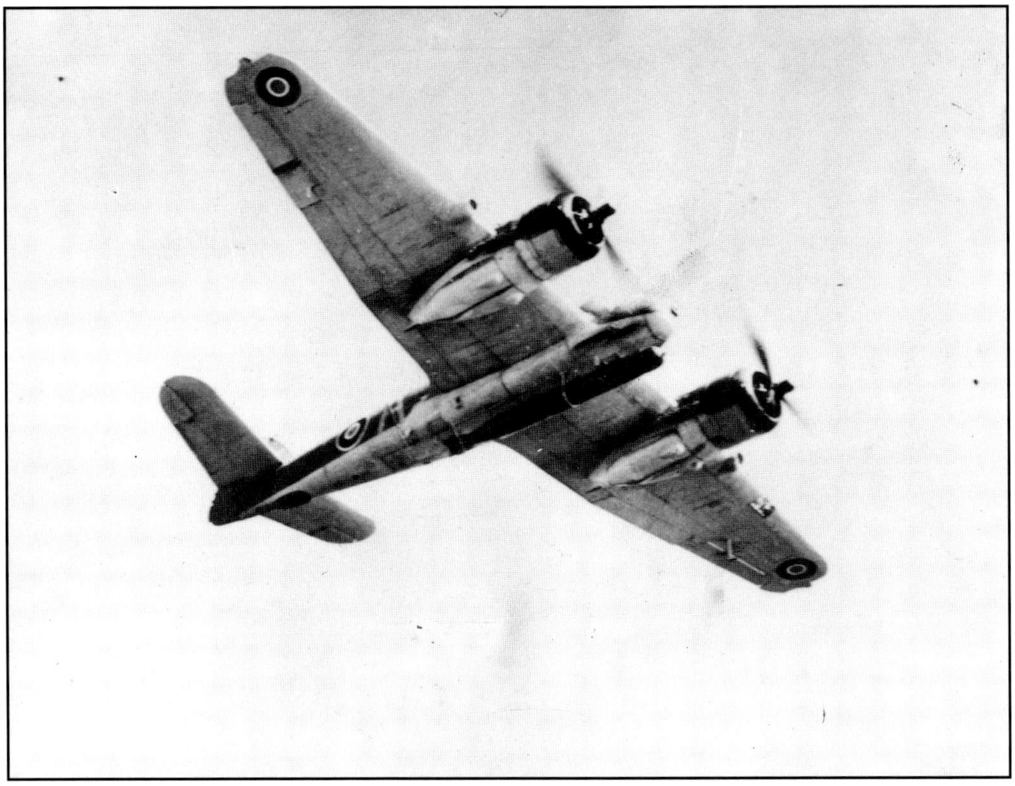

Above: **A torpedo carrying Beaufighter TF Mk.X over India. In October and November 1944 No. 47 Squadron operated Mosquitos, but high humidity caused structural failure and the squadron reverted to Beaufighters until the problems had been resolved.**

Below: **A TF Mk.X over Sardinia. In June 1943 No. 47 Squadron changed their Beauforts for Beaufighter TF Mk.Xs and moved on to Protville II in Tunisia. Here they joined with Nos. 39 and 144 Squadrons to form 328 Wing until October 1943. The German withdrawal from Corsica led to a move to El Adem and re-equipment with torpedoes in October 1943. By January 1944 No. 47 Squadron was one of the last strike squadrons in the eastern Mediterranean, the others being Nos. 227, 252 and 603 Squadrons. They were stationed at Gambut, and commanded by Wing Commander William D L Filson-Young. Their role there was to carry out coastal sweeps along the Greek coast and the Greek islands in the Aegean Sea.**

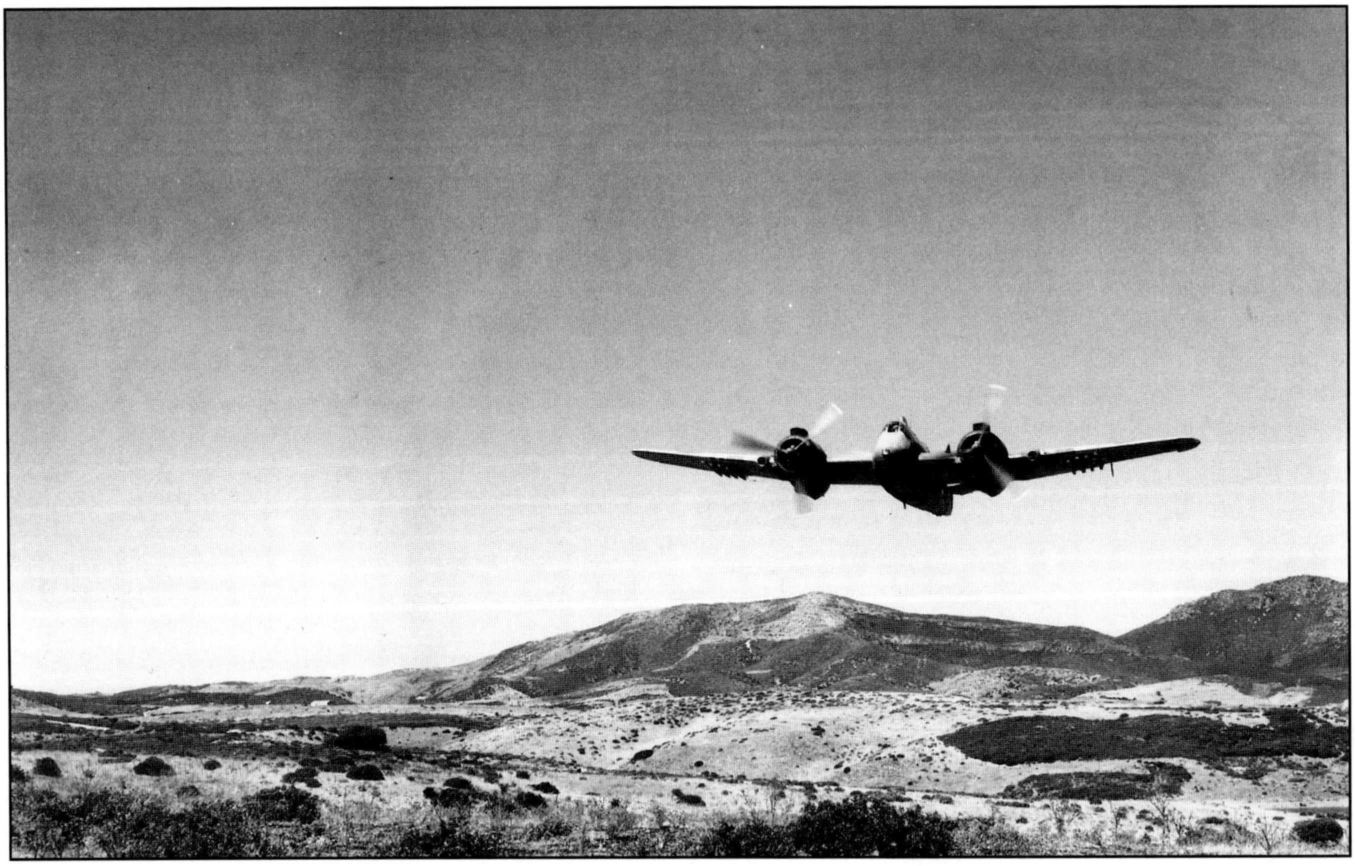

68 SQUADRON

Code Letters:

WM

Vzdy pripraven (Czech)
(Always ready)

Usage:
Mk.If
May 41 to Mar 43
Mk.VIf
Mar 43 to July 44

Rôle:
Night defence of Britain and intruder operations over Europe.

Bases:
High Ercal 5/41 - 3/42
Coltishal 3/42 - 2/44
Coleby Grange 2/44 to 3/44
Fairwood Common 3/44 - 6/44
Castle Camps 6/44 to 7/44

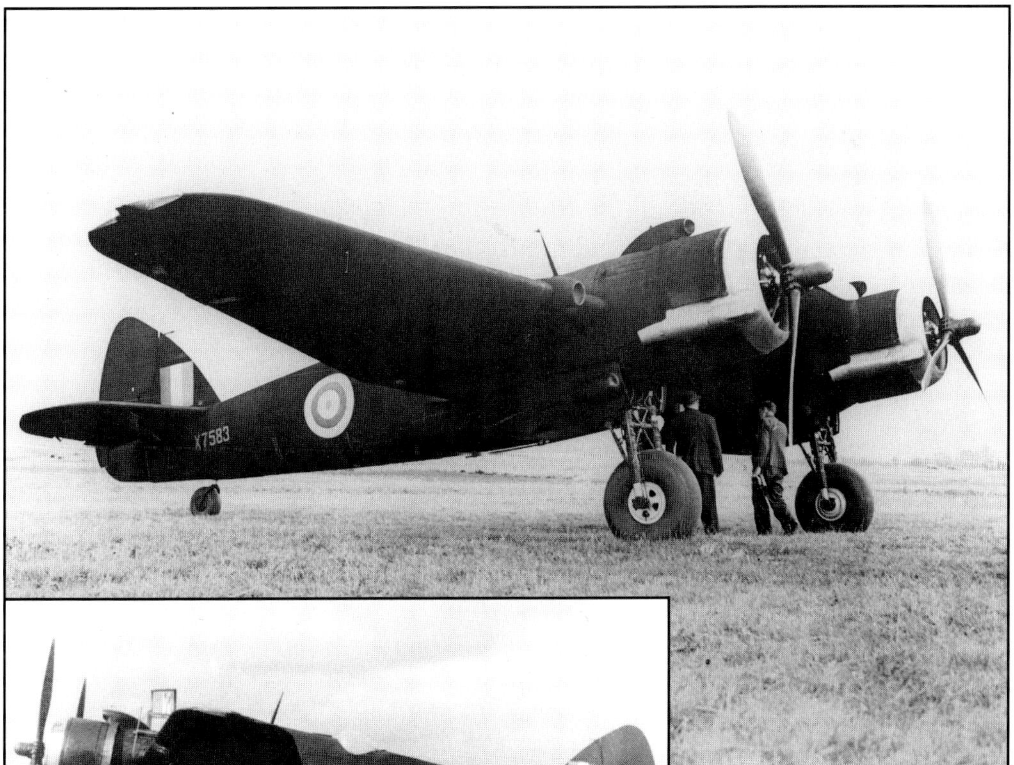

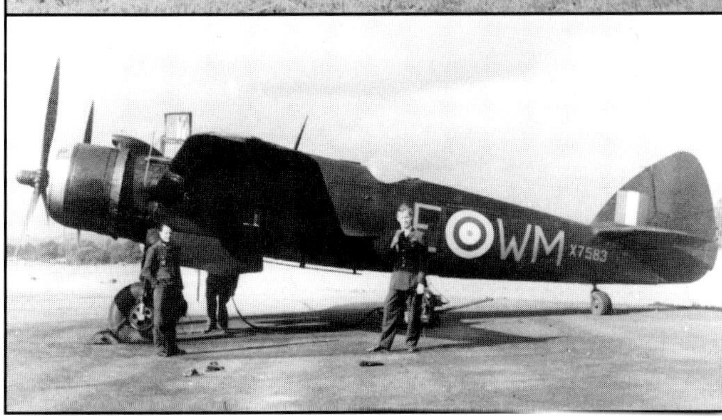

Above: **Two views of X7583, a Weston built Mk.If. The main photograph was taken before delivery and the inset shows the same aircraft after its code letters were applied. The aircraft later went to No. 51 OTU and was broken up at the end of the war.**

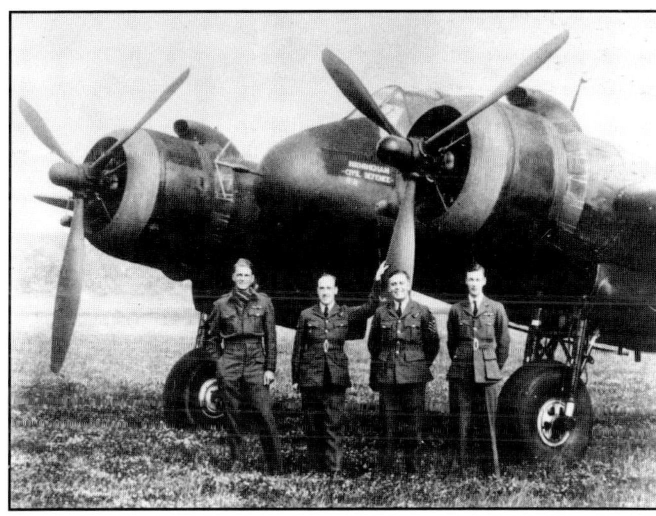

Right: **Appropriately enough for the squadron charged with defending the Midlands, X7842 WM-P was named 'Birmingham Civil Defence'. On 5 September 1942 it caught fire and crashed at Frettenham, Norfolk.**

Below: **The scene at Coltishall on 30 May 1943. During a night flying test an engine on Beaufighter Mk.VIf V8656 failed, forcing its pilot, Flying Officer J Vopalecky to make a single engined landing. On touch down the aircraft veered off the runway and on to wet grass, where the brakes had no effect. Unable to stop, WM-U ran head-on into the parked V8737. Vopalecky and his operator Flight Sergeant R Husar escaped, but the aircraft were damaged beyond repair. (Z Hurt)**

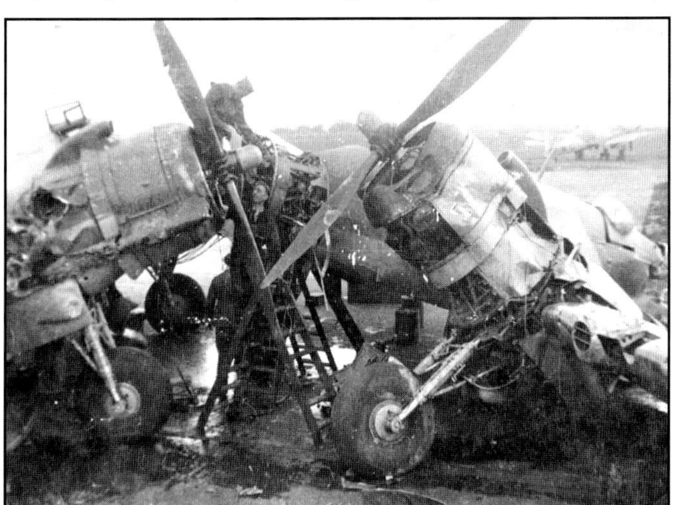

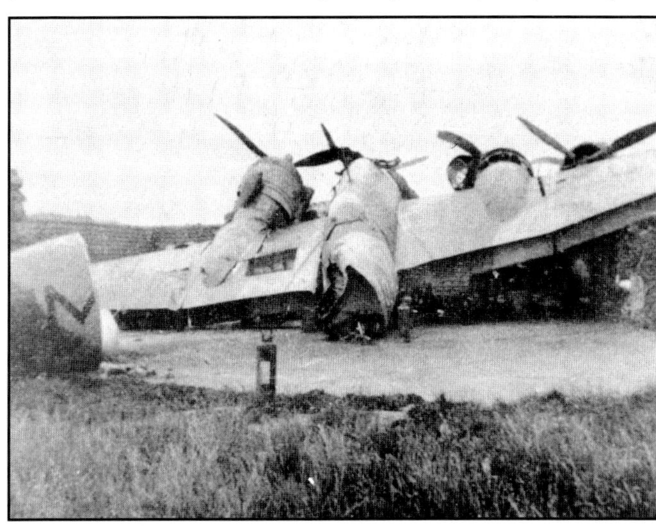

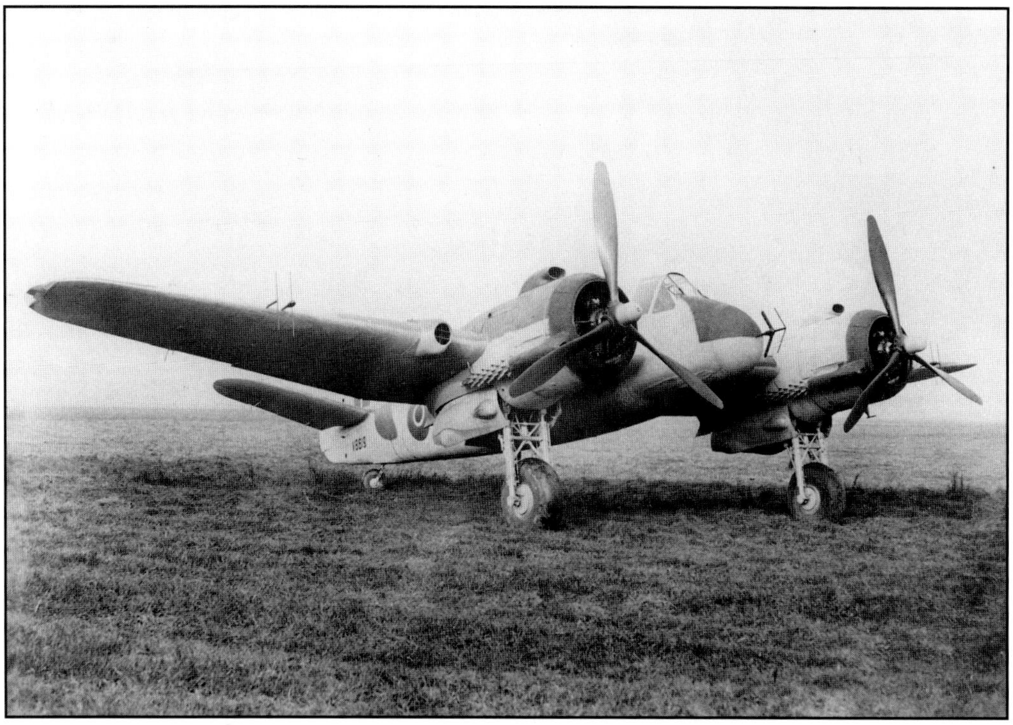

Left: **V8619, a Mk.VIf, was shot down by a Mosquito night fighter over Stowmarket, Suffolk on 10 December, 1943. The pilot, Flight Sergeant S G Irwin baled out safely, but his observer Sergeant R V H Brown was killed.**

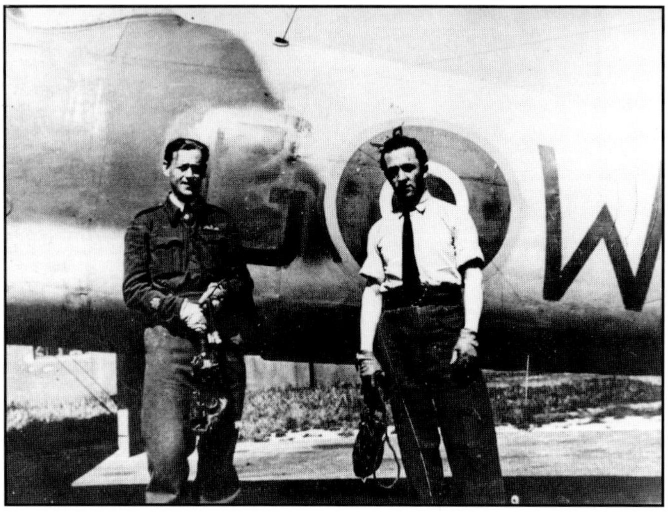

Above: **WM-G, V8749, left No. 68 Squadron and was flown to North Africa by the Overseas Aircraft Delivery Unit. The men are Flight Sergeants Josef Adam and Fridolin Gemrod, two of the Czech men on the squadron.**

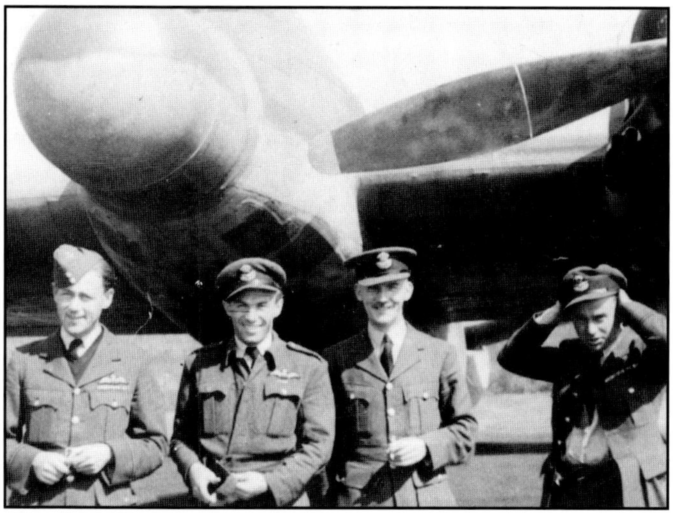

Above: **The thimble nose of an IA Mk.VIII equipped Beaufighter Mk.VIF of No. 68 Squadron at Fairwood Common in the Spring of 1944. L-R P/O J Adam, F/Lt Joe Capka, unknown, F/O L Cupak, who is not quite ready for the photo.**

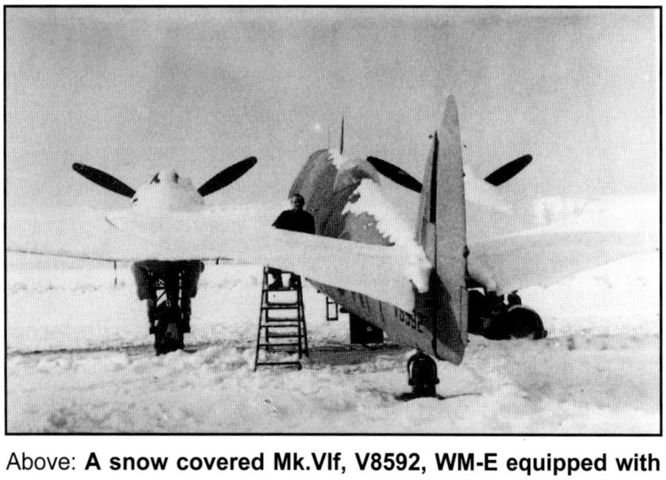

Above: **A snow covered Mk.VIf, V8592, WM-E equipped with AI Mk.VIII, possibly on detachment at Peterhead in the winter of 1942-43. The aircraft soldiered on until 27 April 1944, when it crashed on landing at Fairwood Common.**

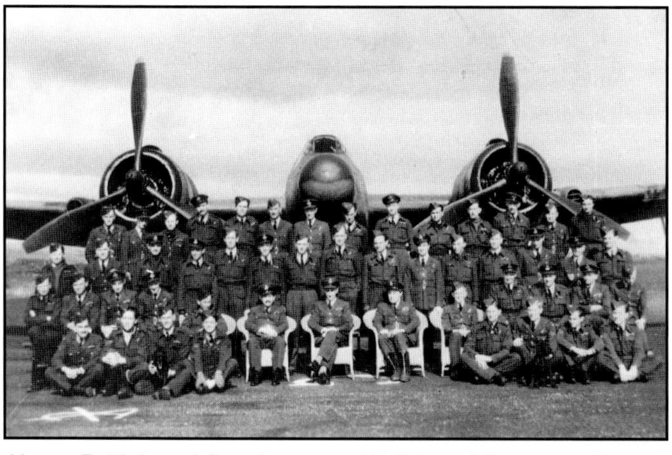

Above: **British and Czech crews at Fairwood Common. Seated in the centre is the CO Wing Commander Hayley-Bell DFC, on the left is Squadron Leader Wright and on the right Squadron Leader Mansfield, the flight commanders.**

69
SQUADRON

With vigilance we serve
Usage:
Mk.1c
Jan 42 to Apr 42

Rôle:
Reconnaissance from Malta

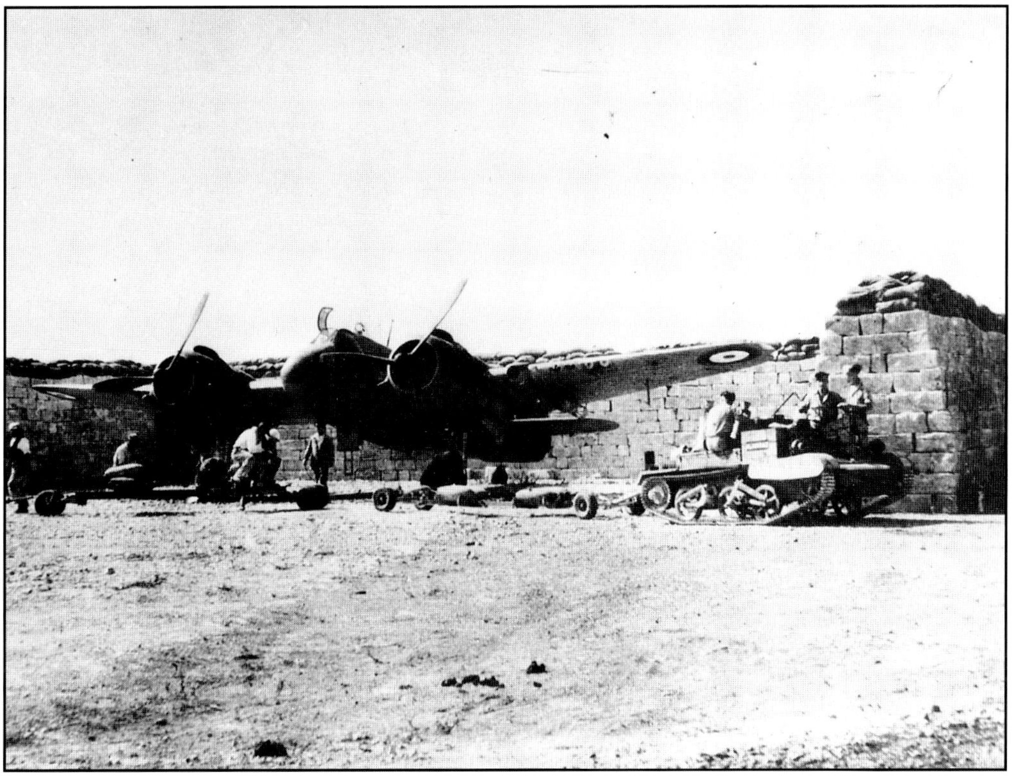

Left: **No. 69 Squadron used Mk.Ics based on Malta for reconnaissance over the Mediterranean. They also had Marylands, Hurricanes and Spitfires during this time.**

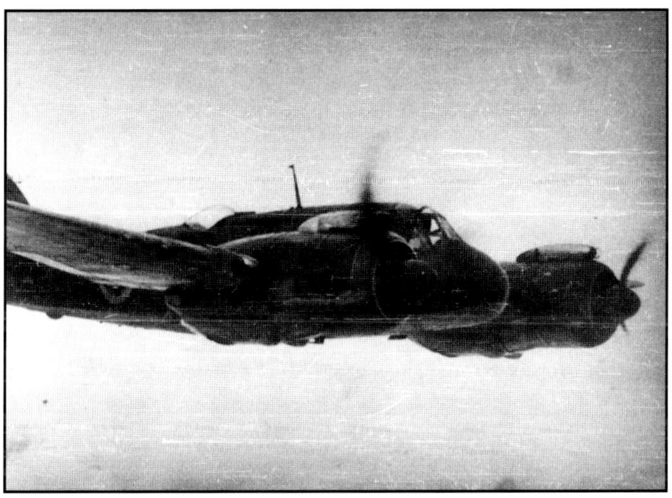

Above: **A Beaufighter Mk.Ic holds a close formation.**

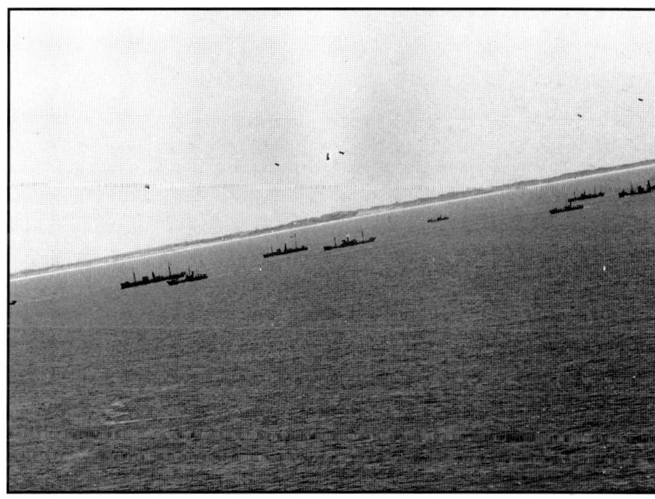

Above: **A typical sight, a convoy and its balloon barrage.**

84
SQUADRON

Scorpiones pungunt
(Scorpions sting)
Usage:
TF Mk.X
Dec 46 to Oct 48
Rôle:
Ground attack in Malaya
Bases:
Seletar 12/46 -9/47
Changi 9/47 - 2/48
Tengah & Kuala Lumpur
2/48 - 10/48

Below: **One of the highly developed TF Mk.Xs used over the Malayan jungle by No. 84 Squadron that used Beaufighters after Mosquitos and before Brigands.**

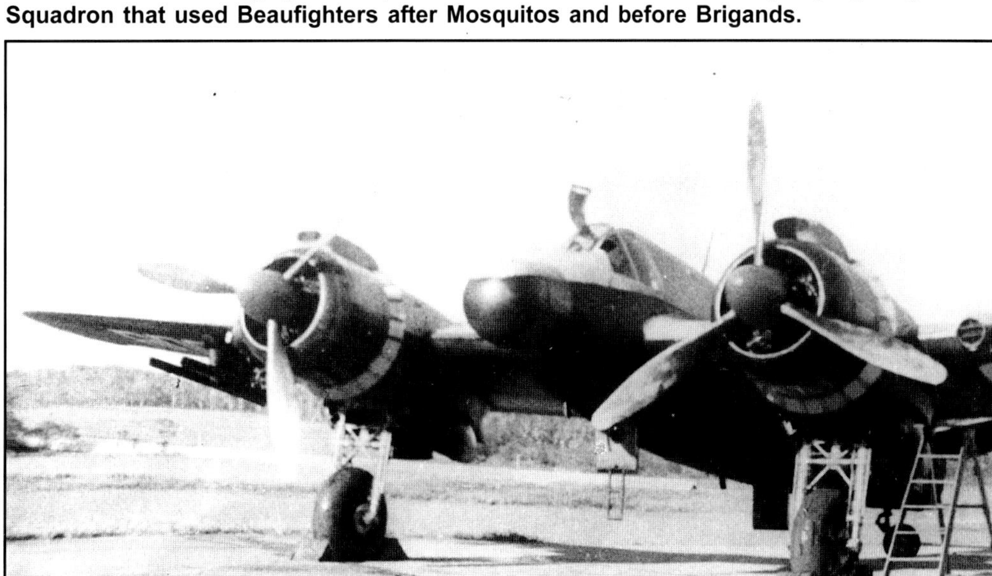

89 SQUADRON

Dei auxilio telis meis
(By the help of God with my own weapons)

Usage:
Mk.If
Oct 41 to Apr 43
Mk.VIf
Aug 42 to June 45

Rôle:
Night defence and intruder operations over Middle East and Ceylon.

Bases:
Colerne 10/41 - 11/41
Abu Sueir 10/41 - 1/43
Bersis 1/43 - 3/43
Castle Benito 3/43 - 8/43
Idku 8/43 - 10/43
Vavuniya 10/43 - 3/44
Minneriya 3/44 - 6/44
Vavuniya 6/44 - 8/44
Baigachi 8/44 - 6/45

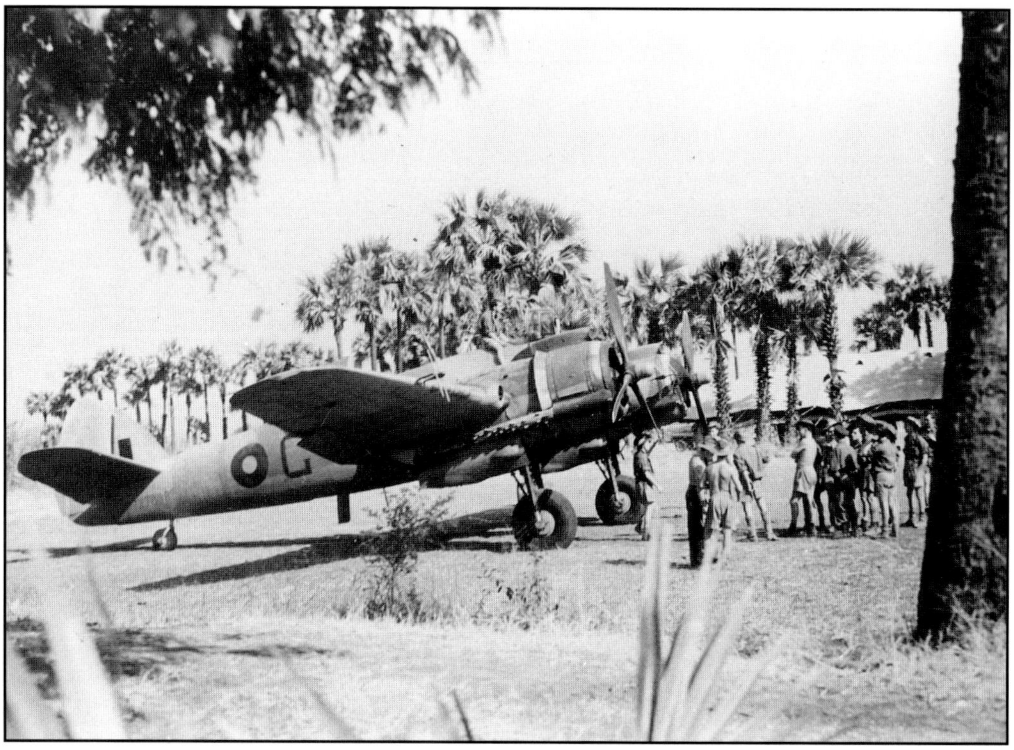

Above: **X7898, 'G' a Mk.VIf, at a forward dispersal near Mandalay Road in 1943. No. 89 Squadron had a nomadic existence, covering Europe, Middle East and Far East. In addition to its main bases aircraft operated from many airstrips on detachment.**

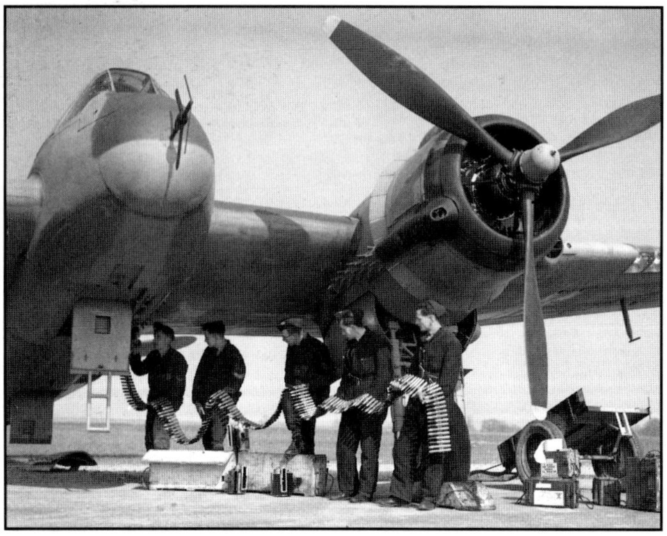

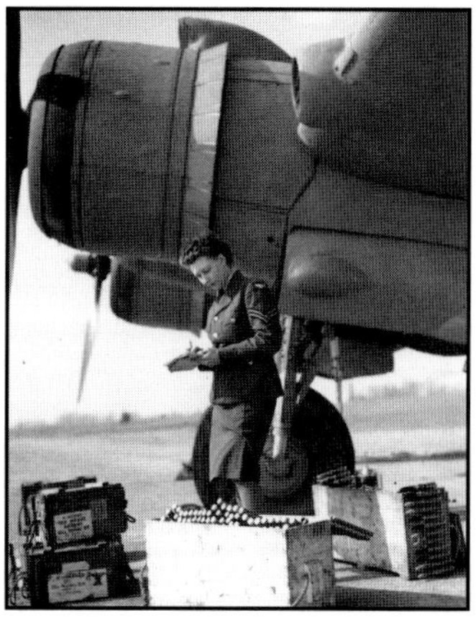

In October 1943 a photographer visited No. 96 Squadron at Drem to record the daily activities and organised the ground crew in front of V8748 ZJ-R, a Mk.VIf. After the squadron converted to Mosquitos in November 1943, V8748 was ferried by the OADU to join No. 89 Squadron.

The usual number of ground crew needed to re-arm a Beaufighter was just two armourers, so the gathering here is clearly for the camera.

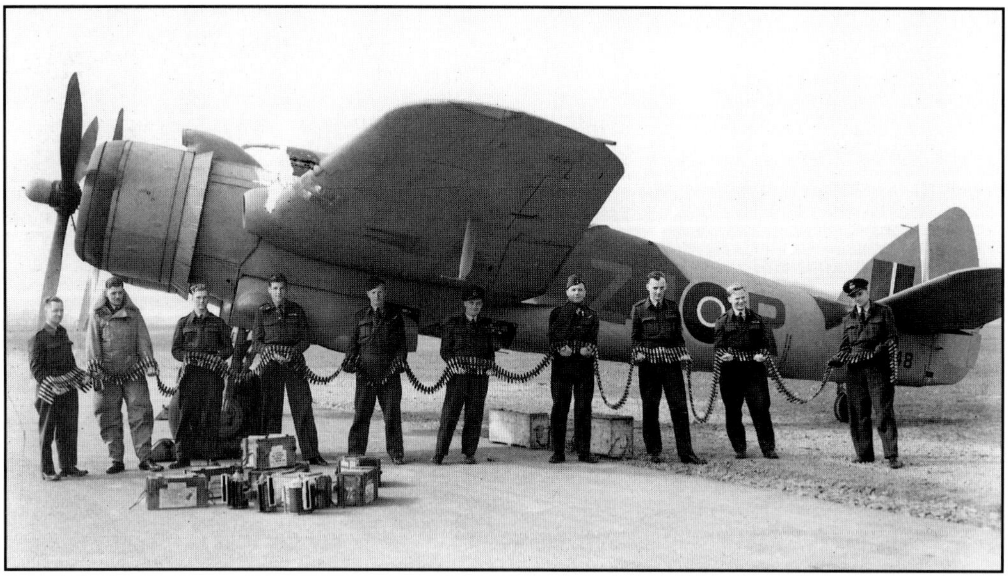

96 SQUADRON

Code Letters:
ZJ

Nocturni obambulamus
(We prowl by night)

Usage:
Mk.IIf
May 42 to Feb 43
Mk.VIf
Sept 42 to Nov 43

Rôle:
Night defence of Britain.

Bases:
Wrexham 5/42 - 10/42
Honiley 10/42 - 8/43
Church Fenton 8/43 - 9/43
Drem 9/43 - 11/43

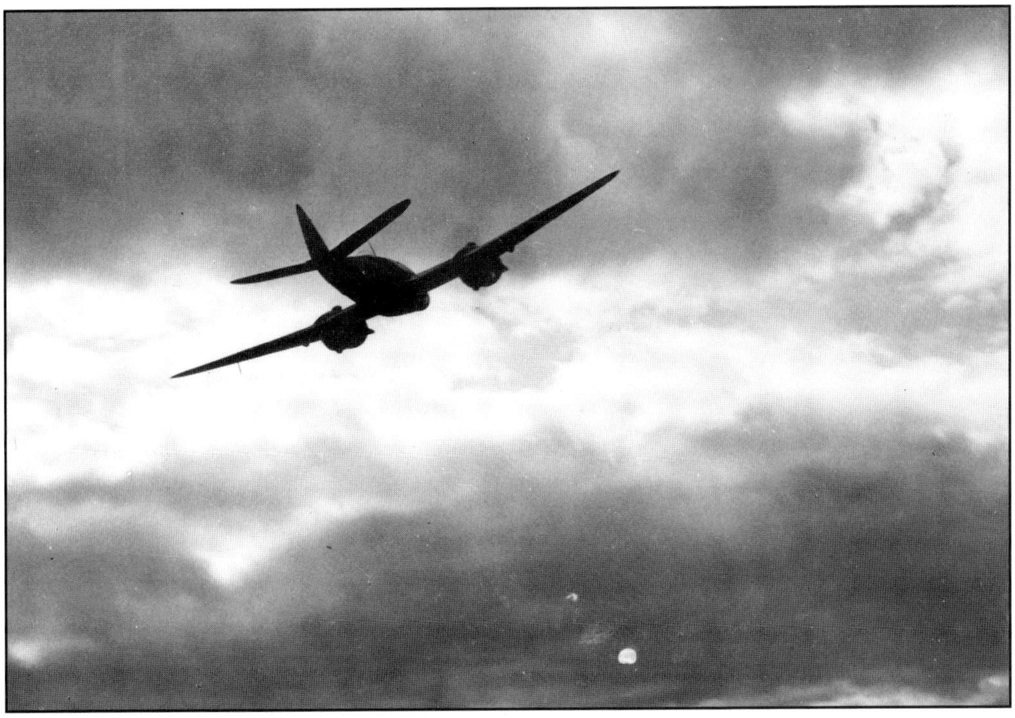

Above: **The silhouette of a No. 125 Squadron Beaufighter. The squadron re-equipped from Defiants to the Mk.IIf in February 1942 and moved on the Mk.VIf in September 1942. Only in February 1944 did they take on their first Mosquito Mk.XVII.**

125
SQUADRON
Code Letters:
VA

Nunquam domandi
(Never to be tamed)

Usage:
Mk.IIf
Feb 42 to Sep 42
Mk.VIf
Sep 42 to Mar 44

Rôle:
Night defence of Britain.

Bases:
Colerne 2/42 - 5/42
Fairwood Common 5/42 - 4/43
Exeter 4/43 - 11/43
Valley 11/43 - 3/44

Right: **No. 29 Squadron's 'Ace' Bob Braham assumed command of No. 141 Squadron on 22 December 1942. With few enemy raids to intercept, Braham began intruder sorties and in mid 1943 commenced 'Serrate' operations against enemy night fighters.**

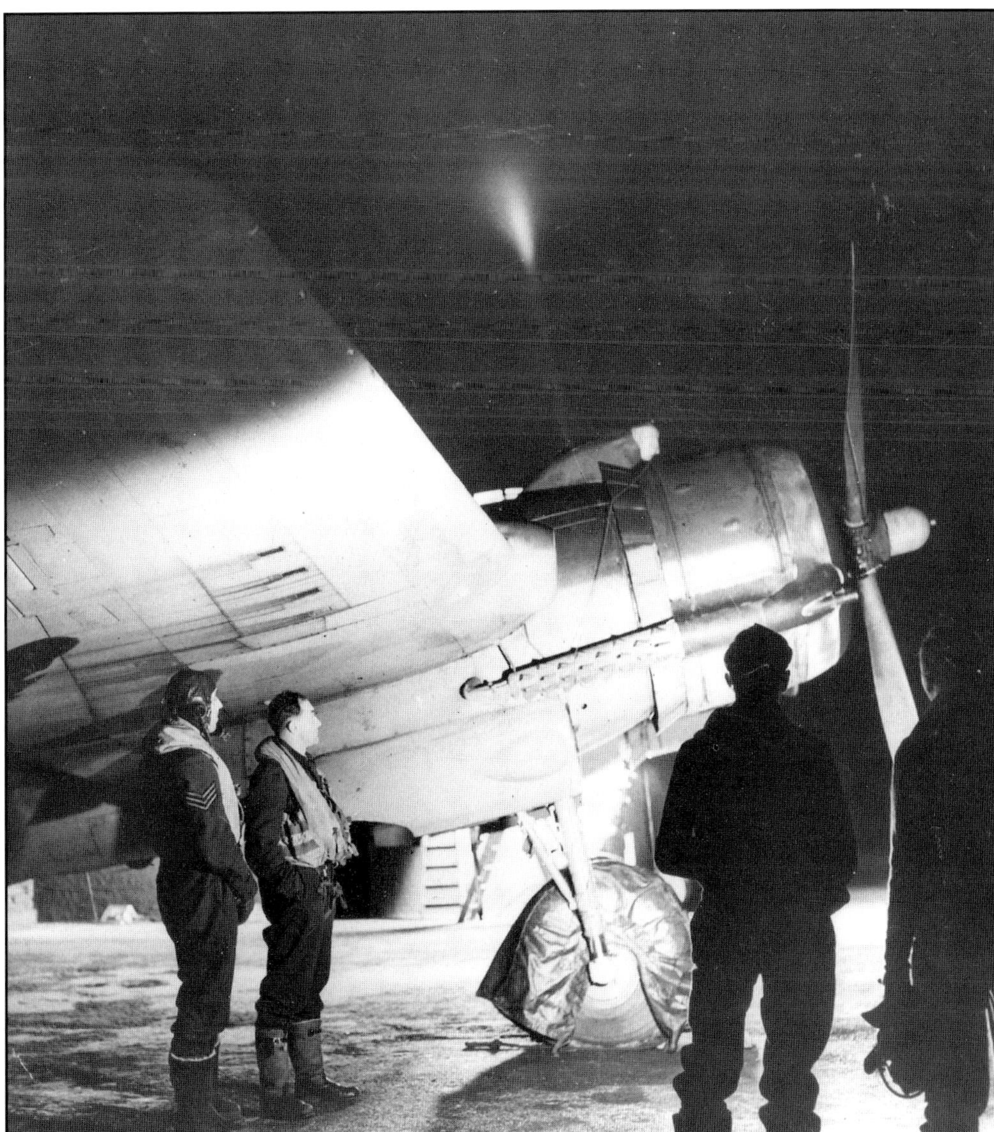

141
SQUADRON
Code Letters:
TW

Caedimus noctu
(We slay by night)

Usage:
Mk.If
June 41 to June 43
Mk.VIf
May 43 to Jan 44

Rôle:
Night defence of Britain and intruder operations over Europe.

Bases:
Ayr 6/41 - 3/42
Acklington 1/42 -6/42
Tangmere 6/42 to 8/42
Ford 8/42 - 2/43
Predannack2/43 to 4/43
Wittering 4/43 - 12/43
West Raynham 12/43 - 1/44

143 SQUADRON

Code Letters:

HO

Vincere est vivere

(To conquer is to live)

Usage:

Mk.1c
June 41 to Nov 41
and
Aug 42 to Sept 42
Mk.IIf
Sept 42 to Mar 43
Mk.XI
May 43 to May 44
TF Mk.X
Sept 43 to Oct 44

Rôle:

Coastal Command anti-shipping operations based in Britain.

Bases:

Aldergrove 6/41
Thornaby 7/41
Dyce 7/41 - 9/41
Sumburgh 9/41 - 12/41
Dyce 12/41
North Coates 8/42 - 8/43
St Eval 8/43 - 9/43
Portreath 9/43 - 2/44
North Coates 2/44 - 5/44
Manston 5/44 - 9/44
North Coates 9/44

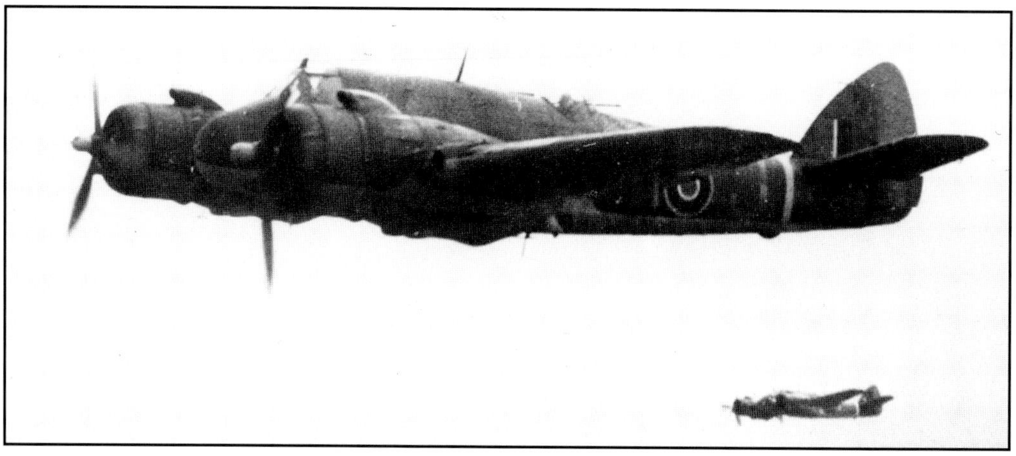

Above: **Beaufighter Mk.VIs of No. 143 Squadron based at Portreath in late 1943. (N. Carr)**

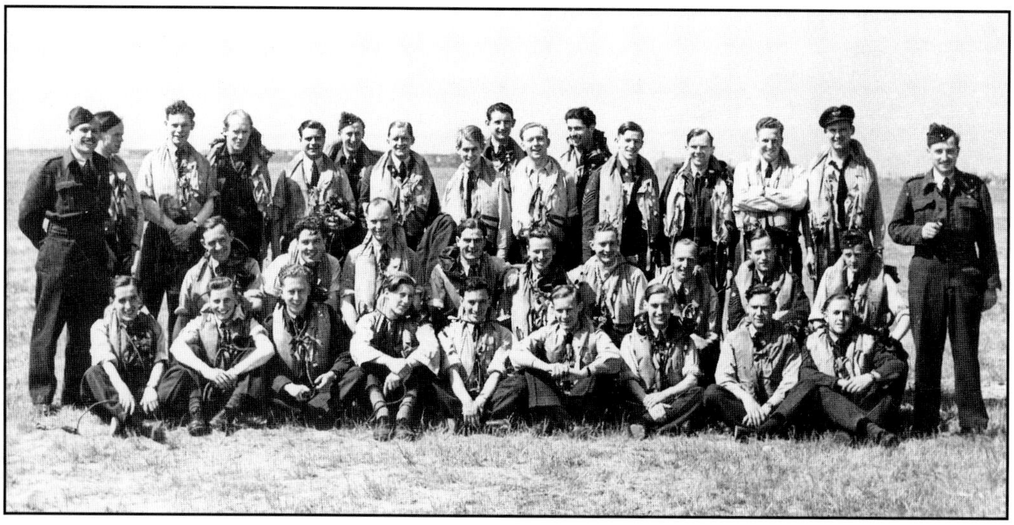

Above: **The aircrews of No. 143 Squadron at Manston in early 1944, shortly before re-equipping with Mosquitos. At least a third of these were later killed in action. (N. Carr)**

Below: **On 17 May 1943, No. 143 Squadron took part with Nos. 236 and 254 Squadrons in an attack on a convoy in the North Sea off Texel. The key to the numbers on the inset as detailed in the original caption reads: 'The Beaufighter from which this picture was taken is about to release a torpedo for an attack on a vessel at (1). Beaufighter at (2) has already released its torpedo (3) for an attack on a ship at (4). Waterborne balloons are carried by merchant vessels at (5) and (6). At (7) and (8) bombs have been dropped by other attacking aircraft, and at (9) cannon fire rakes the water where a vessel has taken evasive action.' The ships sunk in this attack were; MV *Kyphissa*, minesweeper M.414, flakship *Hermann Hindrichs*.**

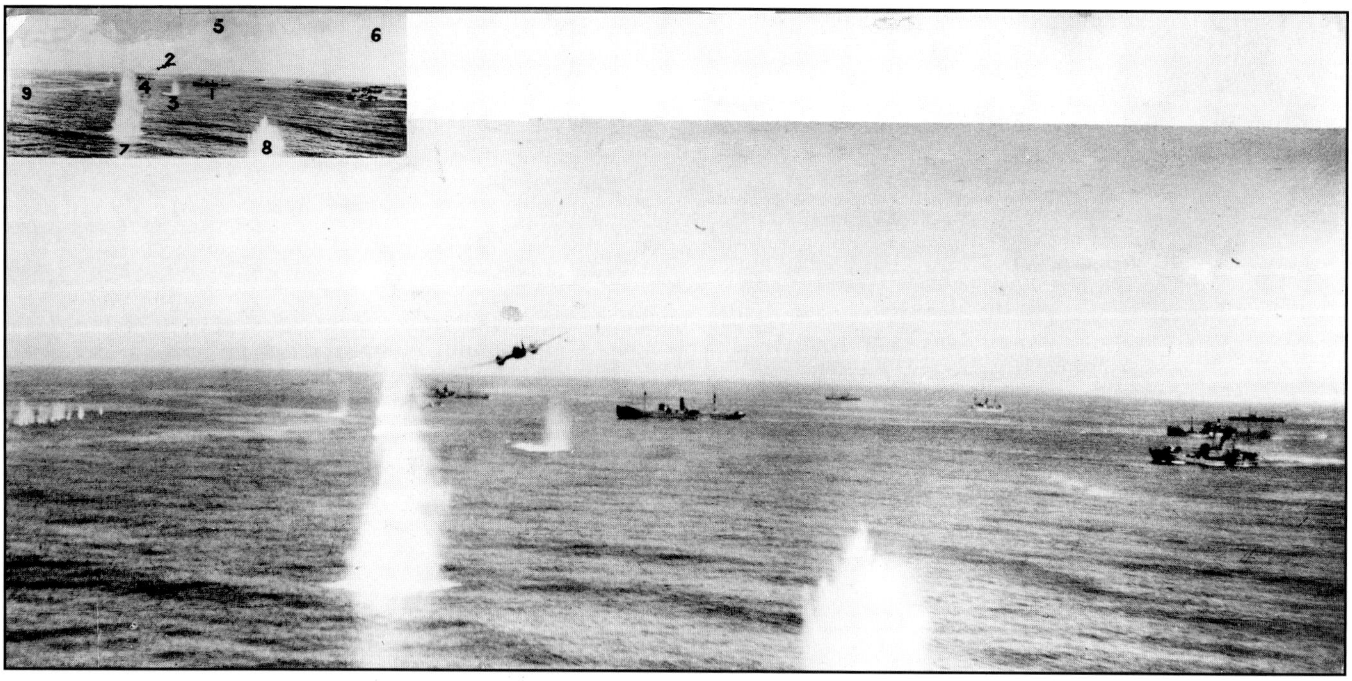

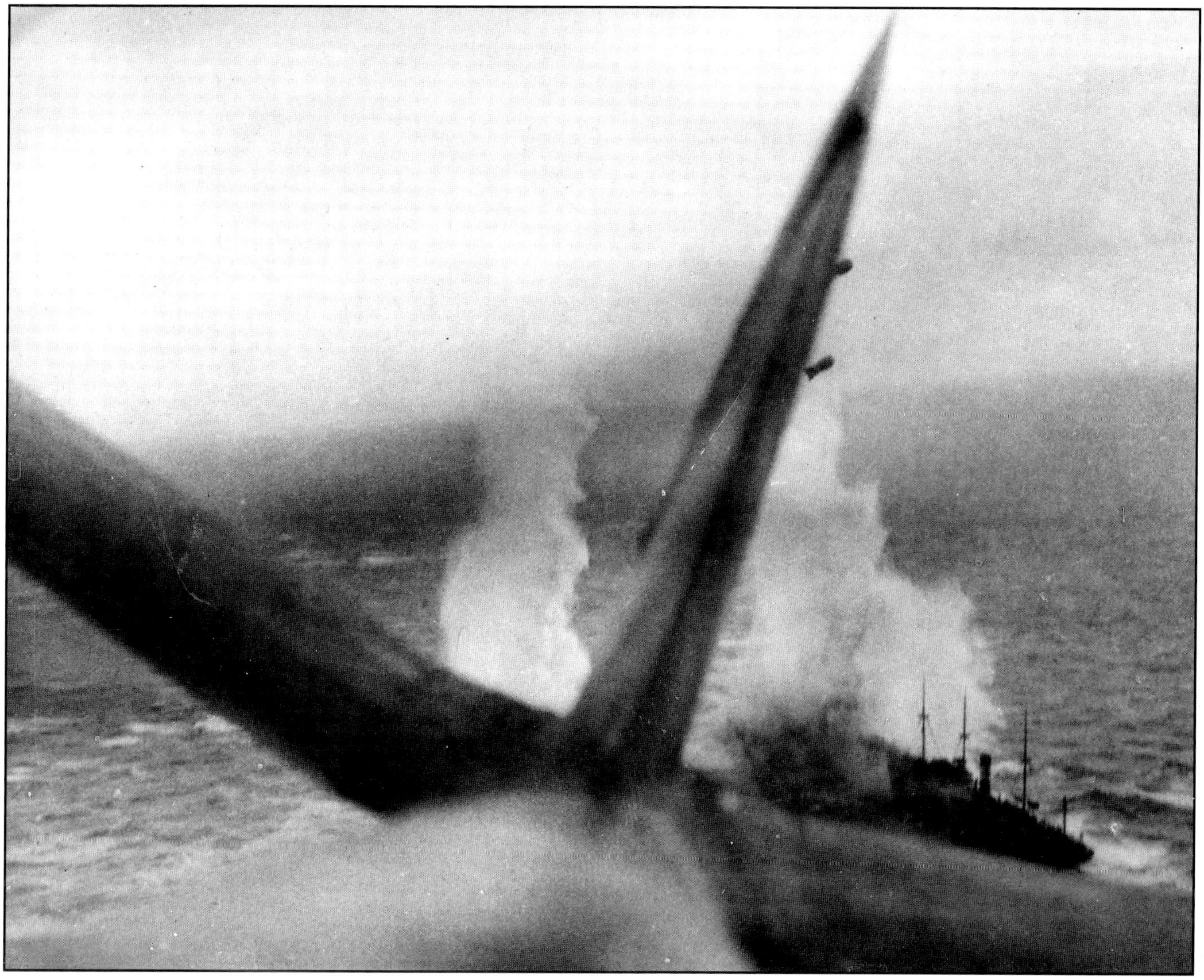

Above: **No. 143 Squadron set out with a Spitfire escort on 1 March 1944 to attack shipping off the Dutch coast and found the merchant ship MV *Maasburg* off Texel. The first wave of attacks disabled the *Maasburg* and a second attack with torpedoes sent her to the bottom.**

Right: **Another attack, this time on 27 June 1943, but on this occasion no ships were sunk.**

Disbanded after the First World War, No. 143 Squadron re-formed at Aldergrove, in Northern Ireland, in June 1941 with Beaufighter Mk.Ics. At this time they absorbed elements of No. 252 Squadron which was going to Malta. In an unusual move the squadron re-equipped with Blenheim Mk.IVs in December 1941, keeping them for seven months before getting Beaufighters again.

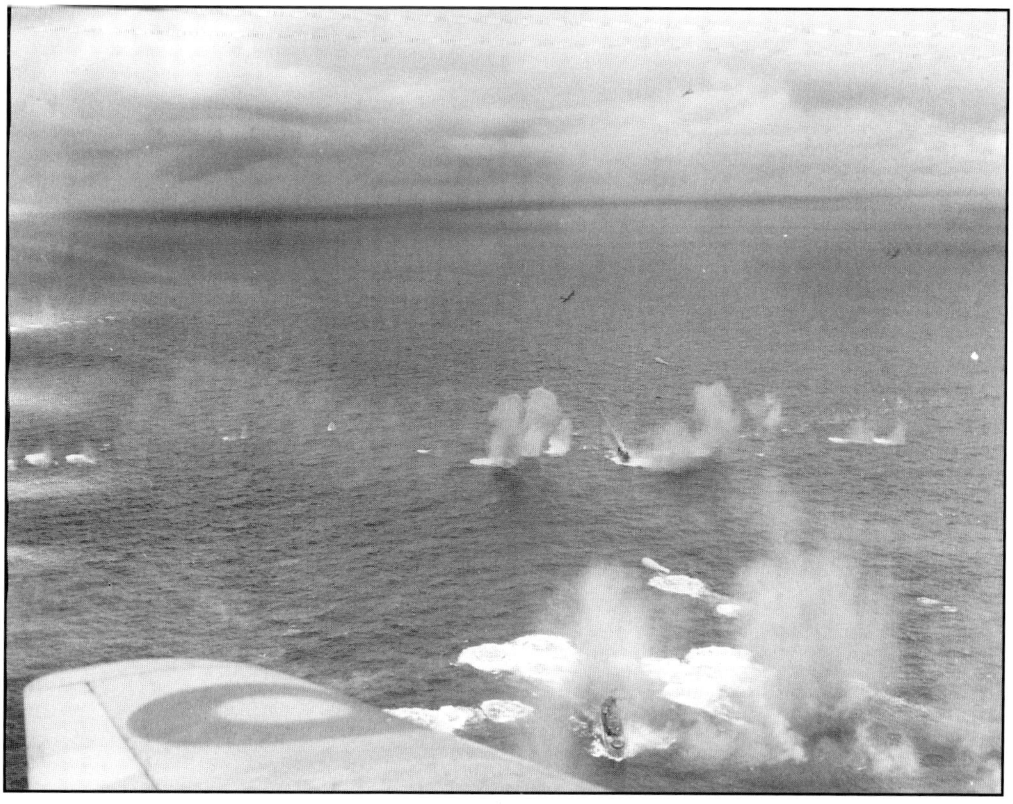

144 SQUADRON

Code Letters:

PL

(Who shall stop us)

Usage:

Mk.VIc
Jan 43 to May 43
TF Mk.X
May 43 to May 45

Rôle:

Coastal Command anti-shipping strike operations mainly based in Britain.

Bases:

Leuchars 3/43 - 4/43
Tain 4/43 - 5/43
Benson 7/43 - 8/43
(Detachment to Protville II 5/43 - 8/43)
Tain 8/43 10/43
Wick 10/43 - 5/44
Davidstow Moor 5/44 - 7/44
Strubby 7/44 - 9/44
Banff 9/44 - 10/44
Dallachy 10/44 - 5/45

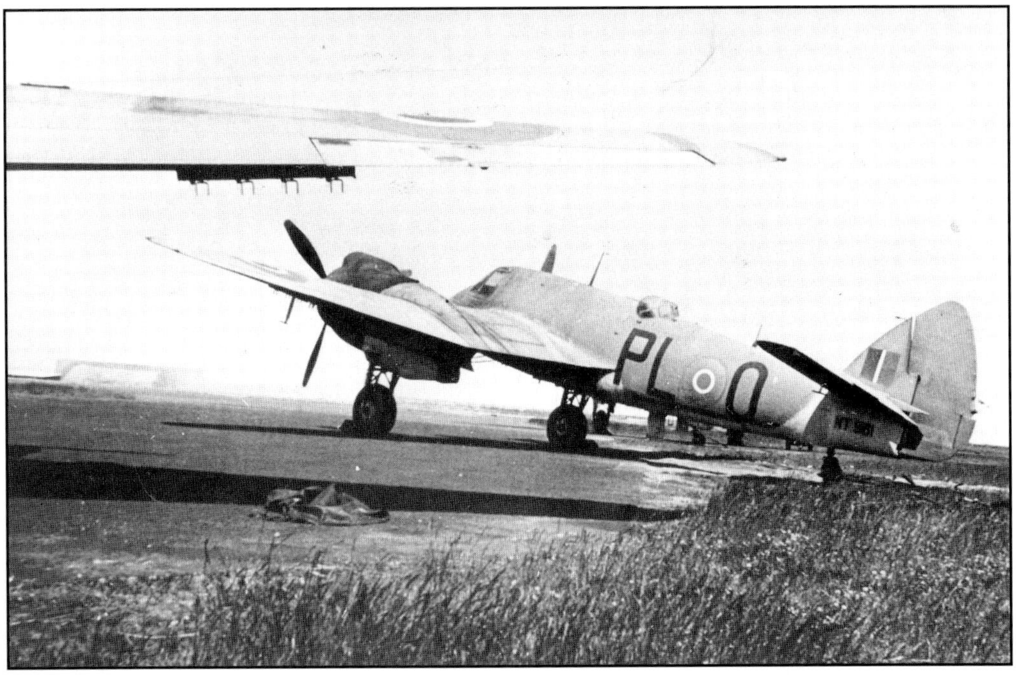

Above: **Showing the squadron's PL code well, this particular PL-O is NT961, which replaced NE831, also coded PL-O, which was wrecked on the 9 February 1945 strike.**

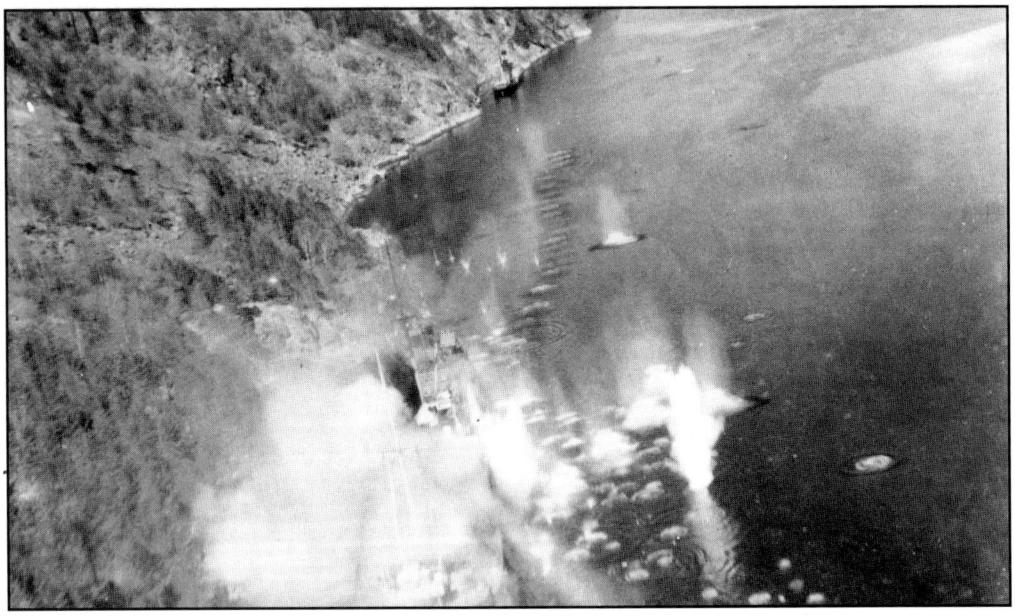

Right: **The squadron making its last attack of the war. The target, as it was so often, was shipping in a Norwegian fjord. The last Norwegian target attacked by No. 144 Squadron was the MV *Ingerseks,* which was sunk in Sognefjord on 23 April 1945.**

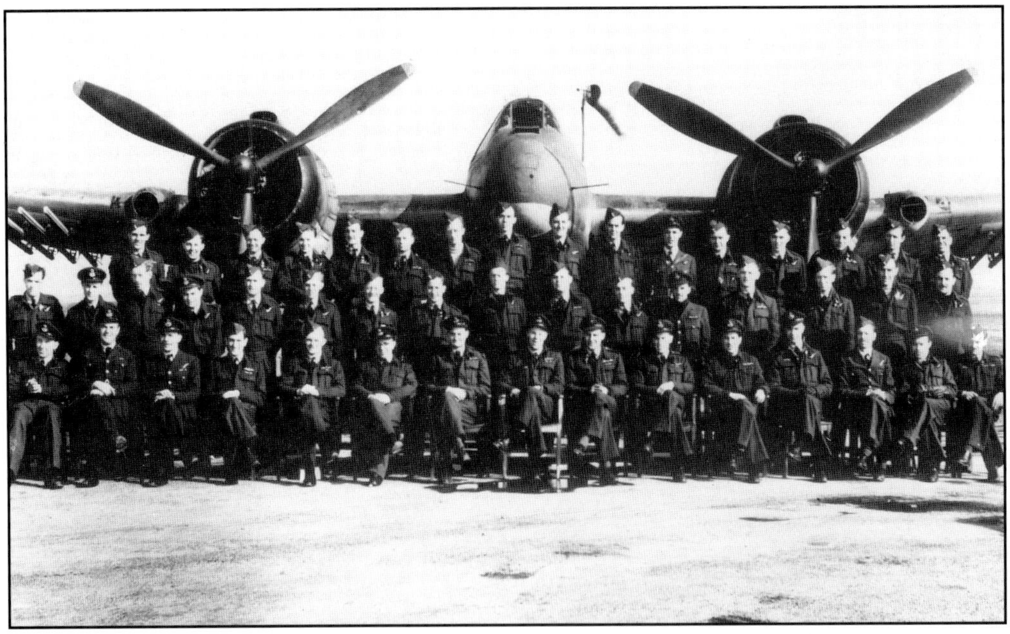

Left: **No. 144 Squadron personnel in Dallachy in early 1945. In the centre on the chair is Tony Gadd DFC and Bar, the vastly experienced Commanding Officer. Gadd had taken over the squadron from Wing Commander David Lunsden in August 1944 when it was part of the Strubby Strike Wing.**

Dallachy Strike Wing's Black Friday

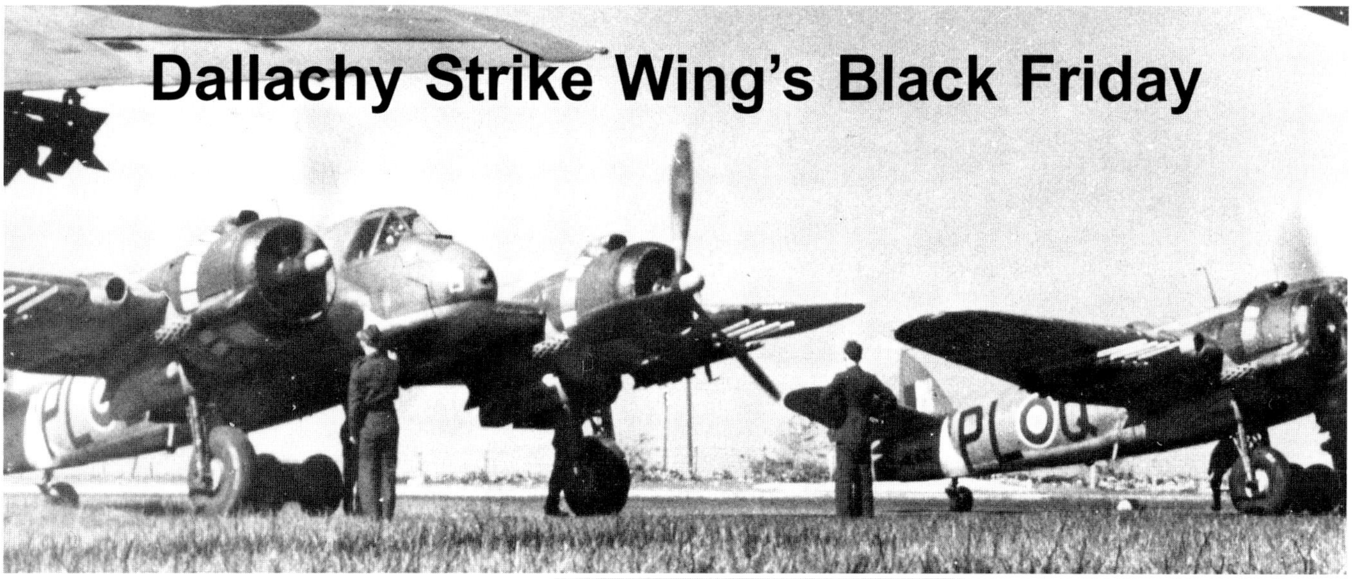

By the February of 1945 the war in Europe was seen by some to be nearing an end, but in many areas it was far from over. The war fought by the Coastal Command Strike Wings based in Scotland was still a life and death matter. Target for the Banff and Dallachy Wing was the shipping in and around the Norwegian coast. The greatest threat in the area to the Allies had been the *Tirpitz*, but that had been sunk in Tromso fjord in November 1944. Destroyers were now the most powerful German vessels left in northern waters. Keeping a regular watch on merchant and naval shipping was a task for the Strike Wings with patrols being flown over the coast, searching the narrow, steep sided fjords. On 9 February 1945 two Beaufighters of No. 489 Squadron were flying just such a reconnaissance. The two New Zealand pilots, Warrant Officer Brightwell and Flight Sergeant Priest, had crossed the Norwegian coast near the Utvar lighthouse and were flying north when a merchant vessel of 1,500 tons was found in Stong fjord. In Førde fjord was something far more interesting, a Narvik class destroyer accompanied by a mine sweeper and two flak ships. Continuing north five large merchant vessels were noted near Nord Gulen and as they passed Bremanger a flak ship and two mine sweepers were seen. The reports were sent to the Dallachy Operations Room by radio and plans for a strike had been made even before the reconnaissance Beaufighters had landed. Temping though the merchant vessels were the Admiralty, under whose command Coastal Command came, had prioritized potential targets and a destroyer was a Class One target.

The continuous attacks by Coastal Command had lead Admiral von Schnader to give the order that all shipping around the Norwegian coast was to move at night and hide in the narrow fjords during the short daylight hours. The Narvik class destroyer, the Z-33 of 2,603 tons had run aground on 7 February and was being towed to Bergen for repair by two tugs. They had chosen to hide in Førde fjord on 9 February. The reconnaissance flight had not gone unnoticed by the commander of the German fleet in the fjord, for he began immediately to move deeper into the fjord to a point where its sides rose vertically from the icy water. Locals watched as gun fire was used to break the ice and slowly the destroyer was shepherded under a steep cliff, known as Jørneset, by two tugs.

Under command of Australian Wing Commander Colin Milson thirty-two Beaufighters of the Dallachy Wing were readied. Nos. 455 and 404 Squadrons contributed eleven rocket armed aircraft each, nine aircraft from No. 144 Squadron and a single machine from No. 489 Squadron were armed with cannons and machine guns only as they were in the process of converting from torpedoes to rockets. Ten Mustangs of No. 65 Squadron would provide fighter escort and finally two air sea rescue Warwicks of No. 279 Squadron would be on hand to attempt to save ditched crews from the ice cold waters. The Mosquito equipped Banff Strike Wing would attack the ships observed at North Gulen. At 13.55 hours the Wing set out for the two hour long low level flight to Førde fjord. In Beaufighter NE831, wearing the codes PL-O of No. 144 Squadron, was Flight Sergeant Stan Butler and his navigator Flight Sergeant 'Nick' Nicholl, this would be their first shipping strike operation.

"Take-off was just before 1400 hours. We formed up and set course at low level in a loose formation of vics of three, lead by our CO Squadron Leader Rogers. The weather was not bad, there were rain squalls here and there, but visibility was reasonably good. Everything was going according to plan. In these fjord attacks, it was usual to fly inland for a while after making a landfall, and then approach the fjord roughly at right angles. You would then turn down the fjord at a height that would allow you both to clear the high ground and to dive in to attack the target when spotted. The aircraft could then break away to seaward on completion of the attack and get a good start for the journey back to base. This type of attack could usually be completed with a minimum amount of time being spent over enemy territory and there was a good chance you would be on your way home before any enemy fighters could reach you. But this time things were different. We made our landfall as normal, and flew inland on the south side of the fjord. We turned north, with the intention of turning west down the fjord and making our attack heading out to sea, but suddenly found ourselves under fire from the ships that appeared almost under us!

"The wing leader did a slow 270 degree turn to starboard to bring us back across the fjord and headed back towards the sea on the south side, parallel to the fjord. Wing Commander Milson had probably decided that the way the ships were anchored under a steep cliff made a successful standard attack at right angles to the fjord almost impossible. We continued flying on the south side of the fjord back towards the sea for some time before turning again north, crossing the fjord for a third time, and gradually worked back round to starboard to head inland on the north side. The wing was then ordered into echelon port before we dropped down into the fjord on our attack dive. Owing to our position on the extreme starboard side of the original vic formation, Nick and I had to be last over into the echelon, making us the tail-enders. There was a further complication of which I was blissfully unaware, all this manoeuvring had taken an awfully long time, long enough for enemy fighters to appear on the scene.

"We were flying fairly close to a high flattish area of ice and snow-covered rock coming up to the north edge of the fjord when the attack order came over the radio from the wing leader. I began the attack procedure: lock the gun sight into position, flip the gun switches from safe to fire, and adjust speed to maintain position as we turned left into the fjord to make our dive. At first I couldn't see any ships, but a few choice words from Nick put me right. I saw two targets and chose the one that was easiest to get at. I throttled back into the dive, ready to start firing when I thought we were just out of range and I could "hosepipe" my fire onto the target. Nick was now wide awake in his backwards-facing position. He wasn't very happy about the cotton-wool puffs of heavy ack-ack shells above us. I suppose they hoped the odd aeroplane might fly into a shower of shrapnel. Agonisingly, to him it seemed an eternity before I pressed the gun button. We got in quite a long burst, bang on target. Hypnotising for a first timer, so hypnotising that there was a danger of not pulling out of

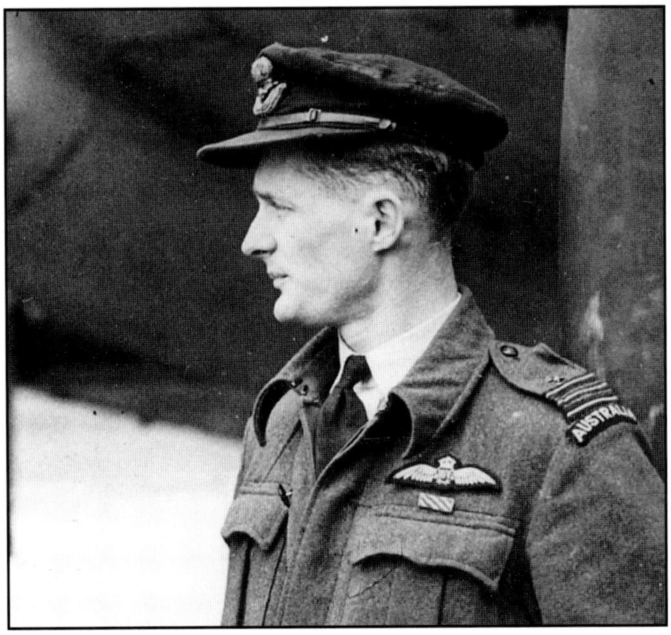

Above: **Squadron Leader Milson**

your dive in time to avoid the water. We flattened out. Nick saw a ship's mast flash past and then, on our port, the destroyer tucked close in to the fjord wall. It seemed to be only yards away and was giving us a continuous broadside with everything it had for far too long as we jinked along its length. Being last into the attack, and probably their only remaining target, we were getting plenty of unwelcome attention. It was a frightening moment.

"Only as I pulled out of my dive did I, too, see the other ships. I opened up the throttles to take-off boost to get clear of the intense flak, but kept close to the water and ice, making no attempt to climb away because to do so would have slowed us down and presented a much easier target for the ship's gunners. In fact we couldn't have climbed if we'd wanted to. Just before we cleared the destroyer there had been a noisy *ber-doingg*, and a spurt of liquid came gushing up from the floor of my cockpit. My jinking was causing blobs of the stuff to splash about all over the "glass" and me. Vision was seriously impaired. Seconds later, Nick saw something which must since have given him nightmares, the unmistakable front silhouette of an FW 190, coming at us with little lights sparkling along its wings. Nick's voice in my earphones nearly blasted my head off: "Weave, for Christ's sake, Weave, Weave," - not a text book air force communication, and so shocking coming from one who benefited from a Victorian church upbringing!

"Meantime, I had gained a little height - it's too dodgy to fly low when you can't see properly – I moved the gunsight to one side and wiped the screen with my glove to improve forward vision. We were now heading along the fjord, which, with a lowering cloudbase, gave the impression of being in a large tunnel. Tracer was streaming from behind on our port side and I immediately went into a drill recommended by a Canadian instructor whose pupil I was at SFTS in Calgary, Alberta. You do a slight left bank with a touch of right rudder and then reverse it to slight right bank with a touch of left rudder, thus proceeding on a generally straight track whilst giving the impression that you are weaving from side to side. This should cause the marksman on our tail - Nick's FW190 - to incorrectly deflect, and as he corrected his aim by reference to his tracer stream, you would bank the opposite way and he would, again, over-deflect. Naturally, if you do this at constant height, his shell stream passes quickly through your path, but we were not flying at a constant height. I was pumping the control column backwards and forwards quite violently at random intervals and, when going down, getting quite close to the ice. This is relatively safe in a Beau, for it has excellent forward vision, but it's very dicey for a single-engined aircraft with a long snout fronted by a dirty great radial engine. Nick's blood pressure returned to near normal at the sight of a saviour - one of our Mustangs who later saw off the 190 after Nick had fired a red Verey cartridge.

"The cloud seemed to be getting lower as we continued inland. The sides of the fjord disappeared into the cloud above us, and the question now was how to get out and head back to the coast without hitting any high ground en route. Fortuitously, there now appeared ahead in this somewhat menacing tunnel an area of snow and ice-covered shale and rock sloping relatively gently into the water - a convenient opportunity to pull up sharply and continue climbing through the cloud, while maintaining a slow turn to our left. I now had no idea of my direction because the instruments had toppled during evasive action. I still resisted the temptation to push the throttles through the gate in order to climb more quickly because I couldn't risk any engine troubles. I hardly expected the engines to have escaped damage and I still couldn't be certain that it was only hydraulic oil that had leaked into the cockpit. The cloud was thin and we were soon through it into a peaceful environment, with just another thin layer of wispy white cloud high above us. There was nothing else in sight and I just sat, stupefied, continuing the slow turn to port until we were heading due west by the sun. Amazingly we appeared to have got away with it. We were both uninjured, sitting in an apparently airworthy aircraft with our two sturdy Bristol Hercules engines performing faultlessly. We might well be sleeping in our own beds that night after all.

"The compass settled down, so I could reset the gyro and set the course for Dallachy guessed by Nick, who also told me that a sizeable chunk of our starboard elevator was no longer with us. This surprised me, for it was having little or no effect on straight and level flight. I knew, though, that it could be a different story when slowing down for landing. We settled down to the return crossing at 3,000 feet, a good height should we need to put out a Mayday call before ditching."

The Focke-Wulfs Attack

Attacking alongside Stan Butler was Pilot Officer Smith and his navigator Pilot Officer 'Spike' Holly. Unlike Stan and 'Nick', both had more than 35 combat missions behind them and were considered among the most experienced in the squadron. They reckoned that this mission would be their last, something that proved to be right. Just as they dived down towards the ships Smith caught a glimpse of a eight FW190s coming from the southeast. Holly heard the familiar pounding from the cannons and saw the tracers from the ships flash past their wings. They got through and turned over Naustdal at 50 meters. He photographed the chaotic scenes behind him and put the camera down on the floor. When he straightened up again he was startled at the sight of a fighter approaching from the rear, a couple of hundred meters behind and a little to the side. Events now happened at frightening speed. The FW190 came straight at them and Holly fired. At the same time the German pilot fired several rounds. One of the cannon shells exploded next to Holly and fragments entered his leg and stomach. He was thrown into his seat, unconscious. Another shell burst into the front cockpit without injuring Smith, but at the same time the port engine was put out of action. Smith struggled to hold the plane level and passed Naustdal, heading for snow clad trees on the eastern side of the fjord. Two of them were a little taller than the rest. He managed to raise the nose a little, but knew that he would hit them. The Beaufighter tore through the treetops, but was still flying. Ahead was Høydals Fjord. At Hopen farm near Høydal Fjord, a plane appeared suddenly, screaming over the roof tops. It was obviously damaged and losing altitude all the time. It chopped the top of a pine tree and vanished. Frida Hopen rushed outside and down to the boat shed where her husband Henrik and her son Arne were at work. They scrambled together to the top of a hill for a good view. There they saw the plane sinking in the water. The men raced to the rowing boat and rowed as hard as they could to the plane where they found two me struggling in the icy water. Smith managed to walk up to the farm house by himself, but Holly needed help. The Hopen family tried to help as best as they could, but it was clear that Holly was in need of a doctor, and for this the Germans must be told.

9./JG5 had dived directly at the stream of Beaufighters on their way into the fjord. A German field report stated: "At 1608 hours we made contact with approximately 30 Beaufighters and 10 escort planes of the Mustang type. We went to attack in formation. I was successful in getting behind and above one of the Beaufighters, and fired a long burst. He began to burn at once and came down vertically approximately 10 km northwest of Førde at 1610 hours." According to German sources this was the first of the planes to be shot down. It came in low over the ice when its tail fell off. It began to burn, tipped over and was seen from Bjørkedol to explode in the air. Parts of the wreckage landed near Holmeneset. Anders Sale relates that later a man was found in the sea. He was a French—Canadian. This is believed to have been the plane of Pilot Officers W. J. Jackson and H. E. Blunderfeld from No. 404 Squadron. Jackson is still missing.

Egil Hjelmelofld and a friend stood on the ice at Lone River when the battle began: "We left the ice to find shelter under some snow drifts and icy bushes ashore. We were shivering both from the cold and fear, but spellbound by the events above us. Two planes came diving over the ridge with fighters giving chase. One Beaufighter escaped over Dals Fjord before the Germans did any real damage, but the other was not so lucky. It turned east and lost altitude before going into a left turn. At first it appeared that it may land on the ridge at Relnkostert near Storcsteinen. But suddenly the plane tipped over into a sharp turn, stalled and hit the ground. It turned on its back and broke in two just in front of the tail. The wreckage slide downhill in the deep snow and stopped only after crossing the old road 500 meters further down.." This was the Beaufighter of 24 year old Flying Officer Lynch. With him as navigator flew Flying Officer Knight. Lynch came from Ontario and Knight from British Columbia. They had only been with No 404 Squadron for three weeks and this was their first strike.

Now there were planes everywhere. Beaufighters were still attacking the ships. The German fighters did all they could to hinder them. Anders Sale watched the planes come sweeping towards the Z-33 at Buanes. He saw anti-aircraft gunners on the destroyer fall after being hit, only to be repeatedly replaced by fresh gunners.

Warrant Officer Morton from No. 144 Squadron was attacked by four fighters. He managed to hide in the clouds after first firing at one of them. Flying Officer Flynn from No. 404 Squadron attacked two German planes on the tail of another Beaufighter. Flight Lieutenant Stewart was chased by two Focke Wulfs and his plane badly damaged, but neither he nor his navigator were injured.

Not all were so lucky. One Beaufighter landed in a swamp by Naustdol. The plane slid across the swamp and down the mountain side towards the river. It burst into flames. The local farmers who tried to reach the airmen had to give up any rescue attempt in the face of intense heat and exploding cannon rounds. The crew was possibly Canadian. Locals heard the German soldiers say: Arme Kanadier.

Another Beaufighter was pursued by an FW190 pilot who wrote later: "I followed a Beaufighter at low altitude and fired two short bursts. The plane swerved a little off course and then after another burst the plane went straight down and began to burn at once. This was approximately 5 km northeast of Naustdol and the time was 1613 hours." Eyewitnesses saw the fight take place at rooftop height along the valley before the Beaufighter fell at Hukset, in a range of little hills where the two young men lost their lives. They were probably from Australia.

On the innermost arm of Førde Fjord, at Steinen, one Beaufighter went down in flames. It exploded at low altitude and the wreckage was strewn over a large area. It was said that the Russian prisoners of war who fetched the bodies wept when they returned to Førde. Outside Kvieneset, between Erdal and Naustdal, another Beaufighter came down. The plane was on fire and a thick halo of smoke was left hanging in the air. It turned sharply, stalled, and crashed through the ice. The burning fuel marked the final resting place for two young men.

Near Svanoy a burning Beaufighter was forced to land in the sea. On board were Flight Lieutenant McColl and Warrant Officer MacDonald, both Australians from No. 455 Squadron. They had got into the rubber dinghy and were rescued by a fishing boat from the Maloy district. They arrived at Atløy unhurt, but wet and frozen. The German guards at Atløy used the home of Sigurd Løkeland as a detention centre. At Løkeland's the men were given dry clothes and shoes, and food of a quality which the Germans had not seen for a long time, to their extreme annoyance.

Flying Officer Savard from No. 404 Squadron struggled to maintain control with his navigator Pilot Officer Jeffrey Middleton seriously injured. Savard came low out the fjord and tried to land on the ice,

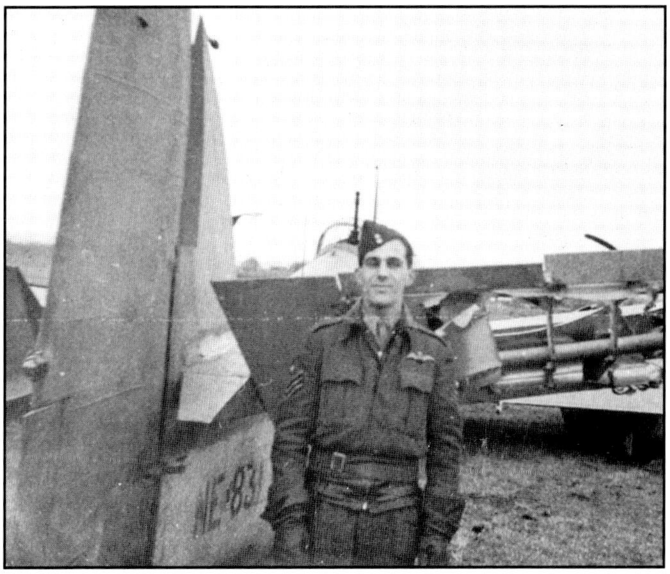

Above: **Thankful to be back in one piece, Stan Butler.**

hoping that it was thick enough. The plane hit the surface and the engines were ripped loose to spin away over the ice, leaving the fuselage on its back. People came running from the shore to help, but German soldiers shouted and fired warning shots. Moses Hougen reached the plane and, hearing the shots, turned in his tracks and rushed back ashore. The soldiers fired and hit him in the leg, an injury that plagued him for the rest of his life. Savard and Middleton were helped out of the plane, but Middleton had massive injuries and died before reaching the shore. Savard fared better. He ended up in a German prisoner of war camp until the end of the war, only a few months later.

The Reckoning

It has not been possible to establish with certainty the identity of the crews lost at Steinen, Kvieneset, Naustdal summer farm, Hukset or Holmeneset. It is known that Flying Officer Myrick of Ontario and Flight Sergeant Berges of Quebec were in one of the planes. Both were found and are now buried in Hougesund. Myrick and Lynch grew up in the same district and had known each other for a long time. Like Lynch, Myrick and Berges had only been with No. 404 Squadron for three weeks. It was their first combat mission. Flying Officer H. Smook and his navigator Warrant Officer Duckworth of No. 404 Squadron are still missing. They had been with the squadron for barely two months. Flying Officer Smerneos and his 26 year old navigator Flying Officer Cochrane of Toronto, did not return that day. Both had been with No. 404 Squadron for six weeks. They are buried in Haugesund. 28 year old Warrant Officer Mutimer from East Brunswick, Victoria, and 20 year old Flight Sergeant Blackshaw from Penhurst, New South Wales, both Australians from No 455 Squadron, are also buried in Hougesund.

The Mustang pilots intervened as soon as they discovered the German fighters, who were now approximately 2000 feet lower. One of the Mustang pilots recounts: "I closed in quickly from the rear and aimed at the plane to the left. When the German pilot discovered me he swerved to the right before he threw the plane into a sharp left turn. I fired and saw hits in the cockpit, the wing and the engine. Suddenly it was engulfed in flames and dived into the water in the vicinity of the ships." This was the plane that came down outside Gjesneset. Onlookers could see that someone had baled out. It was 25 year old Oberfeldwebel Otto Leibfried from Stuttgart attempting to save himself. He was wounded and landed in an inaccessible area near Gjesneset. Night after night the locals saw him send up distress flares. German and Norwegian patrols searched for him, but not until early that summer was he found, dead in a bed of twigs he had made for himself.

At Heilevang onlookers saw a plane plunge into the water. At the same time there appeared a little black dot in the sky. A parachute appeared. The battle was over for Leutnant Koch as he slowly sank down into the fjord. He landed in the water just outside Heilevang. Andreos

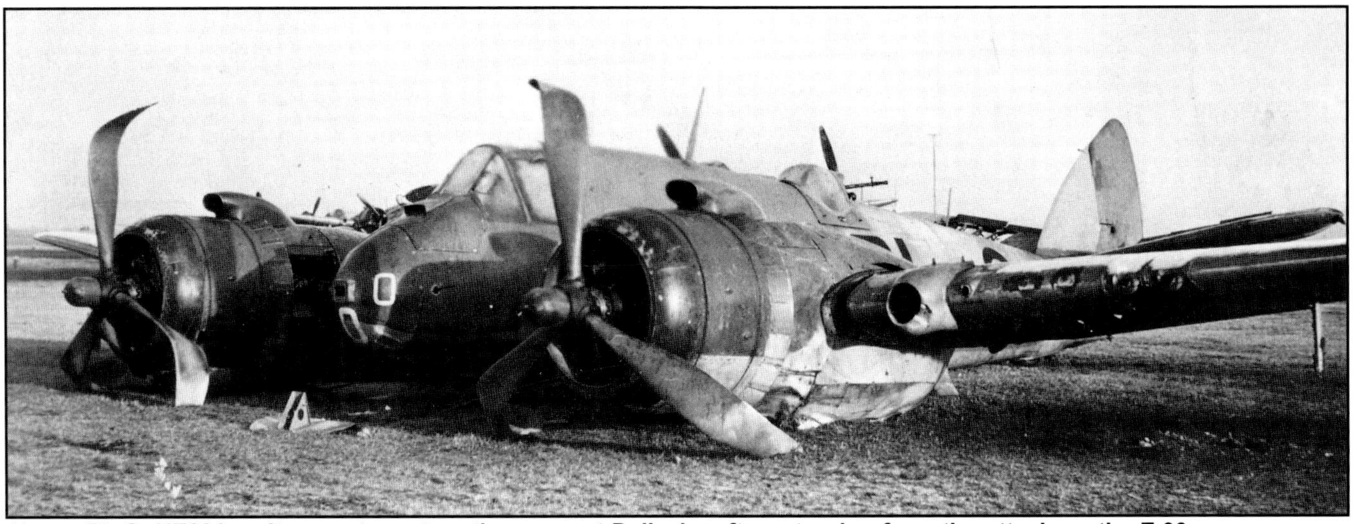
Above: **PL-O, NE831 as it came to rest on the grass at Dallachy after returning from the attack on the Z-33.**

and Jens Heilevang got hold of a rowing boat and rowed over to find the pilot encircled by his parachute; he was in good shape. Only then did they notice that he was German.

At Solhelm north of Naustdal, Trygve Solheim was standing in his yard when two planes flew up the valley and disappeared above Ramsdalshela. There was a flash from the wings of the Mustang. The FW190 flipped over and went into a spin down towards Solheimstolen, trailing black smoke. The pilot was Leutnant Rudi Linz, one of the most experienced German fighter pilots in Norway at that time with seventy victories. He was 28 years old, from Ilmenau, and Staffelkapitän of 12./ JG5. Trygve Solheim clipped on his skis when he saw smoke over Solheim valley. Once up on the rolling grounds he could see the plane near the summer farm. The fire made it impossible to get close, but the pilot was dead.

"A Mustang tried to help the Beaufighters", said Jan Hjelmelend. "and he engaged the German". The stage was set for another tragedy in Bygstod. "Two aircraft were in a dog fight, the Mustang ploughed through the wintry forest looking like a burning torch. It came to rest among the green firs which stood there straight and silent." The pilot was Warrant Officer Caesar, 31 years old from Bristol, England. The FW190 was also badly damaged and its engine caught fire. The pilot turned north at low level and baled out without time for his parachute to open. Fortunately he fell into the snow covered slopes near Fauskestølen, where the deep snow softened his fall and he slid down the mountain in an avalanche of snow. His flare pistol went off and injured him in his foot, but amazingly he was still alive and capable of walking. Jon Hjelmeland was amongst those who watched the plane crash near Fauskestølen. Together with Ingolf Dringelond and another they set off into the hills. Perhaps somebody needed help. It was getting dark when they saw someone making his way over the crest of the hill into the valley beyond and then into an isolated hay barn. Hjelmelond and Bringeland approached the barn together and found the pilot sitting in the dark. He showed them he was wounded and gave them his Luger and his signal pistol.

Stan Smith was now on his way back across the North Sea in PL-O. "We could relax a bit now and eventually made contact with Dallachy control to tell them that our hydraulics were u/s and that we would be making a no-flap belly landing. Dallachy told us to identify ourselves by firing a Verey cartridge when in sight of the airfield and to land on the grass as far down the field as possible, as another aircraft would be belly-landing behind us. I put my flak helmet on again whilst Nick looked for his Verey pistol. Unfortunately, he couldn't find it. We reduced height to cross the coast at low level in line with, and to one side of, the runway. I put the propellers into fine pitch and closed the throttles as we crossed the airfield boundary. All I had to concentrate on then was holding the aircraft straight and level a few feet off the ground. It was still handling well, but did require slightly more exaggerated movements of the control column to get a response as we lost speed. Out of the corners of my eyes, I was fascinated to see the props stop, the starboard first and then ... wallop. We hit the deck. I vividly recall pressing hard on the brake, but I had no wheels! We didn't need brakes anyway and came to rest just before the perimeter track. More by luck than judgement, we had landed exactly as instructed, on the grass, well down the field. Everything was quiet. I sat there dazed, automatically going through my cockpit drill, caging the gyro, all switches off, then collected my stuff together, opened the top hatch, nipped out onto the wing, and dropped onto terra firma.

"Before commencing my landing approach I had reminded Nick to jettison his canopy at the earliest opportunity and get out quickly, before the aircraft came fully to rest if possible. All of this he did. What, unfortunately, he didn't do was to unplug the lead from his headset to the radio. He nearly lost his head and suffered a real pain in the neck for some time afterwards.

"Wing Commander Dinsdale, a New Zealander who was Wing Commander Flying at Dallachy, came rushing up in his utility truck, and then hurried on to another crew immediately he had ascertained that we were OK. Another truck picked us up for transit to the ops room for debriefing. I liked debriefing. There were always cups of fresh hot tea and, better still, a tot of Navy rum. We were Coastal Command, you know! What's more, Nick didn't like rum, so his ration found its way into my tea. Try it some time, it's jolly good. One of our ground crew told me afterwards that we had been hit by a shell. It had pierced the fuselage on the port side at a point about six inches below and in front of the root of the leading edge, continuing on a downward trajectory to puncture a distribution manifold in the hydraulic system near the base of the control column. At least one bullet had gone into a self-sealing petrol tank, and there were a few other holes through the wings and scrapes along the fuselage where bullets had glanced off. The squadron record also mentions a two foot square hole in the elevator, but this, of course, is a gross exaggeration. Surely it was meant to read 'two square feet'!

"It had been our very first shipping strike, and it was against a tough target: a German Narvik class destroyer, two 'M' Class minesweepers and several flak ships. Although all the ships had been damaged, none had been sunk. It was a hairy experience which served us well on a further eight shipping strikes before the end of the war in Europe and the disbanding of 144 Squadron."

Z-33

It has been difficult to establish what damage the ships in the fjord sustained, or how many Germans were killed and wounded on board the ships. Four men were killed on the Z-33. On one of the other ships, VP6808 a converted trawler, three men were killed. There may have been further fatalities on the other boats. In addition a number were wounded and admitted to hospital in Florø. The rockets used were of the armour piercing type, without any explosive charge, and were intended to create leaks below the water line. Nevertheless one explosion occurred in the Z-33 after a cannon attack by Flight Lieutenant Power of No. 144 Squadron. A 'Sperrbrecher' heavily armed mine sweeper was on fire amidships. Several other ships were also damaged. The Australians reported that they had attacked a gun position on the north side of Førde Fjord. After the attack things went quiet on that side.

A further air strike led to more losses on board Z-33, but eventually the destroyer reached Trondheim and later the ship arrived in Germany after repairs. When peace was declared the Z-33 was surrendered to the Soviet Union as war booty. In the years that followed, the locals gathered what might be of use from the wrecked planes. The shops were not overly filled with goods at that time. A wheel and bearings were certainly not easy to get hold of, and had many uses on the farm. The man who tried to salvage an engine was particularly unlucky. He gashed himself on the metal and suffered blood poisoning from the wound. It was difficult to get to the doctor, and the man died about a week later. Those parts that lay on the ice vanished as it thawed. The planes that fell on dry land, stayed there for a long time and many farmers lost cattle because their animals were poisoned after attempting to eat parts.

No. 144 (RAF) Squadron Beaufighter TF Mk.X

PL-R	S/L G. D. W. Rogers	Pilot	
	F/O A. E. Thurgood	Nav	
PL-Y	P/O P. C. Smith	Pilot	PoW
	P/O F. S. Holly Nav	PoW	
PL-Z	W/O R. H. Field	Pilot	
	F/S D. H. Anstey	Nav	
PL-Q	W/O F. E. C. Morton	Pilot	
	W/O D. C. Mascell	Nav	
PL-K	W/O J. G. H. Muriny	Pilot	
	F/S R. R. Winter	Nav	
PL-L	F/S D. E. Reeves	Pilot	
	F/S G. Ogilvie	Nav	
PL.S	F/L J. L. Power	Pilot	
	F/O D. H. Foxall	Nav	
PL-O	F/S S. A. Butler	Pilot	
	F/S C. B. Nicholl	Nav	
PL-D	F/L R. S. Harrison	Pilot	
	W/O T. D. J. Wilkinson Nav		

No. 404 (RCAF) Squadron Beaufighter TFX

EE-U	NE339	S/L W. R. Christison (DFC) Pilot		
		F/L W.J.Toon (DFC)	Nav (RAF)	
EE-T	NE688	F/O N. P. Flynn	Pilot	
		P/O M.H.Michael	Nav	
EE-G	NE825	F/L J. B. A. Stewart	Pilot	
		F/O A. A. Johnston	Nav	
EEC	NV422	F/O H. C. Lynch	Pilot	Killed
		F/O O. W. Knight	Nav	Killed
EE-W	NE761	F/O P. R. Myrick	Pilot	Killed
		F/S C. G. Bergen	Nav	Killed
EE-S	NT916	F/O J. E. Nelson	Pilot	
		WO R. G. Gracie	Nav	
EE-A	NE669	P/O H. W. R. Ramsden		Pilot
		WO R. Rumble	Nav	
EE-Q1	RD136	F/O H. Smook Pilot	Killed	
		WO A. M. Duckworth	Nav	Killed
EE-V	NT922	P/O W. J. Jackson	Pilot	Killed
		P/O W. E. Blunderfield	Nav	Killed
EE-O	NV292	F/O J. R. Savard	Pilot	PoW
		P/O J. Middleton	Nav	Killed (RAF)
EE-F	NT890	F/O C. Smerneos	Pilot	Killed
		F/O N. D. Cochrane	Nav	Killed

No. 455 (RAAF) Squadron Beaufighter TF Mk.X

UB-K	NE347	W/C	C. G. Milson (DSO DFC)Pilot		
		P/O	R.E.Jones (DFC)	Nav(RAF)	
UB-O	NV199	F/L	R. R. McColl	Pilot	PoW
		W/O	L. L. MacDonald	Nav	PoW
UB-H	NV423	W/O	N. P. Turner	Pilot	
		W/O	G. F. Hammond	Nav	
UB-F	LZ407	F/O	W. G. Herbert	Pilot	
		F/S	J. W. Tucker	Nav	
UB.D	NV432	F/O	J. MacDonald	Pilot	
		F/L	W. Bremner	Nav	

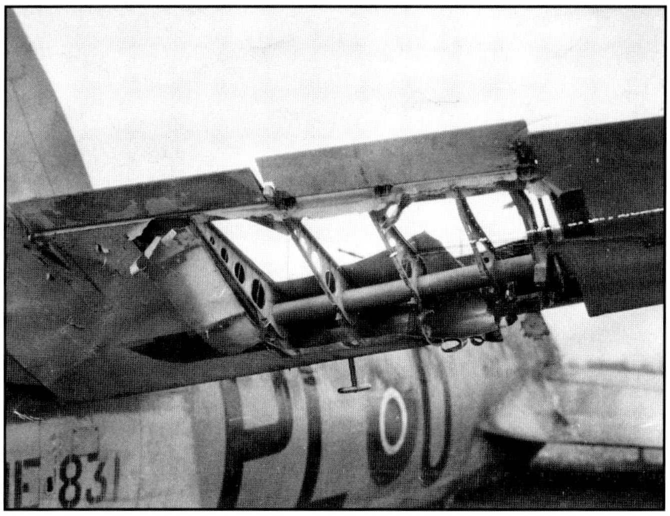

Above: **The damage to PL-O. The close-up detail of the serial stencilling is also unusual. (C B Nicholl)**

UB-B	NE444	W/O	W. T. Furlong	Pilot	
		F/S	A. E. Williams	Nav	
UB-A	NT954	F/O	J. G. Cox	Pilot	
		W/O	A. W. Ibbotson	Nav	
UB-R	NV424	F/O	C. J. Smith (DFC)	Pilot	
		F/O	M.F. Jackson	Nav	
UB-V	NV196	W/O	D. E. Mutimer	Pilot	Killed
		F/S	J. D. Blackshaw	Nav	Killed
UB-X	NV450	F/O	H. R. Spink	Pilot	
		F/O	L. R. Clifford	Nav	
UB-Q	NE798	F/O	C. G. Thompson (DFC) Pilot		
		W/O	I. M. Gordon	Nav	

No. 489 (RNZAF) Squadron Beaufighter TF Mk.X

P6-H	NE213	W/O	J. Brightwell	Pilot	Morning Recce
		W/O	E.Foy	Nav	
P6-K	LZ531	F/S	R. Priest	Pilot	Morning Recce
		W/O	D.Ball	Nav	
P6-W		F/L	J. Brice	Pilot	
		F/O	R. Henson	Nav	

No. 65 (RAF) Squadron P-51C Mustang IIIa

YT-Q	HB878	F/L J. W. Foster	Pilot
YT-	HB831	F/O T. S. Richardson	Pilot
YT-S	KH484	F/L J. Butler	Pilot
YT-	FB360	W/O E. D. Stone	Pilot
YT-P	HB835	F/O W. L. Black	Pilot
YT-L	HB845	F/L G. C. L. Watt	Pilot
YT-	HB836	W/O C. C. Caesar	Pilot Killed
YT-	KH580	F/L D. M. Davidson	Pilot
YT-	FB383	F/L R. L. Sims	Pilot
YT-	KH582	F/O D. W. Davis	Pilot

9./JG 5 Focke Wulf FW 190

White 10	732197	Fw.	Rudolf Artner	FW190A-8
White 22	581876	FjOfw.	Otto Leibfried	FW190F-8 Killed
White 3		Fw.	Martin Ullmann	FW190A-8
White 19		FJUffz.	Heinrich Hellwig	FW190
White 1	931862	Uffz.	Heinz Orlowski	FW190F-8
		Uffz.	Walter Opitz	FW190
White 9		Uffz.	Gerh.Eissermann	FW190A-3
		Uffz.	Ballerstädt	FW190
		Ofhr.	Georg Höhn	FW190

12./JG 5 Focke Wulf FW 190

Blue 4	732183	Lt.	Rudi Linz St.kp.	FW 190A-8 Killed
Blue 9	732070	Lt.	Karl Heinz Koch	FW 190A-8
Blue 1	350177	Uffz.	Herbert Schafer	FW 190A-8

153

SQUADRON

Code Letters:

TB

Noctividus
(Seeing by night)

Usage:
Mk.If
Jan 42 to Jan 43
Mk.VIf
Nov 42 to Sept 43

Rôle:
Night defence of Northern Ireland. Moved to Algeria in December 1942. Did convoy escort work in the Sicilian campaign

Bases:
Ballyhalbert 1/42- 12/42
Portreath 12/42
Maison Blanche
12/42 - 7/43
Reghaia 9/44

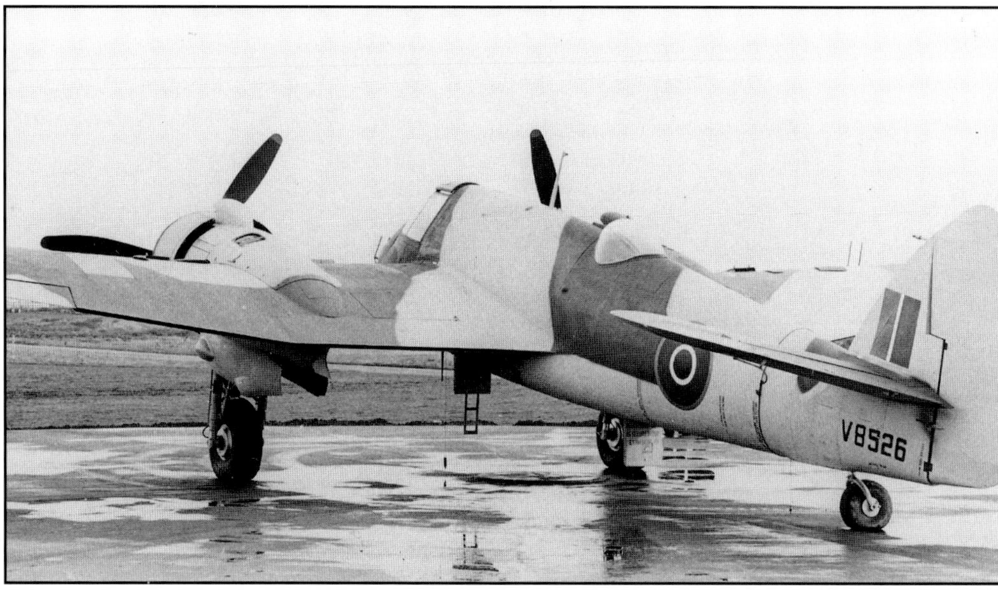

Above: **V8526 a Mk.VIf served with Nos. 153 and 96 Squadrons before being ferried to North Africa by the Overseas Aircraft Delivery Unit to serve with No. 153 Squadron once more.**

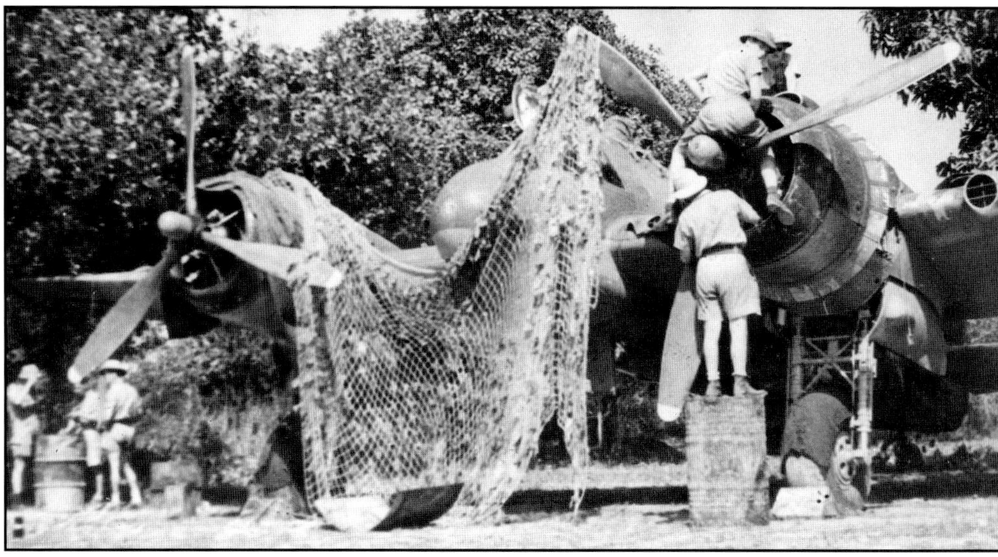

Right: **Under the command of Wing Commander Henry Goddard No. 176 Squadron became operational on 15 January 1943 and scored its first victory, a Type 97 bomber. In 1944 detachments took on the role of low level night sweeps looking for road, rail or river targets in Ceylon.**

Below: **X8164 a Mk.VIf, was hit by return fire from a Ki.21 and was abandoned near Calcutta on 19 January 1943. It was one of the original eight machines taken on by No. 176 Squadron when it was formed at Dum Dum in January 1943 from a detachment of No. 89 Squadron after its arrival there from the Middle East.**

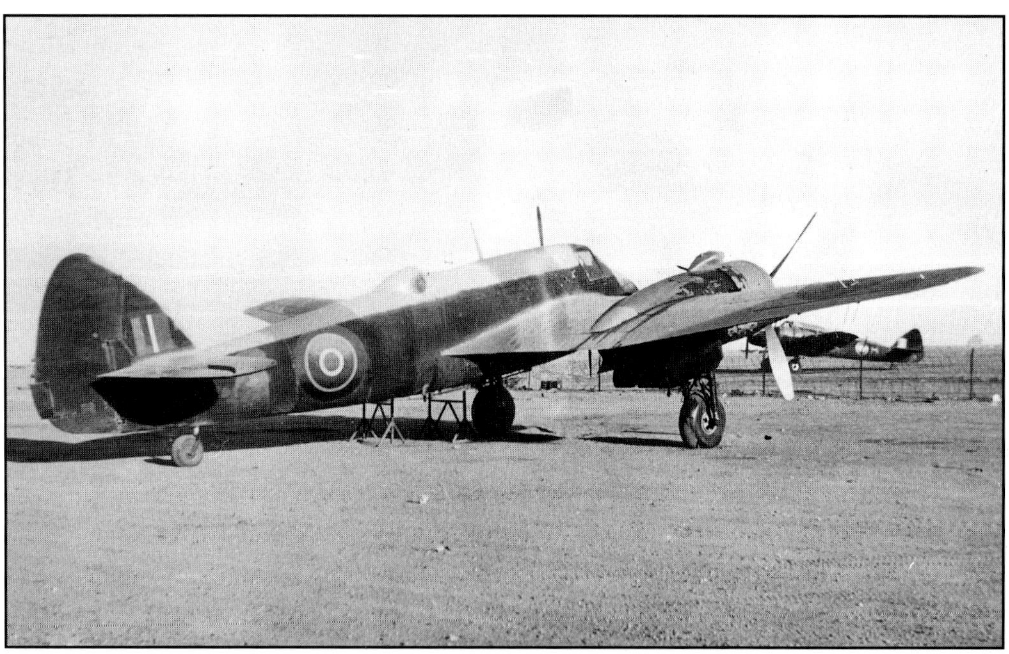

176

SQUADRON

Nocte custodimus
(We keep the night watch)

Usage:
Mk.If
Jan 43 - Aug 43
Mk.VIf
Jan 43 to Aug 45

Rôle:
Night defence of India

Bases:
Dum Dum 1/43 - 2/43
Baigachi 2/43 - 8/44
Vavuniya 8/44
Minneriya 8/44 - 3/45
Baigachi 3/45 - 8/45

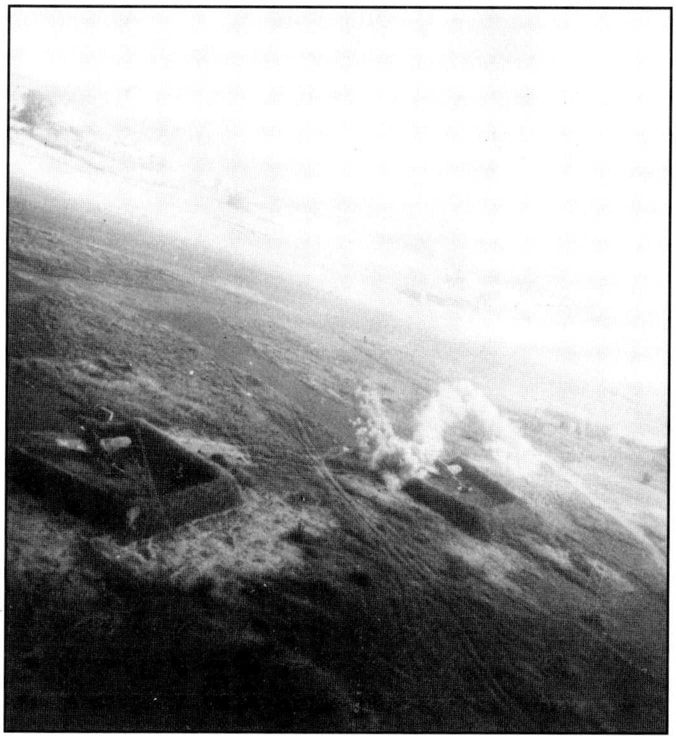

Left: **Lashio airfield under attack by Squadron Leader Hunt, the B Flight Commander of No. 177 Squadron.**
One remarkable jungle survival story involves Wing Commander Nottage, CO of No. 177 Squadron, and his observer Pilot Officer Bolitho. They were forced to crash land in a paddy field on 26 April 1945 after RD376 had been hit by AA fire. The pair began to march back, receiving some food from a village headman, until 6 May when they made contact with a Special Forces unit and were flown out of a small clearing by a Jungle Rescue light aircraft.

177 SQUADRON

Silentur in medias res
(Silently into the midst of things)

Usage:
Mk.VIc
May 43 to May 45
TF Mk.X
Nov 43 to July 45
Mk.XI
Nov 43 to May 44

Rôle:
Ground attack in Burma.

Bases:
Phaphamau 5/43 - 8/43
Chittagong 8/43
Feni 8/43 - 5/44
Ranchi 5/44 - 8/44
Chiringa 8/44 - 2/45
Ranchi 2/45 - 6/45
Hathazari 6/45 - 7/45

211 SQUADRON

Code Letters:
UQ

Toujours a propos (French)
(Always at the right moment)

Usage:
TF Mk.X
Oct 43 to May 45

Rôle:
Ground attack in Burma.

Bases:
Phaphamau 8/43 - 11/43
Ranchi 11/43 - 12/43
Silchar West 12/43 - 1/44
Bhatpara 1/44 - 5/44
Feni 5/44 - 7/44
Chiringa 7/44 - 5/45
Yelahanka 5/45

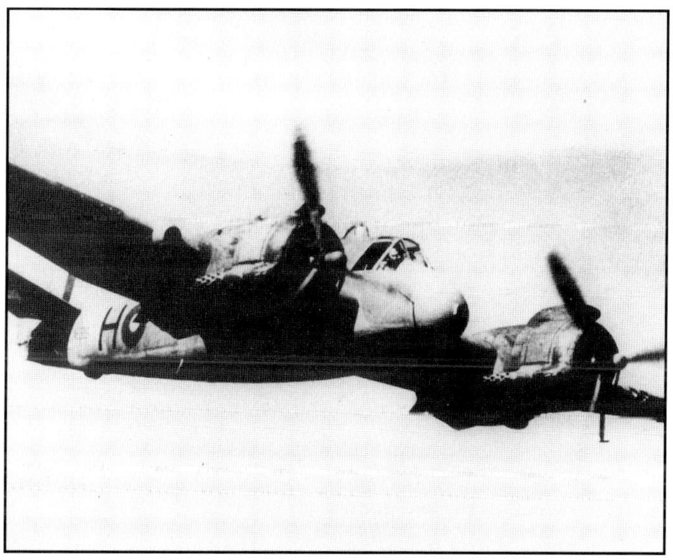

Left: **TFX NE815 'H' of No. 217 Squadron makes a low pass over Ratmalana, Ceylon, in 1944.**

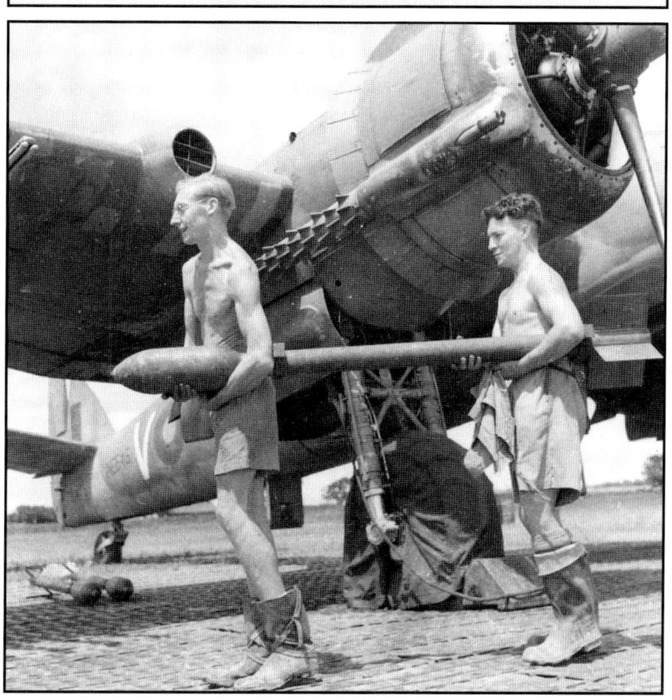

Right: **Two British armourers give a good idea of the size and weight of a rocket projectile as they carry one with a 60lb high explosive head to a waiting Beaufighter TF Mk.X.**

217 SQUADRON

Code Letters:
MW

Woe to the unwary

Usage:
TF Mk.X
July 44 to Sept 45

Rôle:
Anti-shipping from, and defence of, Ceylon.

Bases:
Ratmalana 7/44 - 9/44
Vavuniya 9/44 - 6/45
Gannavaram 6/45 - 9/45

219 SQUADRON

Code Letters:

FK

From dusk to dawn

Usage:

Mk.If
Sept 40 to May 43
Mk.VIf
May 43 to Jan 44

Rôle:

Night defence of Britain.
Night defence North Africa

Bases:

Redhill 9/40 - 12/40
Tangmere 12/40 - 6/42
Acklington 6/42 - 10/42
Scorton 10/42 - 4/43
Catterick 4/43 - 5/43
Bone 6/43 - 8/43
La Sebala 8/43 - 10/43
Sidi Amor 10/43 - 1/44

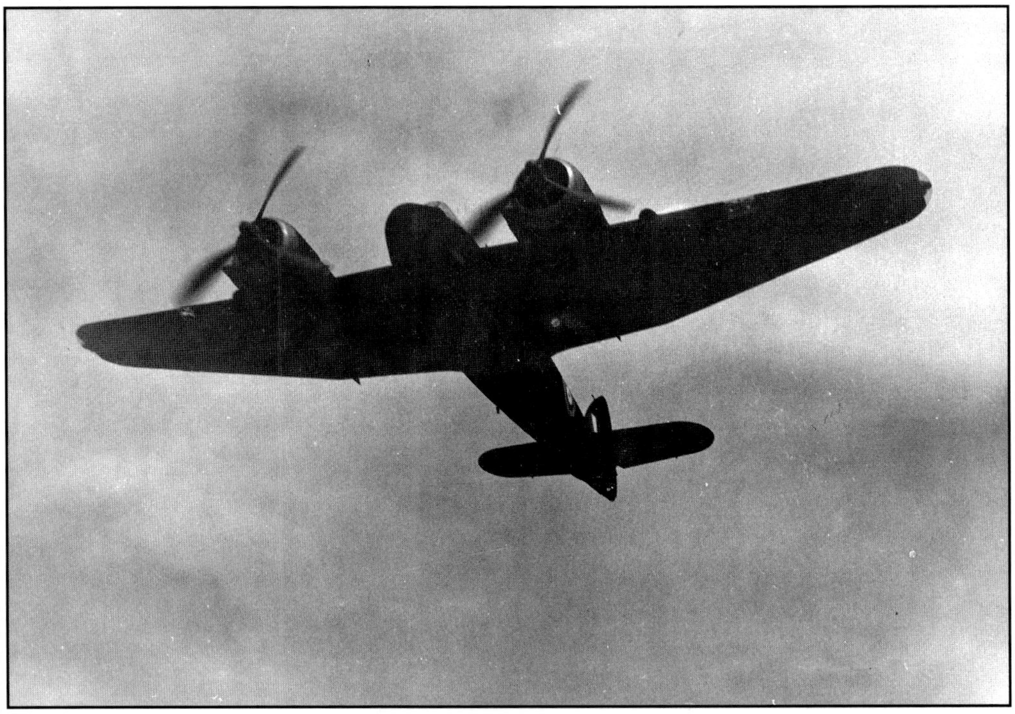

Above: **The classic outline of a Mk.If overhead, a familiar sight at Tangmere when No. 219 Squadron was a main stay against the Blitz.**

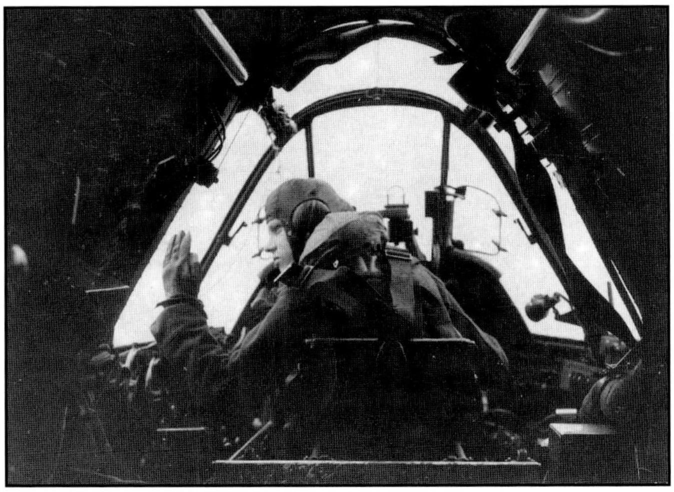

Right: **A night fighter pilot waves the chocks away. No. 219 was one of the original four squadrons to get Beaufighters and made the first Beaufighter 'claim' for shooting down an enemy aircraft, on 25 October 1940. Without aid of AI, Sergeants Hodgekinson and Benn intercepted a Do17, but no Luftwaffe loss can be identified that would relate to their claim.**

Below: **V8881, FK-L was one of the Mk.VIfs used by No. 219 Squadron during their time in the Middle East between June 1943 and January 1944. At this time the squadron was part of the North West African Coastal Air Force. (H Levy)**

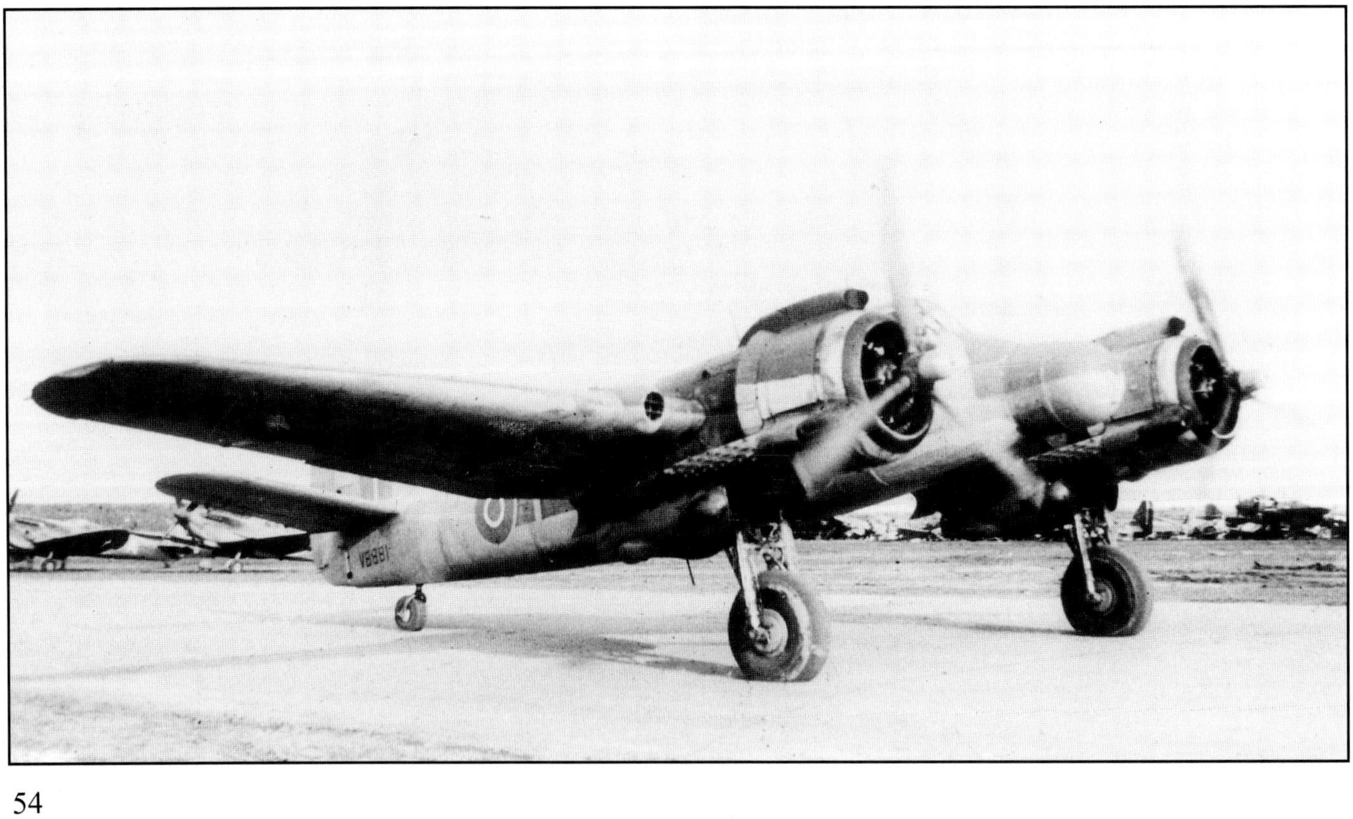

227 SQUADRON

Usage:
Mk.Ic
Aug 42 to Feb 43
Mk.VIc
Aug 42 to Aug 44
Mk.XI
Sept 43 to Aug 44
TF Mk.X
Oct 43 to Dec 43

Rôle:
Anti shipping operations over the Mediterranean

Bases:
Luqa 8/42 - 11/42
Ta Kali 11/42 - 3/43
Idku 3/43 - 5/43
Derna 5/43 - 6/43
El Magrum 6/43 - 7/43
Gardabia West 7/43
Derna 7/43 - 8/43
Limassol 8/43 - 9/43
Lakatamia 9/43 - 11/43
Berka III 11/43 - 8/44
Biferno 8/44

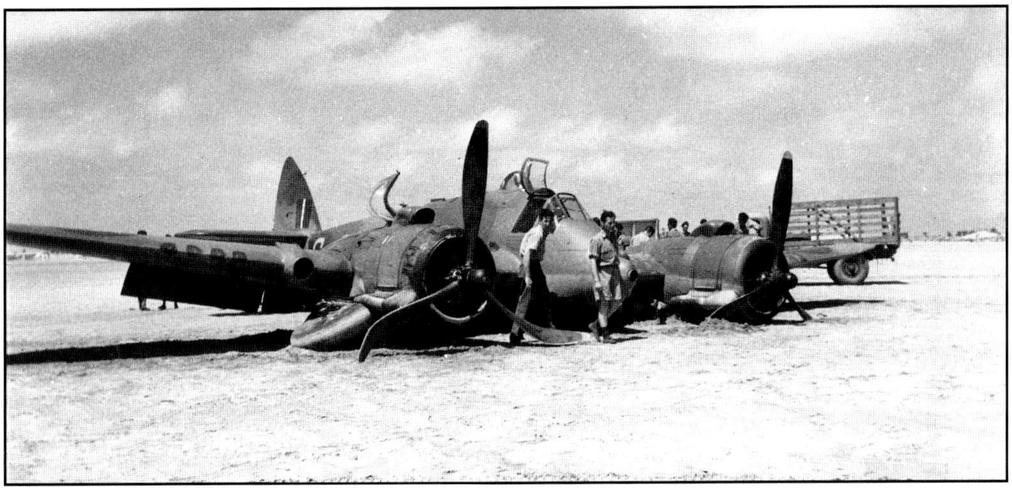

Above: **A ground-looped machine at Idku, March, 1943. No. 227 Squadron and its Beaufighters had an interesting story. Its first incarnation was short lived when a detachment of Beaufighter aircrew in the Middle East was absorbed into No. 272 Squadron. In August 1942 detachments of Nos. 235 and 248 Squadrons at Luqa, Malta, were designated No. 227 Squadron under the command of Wing Commander D Ross Shore, DFC. The squadron continued operations with Beaufighters until August 1944, when it was re-designated No. 19 Squadron (SAAF). Another No. 227 Squadron was formed in October 1944, this time with Lancasters at Bardney.**

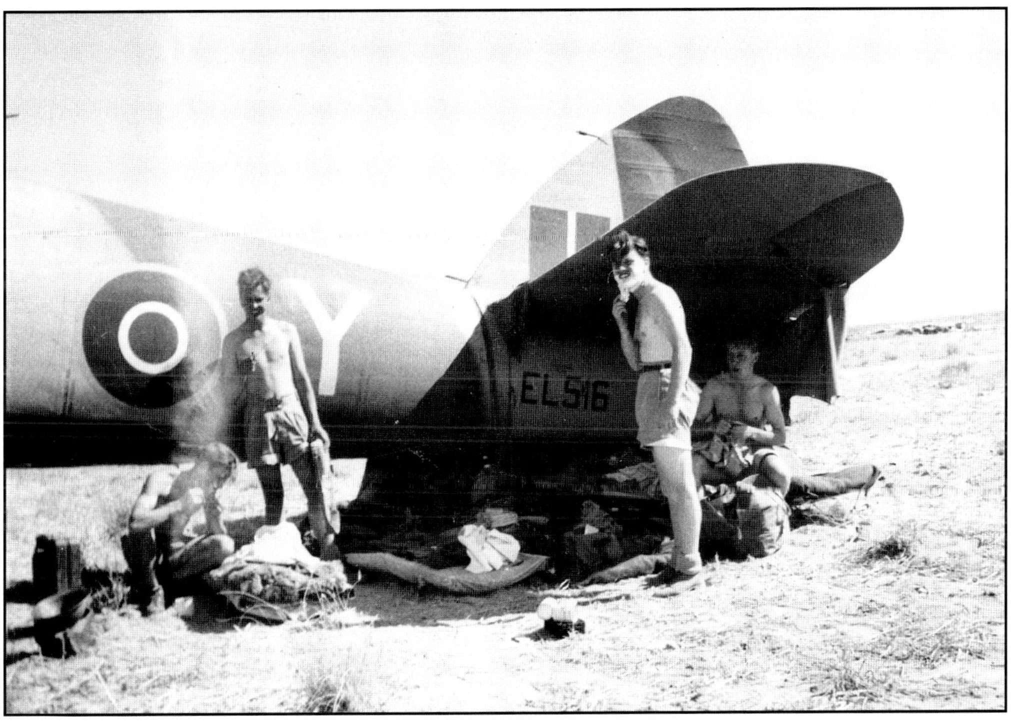

Left: EL516 provides shade at Sidi Magrum, Libya in July 1943. The aircraft was lost when it suffered engine failure and ditched in the Mediterranean in September 1943.

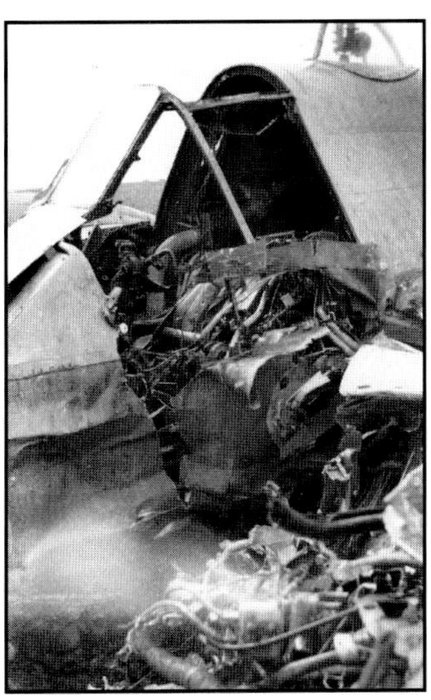

Left: The pilot of this Mk.VIc fell foul to the take-off swing and the port prop smashed through the cockpit. The pilot escaped with a cut arm.

Right: The Radar station at Methoni under attack by No. 227 Squadron after having been discovered by No. 454 Squadron.

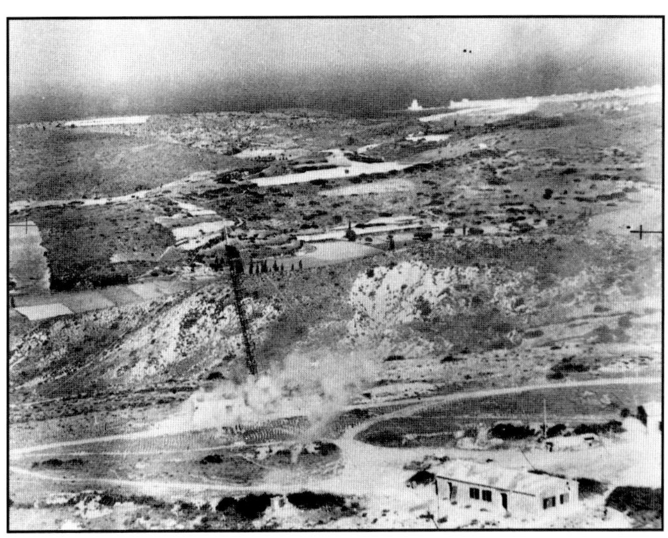

235
SQUADRON
Code Letters:
LA

Jaculamur humi
(We strike them to the ground)

Usage:
Mk.Ic
Dec 41 to Sept 42
Mk.VIc
July 42 to Oct 43
Mk.X
Oct 43 to May 44
Mk.XI

Rôle:
Coastal Command Strike

Bases:
Sumburgh 3/42 - 5/42
Docking 5/42 - 7/42
Chivenor 7/42 - 1/43
Leuchars 1/43 - 8/43
Portreath 8/43 - 2/44
St Angelo 2/44 - 3/44
Portreath 3/44 - 6/44

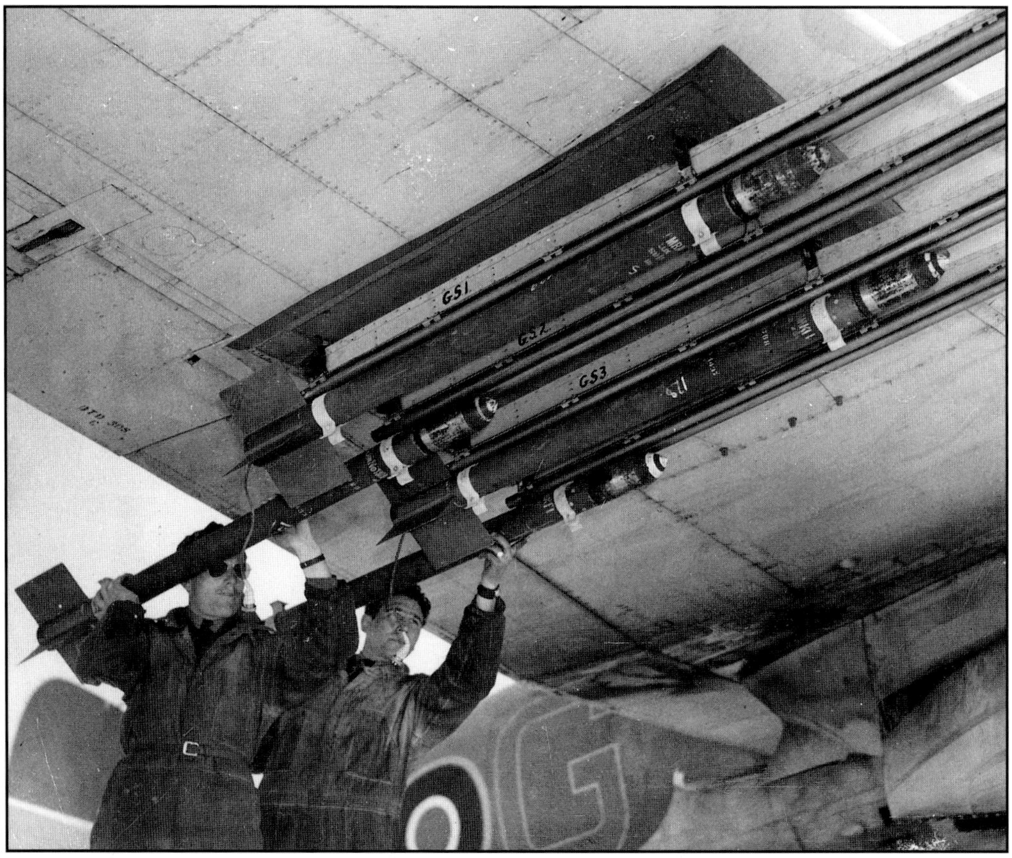

Above: **Loading 25lb armour piercing rockets on to the rails of a Mk.X in 1944.**

No. 235 Squadron was one of the first three Coastal Command Squadrons to receive Beaufighters, the others being Nos. 236 and 248 Squadrons. Originally they used them as long-range fighters over the North Sea hunting for German bombers, several of which they destroyed, and also flew escort to several Hampden bomber raids. By D-Day, Coastal Command had eight Beaufighter squadrons and No. 235 Squadron was moved from St. Angelo in Northern Ireland to Portreath in Cornwall to cover the western approaches to the Channel.

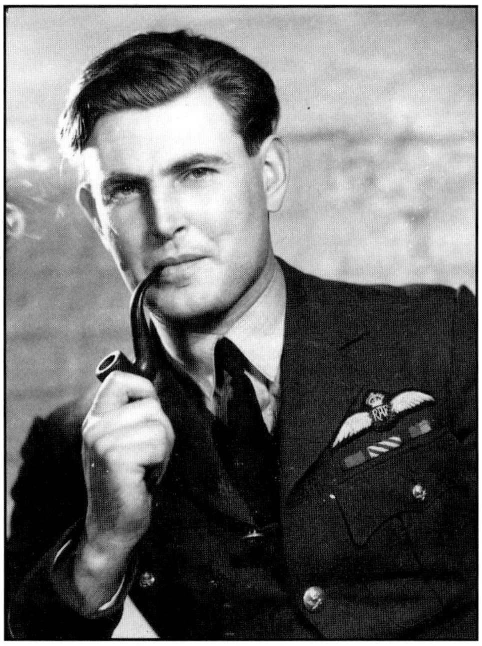
Above: **Wing Commander R H McConnell DSO, DFC, of No. 235 Squadron.**

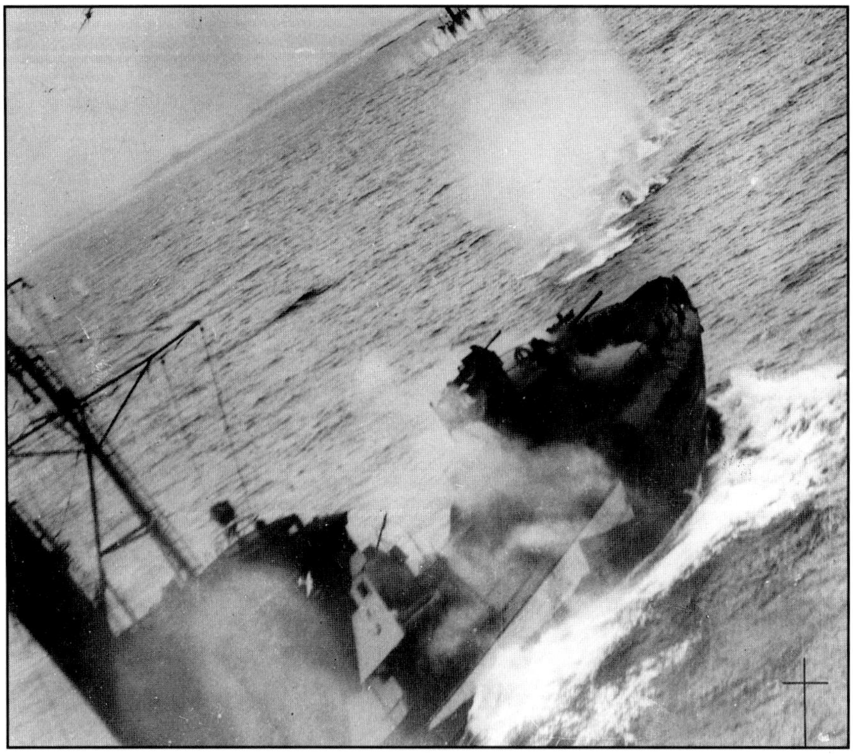
Left: **The original caption to this photo read, 'Flying through cloud down to sea level, Beaufighters of RAF Coastal Command completely surprised a German convoy off the south coast of Norway on Saturday evening. One merchant vessel blew up after being set on fire, a cargo liner was hit with a torpedo and an armed coaster left burning, listing and sinking. Two other vessels were blazing furiously while the rest of the convoy was either on fire or damaged.'**

236

SQUADRON

Code Letters:

ND & MB

Speculati nuntiate
(Having watched, bring word)

Usage:

Mk.Ic
Oct 41 to Feb 42
Mk.VIc
Sept 42 to July 43
Mk.X
July 43 to May 45

Rôle:

Coastal Command reconnaissance, escort and strike

Bases:

Carew Cheriton
10/41 - 2/42
Wattisham 2/42 - 7/42
Oulton 7/42 - 9/42
North Coates 9/42 - 5/45

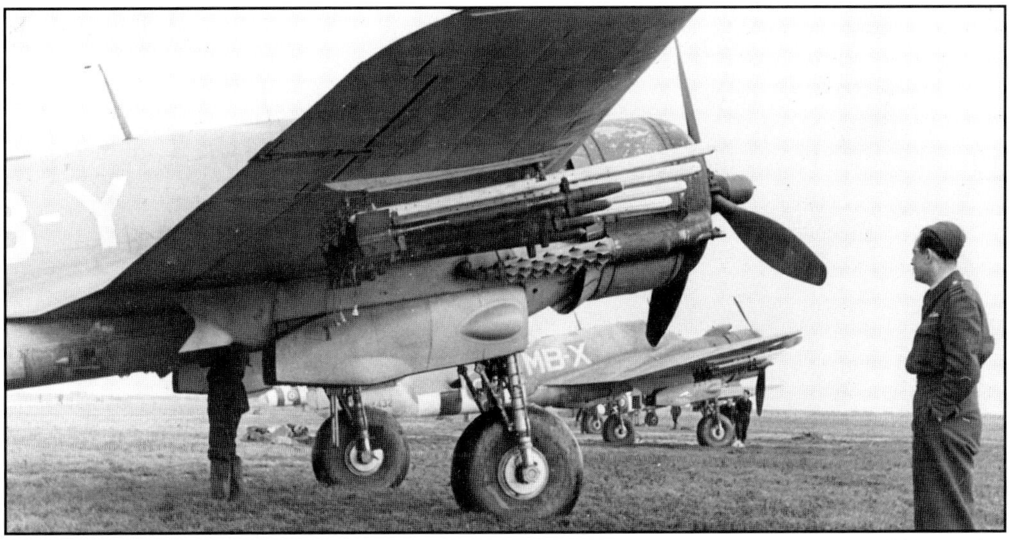

Above: **Fully loaded with 3 inch rockets at North Coates. Note that the rockets still have the 'pig-tails' plugged in to disarm them, the plugs would be removed by the armourers immediately before take-off.**

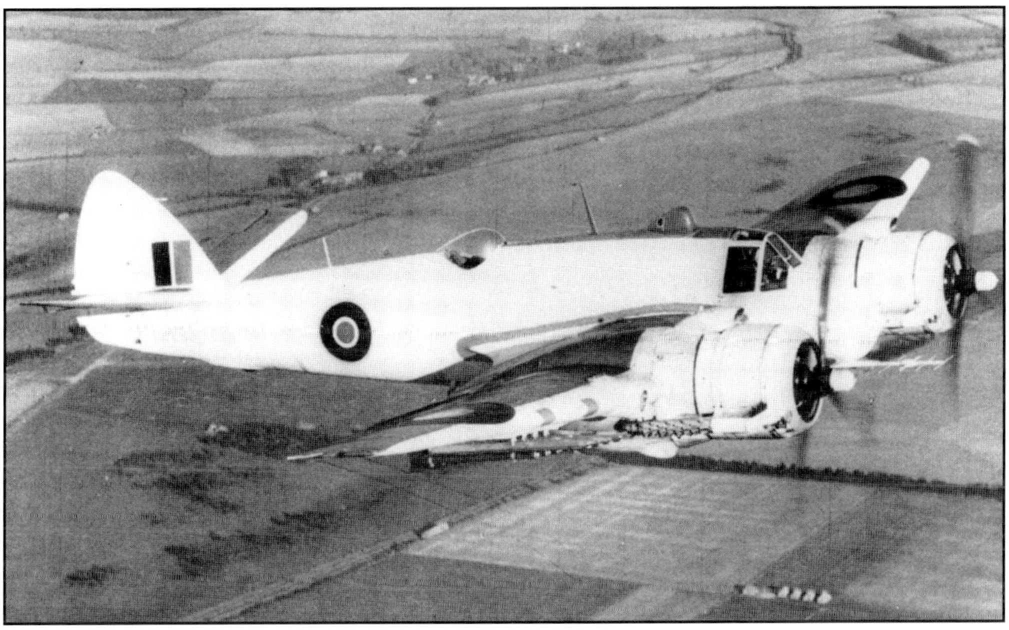

Left: **LZ293 with ASV Radar and Coastal Command colours. This aircraft crashed on 11 August 1944.**

Below: **NT950, MB-T, in D-Day markings.**
No. 236 Squadron was the mainstay of the North Coates Strike Wing from November 1942 to May 1945, with Nos. 143 and 254 Squadrons.

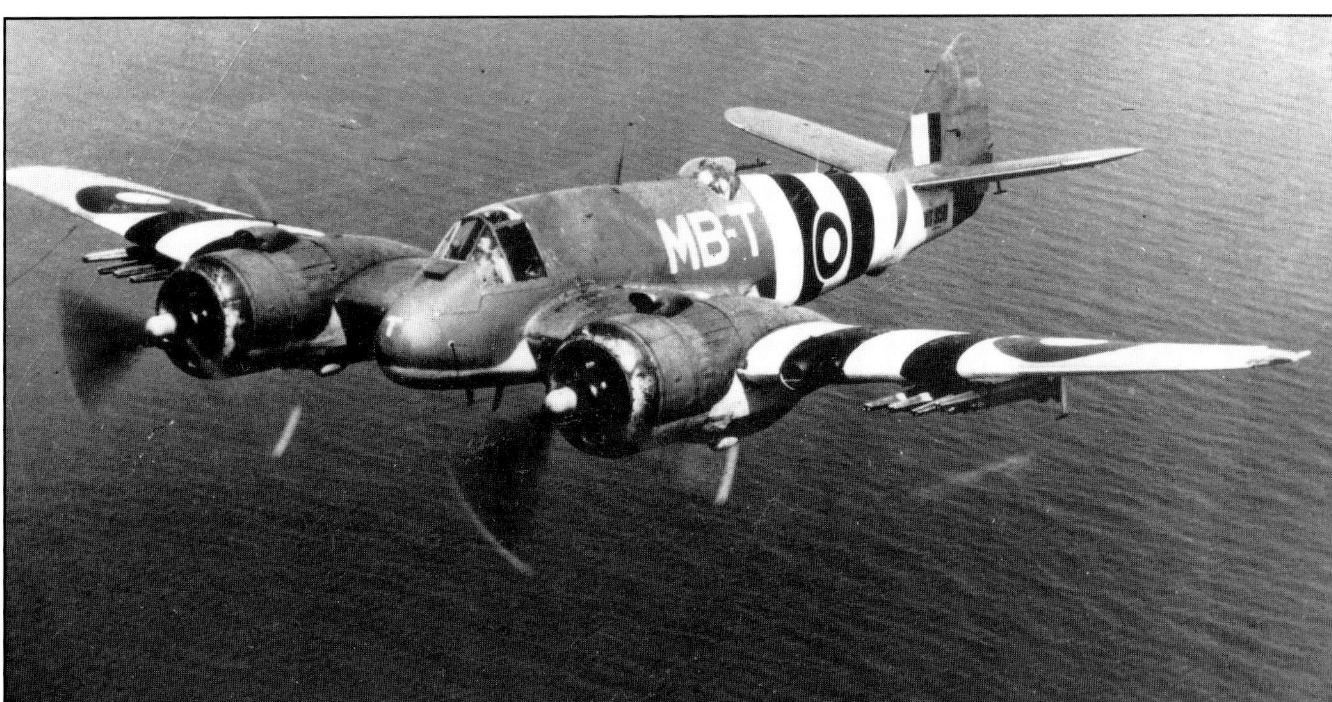

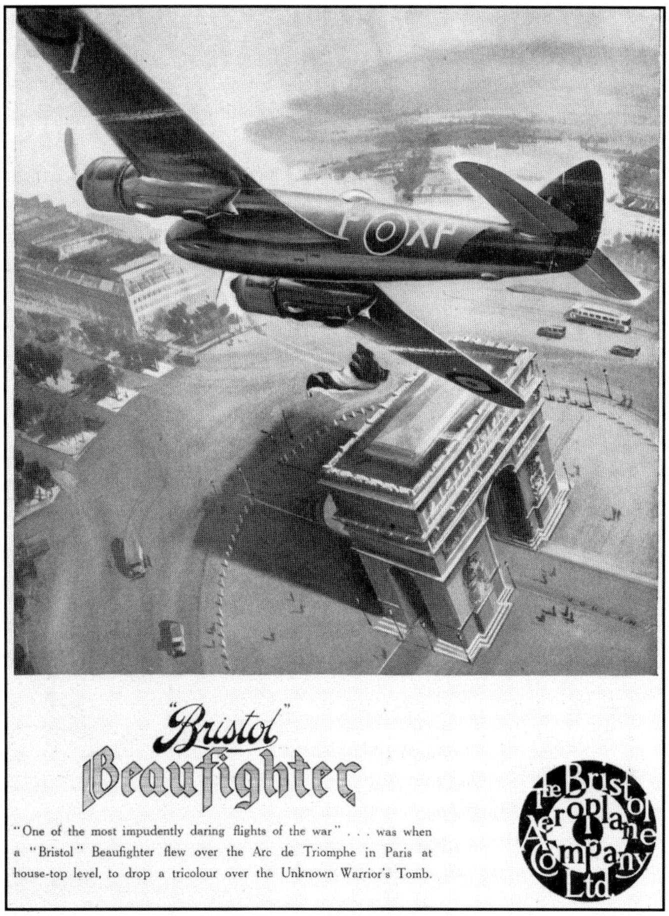

Left: **The Bristol Aeroplane Company used Gatward's exploit in one of its adverts for Beaufighters. The markings are ficticious.**

The Solo Paris Raid

The origins of the audacious lone raid date back to September, 1941, when Major Ben Cowburn of the Special Operations Executive was dropped into occupied Europe. He made his way into Paris where, when strolling along the Champs Elysées one day, he heard in the distance the sound of a military band and as it came nearer he saw a German detachment, led by an officer on horseback, marching towards the Arc de Triomphe. Cowburn noted what a wonderful target the parade would make and what a wonderful boost to French moral an attack would be.

Back in London Cowburn put his proposal to the SOE who approached the AOC-in-C Fighter Command. The original proposal was to send three Spitfires equipped with long-range tanks to lay red, white and blue smoke - the colours of the tricolour – over Paris. The plan was scrapped and instead it was decided to send a single Beaufighter. Volunteers from Coastal Command were called for and Flight Lieutenant Ken Gatward and Sergeant George Fern from No. 236 Squadron were selected. Gatward, then 27, had joined the RAFVR in 1937 and had flown Blenheims on reconnaissance and bombing operations with No. 53 Squadron in 1940. Major Cowburn back in France once again, provided a timetable for the Germans' daily parade along the Champs Elysées and on 5 May 1942, Gatward and Fern began training. Every day they made practice gunnery attacks on a ship wreck in the Channel, pored over detailed maps of Paris and studied photographs of all the buildings in the parade area. They also visited Portsmouth Dockyard to collect a new and grand-looking Tricolore - for which they signed several forms. Back at nearby Thorney Island they cut the flag into two and the parachute section sewed iron bars on each piece. Secretly they practised dropping the wrapped flags from the top of a hangar to see how they unfurled when descending.

On 13 May the weather augured well for the raid, but as they crossed the French coast the cloud cover cleared and, obeying orders, they returned disappointed. Three more attempts were made, but the weather conditions imposed by did not materialise and back to base they came. By the fifth try - on 12 June - Gatward's patience was almost exhausted. He took off from Thorney Island in T4800 and was determined to get through at all costs. Ken Gatward described the raid in 1962:

"Cloud was forecast, but it had broken up when we reached the French coast. This time we carried on. We flew close to the deck all the way, rarely more than 100 feet up and often as low as 30 feet, hedge-hopping trees and buildings. We cruised at 220 mph. Navigating with a map, Fern did a difficult job magnificently and guided me straight into Paris on course. The parade was timed for midday. Just before noon we picked up the shape of the Eiffel Tower and at 12.02 we were over the Champs Elysées. I climbed to 300 feet and banked for the attack - but there was no parade. The boulevards were almost deserted. Somehow, it seemed, the Germans had learned of our mission. Filled with rage and frustration, we dived on to the Champs Elysées, roared along at below-rooftop height and climbed over the Arc de Triomphe. As we flashed past it Sergeant Fern flung the flags out through the flare-chute. They went out rather like harpoons and that was the last we saw of them.

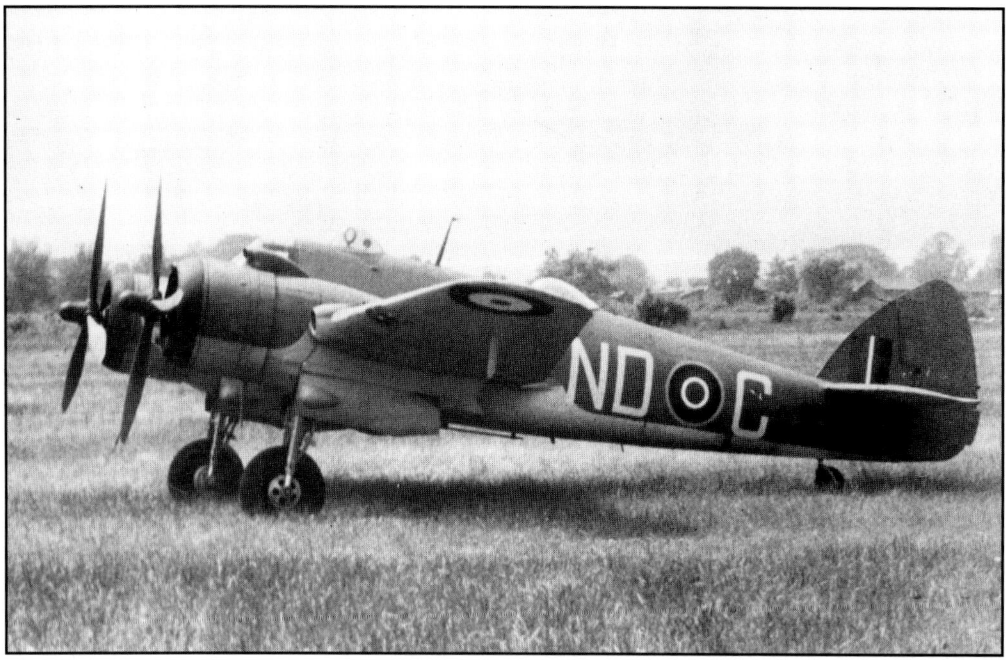

Left: **ND-C the Beaufighter Gatward flew on this Paris trip. The ND code was used until August 1943, when the Coastal Command single number scheme was introduced as No. 236 Squadron was part of the North Coates Strike Wing. From July 1944 the code MB was used by the squadron.**

"By now we were approaching the Place de la Concorde and the *Kriegsmarine* Headquarters. This was my secondary target and as we passed we sprayed the place with cannon shells. We got a glimpse of terrified sentries running for their lives - and then we were on the way home. We flew back to the coast as low as we had come, but met no ack-ack or enemy fighters. We got away with the whole operation scot-free. The only incident was a minor collision with a big crow that crashed into our starboard radiator. Apart from that our only opposition came from swarms of small flies that, we collected in a solid mass on our wind-shield. By the time we got back it was difficult to see out."

The reason for the changed time of the parade that day has never been explained, but the flight was still considered a tremendous success and it convinced many doubting Thomases in France of the efficiency and reliability of the RAF and the SOE organisation. News of it spread through France like wildfire. Frenchmen gleefully told each other of how the Germans had been taken by surprise in broad daylight and how the Beaufighter had cocked a snook at all the hundreds of Luftwaffe fighters based in Northern France.

Gatward was awarded the DFC and Fern the DFM. Later Gatward won the DSO and a bar to his DFC. As Wing Commander he became CO of No. 404 Squadron. Fern, rose to rank of Squadron Leader.

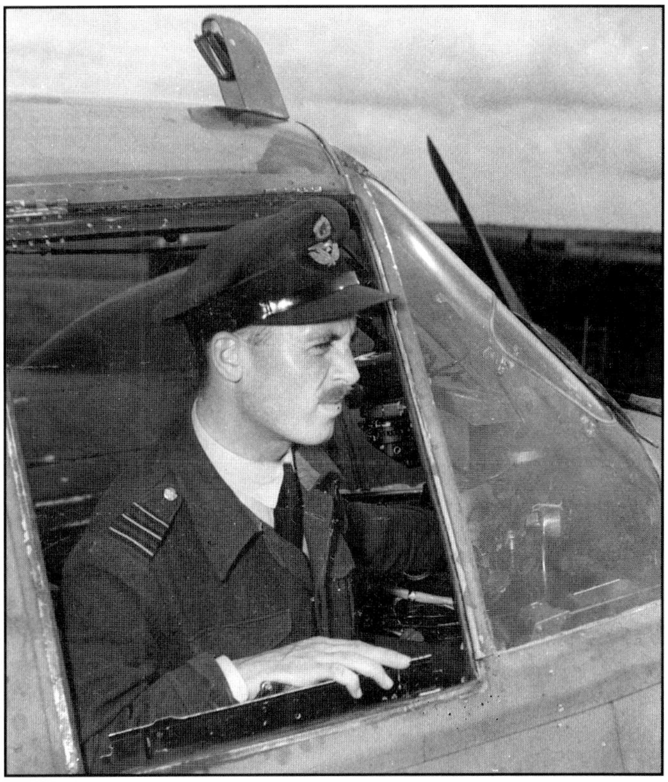

Right: Wing Commander A K Gatward, DSO, DFC at Davidstow Moor in August 1944. At this time he was the Commanding Officer of No. 404 Squadron.

No. 236 Squadron at work

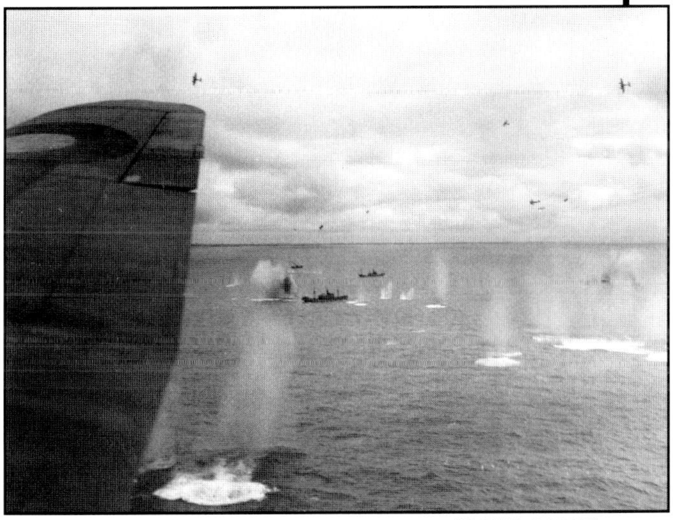

27 June 1943. Attack on enemy convoy 5210N 0410E

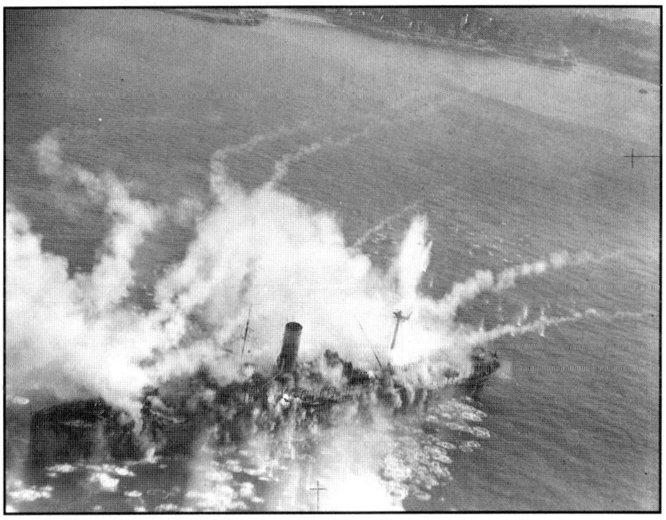

13 August 1944. Armed enemy motor vessel off Royon

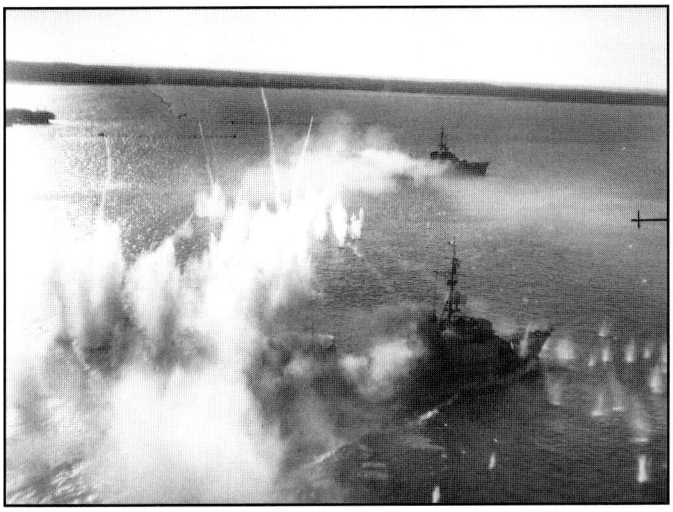

24 August 1944. Enemy destroyers at Le Verdon.

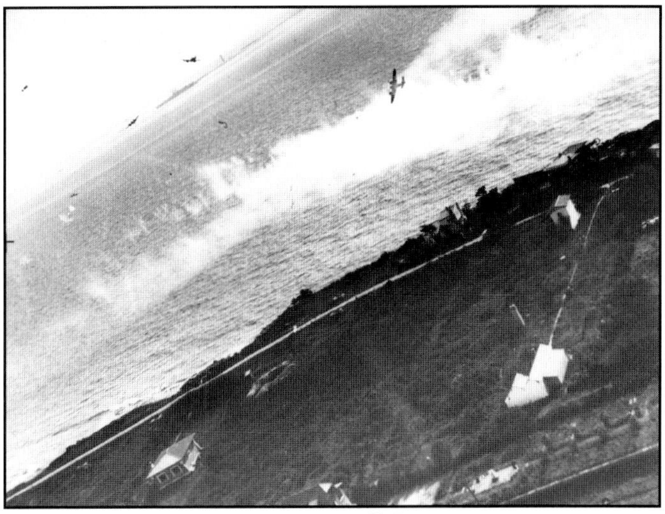

26 August 1944. Motor vessels off Royan.

248
SQUADRON

Code Letters:

WR

Il faut en finir
(It is necessary to make an end of it)

Usage:
Mk.Ic
July 41 to June 42
Mk.VIc
Sept 42 to June 43
Mk.X
June 43 to Dec 43

Rôle:
Coastal Command Strike

Bases:
Bircham Newton
7/41 - 2/42
Dyce 2/42 - 5/42
Sumburgh 5/42 - 8/42
Dyce 8/42 - 9/42
Talbenny 9/42 - 11/42
Pembrey 11/42 - 12/42
Talbenny 12/42 - 1/43
Predannack 1/43 - 12/43

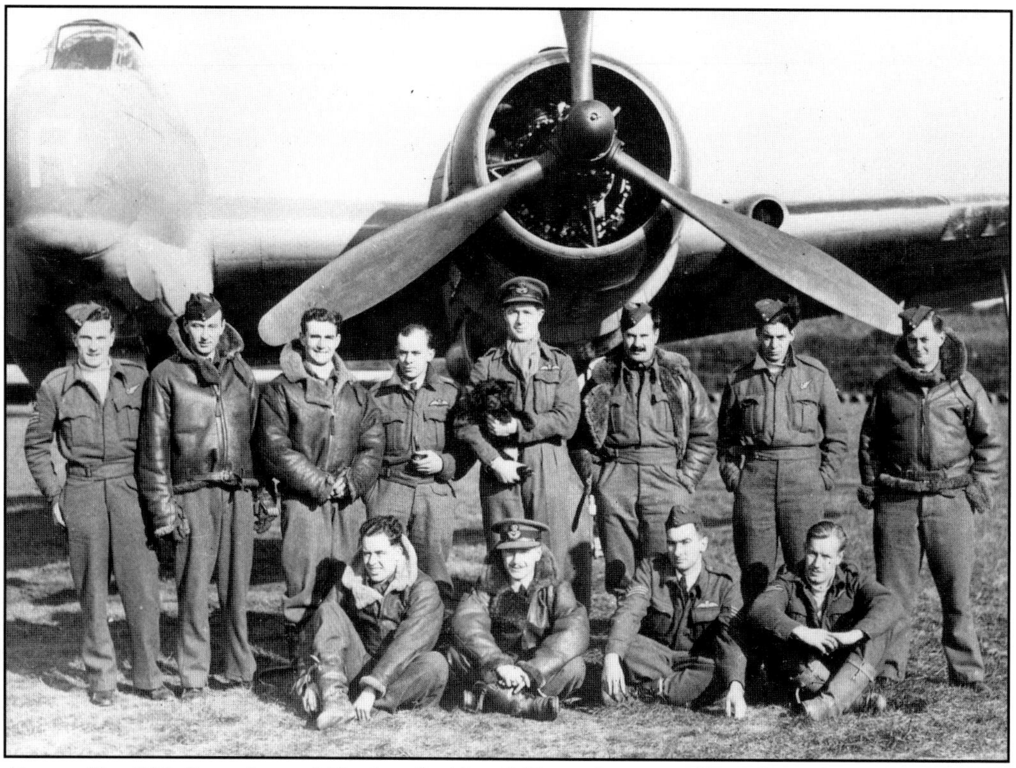

Above: **No. 248 Squadron at Portreath. The Officer Commanding, Squadron Leader Cartridge DFC is holding the dog. (G. Medcalf)**

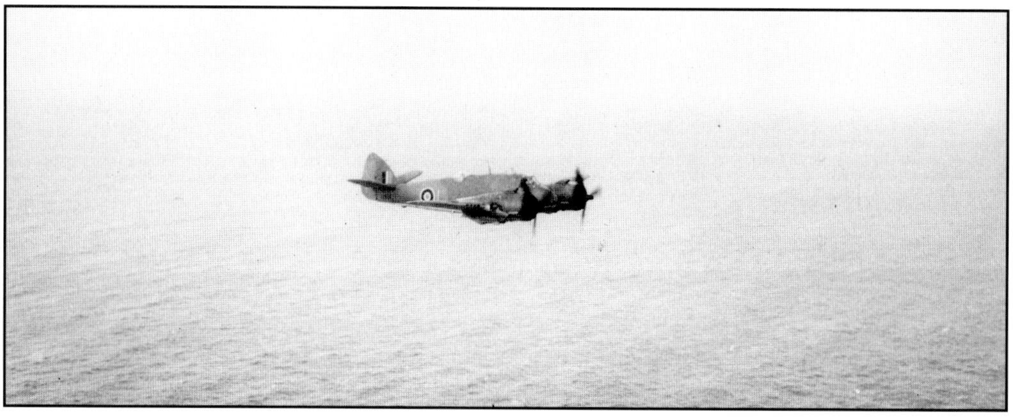

Right: **Between June and September 1942 part of squadron went to Malta, where the aircraft were left to form No. 227 Squadron.**

Below: **JL447 'G' of No. 248 Squadron in the winter of 1942/43.**

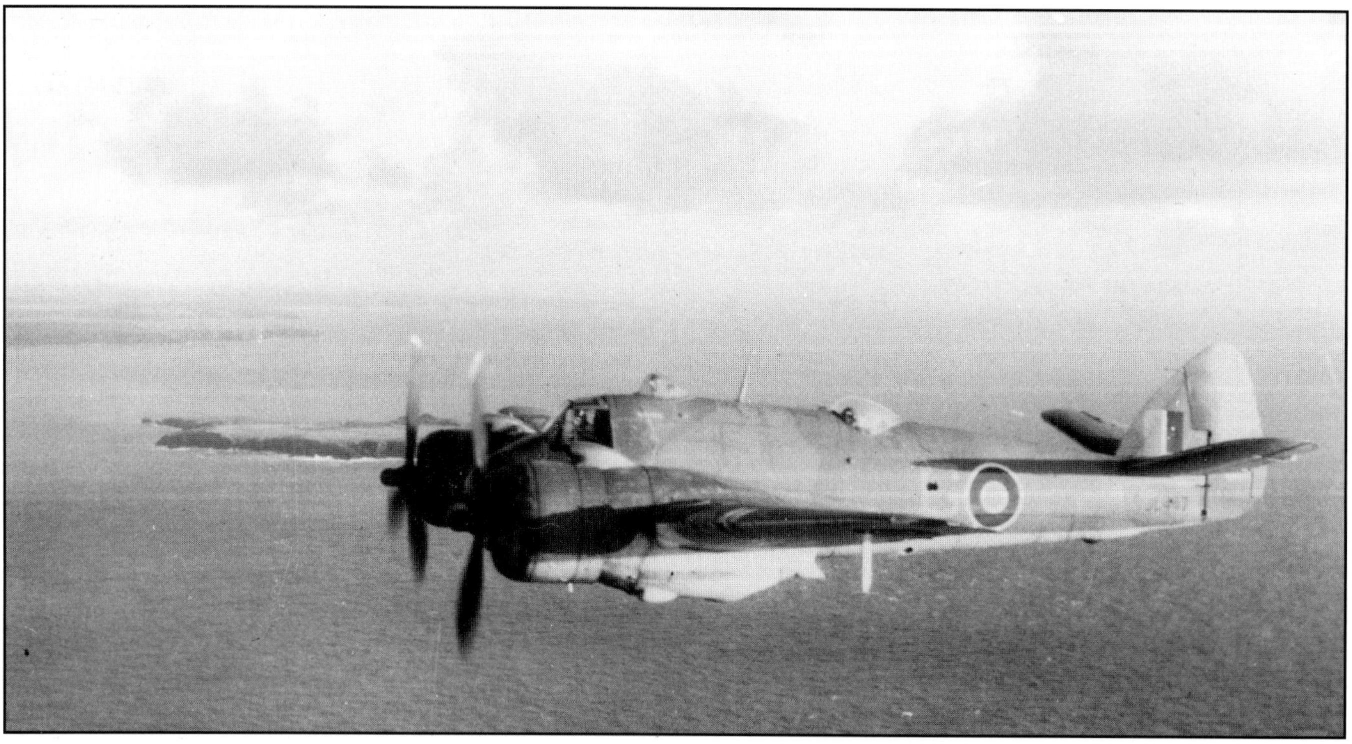

252 SQUADRON

Code Letters:

PN & BT

With or on

Usage:

Mk.If
Dec 40 to Apr 41
Mk.Ic
Mar 41 to Jan 44
Mk.VIc
Sept 42 to Jan 44
Mk.XI
June 43 to Jan 44
TF Mk.X
Jan 44 to Dec 46

Rôle:

Coastal Command.
Middle East shipping strikes

Bases:

Chivenor 12/40 - 4/41
Aldergrove 4/41 - 6/41
Idku 11/41 - 1/43
Berka III 2/43 - 9/43
Limassol 9/43
Lakatamia 9/43 - 12/43
LG91 12/43 - 1/44
Mersa Matruh 1/44 - 6/44
Gambut 6/44 - 11/44
Mersa Matruh 11/44 -2/45
Aboukir 2/45
Gianaclis 2/45
Hassani 2/45 - 8/45
Araxos 8/45 - 12/46

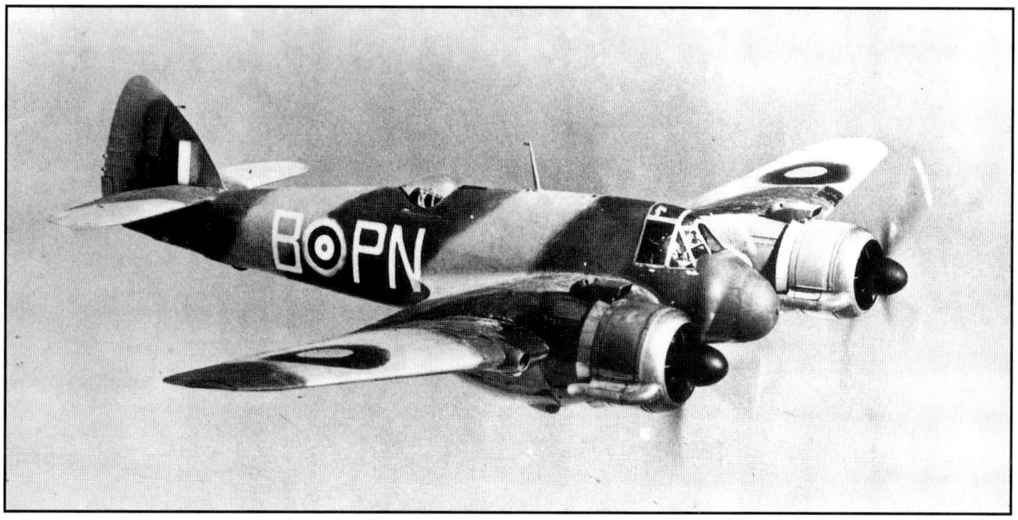

Above: **PN-B, R2153, was one of the first Beaufighters received by No. 252 Squadron when it re-equipped from Blenheims. The code was changed to BT when the squadron was re-formed in the Middle East at Idku in November 1941.**

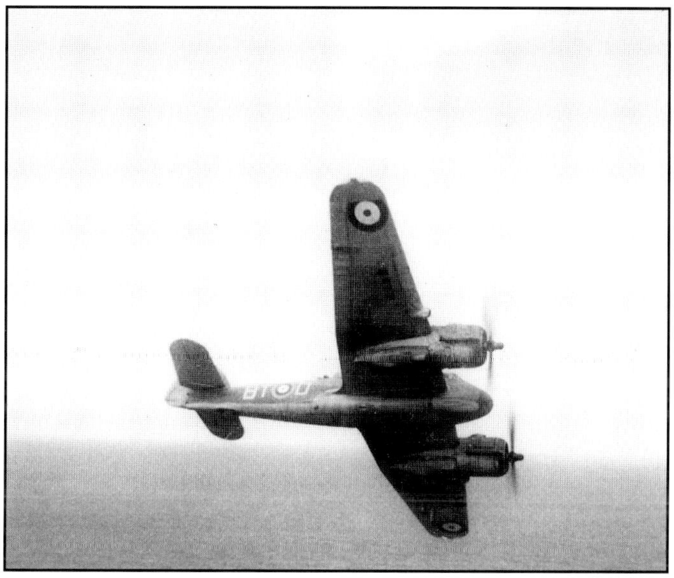

Left: **BT-D in 1942. The squadron had broken up after four months in Northern Ireland. Fifteen aircraft and crews were sent to Luqa, Malta, while that remaining at Aldergrove became No. 143 Squadron in June 1941. The Middle East echelon operated from Heraklion, and Abu Sueir, and Idku alongside No. 227 Squadron.**

Below: **T5040, No. 252 Squadron, undergoing a service at Idku, 1942.**

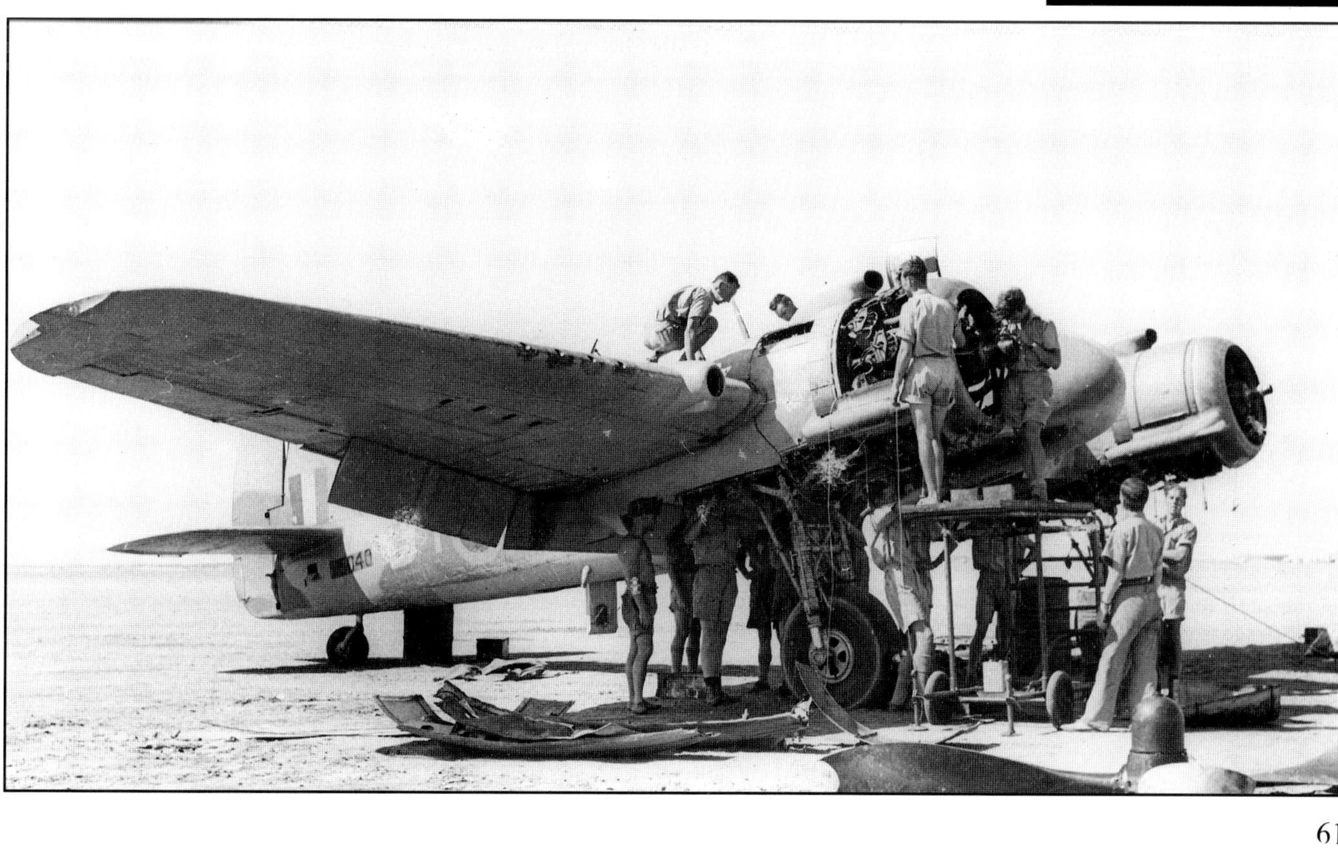

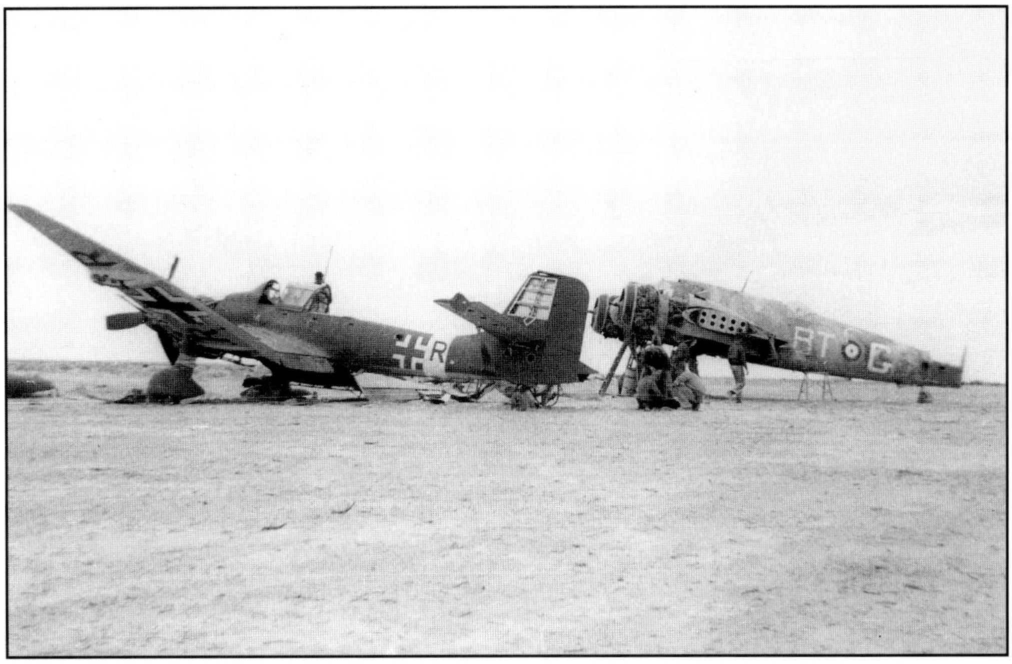

Left: **One of No. 252's Beaufighters, cannibalized for spares, alongside a wrecked Ju87 on a North African airfield.**
Priority target for the squadron was Axis supplies and a 'gift' presented itself on 12 May 1942. Five Beaufighters led by Squadron Leader Wincott and nine Kittyhawks found thirteen Ju52 transports with a single Me110 escort over the coast near Maleme. In the combat that followed nine of the Ju52s and the Me110 escort were shot down. One of the squadron's Beaufighters was lost.

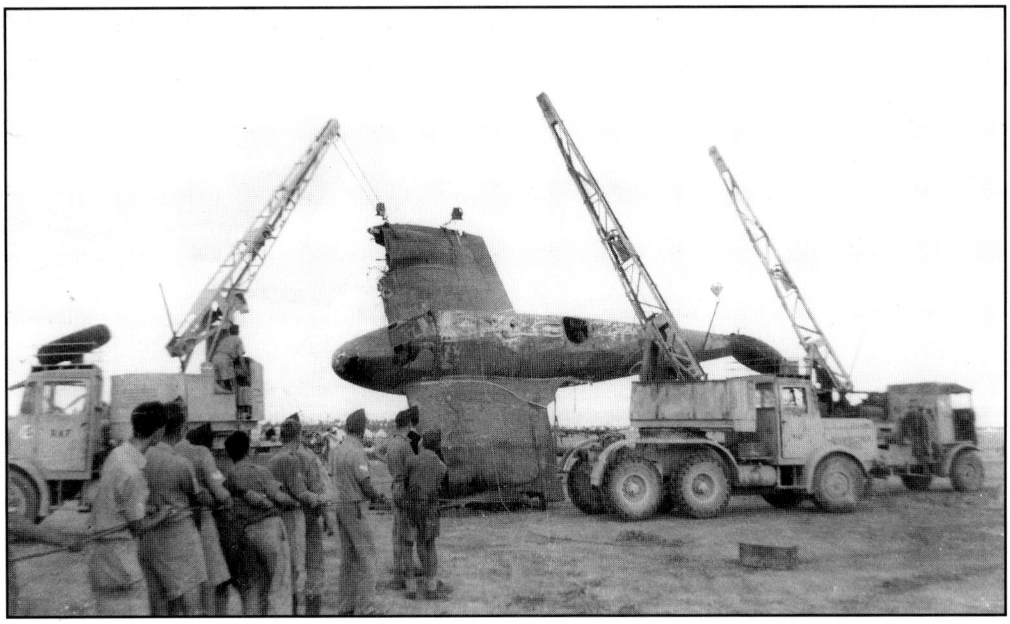

Left: **'E' of No. 252 Squadron turned over on landing after a strafing sortie at El Adem. The low-level operations over the desert proved very hazardous. In January 1943 the CO Wing Commander Bragg was forced to crash land behind enemy lines after strafing a supply line and was captured. His replacement was Wing Commander Ogilvie.**

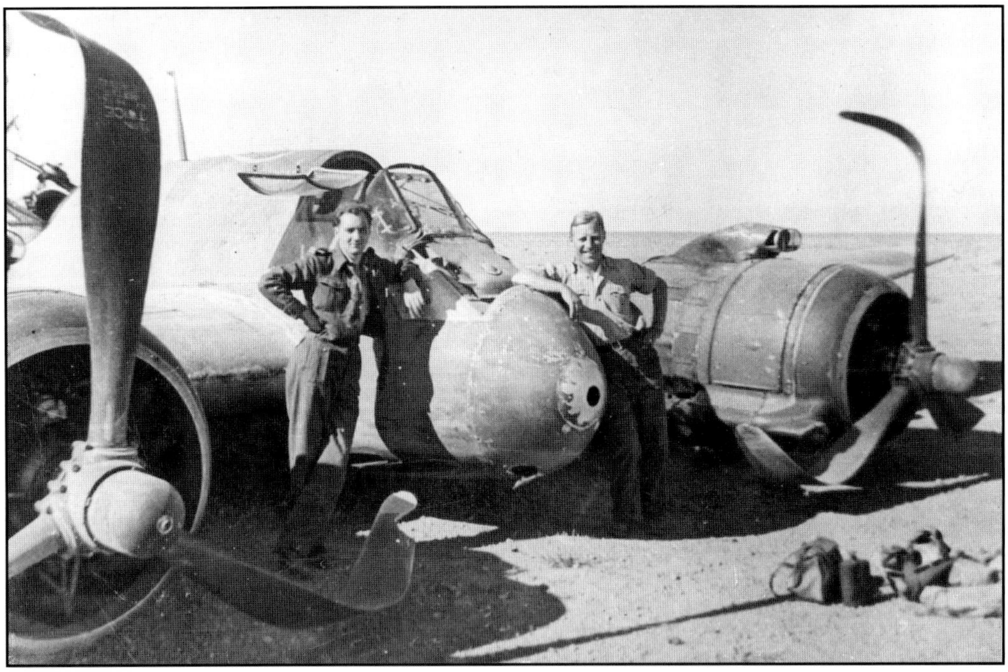

Left: **Squadron Leader A D Frecker DFC, Flying Officer T Armstrong DFC and Flight Sergeant Paddy Clark (a Fitter) crashed behind enemy lines after being hit by flak. Paddy Clark took this picture before they set off to return. They eventually found a British armoured car patrol and returned to the squadron after being 'missing' for 16 days.**

Right: **The men of No. 252 Squadron at Idku in 1942. The men lend scale to the aircraft here, illustrating its 57 feet 10 inch wingspan.**

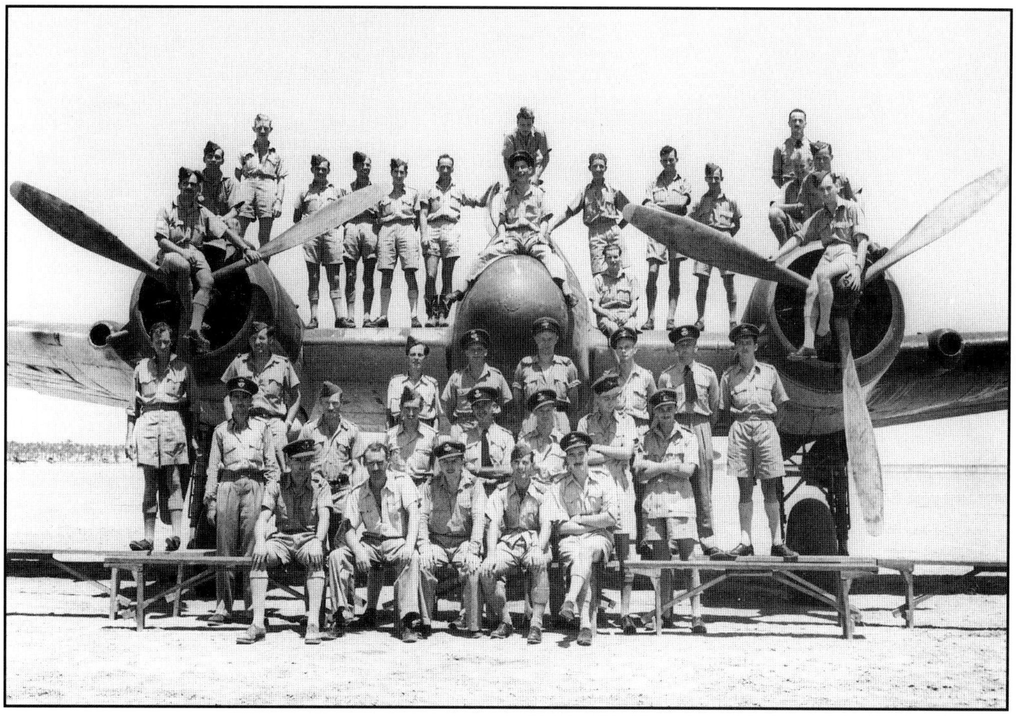

Below right: **The attack on the German barracks at Kalymnos, 24 October 1944.** Below left: **A train at Sidi Barrani attacked by Squadron Leader Frecker on 9 October 1942.**

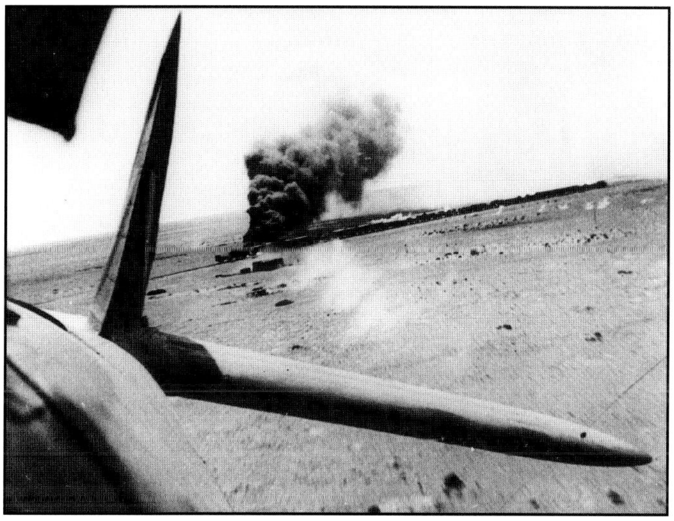

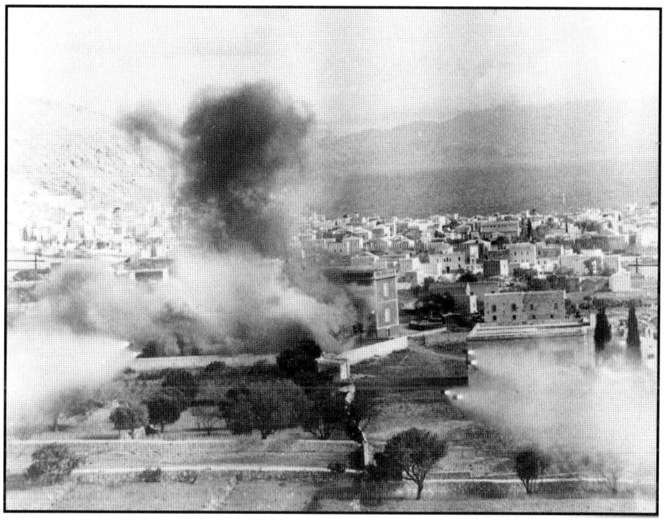

Rocket projectiles race towards the *Sabina* during an attack by No. 252 Squadron on 1 June 1944.

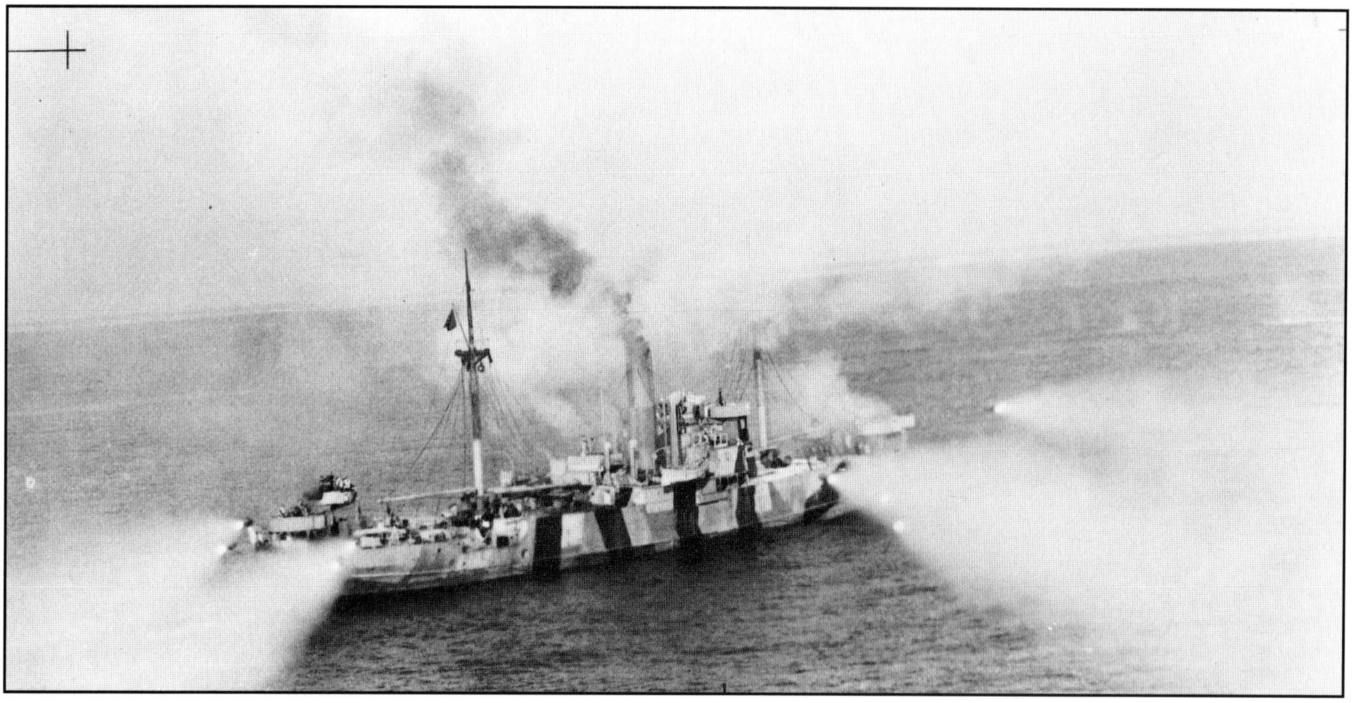

254
SQUADRON

Code Letters:

QM

Fljuga vakta ok ljosta
(Norse)
(To fly, to watch and to strike)

Usage:
Mk.VIf
July 42 to Sept 43
TF Mk.X
Aug 43 to Oct 46

Rôle:
Coastal Command strikes

Bases:
Dyce 7/42 - 10/42
Docking 10/42 - 11/42
North Coates 11/43 - 6/45
Chivenor 6/45 - 11/45
Langham 11/45 - 5/46
Thorney Island
4/46 - 10/46

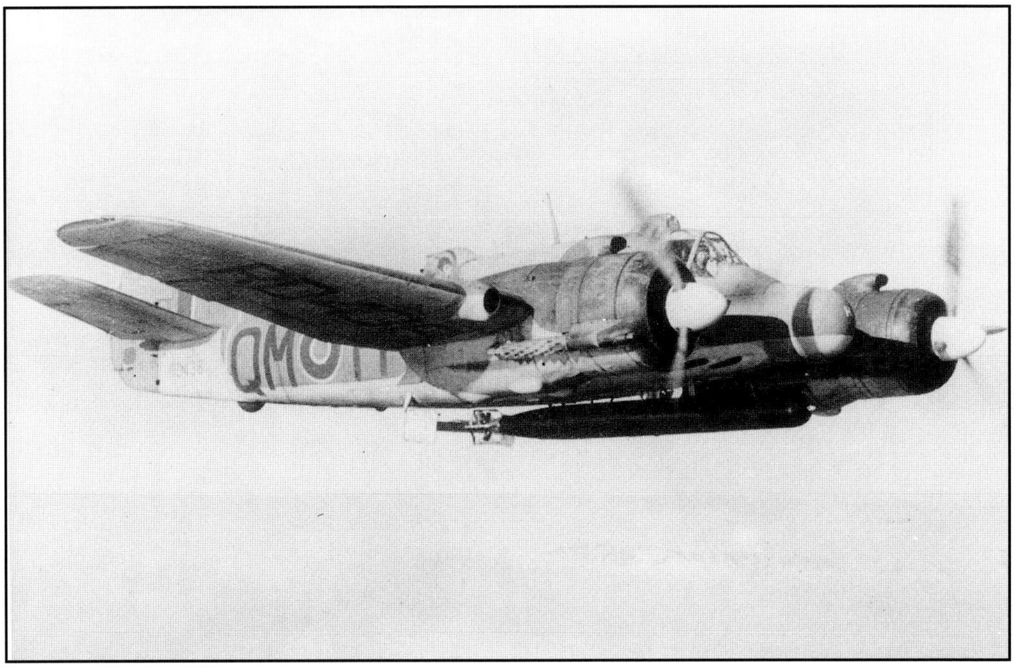

Above: **TF Mk.X RD438 QM-H of No. 254 Squadron carrying a MAT Mk.IV gyro controlled torpedo, the tail fins of which can be seen under the fuselage.**

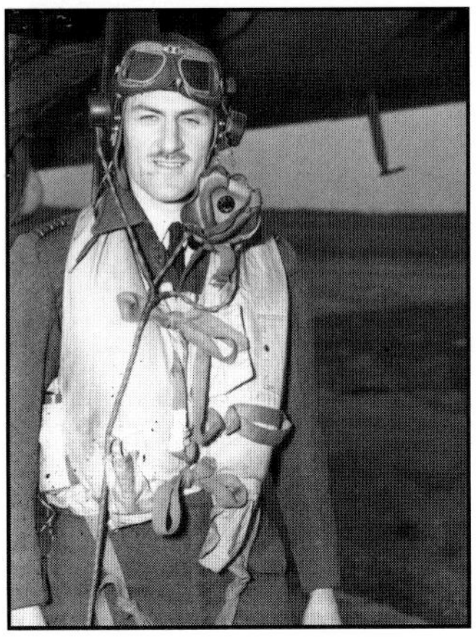

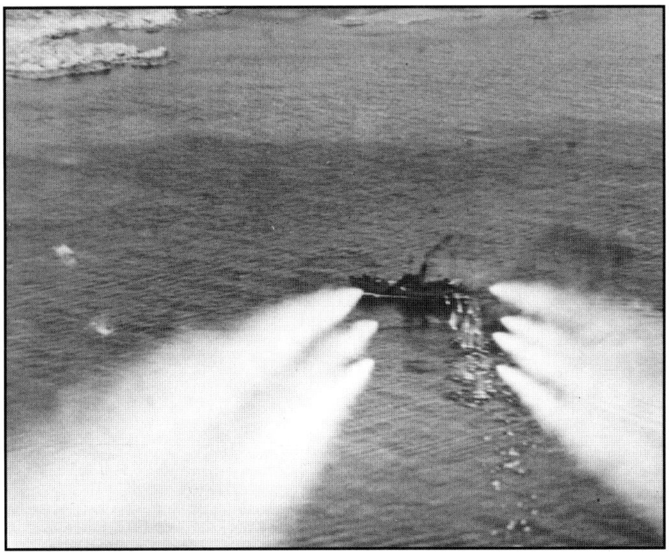

Far left: **Wing Commander R E Burns, DSO DFC, CO of No. 254 Squadron from January to September 1944.**

Left: **On 8 August 1944 a convoy off Bourgeneuf was attacked by the North Coates Strike Wing. Four minesweepers were sunk, but three Beaufighters and three of the escorting 8th Air Force Mustangs were lost.**

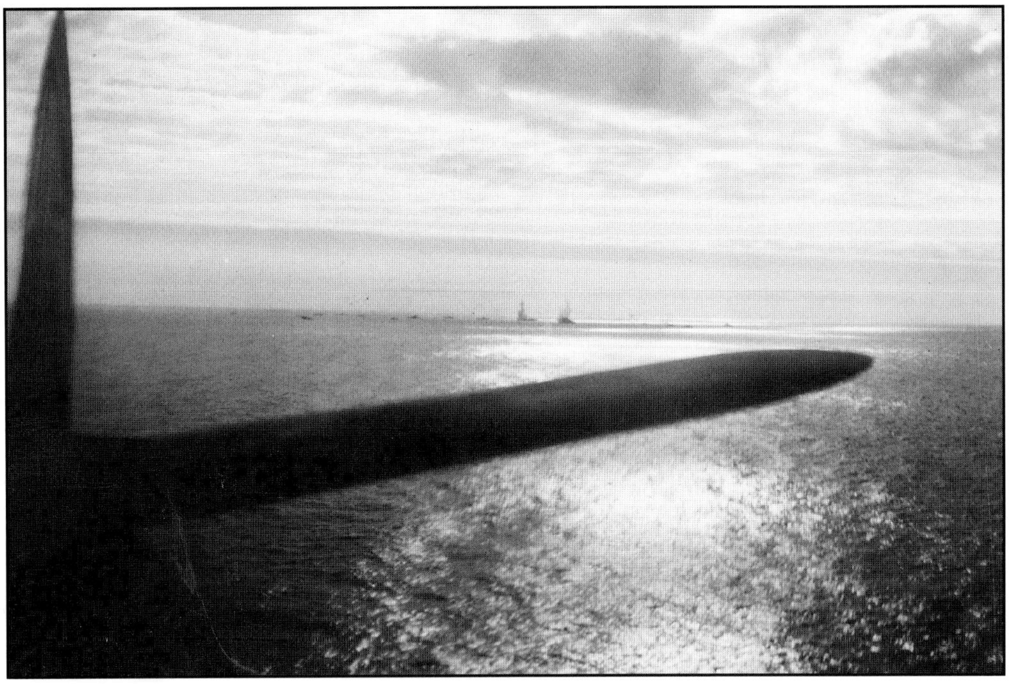

No. 254 Squadron formed part of the North Coates Strike Wing from November 1942 to May 1945, a role it shared with Nos. 236 and 143 Squadrons. It made the first strike from North Coates on 20 November 1942 and the first successful strike against enemy shipping with Torbeaus in April 1943.
In March 1945, operating as usual with No. 236 Squadron, the squadron located and sank five U-Boats in the space of 48 hours.

255
SQUADRON
Code Letters:
YD

Ad auroram
(To the break of dawn)

Usage:
Mk.IIf
July 41 to May 42
Mk.VIf
Mar 42 to Feb 45

Rôle:
Night defence of Britain, later Middle East

Bases:
Hibaldstow 7/41 - 9/41
Coltishall 9/41 - 3/42
High Ercall 3/42 - 6/42
Honiley 6/42 - 11/42
Maison Blanche 11/42 - 12/42
Bone 12/42
Setif 12/42 - 5/43
La Sebala 5/43 - 8/43
Bo Rizzo 8/43 - 11/43
Grottaglie 11/43 - 1/44
Foggia Main 1/44 - 2/45

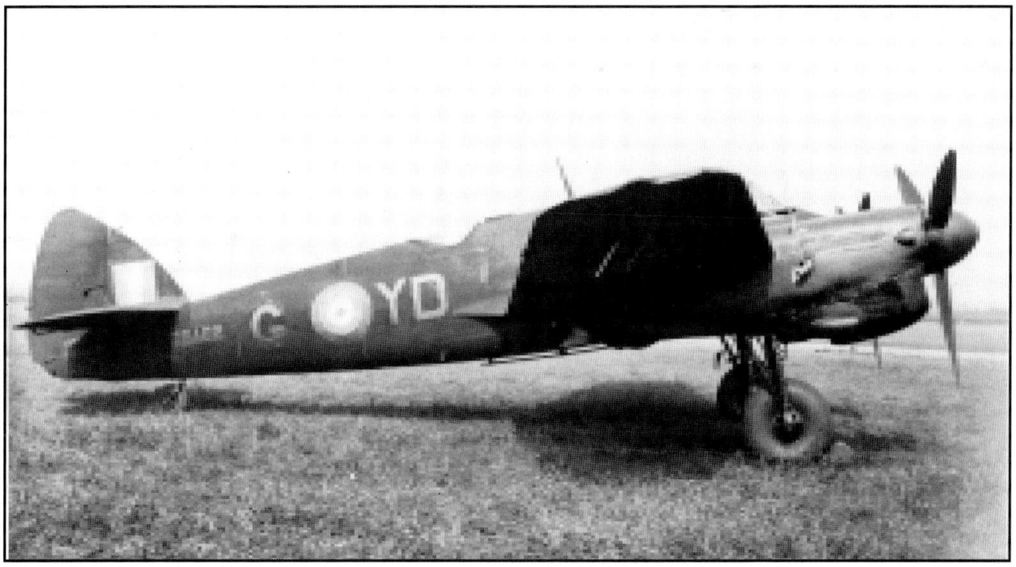

Above: **R2402, YD-G, one the Merlin engined Mk.IIfs used by No. 255 Squadron when based at Coltishall. This aircraft went on to serve with No. 410 Squadron and No. 54 OTU.**

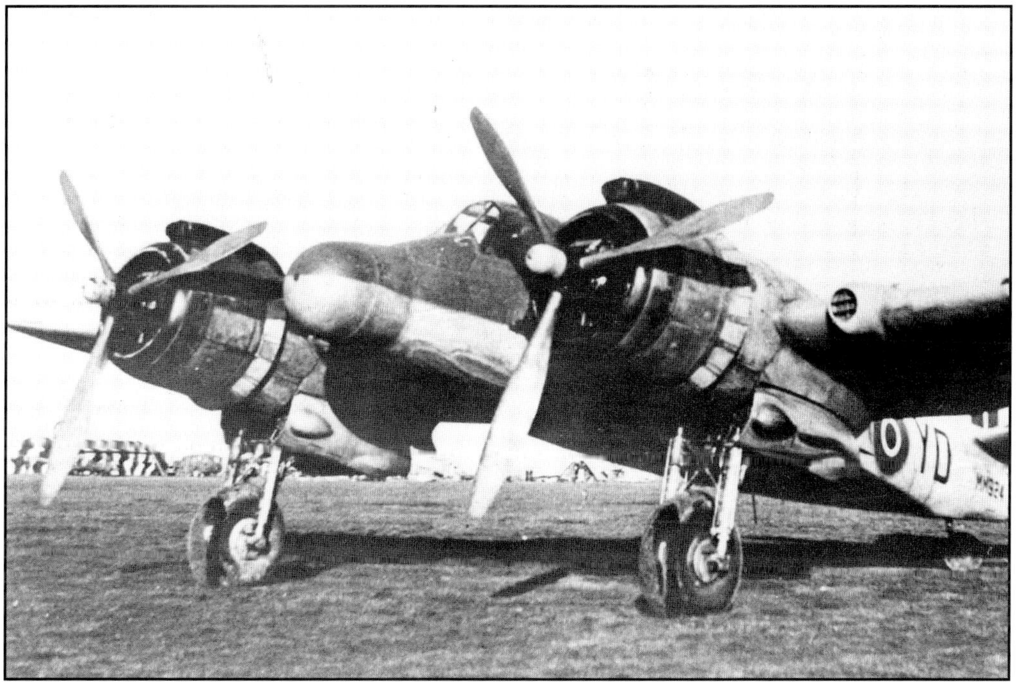

Left: **Mk.VIf MM924, YD-L of No. 255 Squadron in the Middle East, circa 1943.**

Below: **'C' of No. 255 Squadron, V8462, ran in to Hurricane HL978 of No. 225 Squadron when landing at Souk el Arba on 15 December 1942, leaving this mess behind.**

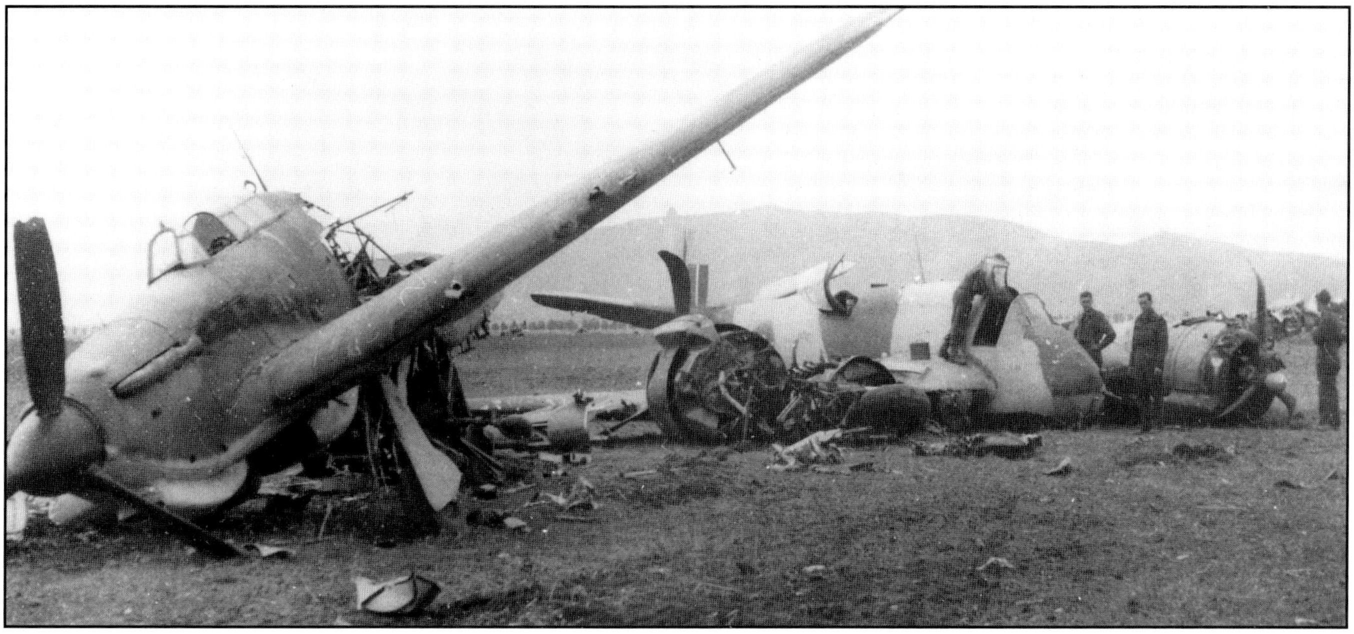

256
SQUADRON
Code Letters:
JT

Addimus vim viribus
(Strength to strength)

Usage:
Mk.If
May 42 to Nov 42
Mk.VIf
Oct 42 to May 43

Rôle:
Night defence of Britain

Bases:
Squires Gate 5/42 - 6/42
Woodvale 6/42 - 4/43
Ford 4/43 - 5/43

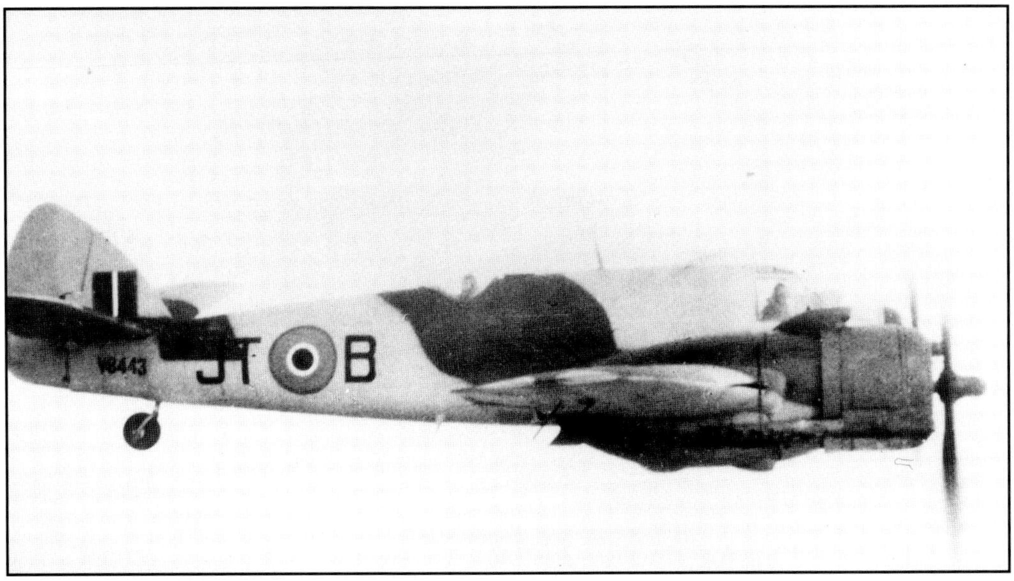

Above: **V8443, JT-B, a Mk.VIf of No. 256 Squadron based at Woodvale.**

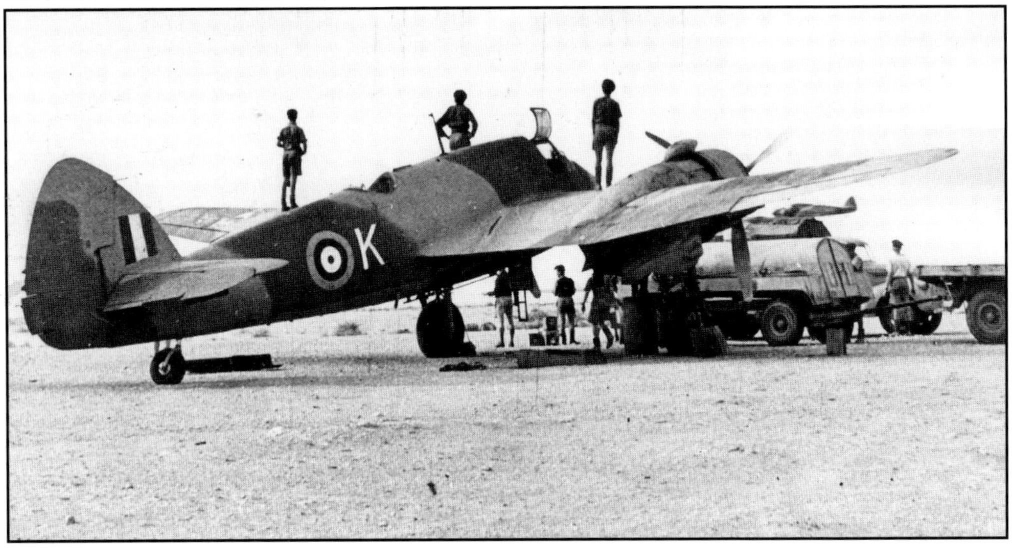

Left: **Ground crew of No. 272 Squadron based at Idku look on as a Beaufighter, visible between the tanker and the wing, beats up the airfield. The squadron had the first Beaufighters available for long range fighter, convoy escort and strike operations in the Mediterranean.**

Below: **T3316, an early Mk.Ic with No. 272 Squadron, was lost on 6 September 1941. Shortly after the squadron's arrival at Idku it absorbed No. 252 Squadron, the Commanding Officer at that time was Squadron Leader Fletcher DFC.**

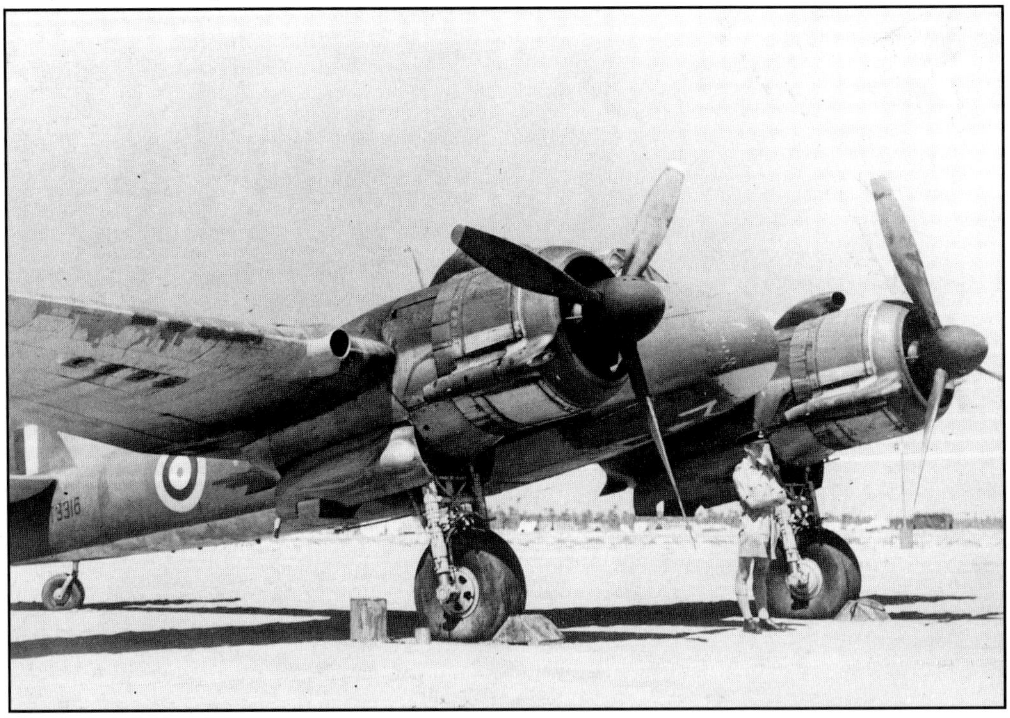

272
SQUADRON
On, on!

Usage:
Mk.Ic
Apr 41 to July 43
Mk.VIc
Nov 42 to Feb 44
Mk.XI
Sept 43 to May 44
TF Mk.X
Dec 43 to Apr 45

Rôle:
Coastal operations in the Middle East

Bases:
Chivenor 4/41 - 5/41
Abu Sueir 5/41 - 6/41
Idku 6/41 - 1/42
LG10 1/42 - 3/42
Idku 3/42 - 11/42
Ta Kali 11/42 - 6/43
Luqa 6/43 - 9/43
Bo Rizzo 9/43 - 2/44
Alghero 2/44 - 9/44
Foggia 9/44 - 3/45
Falconara 3/45 - 4/45

Right: **'V' of No. 272 Squadron over Malta where the squadron's main base was Luqa.**

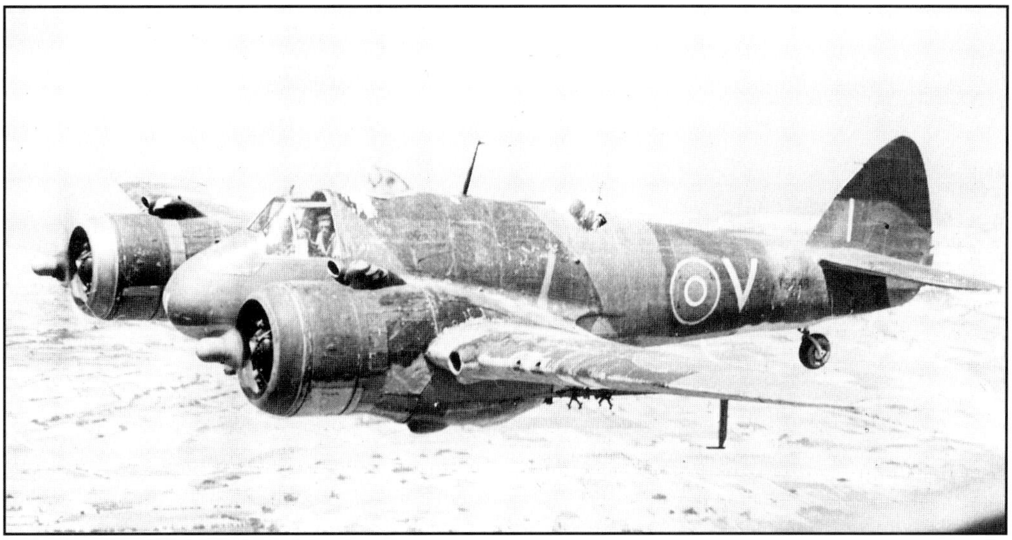

Sinking The Rex

On 7 and 8 September 1944, No. 272 Squadron mounted an attack on the MV *Rex*. Known as the 'Pride of Mussolini' the Italian between-the-wars luxury liner of 51,062 tons had at one time won the Atlantic Blue Riband for the fastest passenger liner crossing. It was drafted into wartime service and was to be used as a block-ship at Trieste. On 7 September 1944, a detachment of Beaufighters flew over to Falconara. The following day, on 8 September, the eight Beaufighters of No. 272 Squadron helped sink the ship in one attack, firing a total of 59 rockets and 4,000 cannon shells.

Right: **The eight crews who destroyed the Italian liner *Rex* on 8 September 1944.**

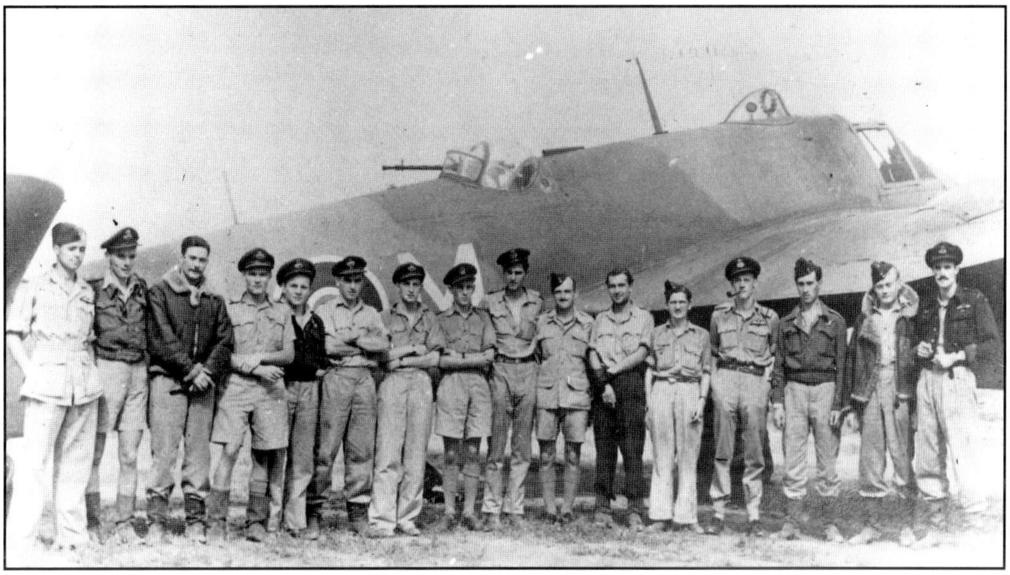

Below: **The *Rex*, under attack. It sustained 123 hits and rolled over to port in shallow water (inset).**

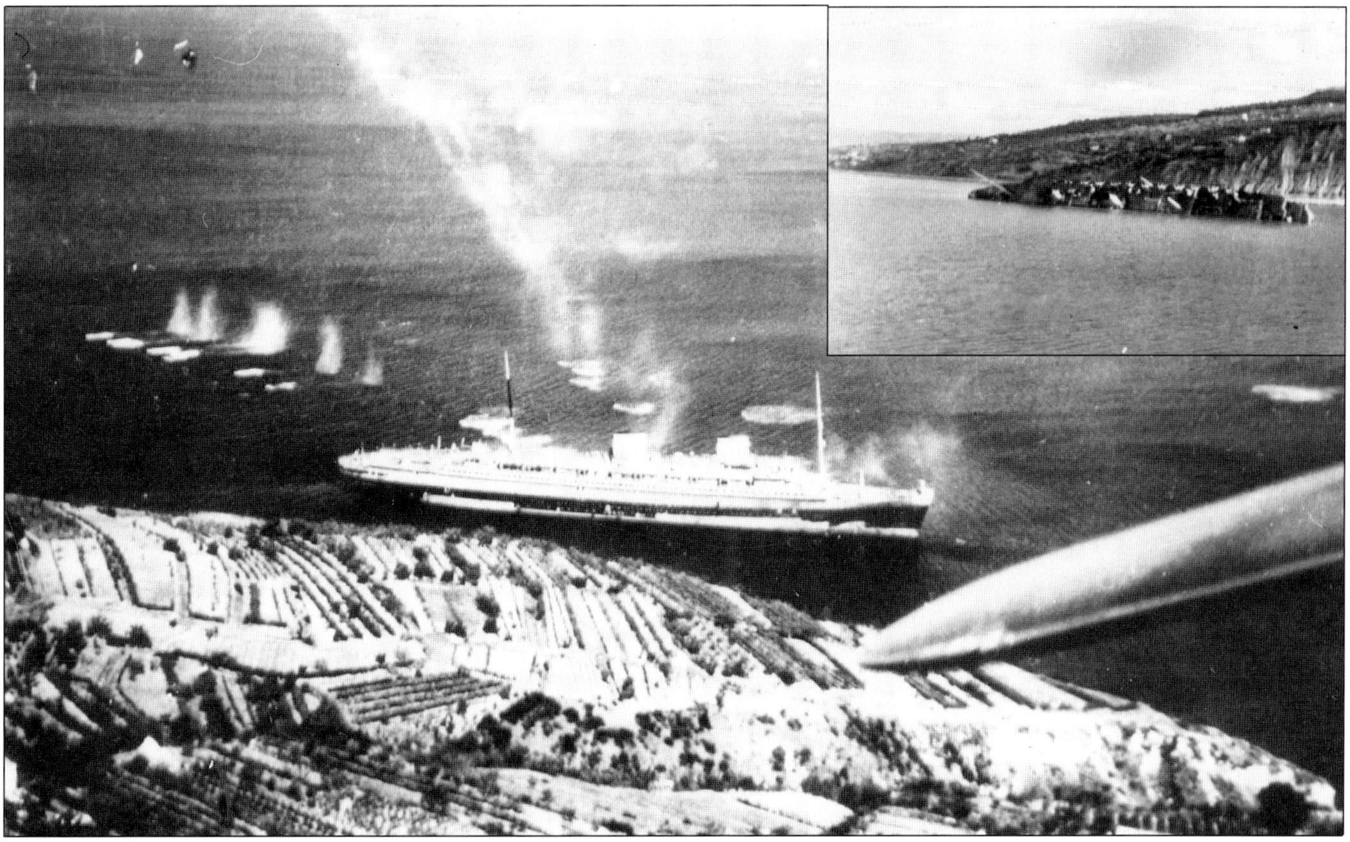

285 SQUADRON

Code Letters:
VG

Respice finem
(Consider the end)
Usage:
Mk.If
Sept 43 to Nov 44

Rôle:
Anti-aircraft target towing
Bases:
Woodvale 9/43 - 11/44

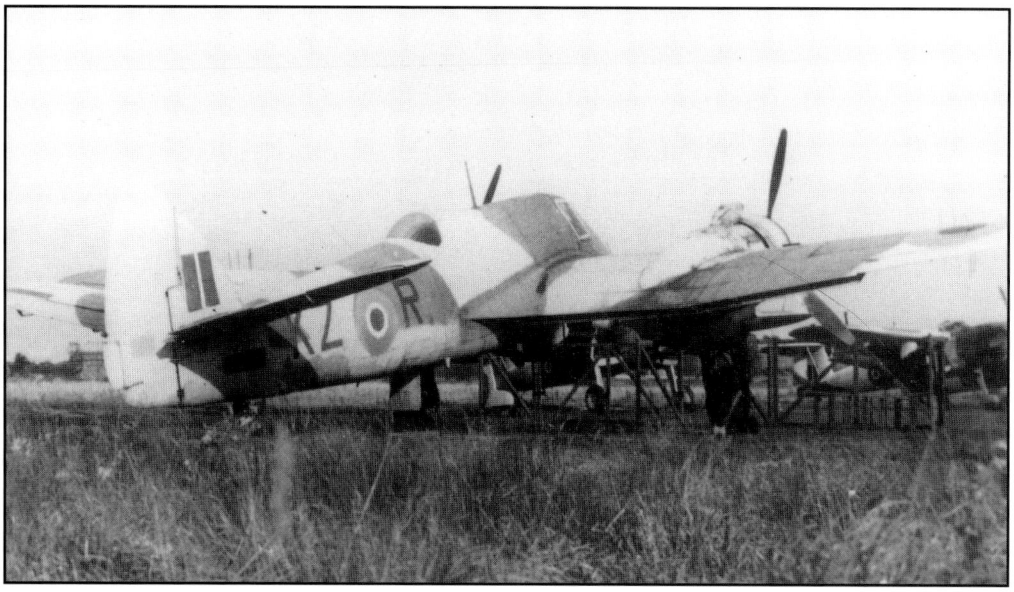
Above: **KZ-R of No. 287 Squadron at Locking in September 1945.**

287 SQUADRON

Code Letters:
KZ

C'est en forgeant
(Practice makes perfect)
Usage:
Mk.VIf
Sept 44 to July 45

Rôle:
Anti-aircraft target towing
Bases:
Gatwick 9/44 - 1/45
Redhill 1/45 - 5/45
Hornchurch 5/45 - 6/45
Bradwell Bay 6/45 - 7/45

288 SQUADRON

Code Letters:
RP

C'est en forgeant
(Practice makes perfect)
Usage:
Mk.VIf
Mar 44 to Nov 44

Rôle:
Anti-aircraft target towing
Bases:
Collyweston 3/44 - 11/44

Below: **One of No. 307 (Polish) Squadron's Mk.VIfs bringing General Sikorski, the Commander in Chief to Exeter in September 1942. No. 307 Squadron under the command of Squadron Leader J Antonowicz began to replace their venerable Defiants with Merlin engined Mk.IIs in August 1941.**

The first successful combats for the squadron came on 1 November 1941 when Sergeants Turanski and Ostrowski intercepted two Do217s and claimed them both destroyed. One Do217 did crash into the sea off Sidmouth, Devon. It was U5+EM of 4./KG2, briefed to attack Liverpool, whose crew of four was killed.

307 SQUADRON

Code Letters:
EW

'Lwowski'

Usage:
Mk.IIf
Aug 41 to May 42
Mk.VIf
May 42 to Jan 43

Rôle:
Night defence of Britain
Bases:
Exeter 8/41 - 1/43

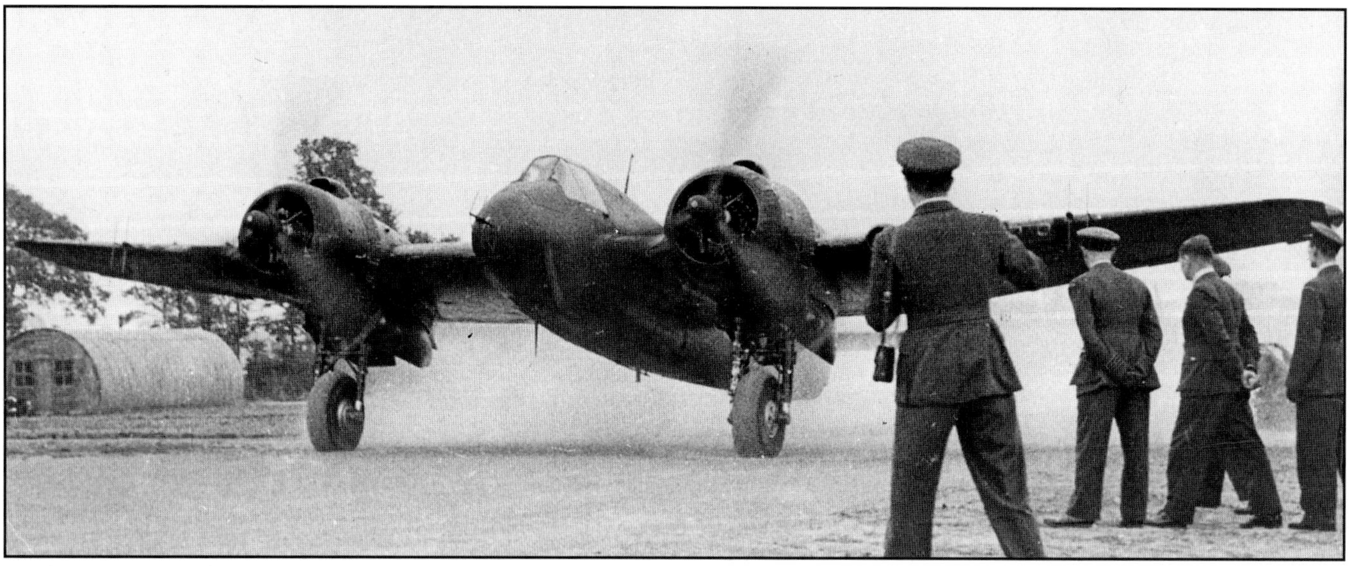

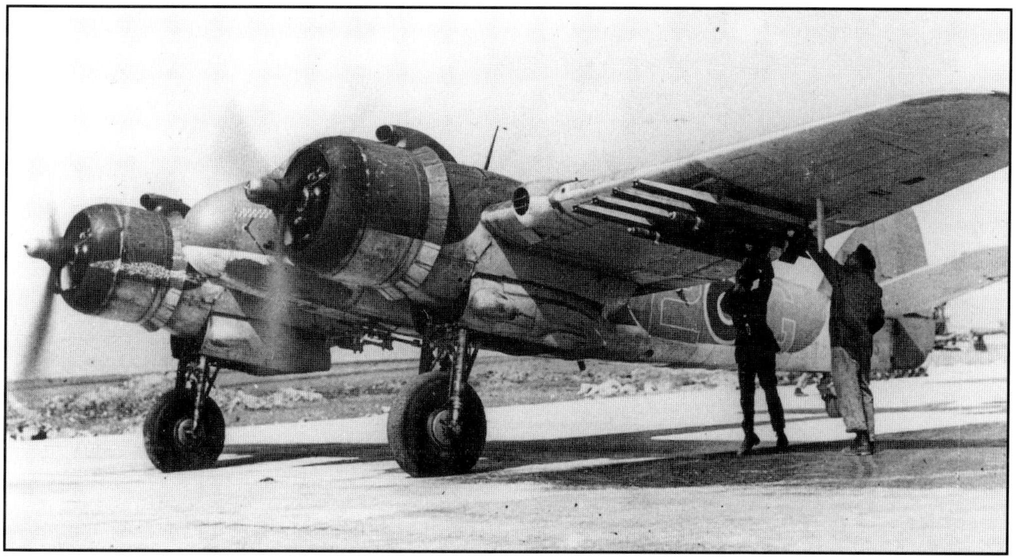

Above: **A Mk. XI of No. 404 Squadron. The '2' code on the fuselage was used by the squadron when part of the Wick Strike Wing.**

404

(Buffalo) SQUADRON RCAF

Code Letters:

EE & EO

(Ready to fight)

Usage:

Mk.IIf
Sept 42 to Apr 43
Mk.XI
Mar 43 to Nov 43
TF Mk.X
Sept 43 to Mar 45

Rôle:

Coastal Command Strike

Bases:

Dyce 9/42 - 1/43
Chivenor 1/43 - 4/43
Tain 4/43
Wick 4/43 - 5/44
Davidstow Moor 5/44 - 7/44
Strubby 7/44 - 9/44
Banff 9/44 - 10/44
Dallachy 10/44 - 3/45

Escort for HMS Belfast

On 28 July 1943 Squadron Leader Al de La Haye led Flying Officer Sid Shulemson on his first operation. They were to provide cover for HMS Belfast and her ten escorting ships heading towards Norway. The reconnaissance unit *Kustenfliegergruppe* 406 sent three of its BV138 seaplanes to search for the British force. Two Grumman Martlet fighters launched from HMS *Illustrious* shot down one of the seaplanes and then the two Beaufighters appeared and shot down the other BV138s. The three BV138s had vanished, so two more were sent out from Trondheim to head towards the Shetland Isles, but they too fell foul of No. 404 Squadron's Beaufighters. Flying Officers Keefe and Flight Sergeant Miller were now patrolling the Belfast and shot both down.

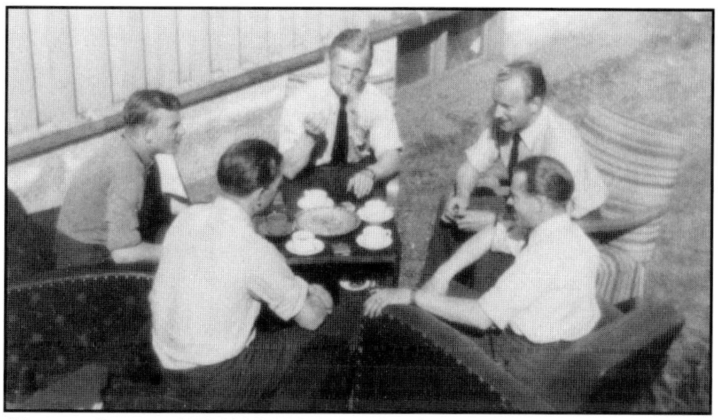

Above: **Crew of BV138 K6+BK of 2./Kuflgr 406 shot down by Flying Officer Keefe. Three of the crew were rescued by a U-Boat which was sunk on 1 August and the crew captured**

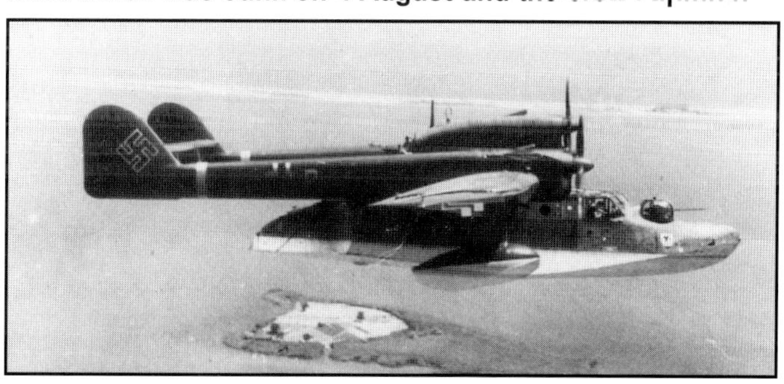

Above: **A BV138C-1 used for maritime reconnaissance.**

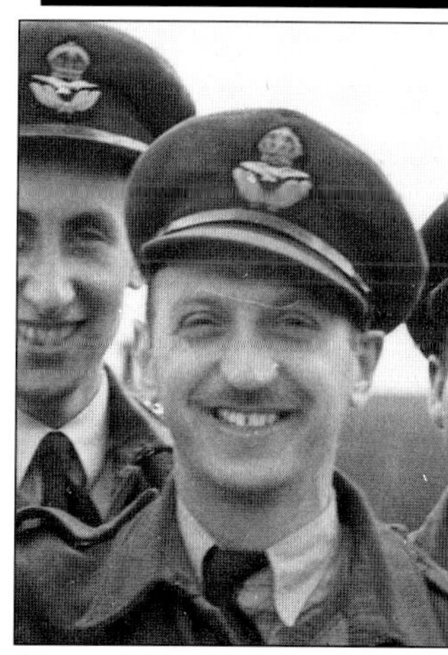

Above: **F/O Sid Shulemson.**

Below: **Sid 'Slippery' Shulemson's observer photographed the BV138 they had attacked going down into the sea.**

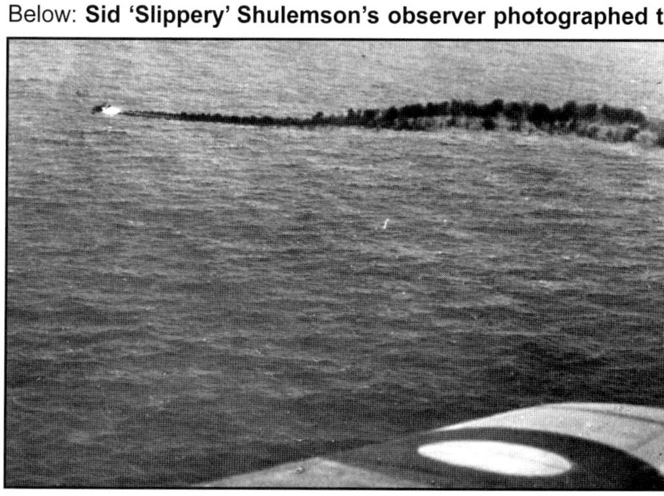

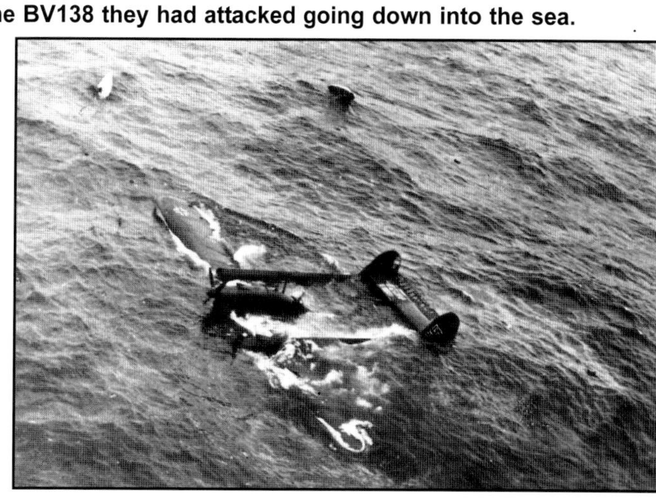

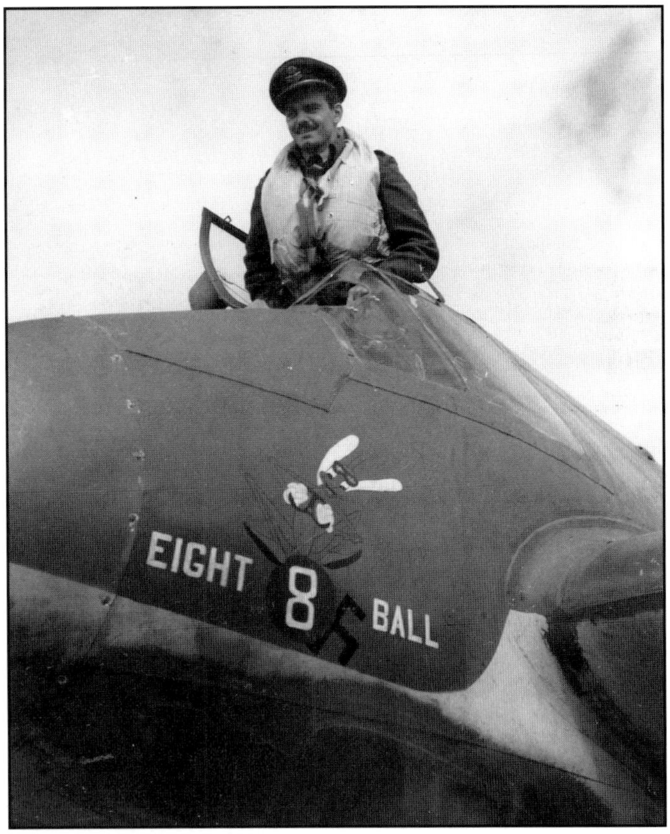

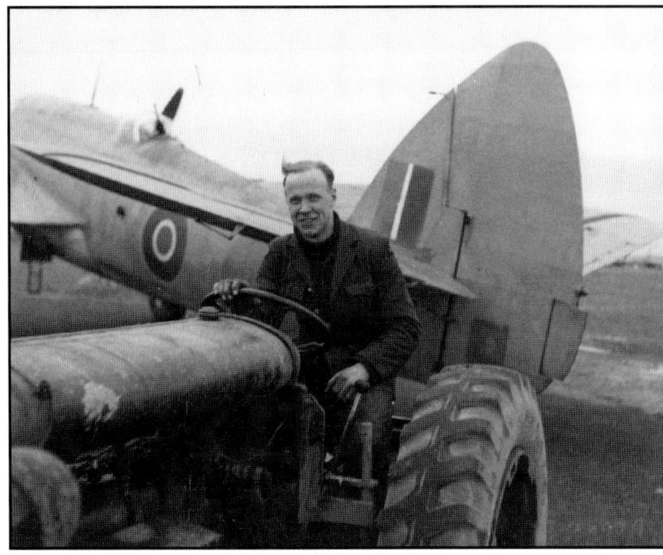

Above: **LAC C N White, one of No. 404 Squadron's ground staff, at the wheel of a tractor towing a Mk.XI. In July 1944 the squadron adopted the code 'EE' when Coastal Command abandoned its own marking scheme.**

Left: **Flying Officer J S Cummins in his Beaufighter Mk. XI 'Eight Ball' on 29 July 1943. In December 1943 he crashed a Beaufighter on take-off from Wick after its engines failed. The aircraft burst into flames and his navigator, 'Red' McGrath pulled him to safety, although both suffered burns. For his bravery 'Red' was awarded the George Cross. Later he was instrumental in saving his commanding officer, Ken Gatward (see opposite).**

Below: **No. 404 Squadron, in July 1943. The refreshments are being provided by a Church of Scotland van.**

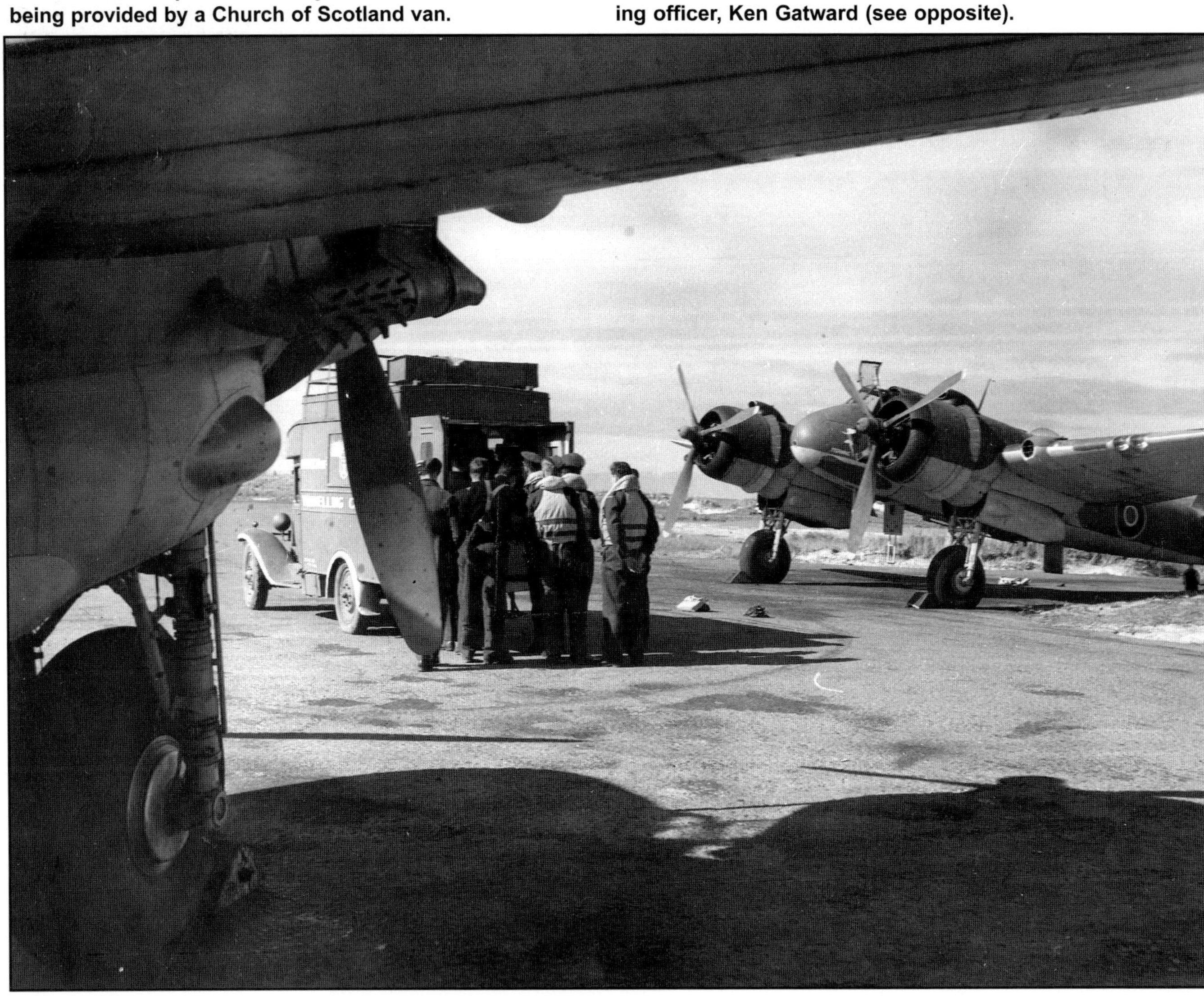

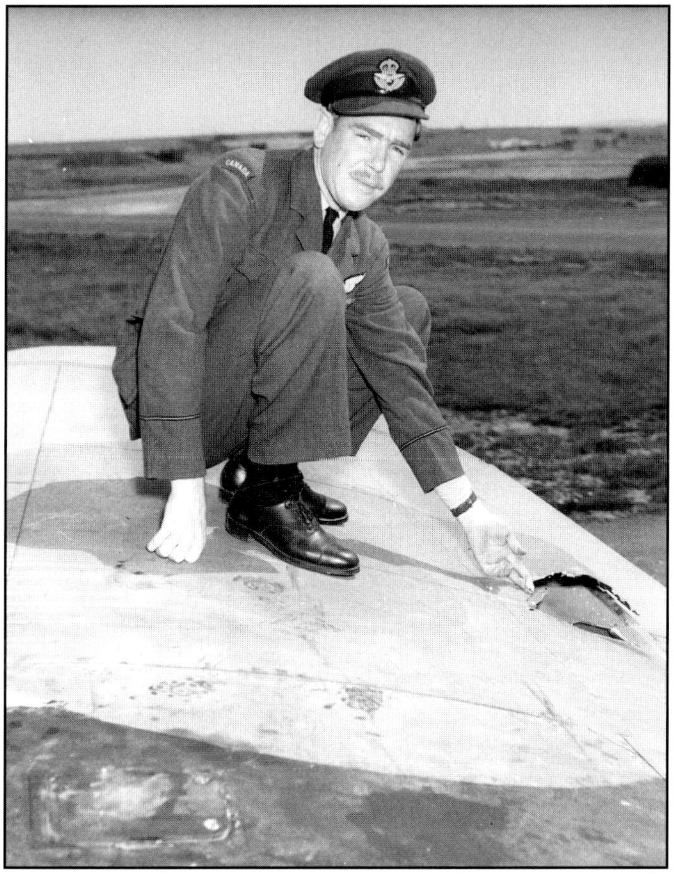

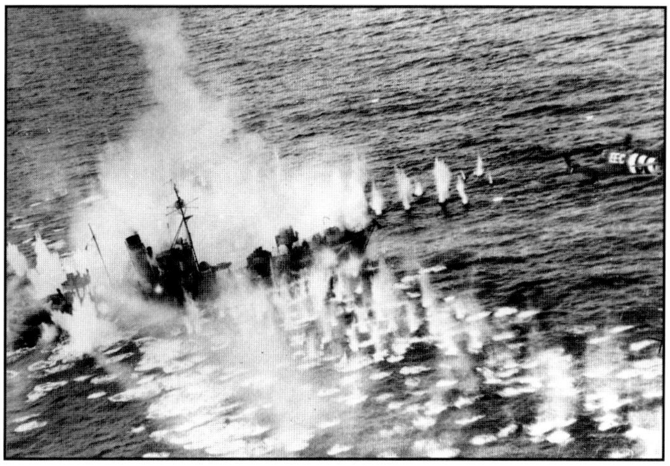

Above: **EE-C bedecked in invasion stripes over flies a flak ship during an attack off Christiansand on 15 October 1944. On this day No. 404, together with Nos. 144, 235 and 248 Squadrons making up the Banff Strike Wing, sank the Norwegian tanker *Inger Johanne* and the flak ship Vp1605 *Mosel.***

Left: **Flying Officer 'Red' McGrath, Gatward's navigator, points out the flak damage sustained on 14 August 1944 to Wing Commander Gatward's TF Mk.X. This was Gatward's last operation and both he and McGrath had been wounded by the flak over the French coast at Arachon. The Beaufighter was almost unflyable and McGrath used the fire axe to jam the control column to the left so that Gatward could use the throttles and limp back home.**

Below: **Rockets under Beaufighter TF Mk.X NE355 EE-H of No. 404 Squadron at Davidstow Moor. The Davidstow Moor Strike Wing existed from May to August 1944 to provide cover for the D-Day landings and subsequent operations in the Western Approaches and comprised of Nos 404 and 144 Squadrons.**

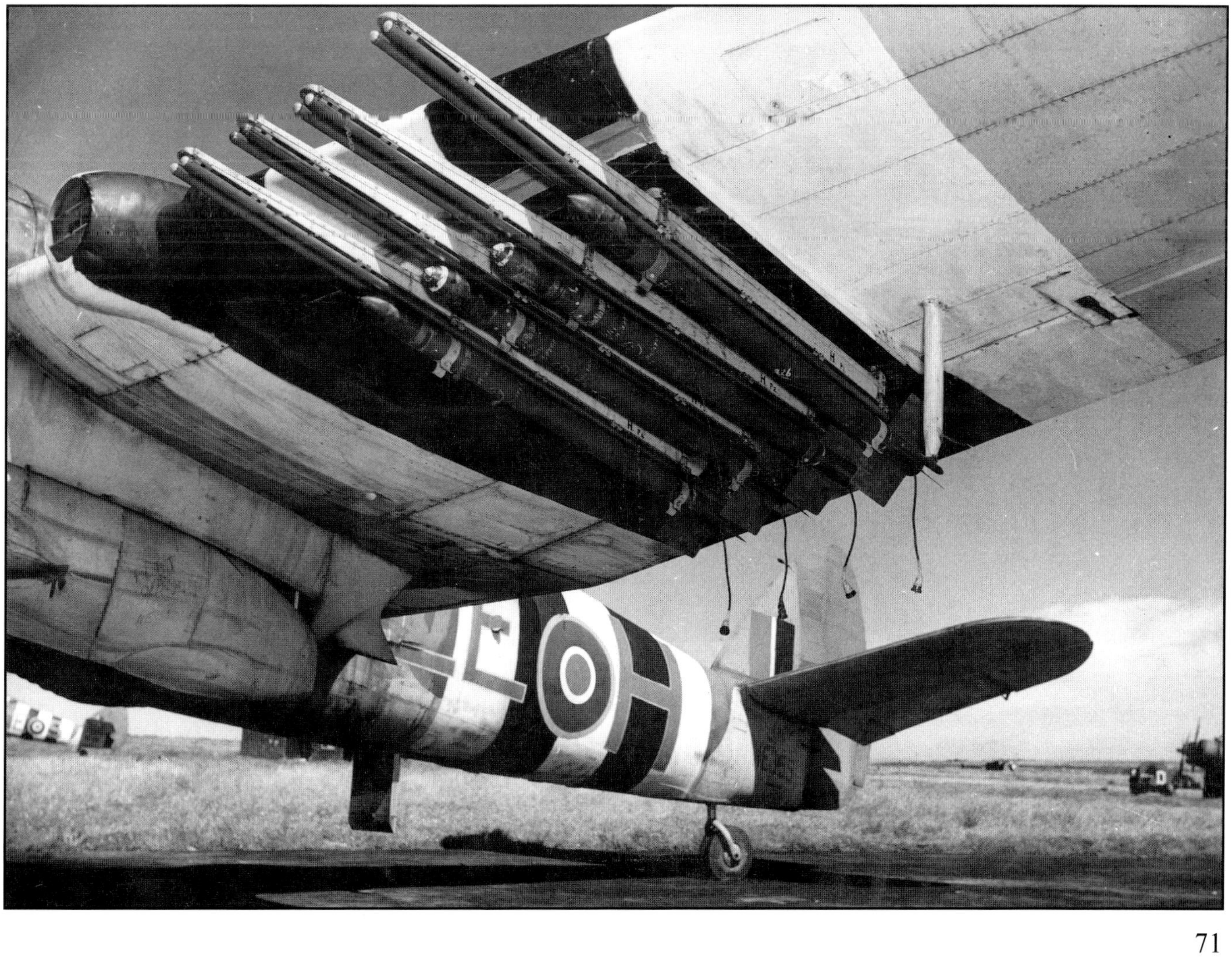

406

(Lynx) SQUADRON RCAF

Code Letters:

HU

Usage:

Mk.IIf
June 41 to July 42
Mk.VIf
June 42 to Aug 44

Rôle:

Night defence of Britain

Bases:

Acklington 5/41 - 2/42
Ayr 2/42 - 6/42
Scorton 6/42 - 9/42
Predannack 9/42 - 12/42
Middle Wallop 12/42 - 3/43
Valley 3/43 - 11/43
Exeter 11/43 - 4/44
Winkleigh 4/44 - 8/44

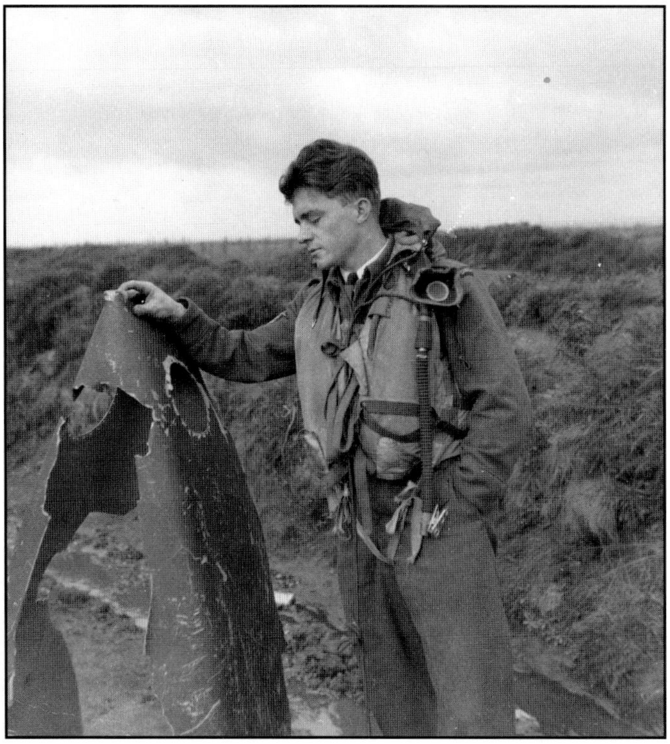

Above: **Flight Sergeant E S Fox, of No. 406 Squadron poses with tail of the Do 217 shot down by Squadron Leader Furse on the night of 25-26 September 1942. U5+IH of 1./KG2 fell on to a house at St Just in Cornwall, not far from the squadron's base at Predannack.**

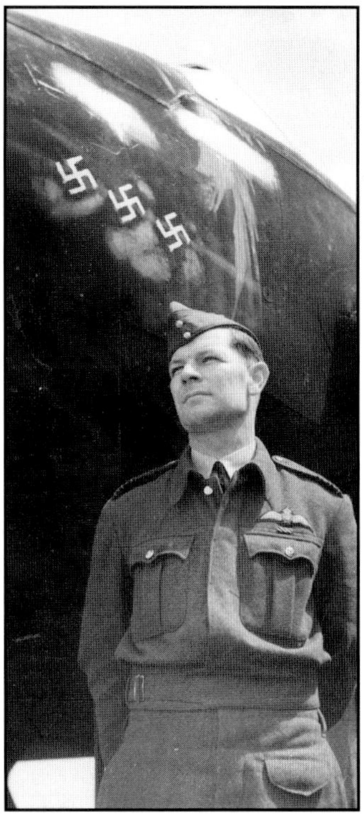

Above: **Wing Commander D G Norris, Commanding Officer of No. 406 Squadron at Scorton, Yorkshire, 2 July 1942.**

Below: **No. 406 Squadron at Acklington, Northumberland, on 15 September 1941. The code letters HU are clear.**

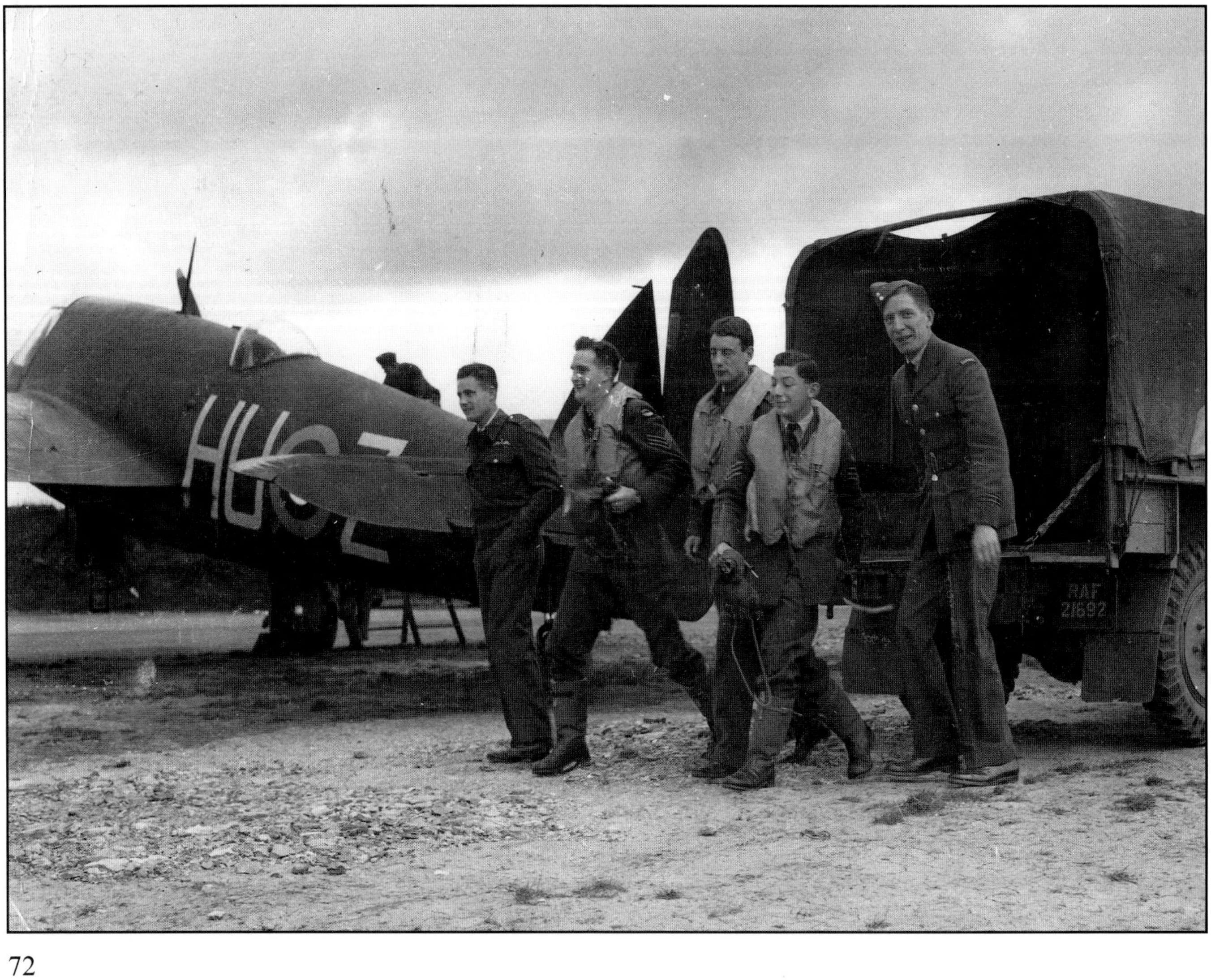

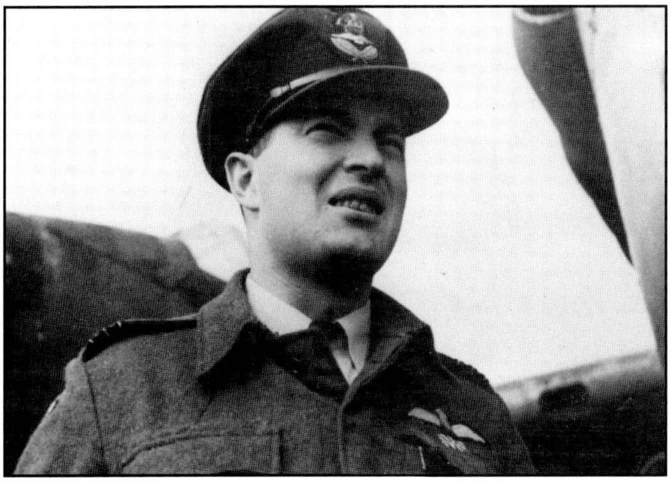

Left: **Robert 'Moose' Fumerton from Quebec, joined the RCAF in 1939 and was eventually posted to No. 406 Squadron in June 1941. On the night of 1-2 September 1941 he and his observer Sergeant Bing in Beaufighter Mk.IIf R2336 shot down a Ju88 of Stab III/KG30 over Northumberland. The aircraft, coded 4D+BD, broke up in the air over Bedlington and killed its four crew. This was the first night victory claimed by an RCAF pilot. In October 1941 Fumerton and Bing were posted to No. 89 Squadron in Egypt, again flying Beaufighters, and he became the highest scoring Canadian night fighter pilot, when operating from Malta in 1942 and 1943. In August 1943 he was posted back to No. 406 Squadron, as its commanding officer, with the rank of Wing Commander.**

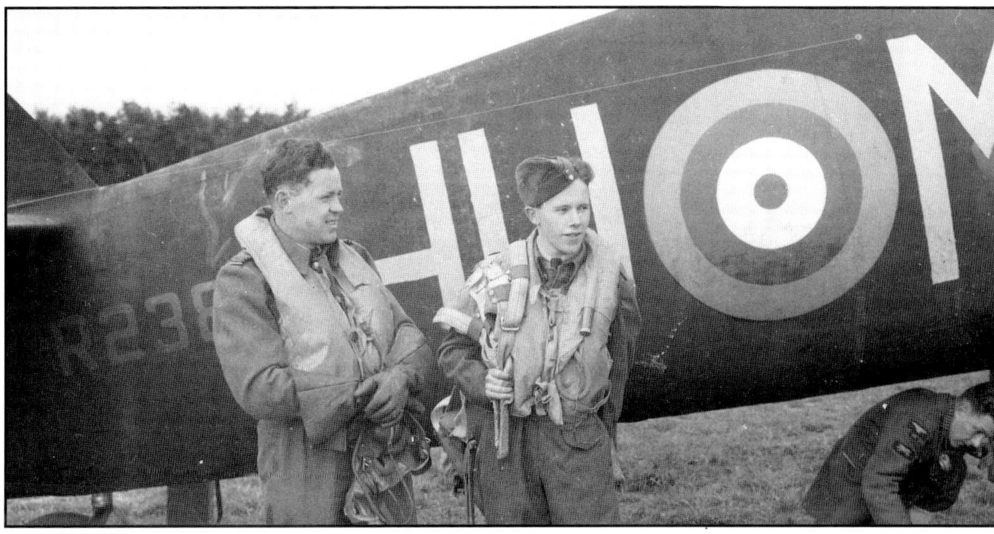

Right: **Flight Lieutenant Johnson and Sergeant Morris beside a Mk.IIf coded HU-M. The photo was taken on 15 September 1941 when the squadron was based at Acklington.**

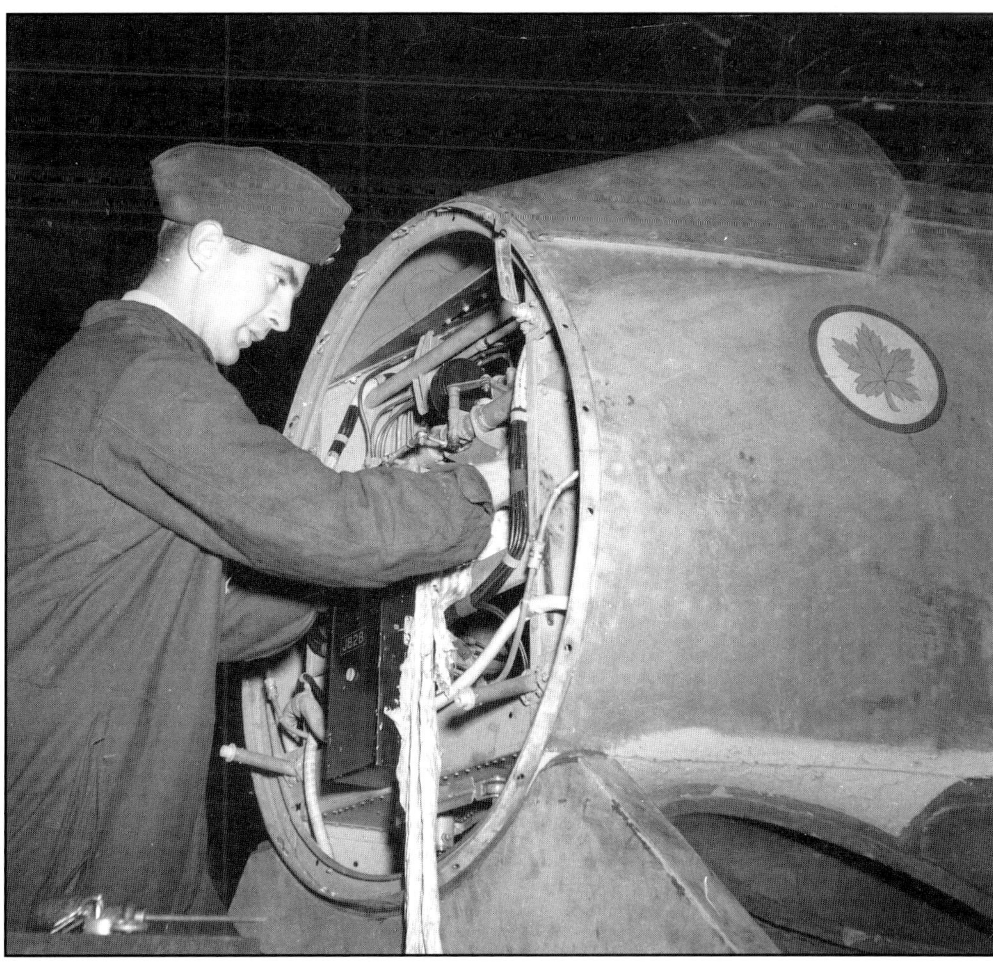

Right: **LAC Trusty working on the AI equipment of a Beaufighter Mk. VI at Valley, 22 April 1943. This unusual view shows well thew nose cone attachment points and gun troughs, as well as the Canadian Maple Leaf emblem.**
The area available for the AI equipment is evident in this photo. The first operational set was the AI Mk.IV, followed by the AI Mk.VII. The advent of 10cm AI brought the superior AI Mk.VIII and Mk.IX. But even the Beaufighter could not carry the new American built SCR520. It was then decided to modify the SCR520 by using parts from the British AI Mk.VIII to save space, thus creating the AI Mk.X.

409
(Nighthawk) SQUADRON RCAF

Code Letters:
KP

Usage:
Mk.IIf
Aug 41 to June 42
Mk.VIf
June 42 to Apr 44

Rôle:
Night defence of Britain

Bases:
Coleby Grange 7/41 - 2/43
Acklington 2/43 - 12/43
Coleby Grange 12/43 - 2/44
Acklington 2/44 - 4/44

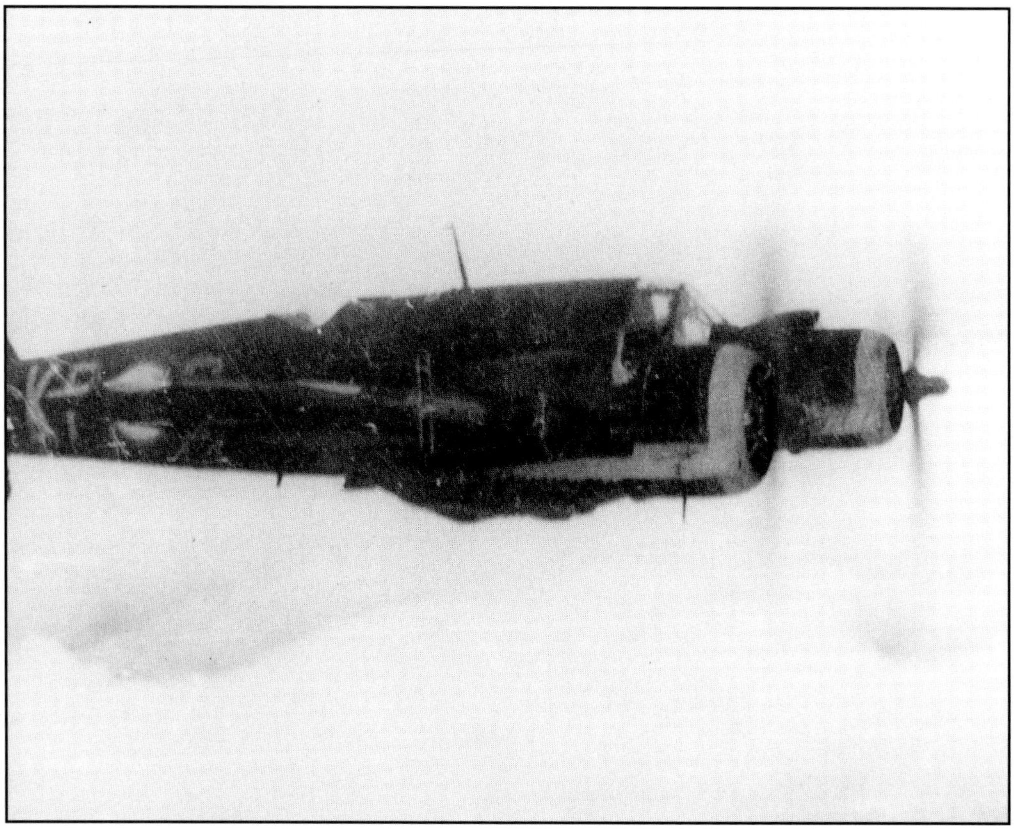

Above: **KP-S, a veteran Mk.If serving No. 409 Squadron RCAF, 1942. The squadron's commanding officer during 1941 and 1942 was Wing Commander P Y Davoud.**

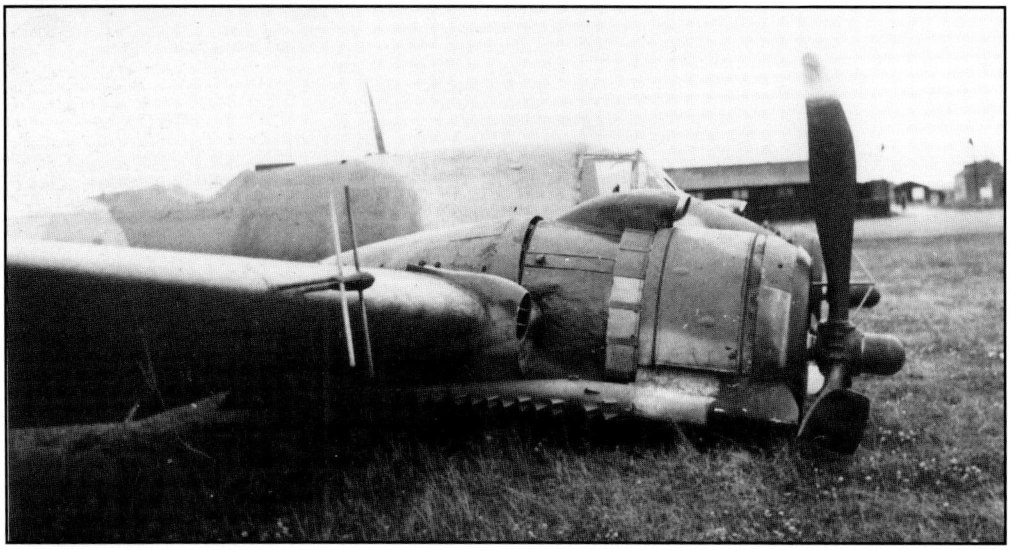

Left: **A Beaufighter Mk.VIf of No. 409 Squadron after ground looping at Acklington.**

Below left: **Mk.VIf X8216, KP-M, of No. 409 Squadron suffered engine failure on take off from Acklington on 12 June 1943 and broke-up on hitting the ground.**

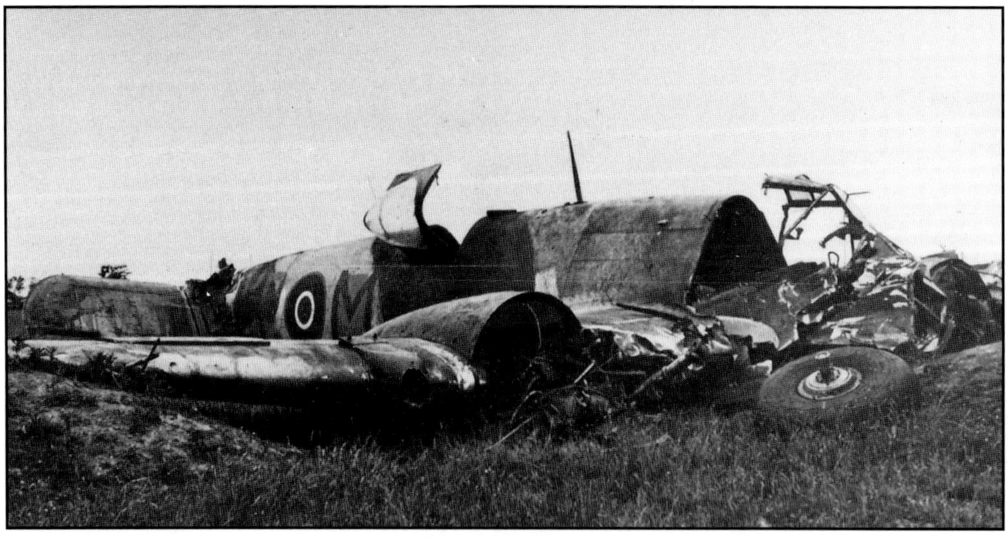

410
SQUADRON RCAF

Code Letters:
RA

Usage:
Mk.IIf
Apr 42 to Jan 43

Rôle:
Night defence of Britain

Bases:
Drem 4/42 - 9/42
Acklington 9/42 - 1/43

455 SQUADRON RAAF

Code Letters:
UB

Usage:
TF Mk.X
Dec 43 to May 45

Rôle:
Coastal Command Strike

Bases:
Leuchars 12/43 - 4/44
Langham 4/44 - 10/44
Dallachy 10/44 - 5/45

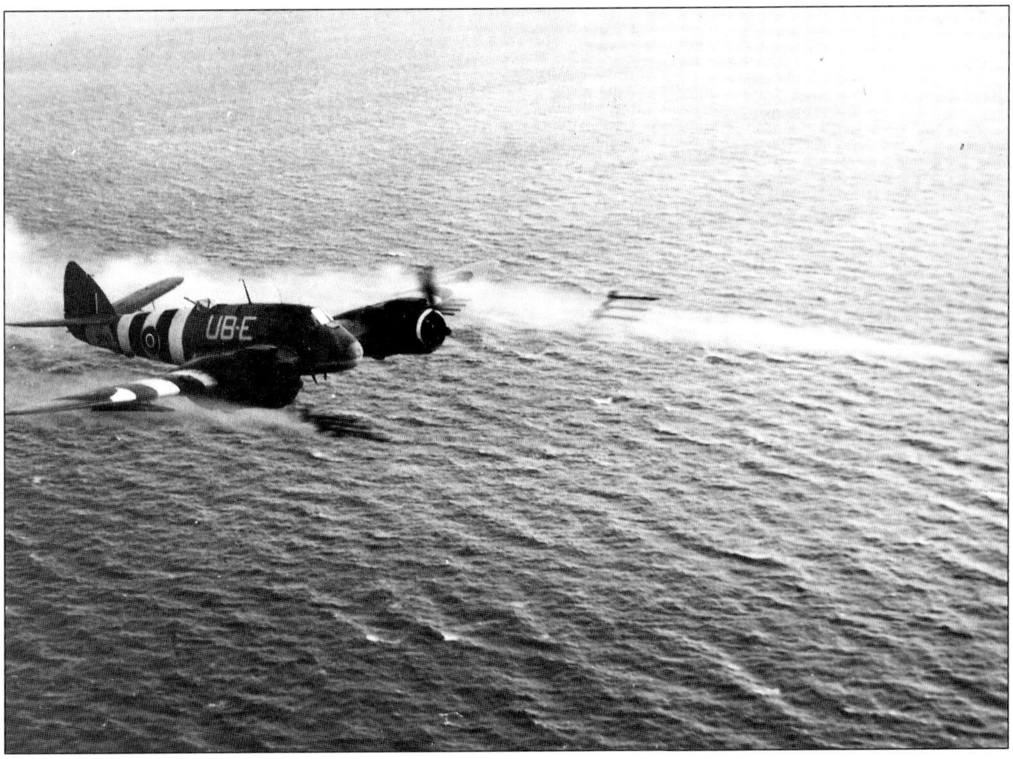

Above: **NE543, UB-E, lets fly with rockets over the Bay of Biscay in September 1944.**

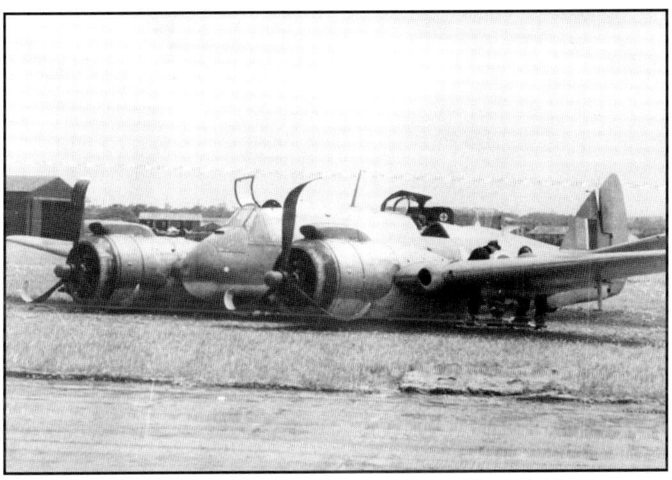

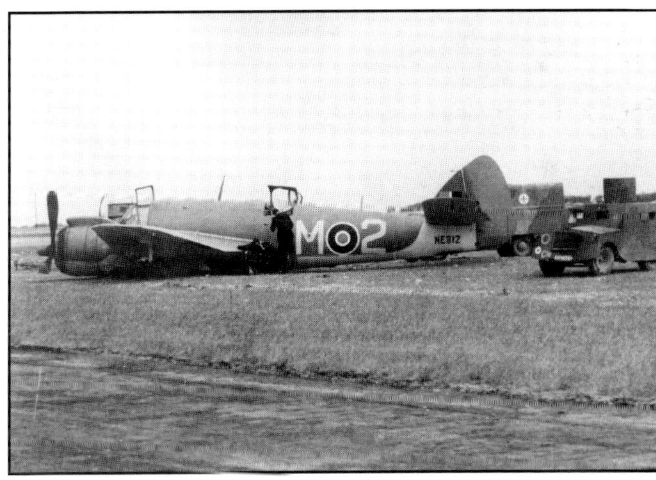

Above: **NE802, M-2, at Langham. Flying Officer I Masson and Flight Sergeant Knight crash landed on return from Borkum with flak damage on 14 May 1944. The squadron, with No. 489 Squadron, had sunk the MV *Vesta* and minesweeper M.435.**

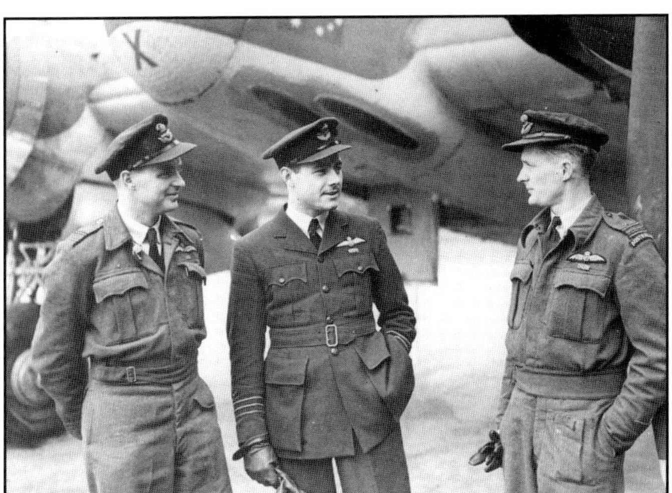

Above: **No. 455 Squadron's commanding officers, left to right: Squadron Leader A L Wiggins (OC A Flight) Wing Commander J N Davenport (OC Squadron) Squadron Leader C G Milson (OC B Flight) at Leuchars 1944.**

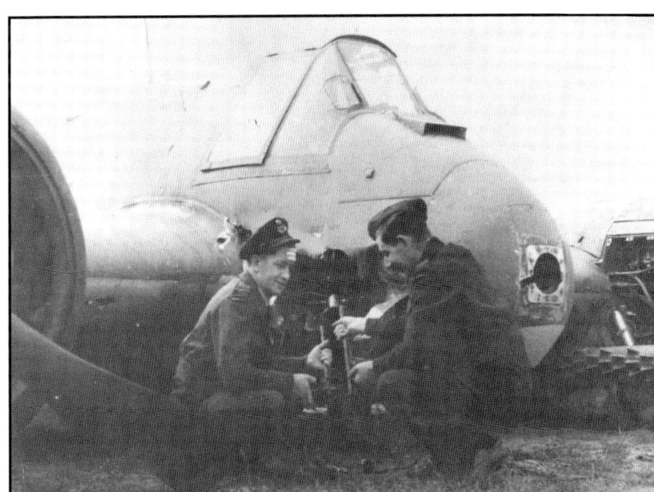

Above: **Flying Officer Steve Sykes (right) from New South Wales and his navigator Flying Officer Lee Turner of Adelaide returned on 12 September 1944 with part of a mast embedded in their Beaufighter. The attack had been against shipping off Den Helder.**

456 SQUADRON RAAF

Code Letters:

RX

Usage:

Mk.IIf
Sept 41 to Mar 43
Mk.VIf
July 42 to Jan 43

Rôle:

Night defence of Britain

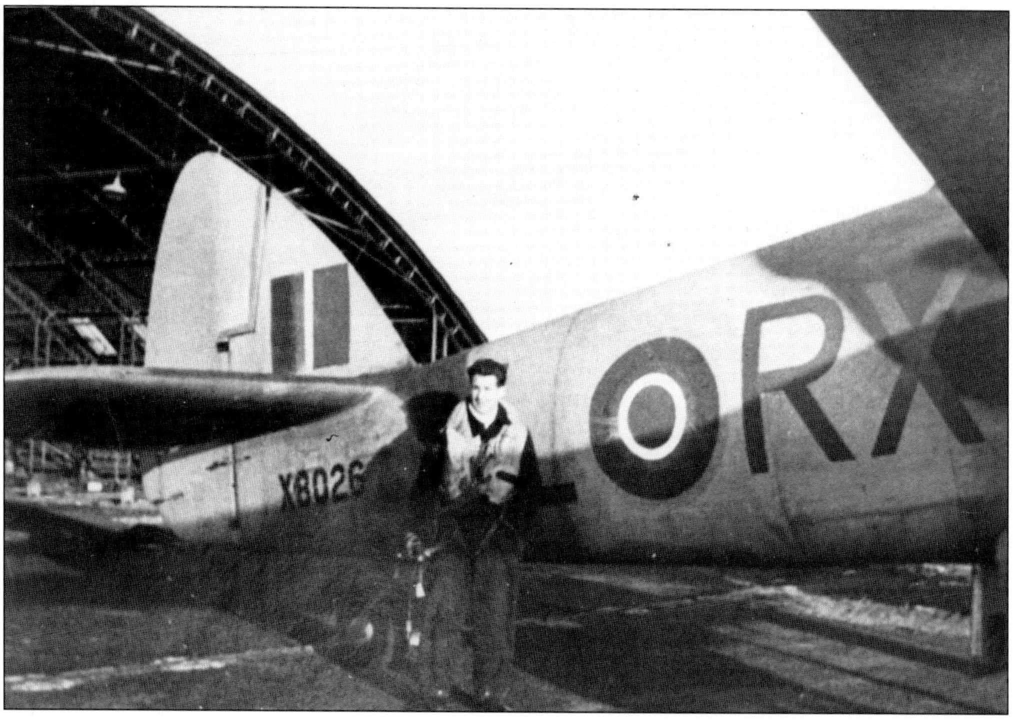

Right: **Mk.VIf X8026 served with No. 456 Squadron, then moved to No. 256 Squadron. It was wrecked when the pilot undershot landing at Woodvale on 10 March 1943.**

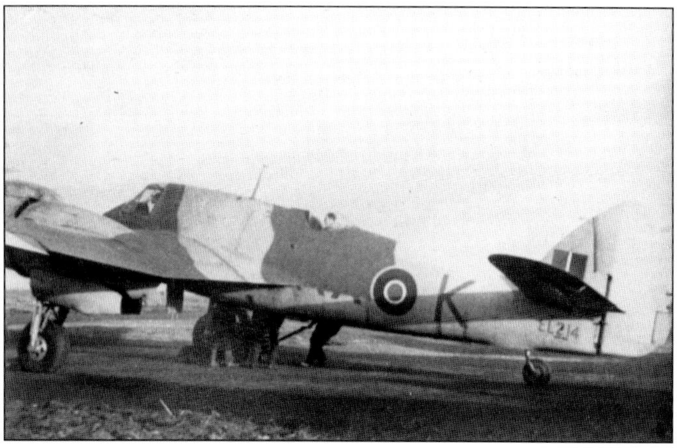

Above: **Mk.VIf EL214, RX-K, at Valley. On 30 January 1943 this aircraft dived into the sea during a camera gun exercise.**

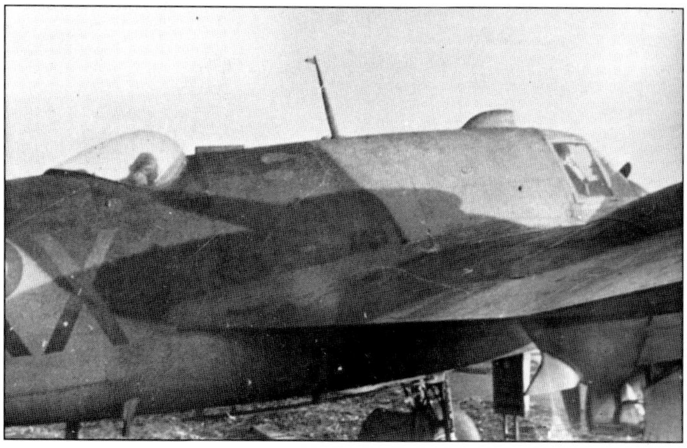

Above: **This close-up shows well the observer / navigator canopy and the camera gun fairing above the cockpit. The lower entrance hatch and ladder is open.**

Below: **Merlin engined Mk.IIfs photographed at RAF Valley while running up their engines.**

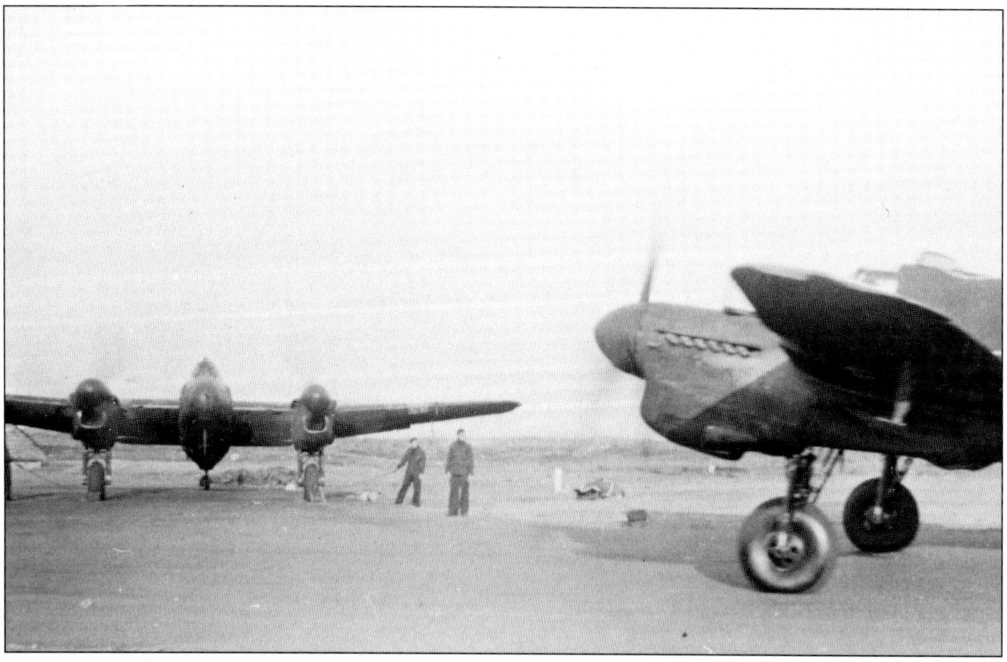

488 SQUADRON RNZAF

Code Letters:

ME

Usage:

Mk.IIf
Jun 42 to May 43
Mk.VIf
Mar 43 to Sept 43

Rôle:

Night Defence of Britain

Bases:

Church Fenton 6/42 - 9/42
Ayr 9/42 - 9/43

489 SQUADRON RNZAF

Code Letters:
P6

Usage:
TF Mk.X
Oct 43 to May 45

Rôle:
Coastal Command Strike

Bases:
Leuchars 10/43 - 4/44
Langham 4/44 - 10/44
Dallachy 10/44 - 5/45

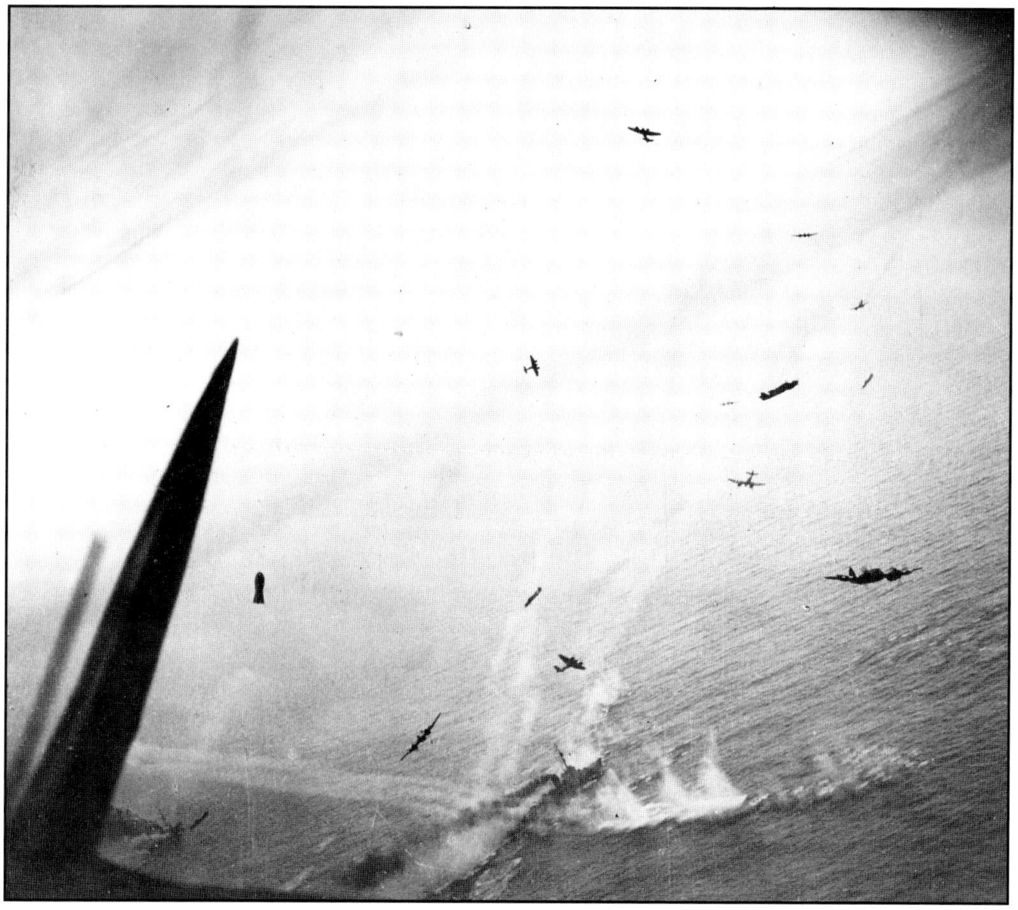

Left: **Nos. 489 and 455 Squadrons during an attack off Borkum, Heligoland, on 25 August 1944. One mine sweeper was sunk in the attack.**

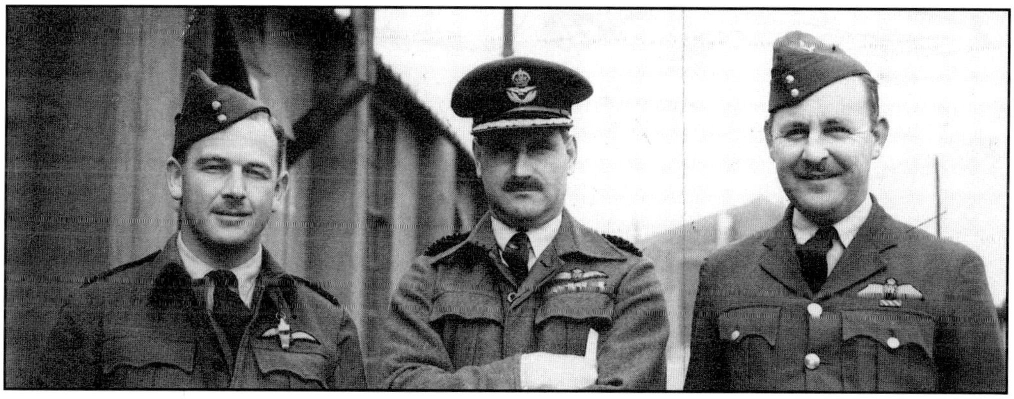

Left: **The commanding officers of No. 489 Squadron, left to right: Squadron Leader L A Robinson (Auckland) Group Captain A E Clouston (Moutoeka) Wing Commander C J S Dinsdale (Te Kuiti).**

Below: **The Langham Strike Wing (Nos. 455 and 489 Squadrons). The nearest aircraft carry the P6 code of No. 489 Squadron.**

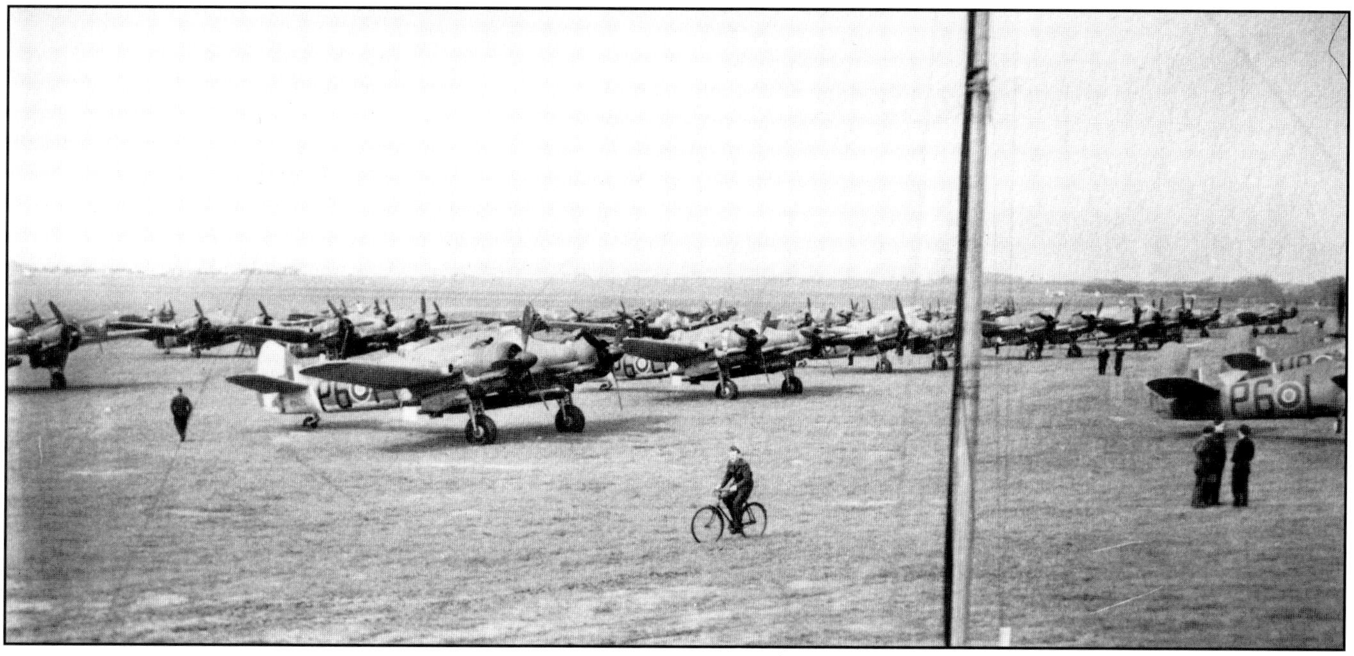

600

County of London SQUADRON

Code Letters:

BQ

Usage:
Mk.If
Sept 40 to Jun 41
Mk.IIf
Apr 41 to Apr 42
Mk.VIf
Mar 42 to Feb 45

Rôle:
Night defence of Britain, later Middle East

Bases:
Redhill 9/40 - 10/40
Catterick 10/40 - 3/41
Drem 3/41 - 4/41
Colerne 4/41 - 10/41
Predannack 10/41 - 9/42
Church Fenton 9/42 - 11/42
Blida 11/42 - 12/42
Maison Blanche 12/42 - 1/43
Setif 1/43 - 6/43
Luqu 6/43 - 7/43
Cassibile 7/43 - 9/43
Montecorvino 9/43 - 2/44
Marcianese 2/44 - 3/44
Pomigliano 3/44 - 4/44
Marcianese 4/44 - 6/44
La Banca 6/44
Voltone 6/44 - 7/44
Follonica 7/44
Rosignano 7/44 - 8/44
Falconara 8/44 - 12/44
Cesenatico 12/44 - 2/45

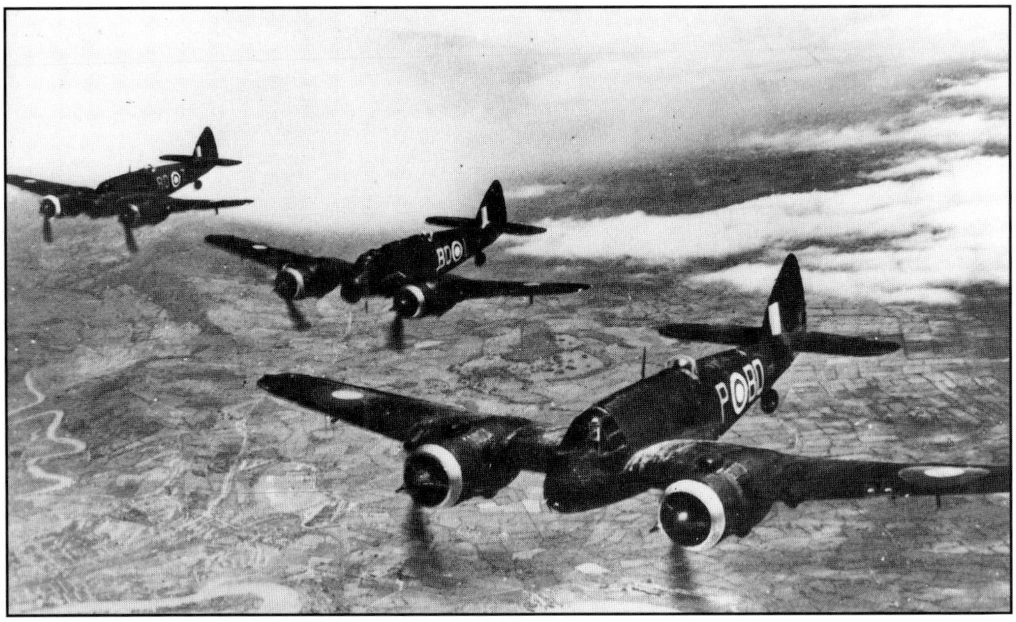

Above: **No. 600 Squadron Mk.Ifs from Colerne photographed on 23 May 1941. The squadron left Britain for the Middle East in November 1942**

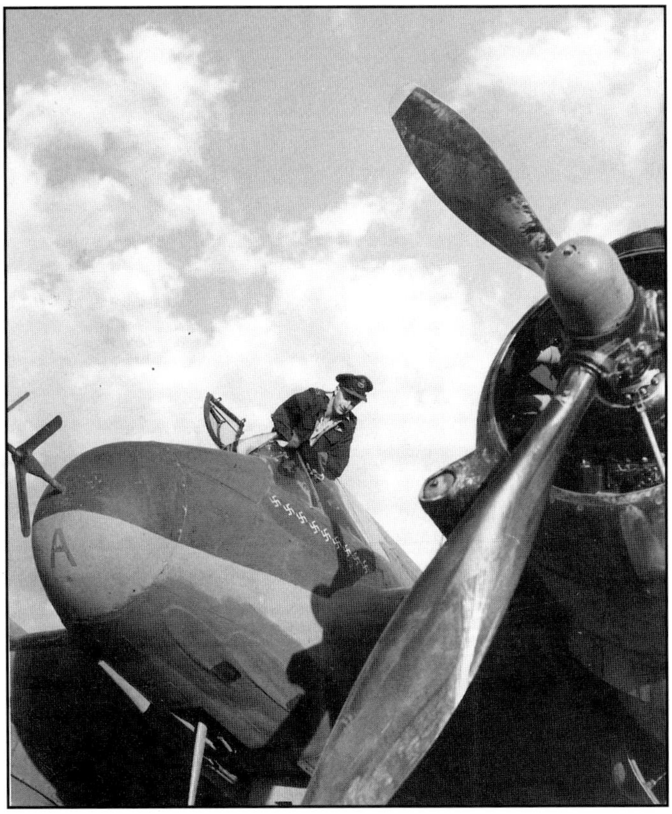

Left: **Wing Commander C P Green's Mk.VIf 'A-Apple' with nine victory swastika symbols. Green commanded 'A' Flight of No. 600 Squadron from November 1941 to June 1942, but left to command No. 125 Squadron. In December 1942 he moved to the Middle East to command No. 600 Squadron. He destroyed six German bombers and damaged another three before being promoted to Group Captain and given command of No. 1 Mobile Operations Unit, Desert Air Force, in January 1944.**

Below: **V8388, a Mk.VIf with No. 600 Squadron had a long life, but was struck off charge on 31 March 1945.**

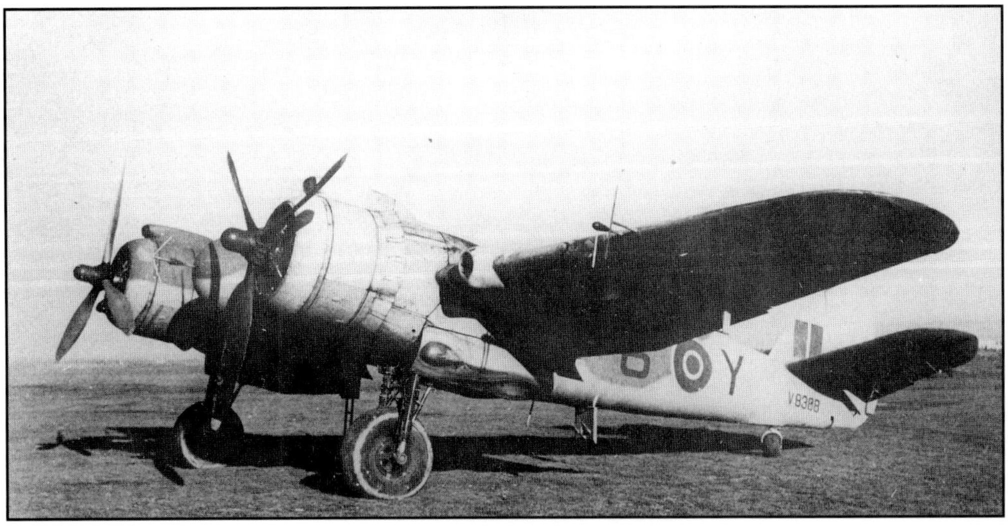

515

SQUADRON

Usage:
Mk.IIf
June 43 to Apr 44

Rôle:
Radar counter measures

Bases:
Hunsdon 6/43 - 12/43

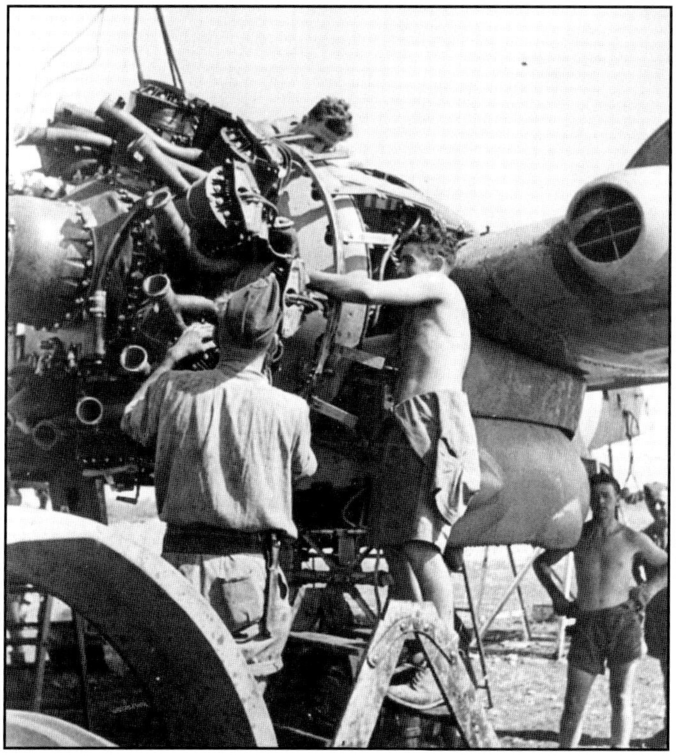

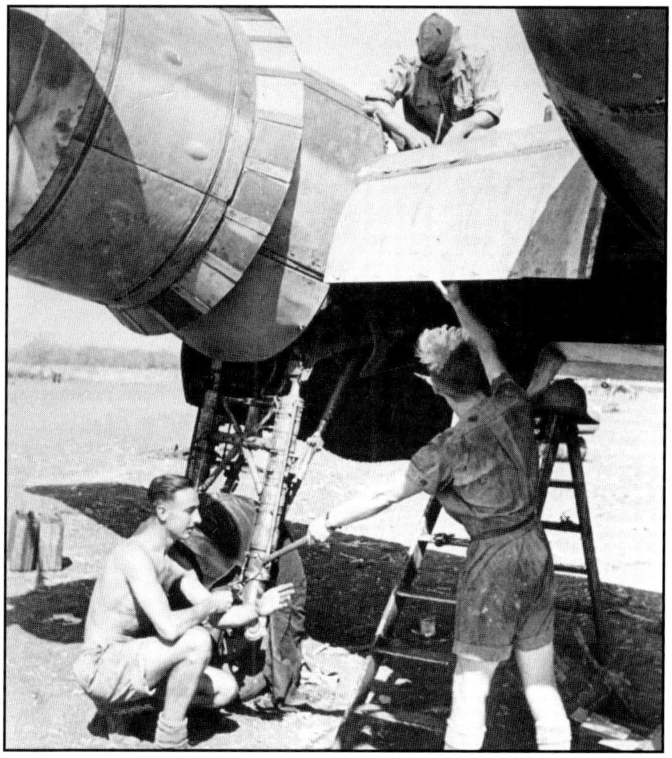

Above: **No. 600 Squadron's nomadic existence in the Mediterranean led to the squadron moving regularly from one air strip to the next with few facilities. Routine maintenance had to be carried out and the ground crews worked wonders with what they had available.**

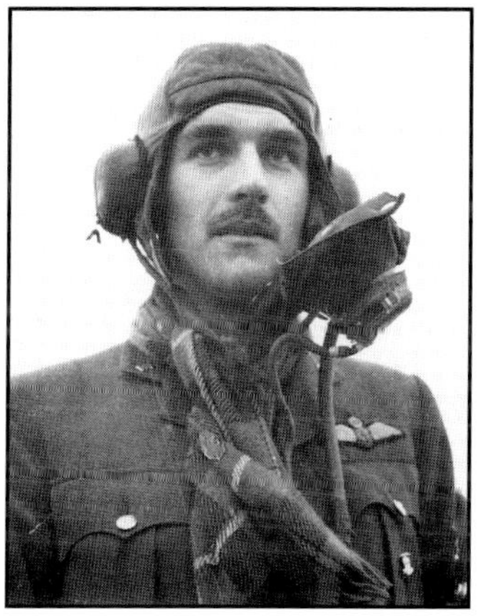

Left: **A D McN Boyd, later Wing Commander and CO of No. 219 Squadron, achieved No. 600 Squadron's first Beaufighter victory on 16 May 1941 when he and his Operator, Pilot Officer A J Glegg, shot down Ju88 V4+IR of 7./KG1 over Devon. He shot down four more enemy aircraft with the squadron and a further five with No. 219 Squadron.**

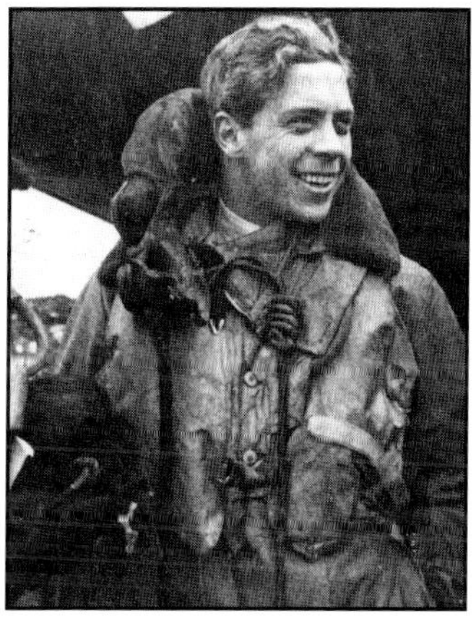

Left: **F D Hughes had a successful career with No. 264 Squadron flying Defiants and then with No. 125 Squadron as flight commander. He joined No. 600 Squadron in December 1943 and claimed ten enemy aircraft before moving back to Britain in early 1944. His total of claims by the war's end was eighteen aircraft destroyed and two damaged.**

Below: **The contrasting conditions faced by No. 600 Squadron, from torrential rain to baking sun.**

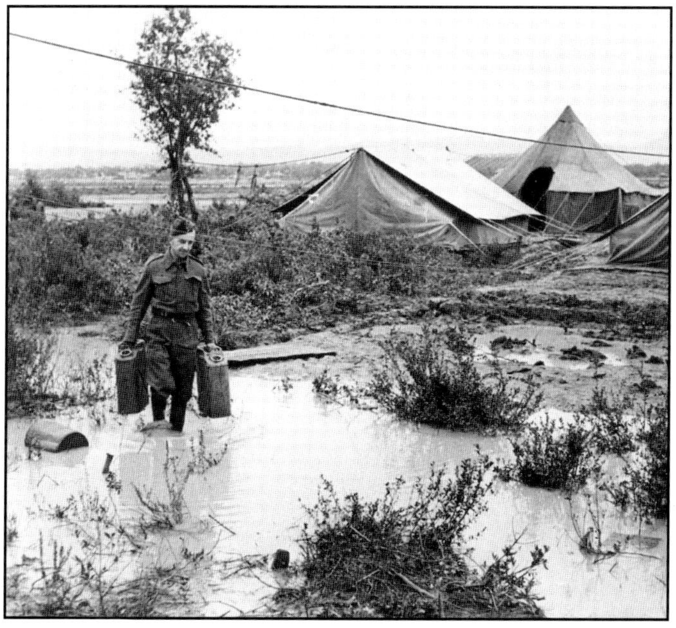

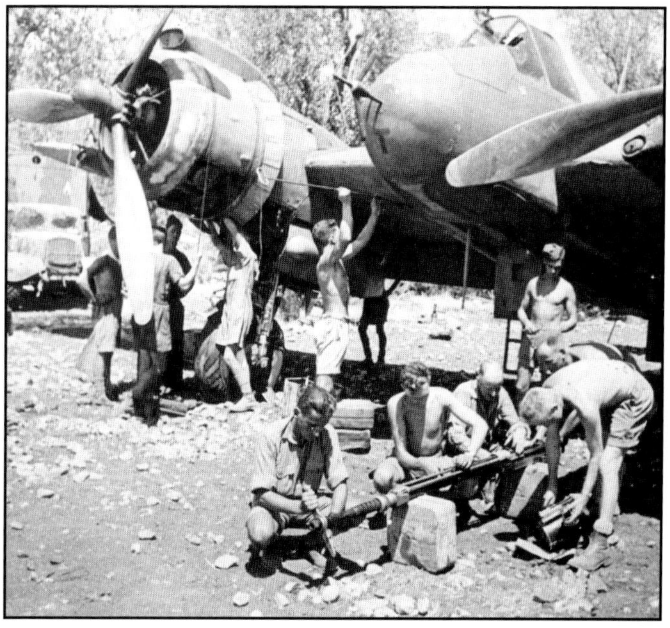

603

City of Edinburgh SQUADRON

Gin ye daur
(If you dare)

Usage:
Mk.Ic
Feb 43 to Nov 43
Mk.VIc
Feb 43 to Oct 43
Mk.XI
Aug 43 to Oct 43
TF Mk.X
Oct 43 to Dec 44

Rôle:
Shipping strikes in the Mediterranean

Bases:
Idku 2/43 - 3/43
Misurata West 3/43 - 9/43
Bo Rizzo 9/43 - 10/43
LG91 10/43
Gambut 3 10/43 - 12/44

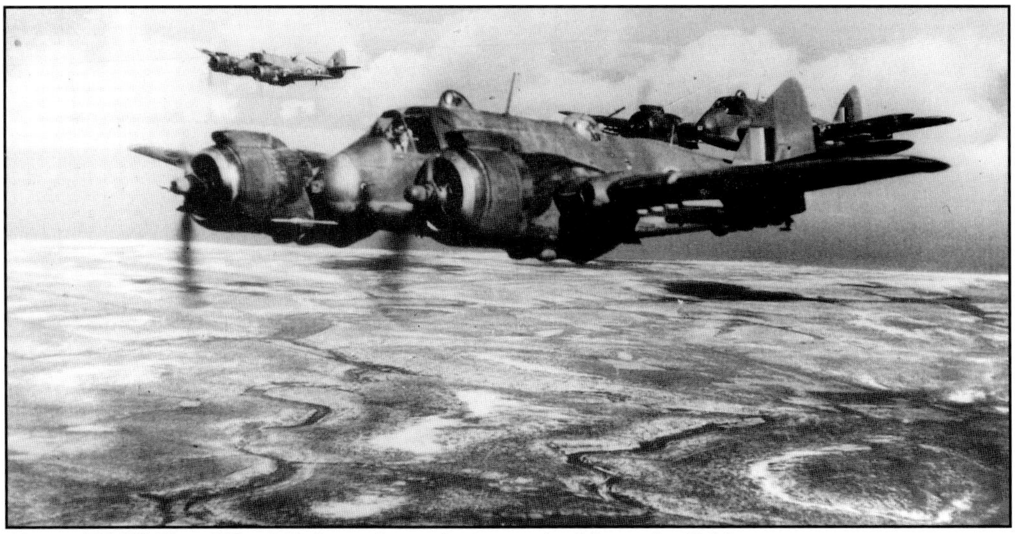

Above: **TF Mk.Xs of No. 603 Squadron photographed in early 1944.**

Right: **In the first six months of 1944, the squadron's TF Mk.Xs fitted with extra tanks had an endurance of eight hours. Every airfield and port in Northern Greece came within range.**

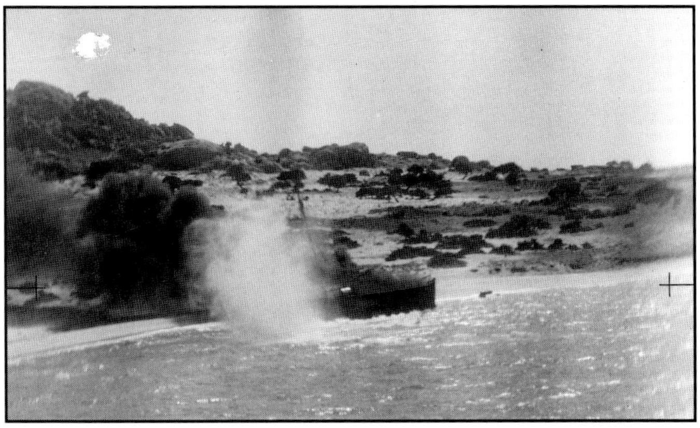

Below: **A float equipped Ju52 set on fire and sunk near Thermia, Greece in 1943.**

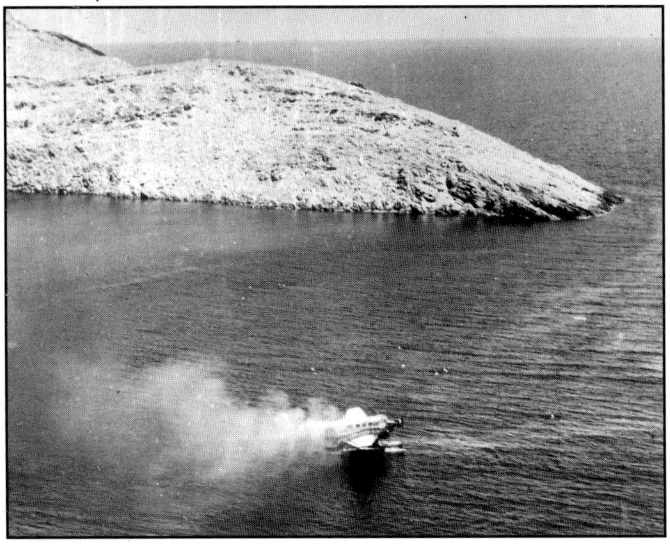

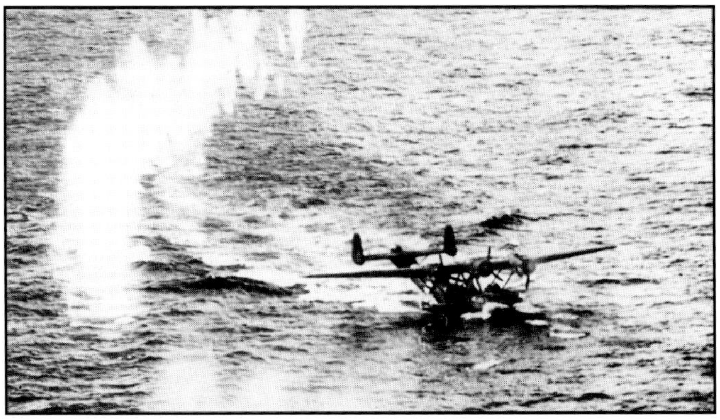

Above: **A Dornier Do24 brought down north of Crete during a sweep.**

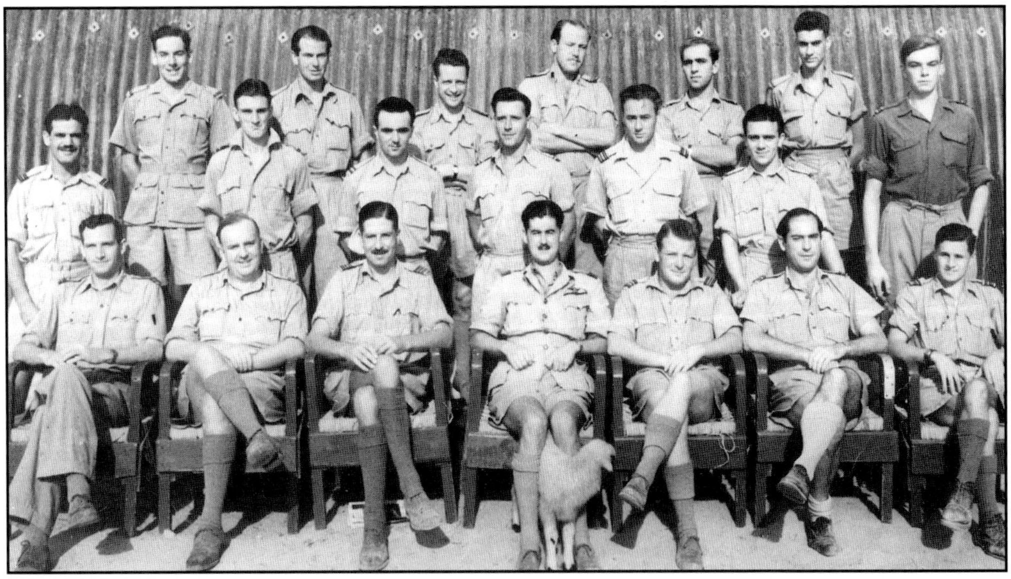

Left: **Wing Commander Foxley-Norris (seated centre) with aircrew officers of No. 603 Squadron at Gambut in Autumn 1944.**

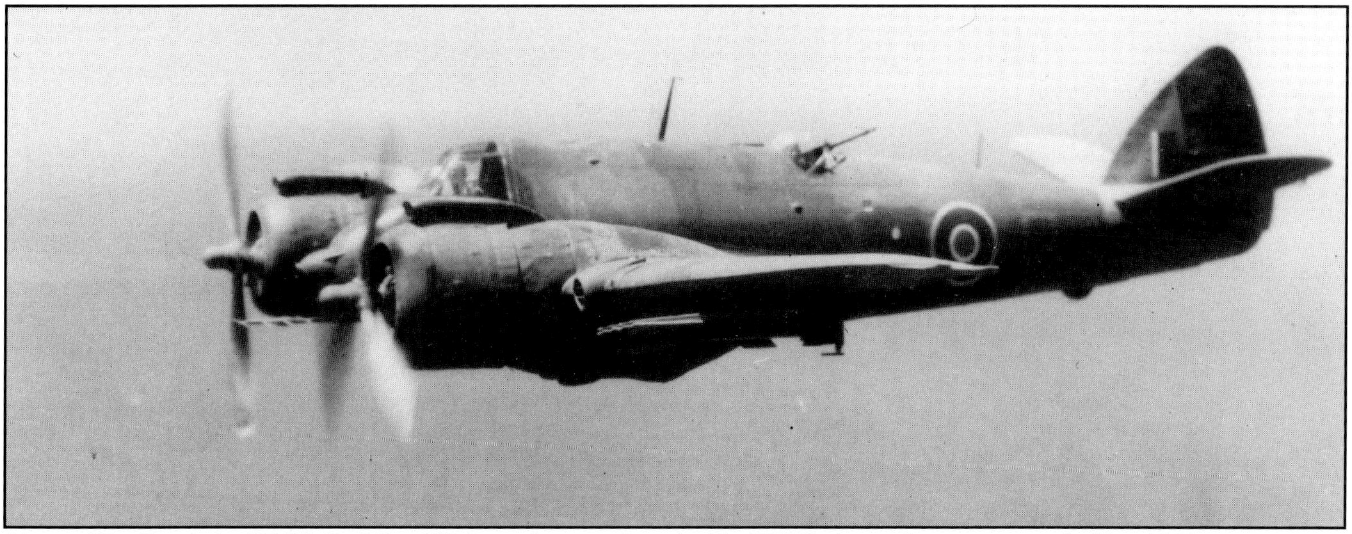

Above: 'G - George' a TF Mk.X of No. 603 Squadron equipped with ASV Radar and nose camera in May 1944.

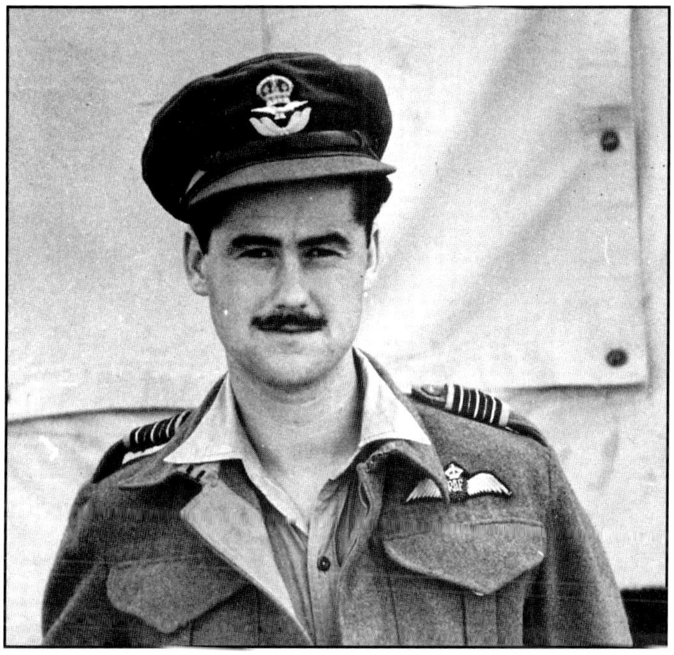

Above: **Wing Commander Christopher Foxley-Norris took command of No. 603 Squadron after leaving No. 252 Squadron in September 1944. (Foxley-Norris)**

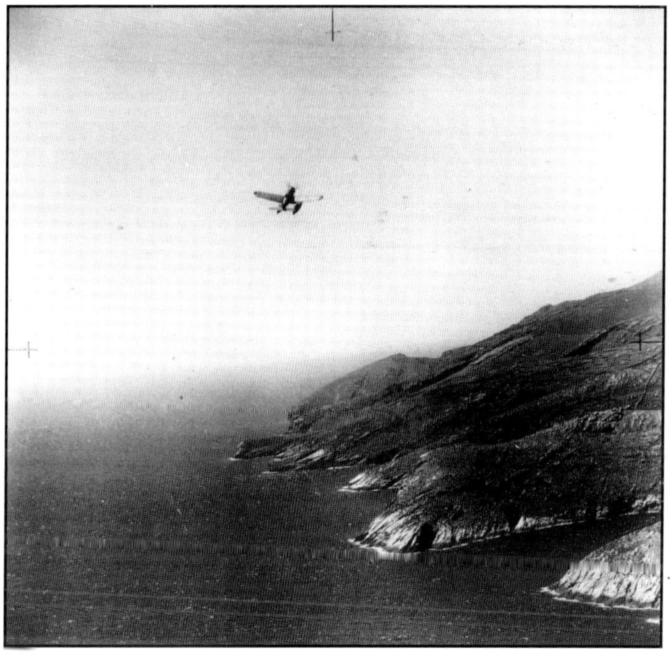

Above: **An Arado Ar196 float plane was no match for a Beaufighter. This one had the misfortune to be caught out on 6 September 1944.**

Right: **TF Mk.X NE400 'H - Harry' again with the prominent 14 inch nose camera.**

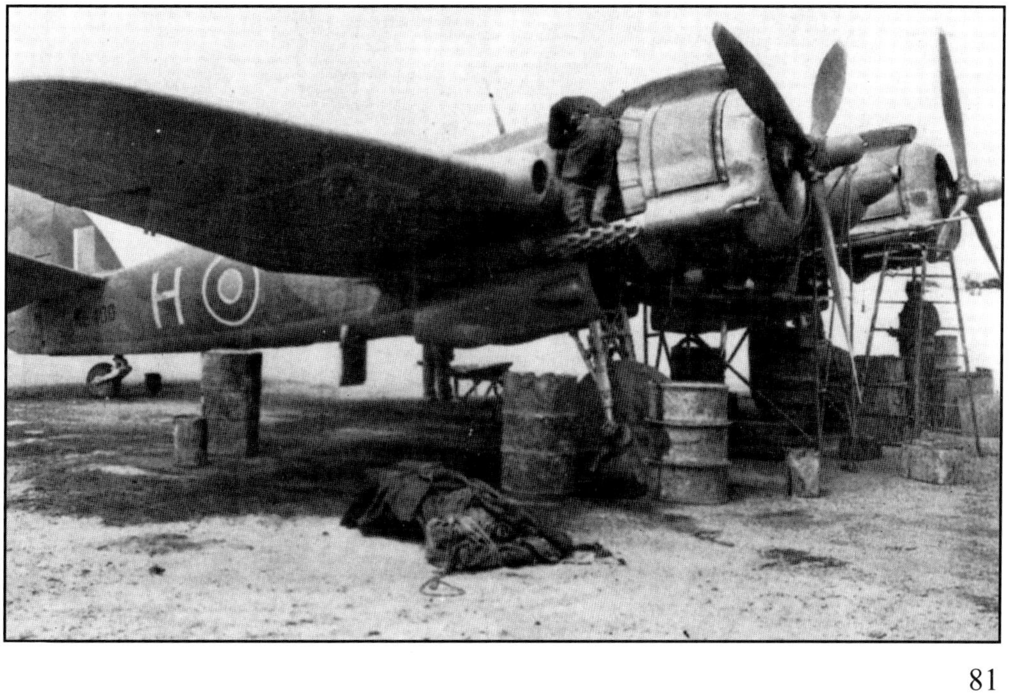

Below: **The symbol of a rocket and slide rule carried by NE400.**

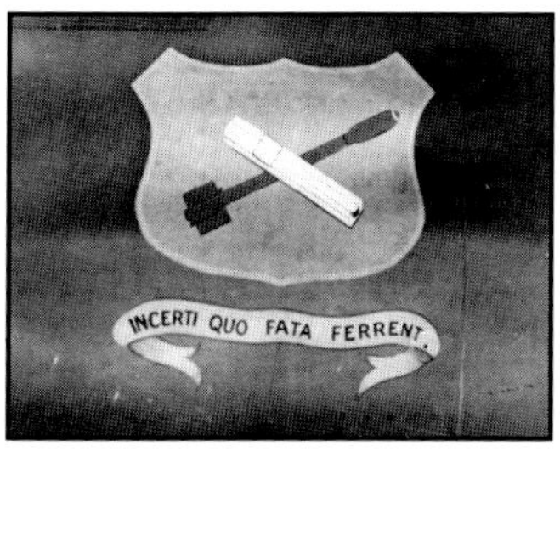

604

County of Middlesex

SQUADRON

Si vis pacem, para bellum

(If you want peace, prepare for war)

Usage:

Mk.If

Sept 40 to Apr 43

Mk.VIf

Apr 43 to Apr 44

Rôle:

Night defence of Britain

Bases:

Middle Wallop 9/40 - 8/42

Warmwell 8/42 - 12/42

Predannack 7/42 - 2/43

Ford 2/43 - 4/43

Scorton 4/43 - 4/44

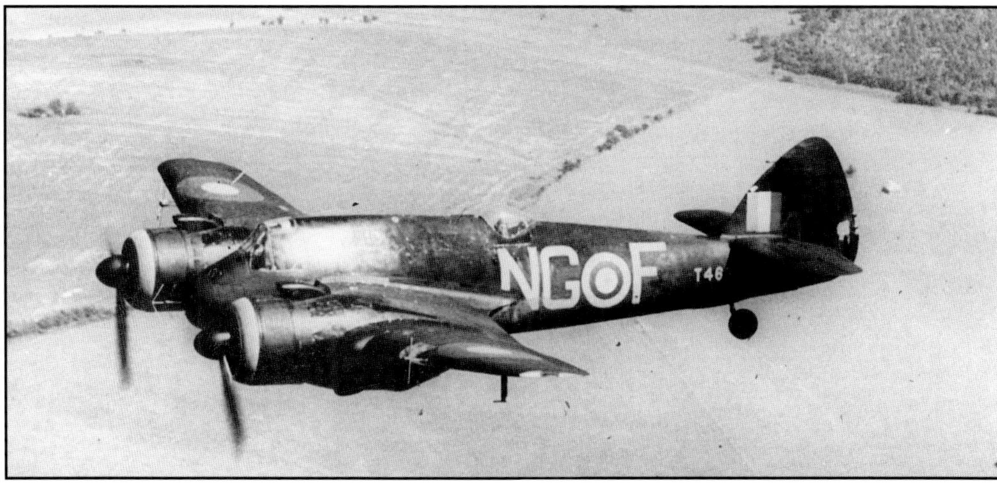

Above: **T4638, a Mk.If built by Fairey at Heaton Chapel, flew into the ground while trying to land at Middle Wallop on 10 November 1941.**

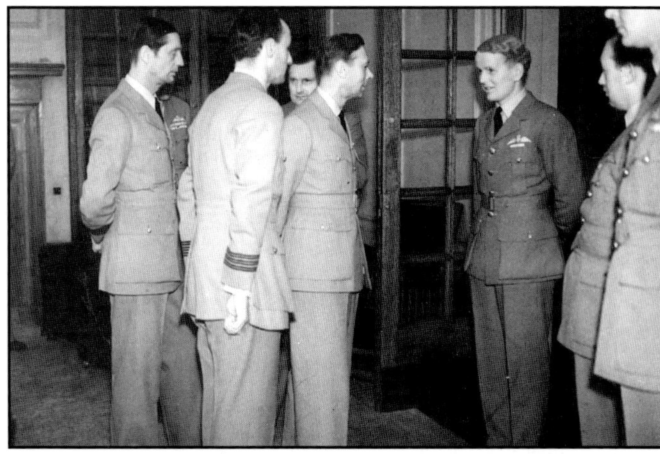

Above: **The King is introduced to John Cunningham.**

By Royal Command

On the night of 7 May 1941 His Majesty King George VI visited No. 604 Squadron at Middle Wallop to see for himself the work of the night fighter units defending Britain in the Blitz. After inspecting the men and aircraft, he moved to the Ground Control Interception Station known as *Starlight*, at Sopley, near Christchurch. Meanwhile Cunningham and Rawnsley had taken off in R2101, coded NG-R, to perform an interception controlled by *Starlight* that would demonstrate the principle to the King. Cunningham intercepted He111 1G+DR of 7./KG27 over Somerset and brought it down at Weston Zoyland. This became known as his 'Royal Command Performance'. Sergeants Wright and Vaughan then took over R2101 and shot down an He111 of 3./ KG55 off Portland. On their return the Beaufighter caught fire and the crew baled out to be rescued from the sea off Bournemouth. If, as is reported, the King, saw an aircraft falling in flames on leaving *Starlight*, it could have been Wright's Beaufighter, not a Luftwaffe raider!

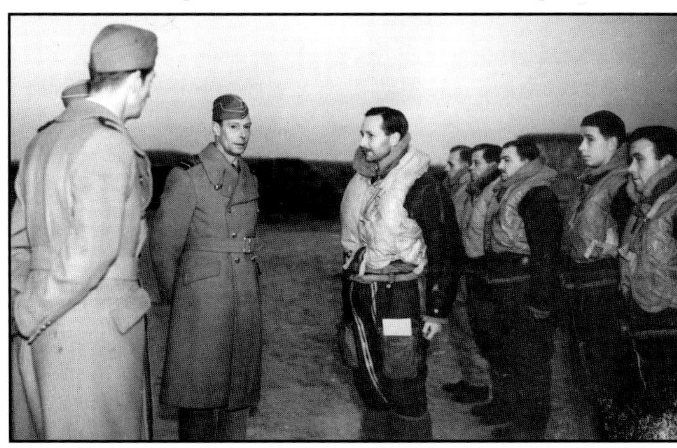

Above: **Aircrew of No. 604 Squadron inspected by the King.**

Below: **The Pheasant Hotel, on the Andover to Salisbury Road near Middle Wallop acted as the Officer's Mess in 1942. The character on the right in the coat is Sergeant Jimmy Rawnsley DFM, Cunningham's Radio Operator.**

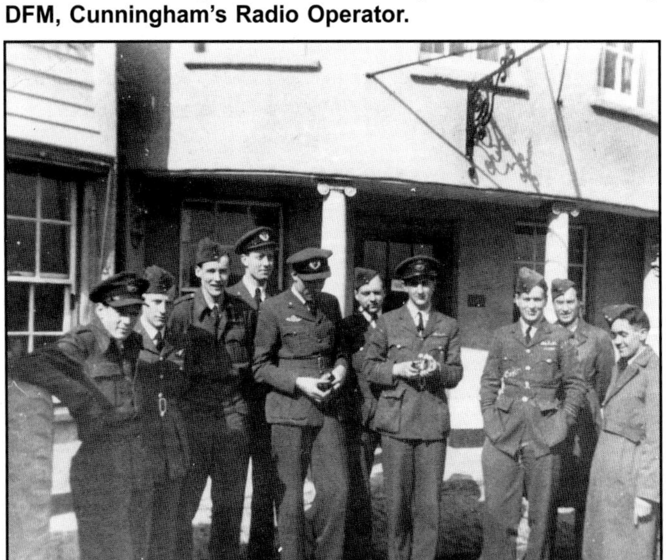

Below: **The King peers into the cockpit of a Beaufighter. These three pictures were taken at night with infra red plates.**

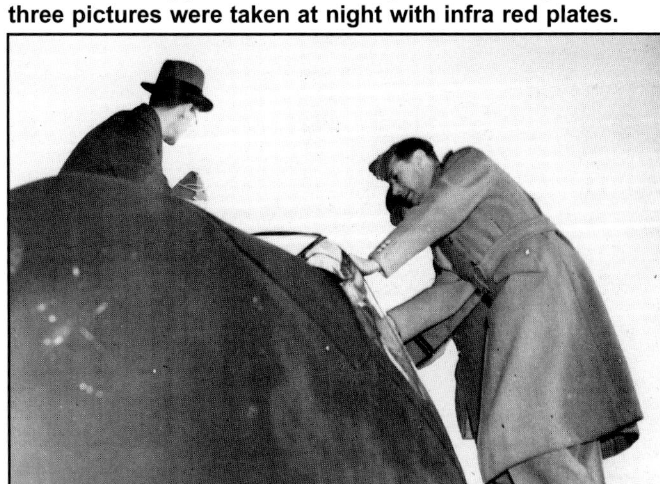

The Night Fighting Legend

John Cunningham was born in 1917 in the London suburb of Croydon and at the age of 18 joined the De Havilland Technical School. He also joined No. 604 Squadron, Auxiliary Air Force, and in 1938 took over as No. 4 Test Pilot from Geoffrey De Havilland. After a time testing 'Long Aerial Mines' in 1940 Cunningham re-joined the now operational night-fighting No. 604 Squadron and began his long association with the Beaufighter. His first claim for an aircraft destroyed was made on the night of 19 November 1940 with Aircraftsman J R Phillipson as his radio operator. The enemy was a Ju88, B3+YL of 3.KG54 which was intercepted over the Midlands and finally crashed near East Wittering, Sussex. This is recorded as the first successful interception by an IA equipped Beaufighter. The press were greatly interested in Cunningham and, apparently in an attempt to conceal from the enemy the presence of airborne interception equipment, the story was 'leaked' that he had phenomenal night vision, 'like a cat'. Thus was born the legend of 'Cat's Eyes Cunning' a sobriquet that John Cunningham detests, but one that stayed with him even after the war had finished.

In Early 1941 Cunningham took on a new radio operator, Sergeant C F Rawnsley, known as 'Jimmy' who had been his gunner in pre-war years when flying Hawker Demons. An association also began with Beaufighter R2101 and the team began to run up an amazing series of night interceptions, making claims for ten He111s destroyed and others damaged. Three He111s were claimed on the night of 15/16 April 1941. On the night of 7/8 may 1941, after his successful combat on the night of the King's visit, Cunningham handed his trusty R2101 to Sergeants Wright and Vaughan. After a successful combat off Portland during which the Beaufighter had taken heavy return fire, it caught fire in the air and it was abandoned.

Cunningham and Rawnsley, now using T4625, carried on their run of success and by June 1941 he had thirteen night victories, becoming the CO of No. 604 Squadron in August 1941. In May 1942 they were both 'rested' from operations, but were back together again in January 1943 when Cunningham was given command of No. 85 Squadron flying Mosquitos. His final total was 20 destroyed, 3 probables, and 7 damaged.

When the war ended Cunningham re-joined De Havillands as a test pilot and became Chief Test Pilot after Geoffrey De Havilland's death. He later tested the Comet and Trident airliners.

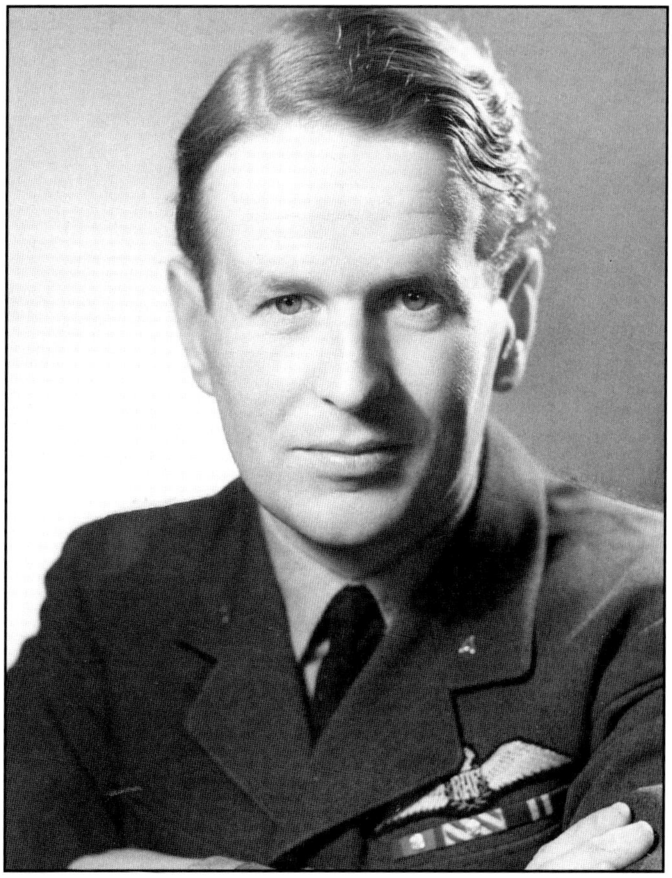

Above: **Group Captain John Cunningham CBE, DSO and 2 Bars, DFC and Bar, OBE, Order of Patriotic War 1st Class (Russian) and US Silver Star.**

Below: **Squadron Leader George McLannahan (Right) and Flight Lieutenant R C 'Bob' Wright with NG-O, T4637.**

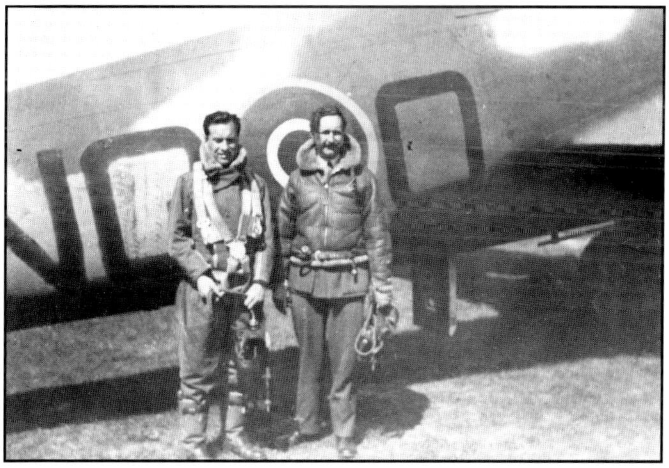

Below: **A radio operator's view of his pilot's head, in this case Squadron Leader McLannahan.**

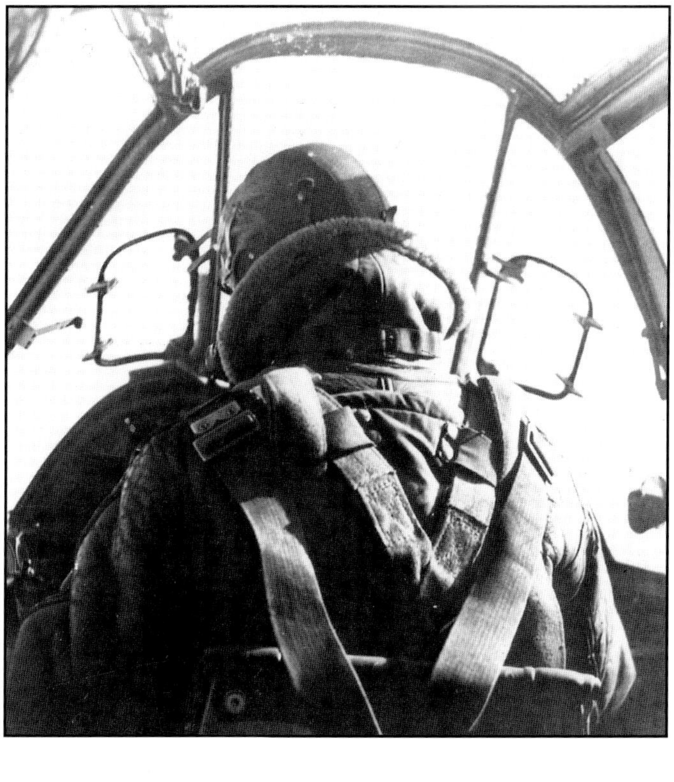

Below: **MM856, a Mk.VIf showing the codes of No. 604 Squadron and with the thimble nose radar.**

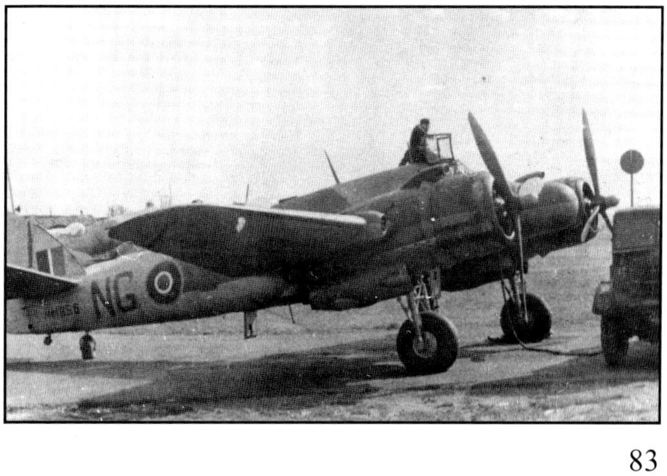

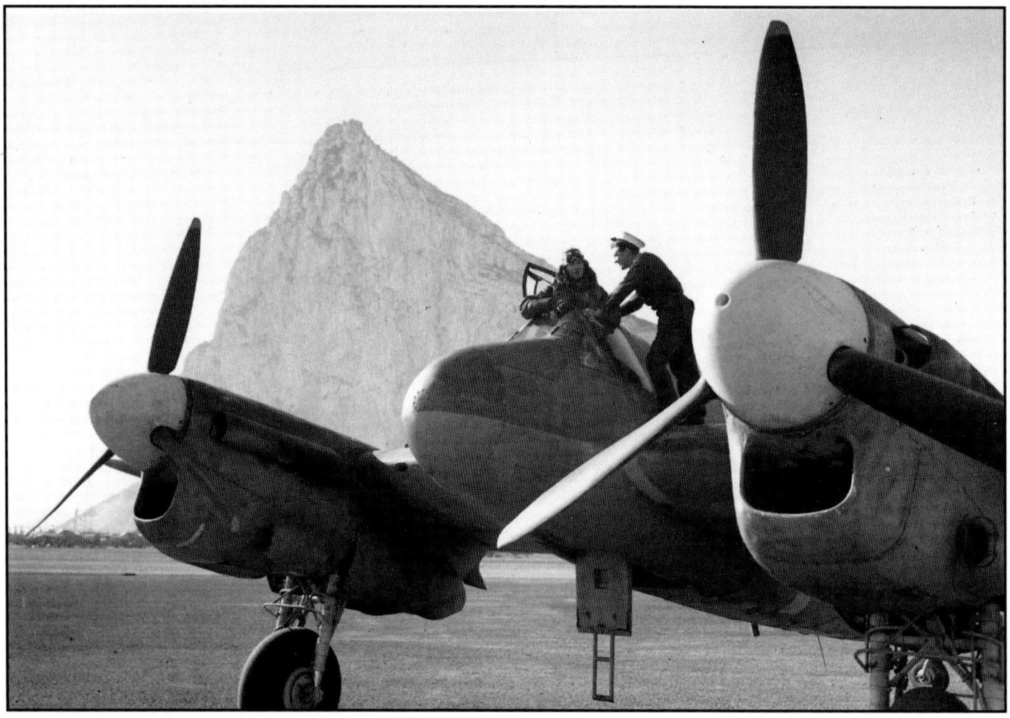

In addition to their use by RAF squadrons, the Fleet Air Arm used Beaufighters with Nos. 721, 723, 775, 779, and 789 Squadrons.

Left: **One of No. 779 (Fleet Requirements Squadron's) Mk.IIs at HMS Cormorant II (Gibralta) The station was commanded by Cdr (A) C E Eckersley-Maslin, RN.**

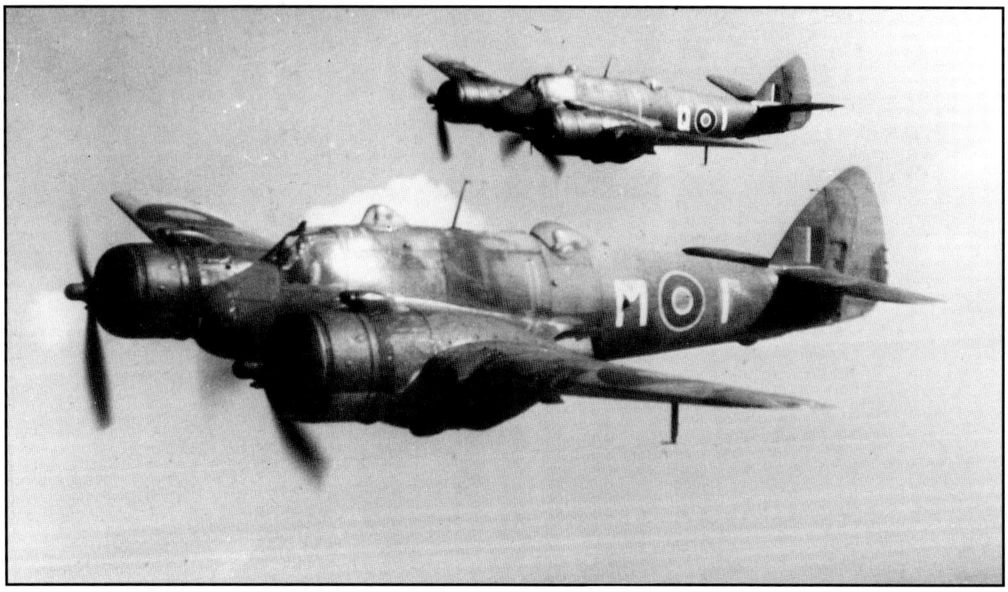

Left: **No.2 (Coastal) OTU at Catfoss, one of many units training crews for operational duties with Beaufighters. Piloting 'M - Mother' is Squadron Leader Randall.**

Below: **One of the post war target towing TT10s showing the wind driven winch on the starboard side of the fuselage.**

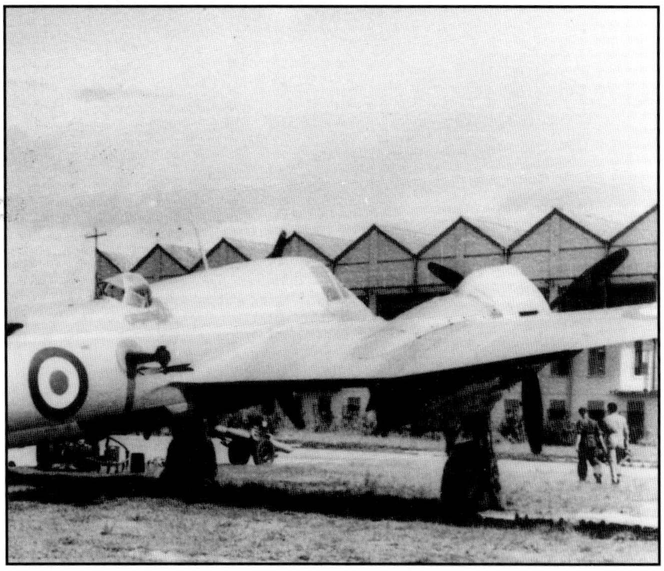

684 SQUADRON

Invisus videns

(Seeing though unseen)

Usage:

Mk.VIc
May 45 - July 45
TF Mk.X
July 45 to July 46

Rôle:

Photo reconnaissance

Bases:

Alipore 5/45 - 7/45

695 SQUADRON

We exercise their arms

Usage:

TT Mk.10
Dec 48 to Feb 49

Rôle:

Target towing

Bases:

Horsham St Faith
12/48 - 2/49

USAAF Beaufighters

Four USAAF Squadrons operated Beaufighters, their aircrews crossing the Atlantic by ship in early 1943. The fully trained pilots were no problem, but a secret training unit in Florida was formed for radio operators. Operational conversion to Beaufighters was done at Cranfield and the AI operators converted to AI Mk.IV at Usworth. The squadrons were Nos. 414, 415, 416, and 417 and all four squadrons were sent to the Middle East Theatre in August 1943 to carry out night fighter operations under the control of the US 12th Army Air Force.

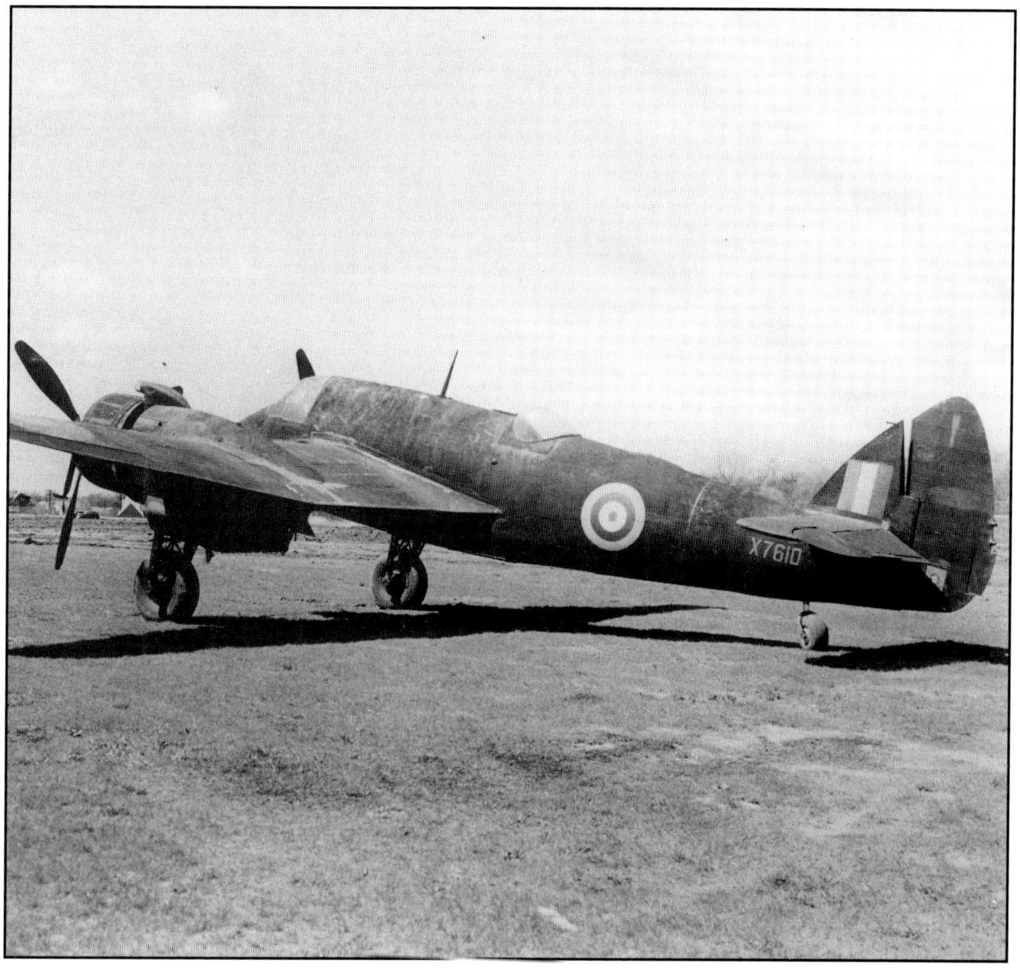

Right: **X7610, a Mk.If, is recorded as being delivered to the USAAF on 10 October 1941 for evaluation.**

Below: Three losses suffered by No. 416 (USAAF) Squadron during training at Acklington. (P Small)

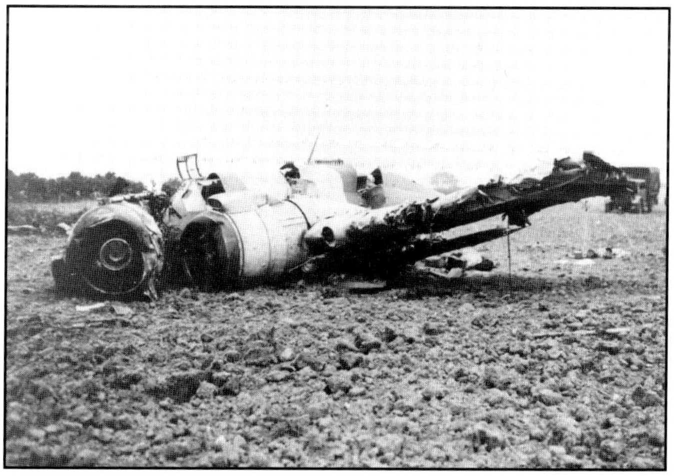

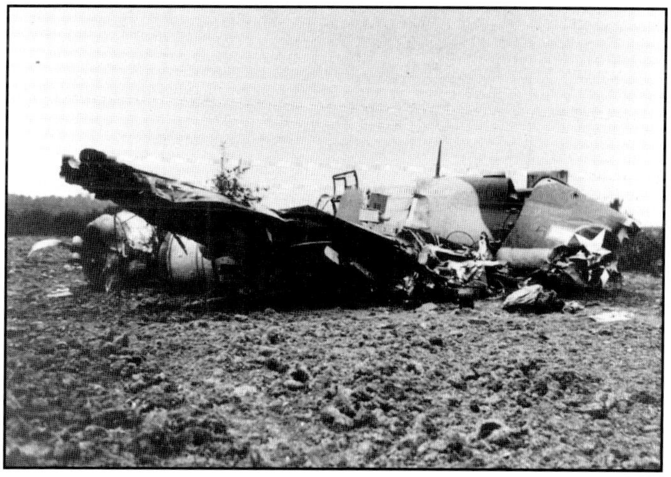

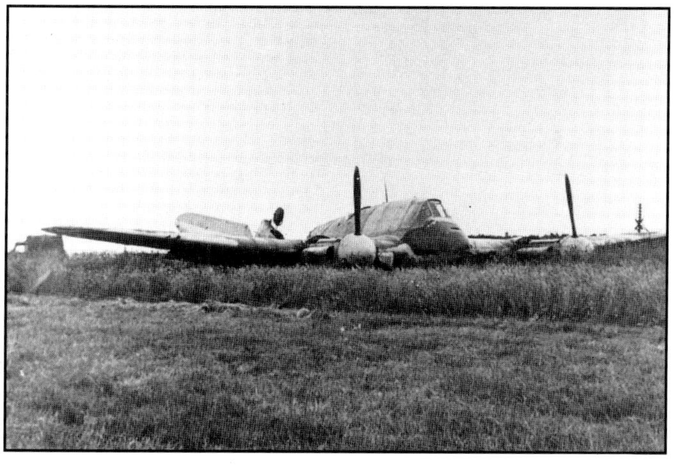

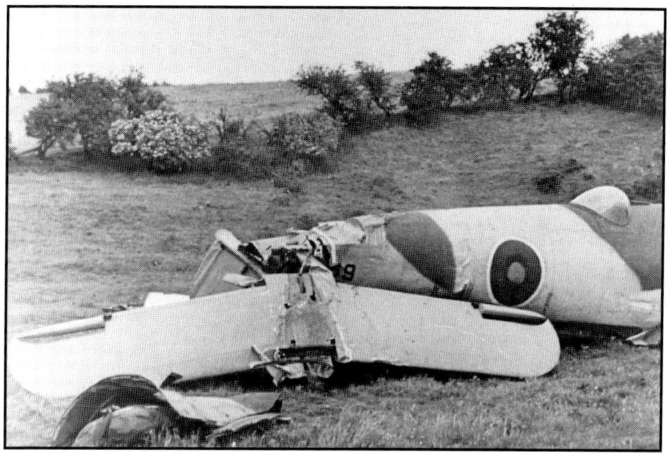

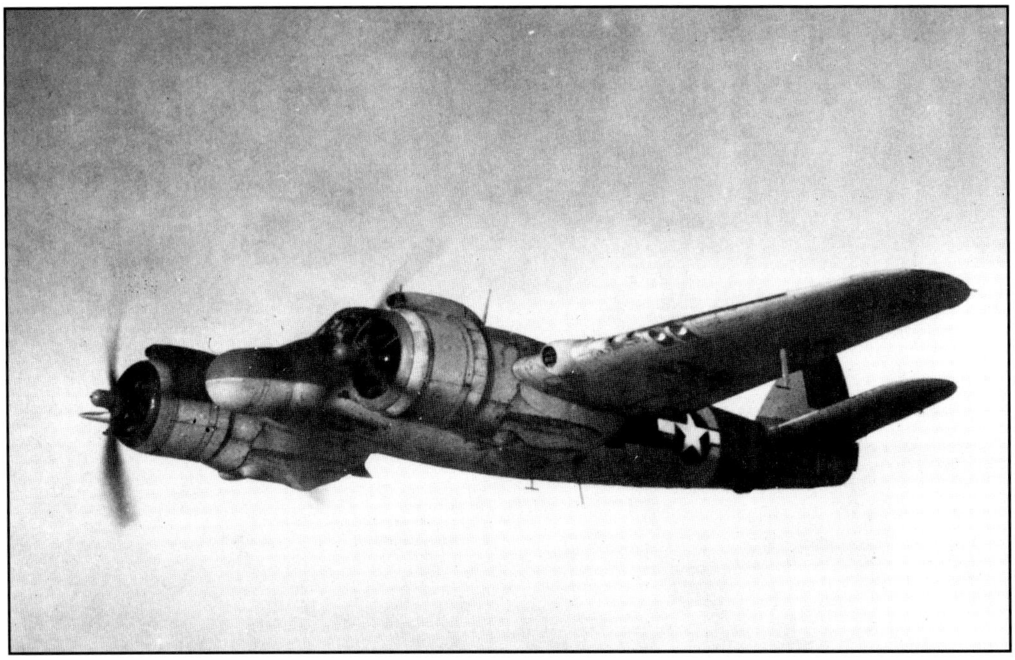

Above: **A Mk.VIf equipped with Mk.VIII AI with No. 417 (USAAF) Squadron at Grottaglie.**

USAAF Beaufighter Operations

414th Night Fighter Squadron. Became operational 10 May 1943. Based at La Senia, Algeria, equipped with Mk.VIf Beaufighters. Replaced Beaufighters with P-61 Black Widows in mid 1944. Total victories - eight.

415th Night Fighter Squadron. Became operational 1 May 1943. Based at La Senia, Algeria, equipped with Mk.VIf Beaufighters. The 415th made the first USAAF Beaufighter 'kill' on 24 July 1943. Replaced Beaufighters with P-61 Black Widows in mid 1944. Total victories - eleven.

416th Night Fighter Squadron. Became operational on 8 August 1943. Based at Algiers, equipped with Mk.VIf Beaufighters. Replaced their Beaufighters with Mosquitos. Total victories - four.

417th Night Fighter Squadron. Became operational on 8 August 1943. Based at Tafaraoui equipped with Mk.VIf Beaufighters. Total victories - nine.

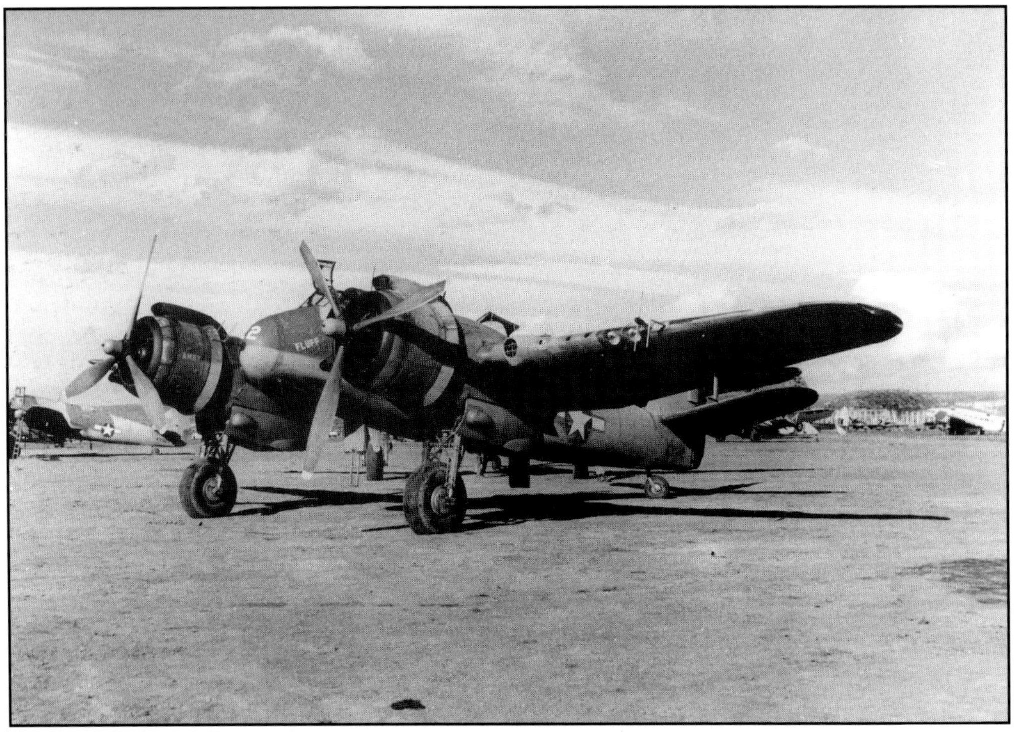

Left: **AI.Mk.IV equipped Beaufighter Mk.VIf KV912 'Fluff' based at Grottaglie photographed on 17 November 1943.**

Below: **The camouflage and unusual rudder trim tabs marks are shown well against the threatening background.**

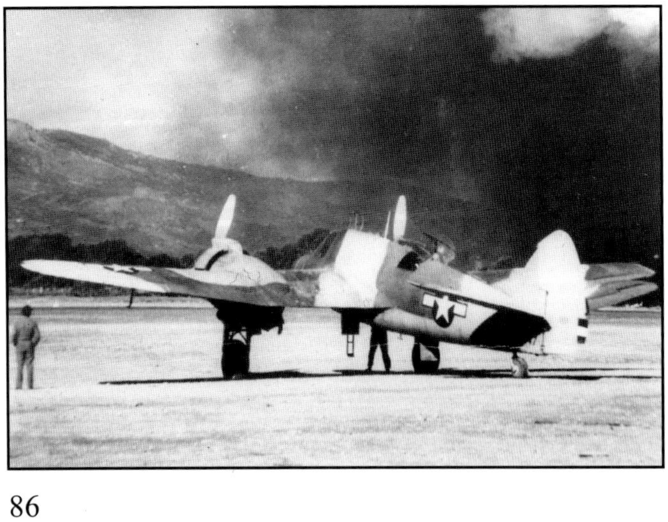

Below: **Taxiing out in the snow is another thimble nosed AI Mk. VIII equipped Mk.VIf.**

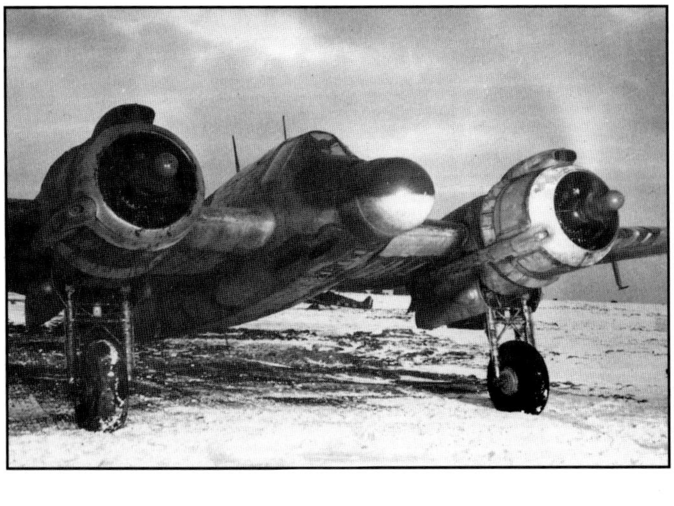

SAAF Beaufighter Operations

No. 16 (SAAF) Squadron

The squadron had served alongside RAF units in the Mediterranean Theatre flying Beauforts and, in line with the RAF squadrons updated to Beaufighter TF Mk.Xs in December 1943. The squadron often operated alongside No. 227 Squadron which was crewed largely with South Africans as well.

No. 19 (SAAF) Squadron

On 11 August 1944, No. 227 Squadron moved to Biferno where it was formally disbanded the following day and the aircraft and personnel formed No. 19 SAAF Squadron.

From August 1944 both squadrons flew as part of the Balkans Air Force, based initially at Biferno in Italy.

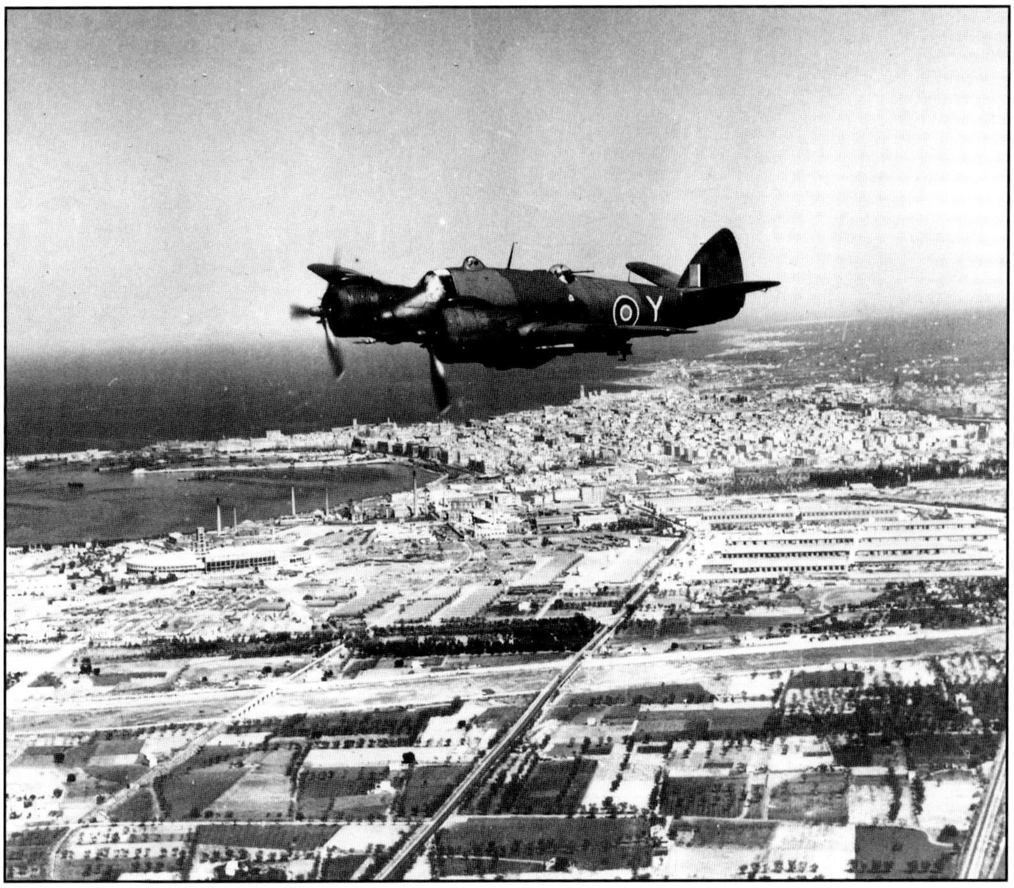

Above: **A Beaufighter TF Mk.X of No.16 South African Air Force over Benghazi.**

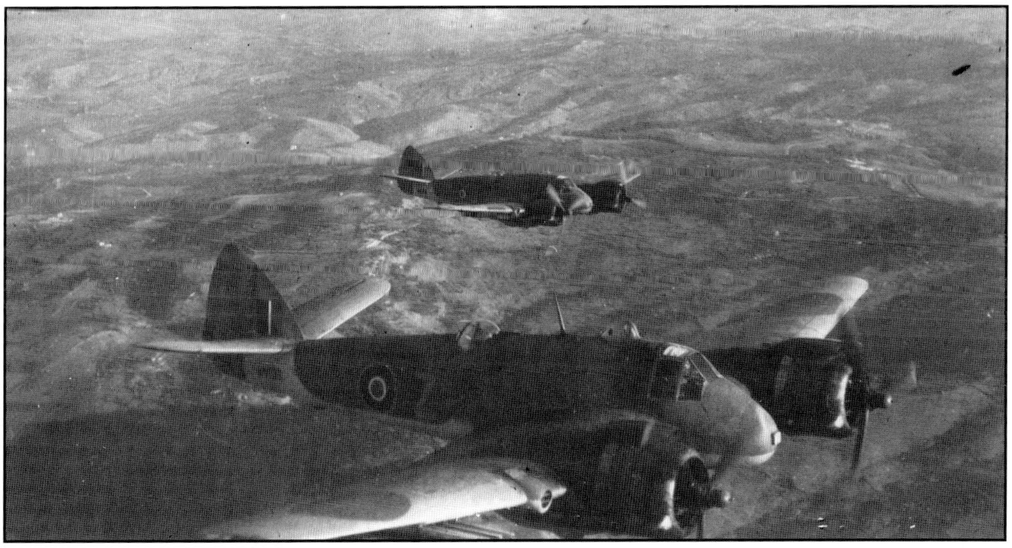

Right: **South African TF Mk.Xs of the Balkan Air Force flying over the hilly terrain of Yugoslavia. Nearest is NV139 'Z - Zebra' a Weston built machine of No. 16 Squadron.**

Below: **The nose art carried on one of No. 16 Squadron's Beaufighters. The ASV Radar aerials are also evident.**

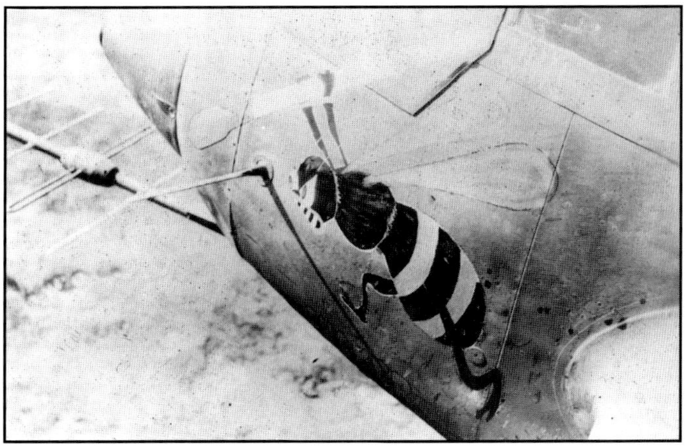

Below: **Rockets from a No. 16 Squadron Beaufighter streak towards the yacht *Kithers* on 15 April 1944.**

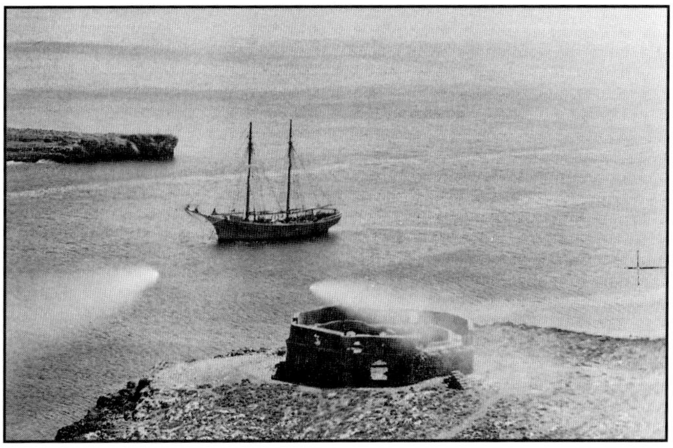

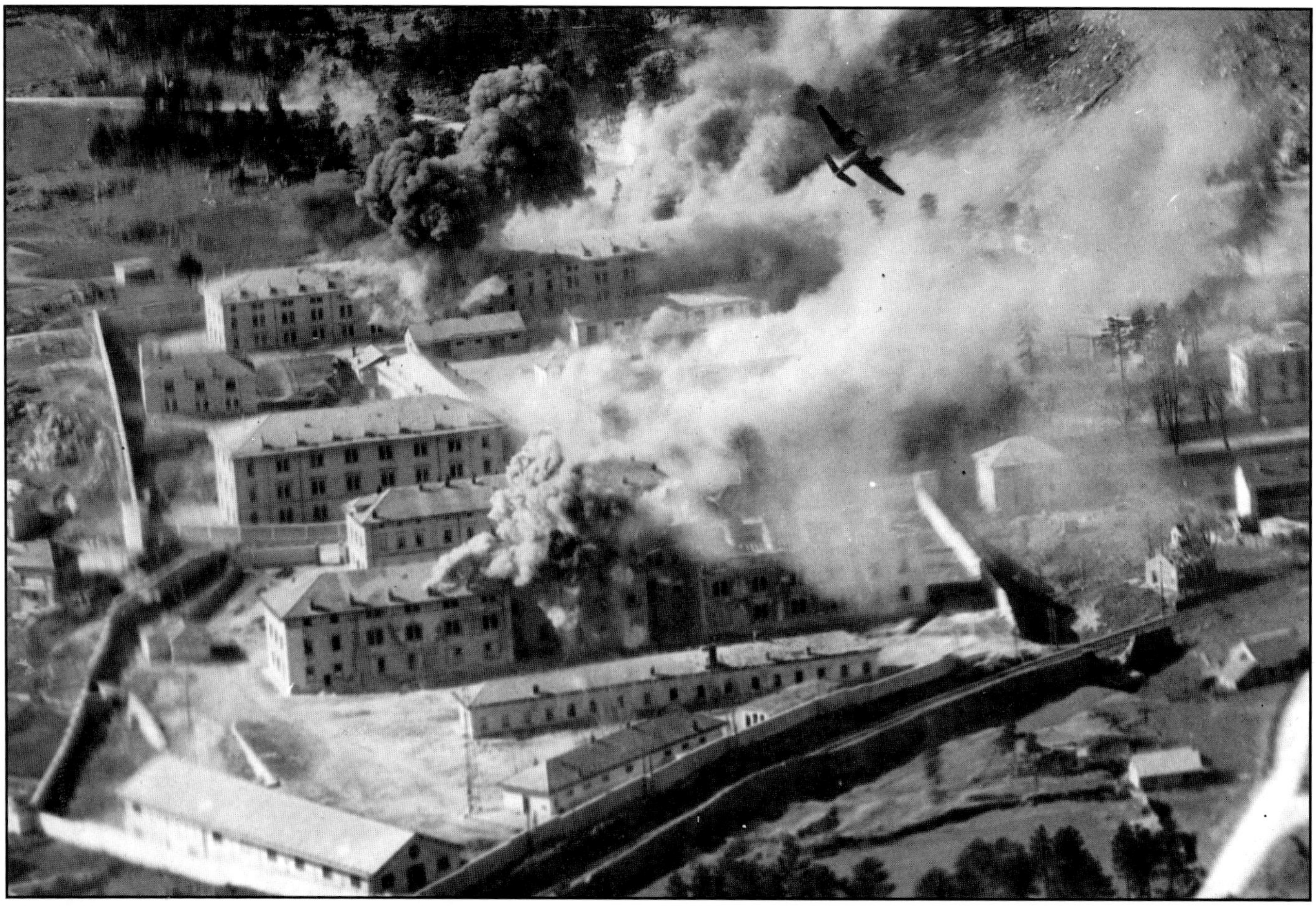

Above: **Attack on German barracks on 23 March 1945. The attack was carried out in support of the Yugoslav National Army of Liberation and scored 84 rocket hits at Postumia, 23 miles east Trieste.**

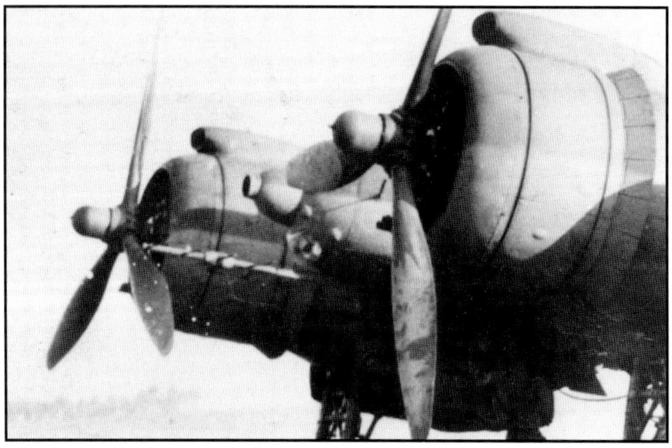

Above: **The nose camera and ASV aerial fitments.**

Below: **The *SS Drache* under attack at Samso in the Aegean, 22 September 1944.**

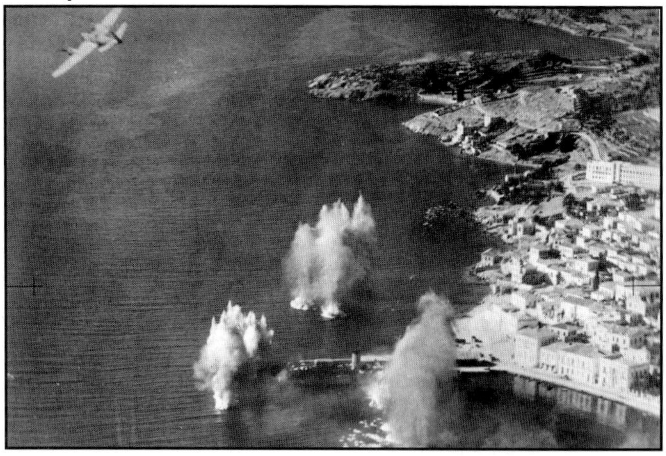

Zuzemberk
13 February 1945

By early 1945 Yugoslavian Partisans were fighting a ground war against the occupying German forces and had come upon a stumbling block at Zuzemberk. The Medieval fortress and the buildings of the small town surrounding it provided a strong defensive position for the German troops and the Partisans made it known to the Balkan Air Force that some air support in the shape of an attack on the town would help them take it. The Yugoslavians had positioned themselves in nearby woodland and would launch an attack when the aircraft arrived.

Four Beaufighter crews of No. 19 (SAAF) Squadron were briefed for the attack to take place on 13 February. The squadron was based at Biferno on the Italian coast and the attack involved a flight across the Adriatic to Yugoslavia, then a difficult navigational exercise over snow covered countryside to the small town. One of the Beaufighter pilots, Staphanus Schonfeldt from Bloemfontein planned to photograph the attack with the idea of getting both the target and a Beaufighter firing its rockets in the same shot.

As the four aircraft approached the target they climbed steeply to 1,000 feet and Schonfeldt manoeuvred close in behind 'K-King' flown by Steve Stevens. Holding position as the Beaufighter ahead nosed over into a dive a hail of spent cannon shells flew back and dented the wings and nose of his aircraft. As the spent shells struck he pressed the camera release button on his control yoke to take a series of exposures at approximately one second intervals, then began his own attack.

The rockets and cannon shells of the four Beaufighters caught the defending forces by surprise and caused confusion in the town that allowed the Yugoslavians on the ground a head start for their attack that was eventually successful. This was one of the many ground support strikes flown by the Balkan Air Force, but is captured forever in Schonfeldt's dramatic photograph reproduced opposite.

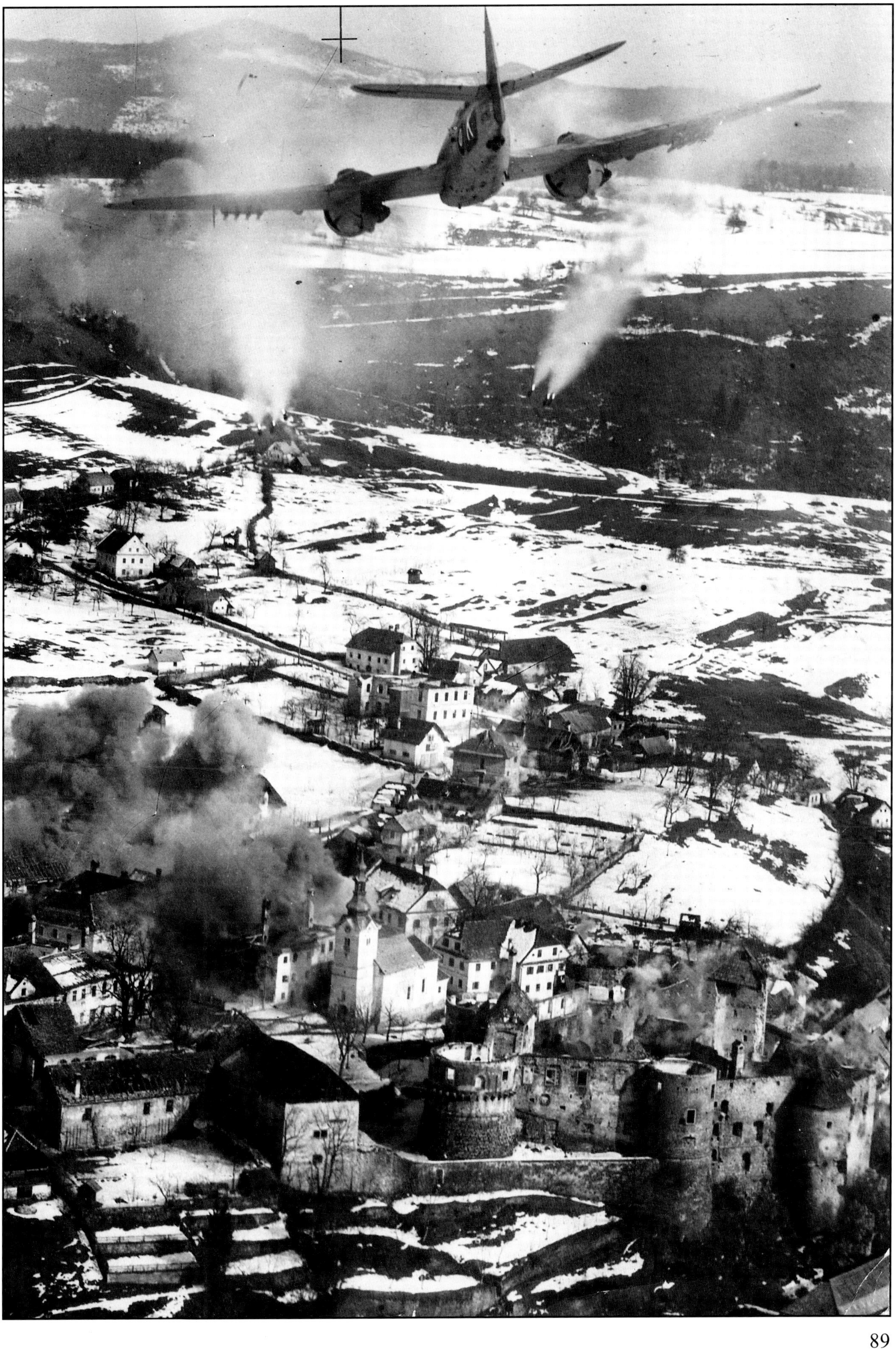

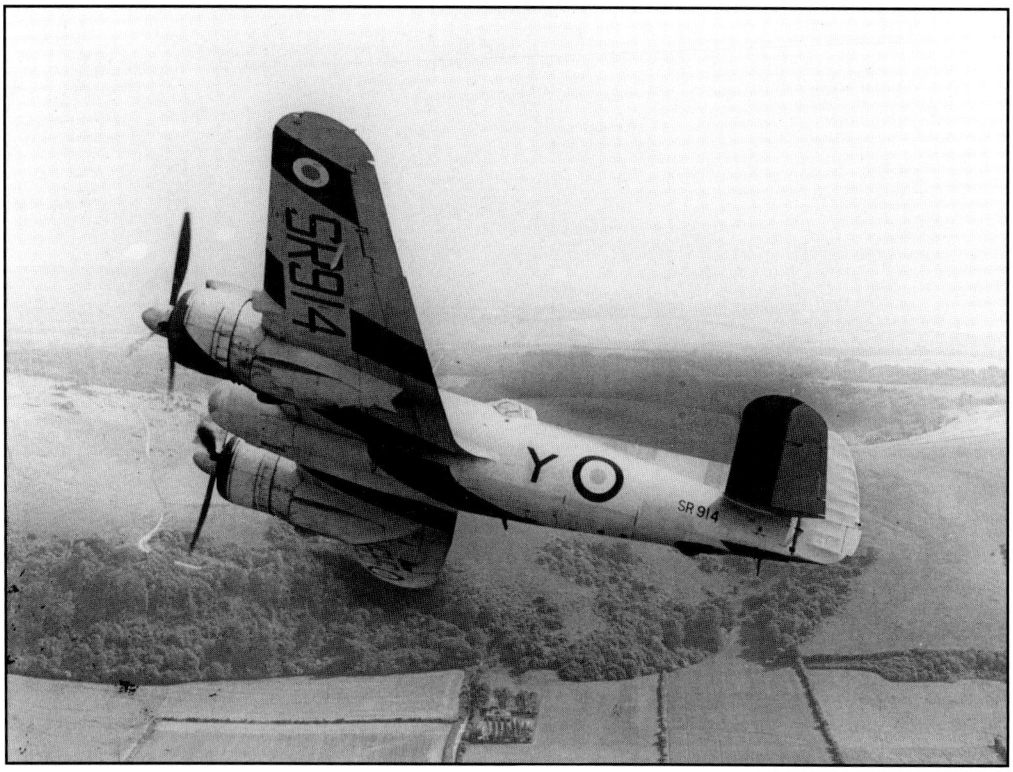

Target Tugs

The last serving Beaufighters were the TT10 target tugs used in Gibraltar, Cyprus, Malta and Malaya. The last RAF unit to fly the Beaufighter was the Seletar Base Flight and the very last flight was flown on 16 May 1960.

Left: **SR914 converted to TT10 specification and photographed in its black and yellow stripes over Somerset.**

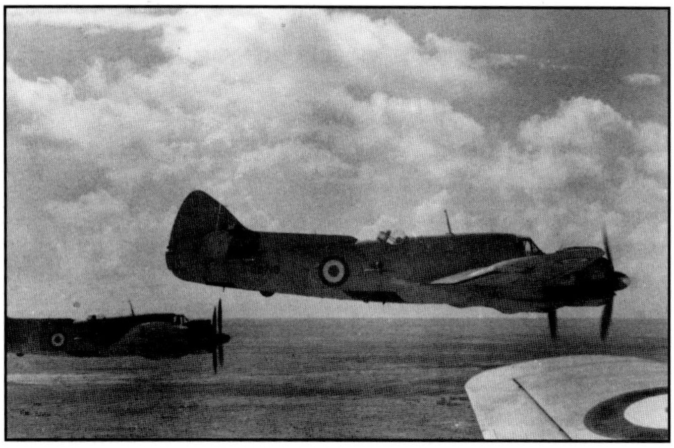

Above: **RD710 one of the TT10s used as target tugs from Shallufa in Egypt until October 1954.**

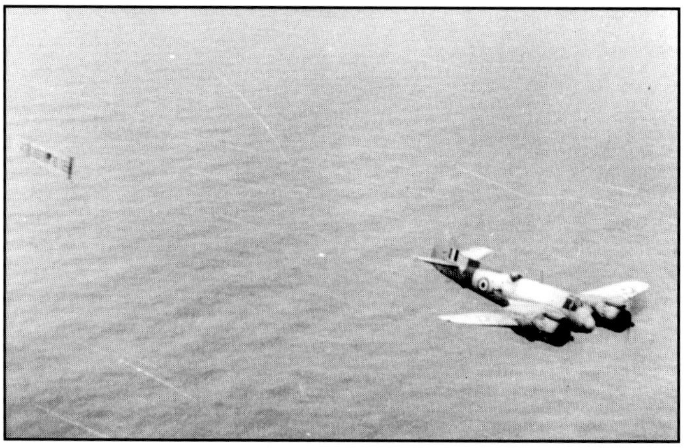

Above: **Target towing from Seletar Base Flight in 1955. (R F Chandler)**

Below: **An unusual view of one of Seletar Base Flight's machines taken in formation over Singapore in 1955. (R F Chandler)**

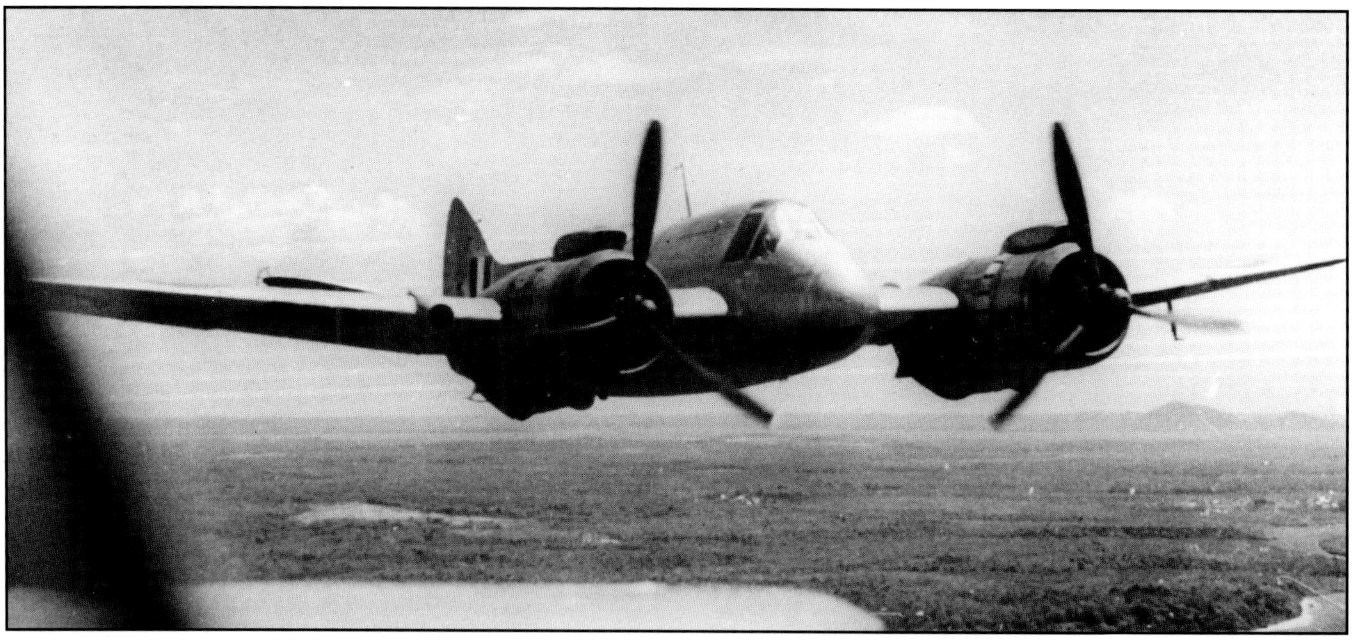

Royal Australian Air Force

The RAAF took an early interest in the Beaufighter to escort its Beauforts in operations against the Japanese in the Pacific. The first fifteen Filton built Mk.Ics arrived in Australia in mid 1942, followed by 57 Fairey built Mk.Ics, 64 Mk.VIcs, 62 TF Mk.Xs and twenty Mk.XIcs. A total of 218 aircraft were delivered, the last arriving in August 1945. The aircraft were allotted serials in the range A19-1 to A19-218.

Australian Production

Beaufighters were also manufactured in Australia by the Department of Aircraft Production at Fishermen's Bend. Bristol copied the drawings required onto 55,000 frames of microfilm and sent them to Australia. The home built Beaufighter was based on the TF Mk.X, fitted with Hercules Mk.XVIII engines supplied from Britain. The Beaufighters built at Fishermen's Bend were designated Mk.21s and allocated serials with an A-8 prefix. 364 Beaufighter Mk.21s were completed at the Fishermen's Bend plant.

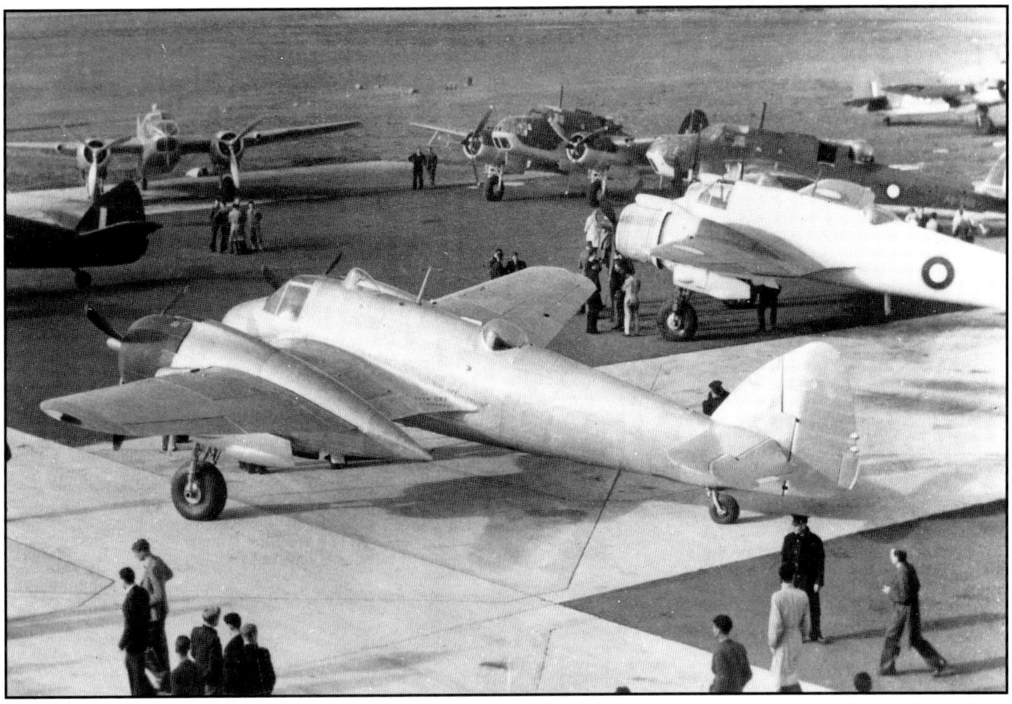

Above: **Department of Aircraft Production at Fishermen's Bend. The unmarked aircraft in front is A-19-2 (RAF serial T4921) that was fitted in Australia with Wright Double Cyclone engines that would have been used if a shortage of Hercules engines from Britain had developed. In the background is LX815, the last British built Beaufighter delivered. (H Shelton)**

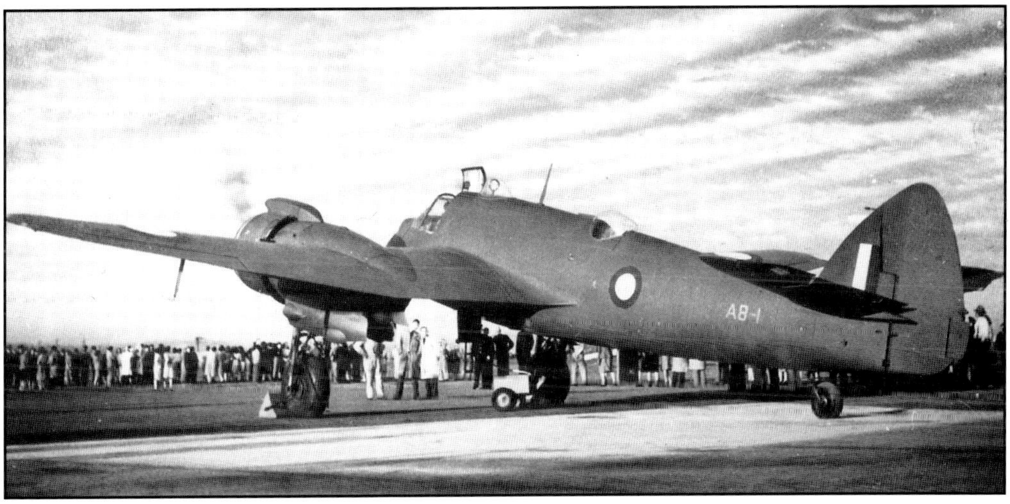

Right: **A8-1, the first Australian built Beaufighter, first flew on 26 May 1944 and later served with No. 1 Air Photo Unit.**

Below: **A8_265 of No. 30 Target Tug Squadron in 1950. This Australian tug wears the usual black and yellow colours.**

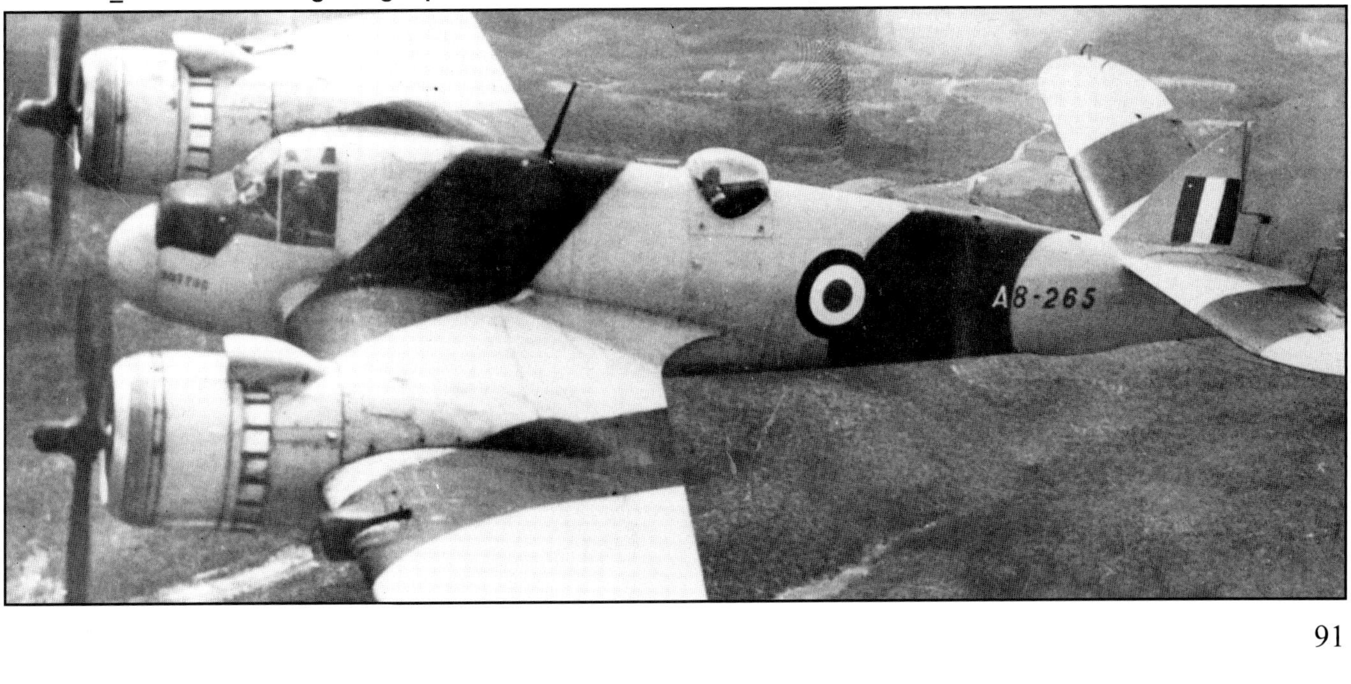

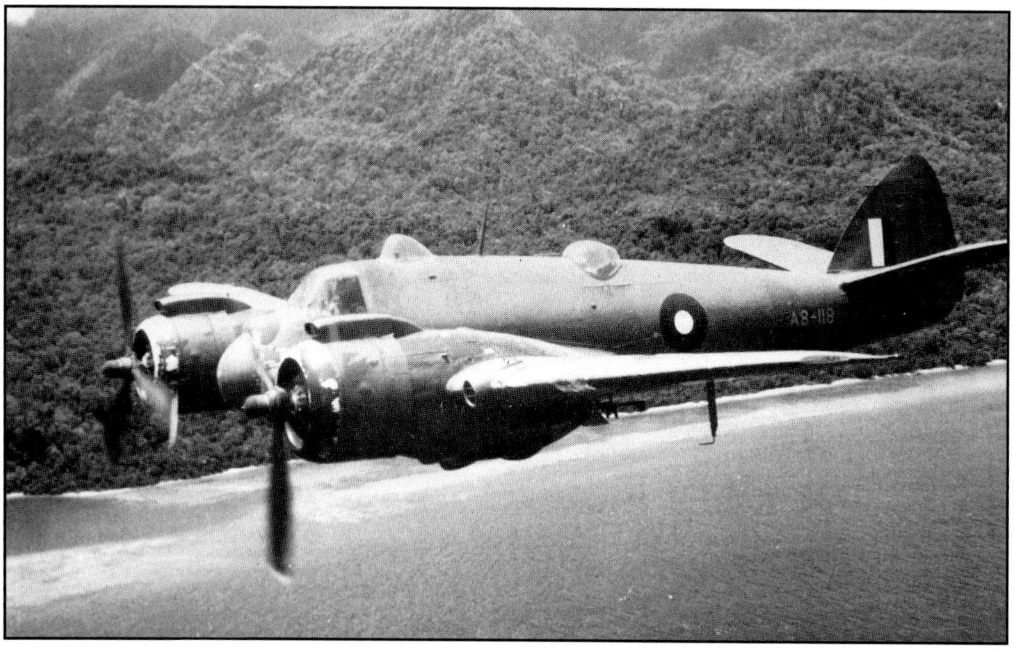

No. 22 Squadron (RAAF)
Code letters - DU
Formed in late 1944 at Noemfoor under the command of Wing Commander C E Woodman. Began operations in February 1945.

Right: **A8-118, Australian built Mk.21 with No. 22 Squadron (K L Collett)**

Below: **Ground crew swarm over a British built Beaufighter during full scale maintenance operations under the baking sun.**

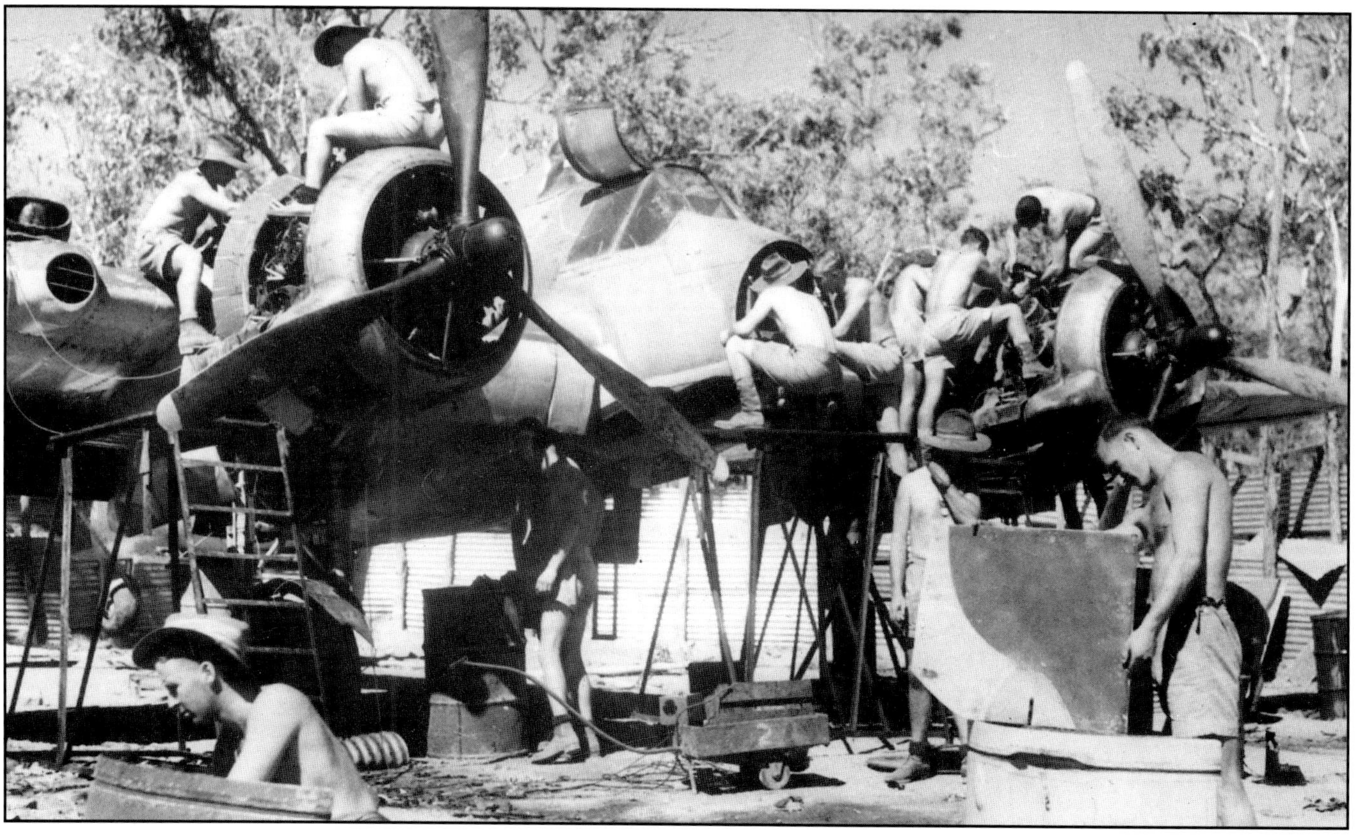

Below: **This Mk.21 of No. 22 Squadron, A8-89, crash landed at Tarakan on 29 June 1945.**

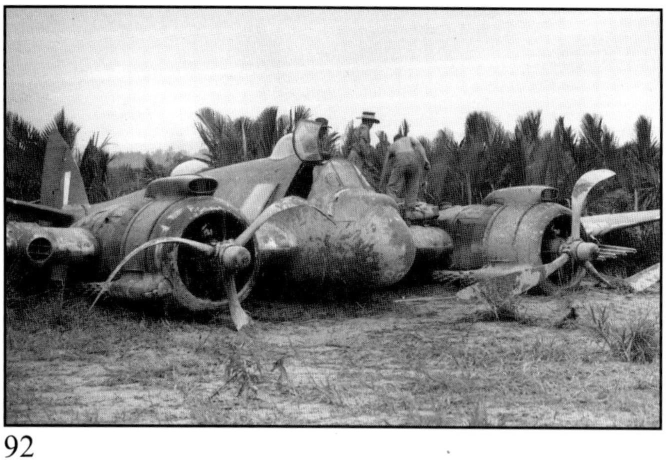

Below: **No. 22 Squadron at Sanga Sanga in the Phillipines in late 1944. Note DU code letters on the fuselages.**

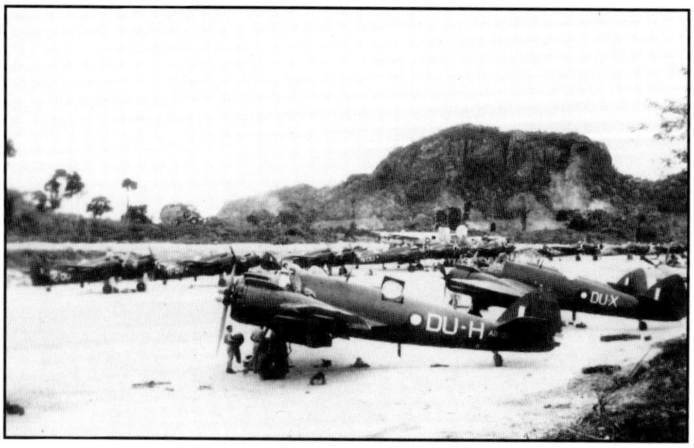

Australian Colours

The British built Beaufighters (A-19 serial prefix) arrived in Australia with standard RAF Coastal Command camouflage colours. When re-painted Dark Green, or Foliage Green, and Dark Brown were used. The underside of all Australian Beaufighters was Sky Type S. A further change was the deletion of the red centre of the roundels, a move decided upon after several Australian aircraft had been attacked by American fighters!

No. 30 Squadron (RAAF)
Code letters - LY
The first RAAF Beaufighter squadron, formed in June 1942 with Mk.Ics under the command of Wing Commander B Walker. Based originally at Port Moresby, the squadron began operations in September 1942 and continued throughout the war, not giving up its aircraft until the 1950s.

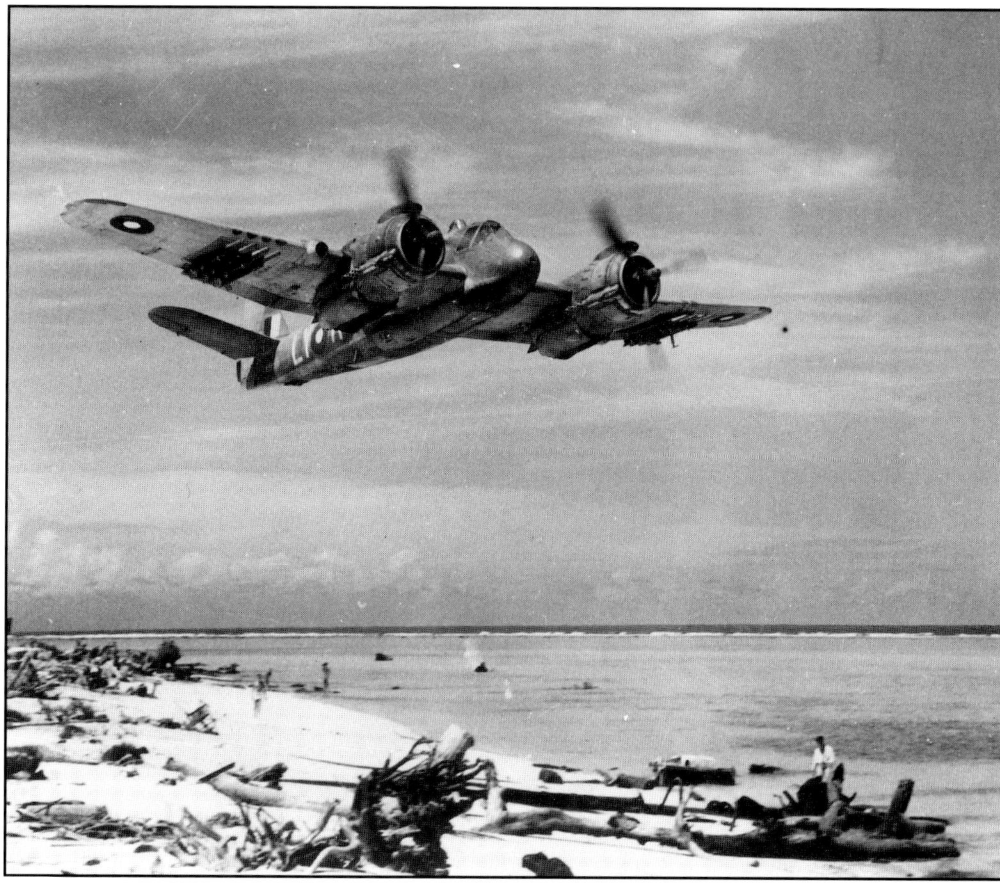

Above: **Low-level work over the Pacific islands was the task for the Australian Beaufighter crews. This No. 30 Squadron machine was photographed on 10 November 1944.**

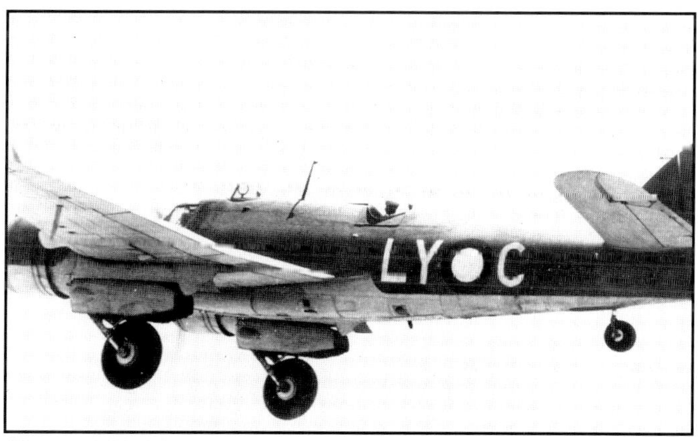

Above: **A19-141 (RAF serial JM168) LY-C, a Mk.XIc with No. 30 Squadron. This machine was lost on 17 December 1943 off Cape Koas.**

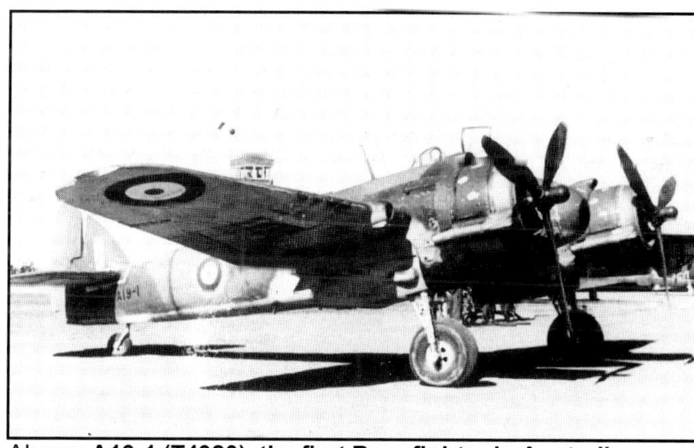

Above: **A19-1 (T4920), the first Beaufighter in Australian service, joined No. 30 Squadron on 27 June 1942. It was lost on 23 September 1942 when hit by AA fire in attack on Buna.**

Below: **No. 30 Squadron at Wama Strip, Morotai in 1945.**

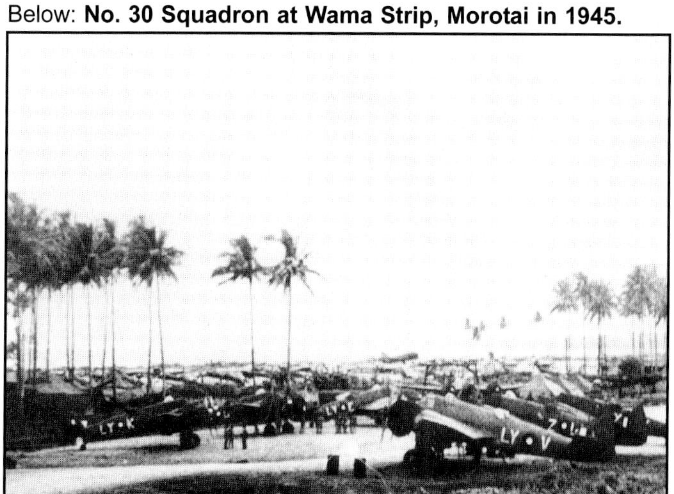

Below: **Servicing with No. 30 Squadron, 26 December 1943.**

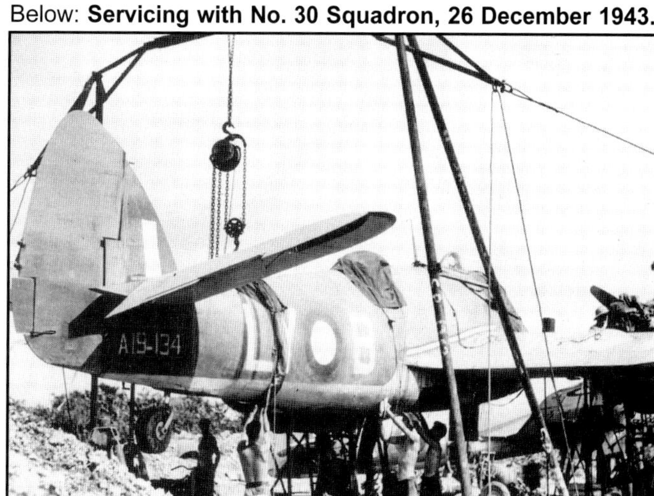

Right: **Men of No. 31 Squadron stationed at Coomalie Creek, Northern Territory, on 20 January 1943. The aircraft is Mk.Ic A19-56 (RAF serial T5081).**

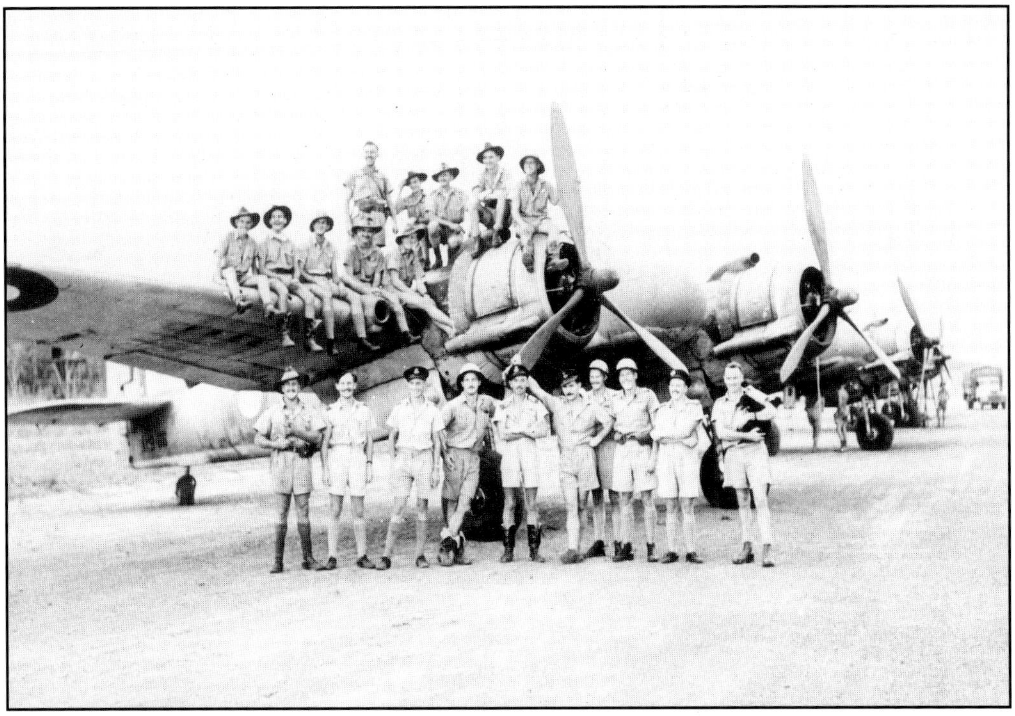

No. 31 Squadron (RAAF)
Code letters - EH
The second RAAF Beaufighter squadron, formed in August 1942 with Mk.Ics at Coomalie Creek. The squadron's first operation was in November 1942 and it continued with Beaufighters until the end of hostilities in the Pacific.

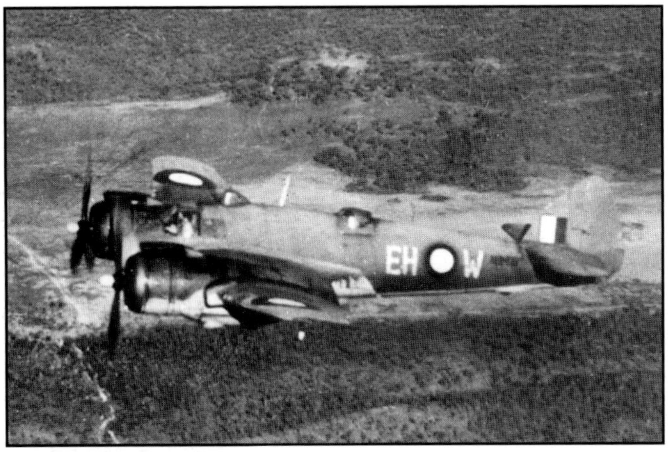

Above: **Mk.VIc A19-118, of No. 31 Squadron was lost attacking Taberfane on 24 July 1943. The British, Dark Green / Dark Earth / Sky finish, is carried with pale grey codes and a black serial number. The huge upper wing roundels are clear.**

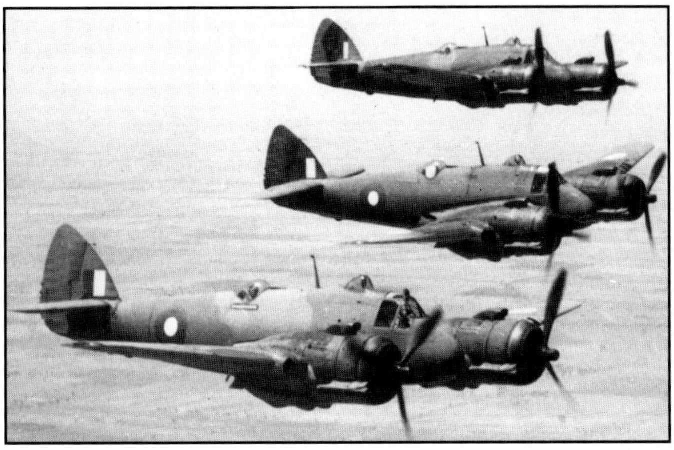

Above: **On 23 December 1942 No. 31 Squadron moved from Coomalie to Timor.**

Below: **No. 31 Squadron in 1943, with A-19-18 in foreground.**

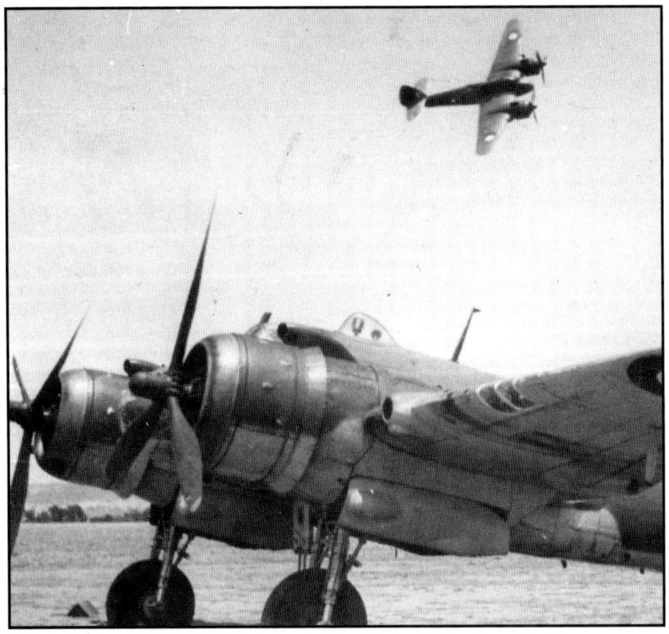

Below: **One of No. 31 Squadron's Mk.21s makes a landing between the airfield construction machinery at Balikpapan on 15 July 1945.**

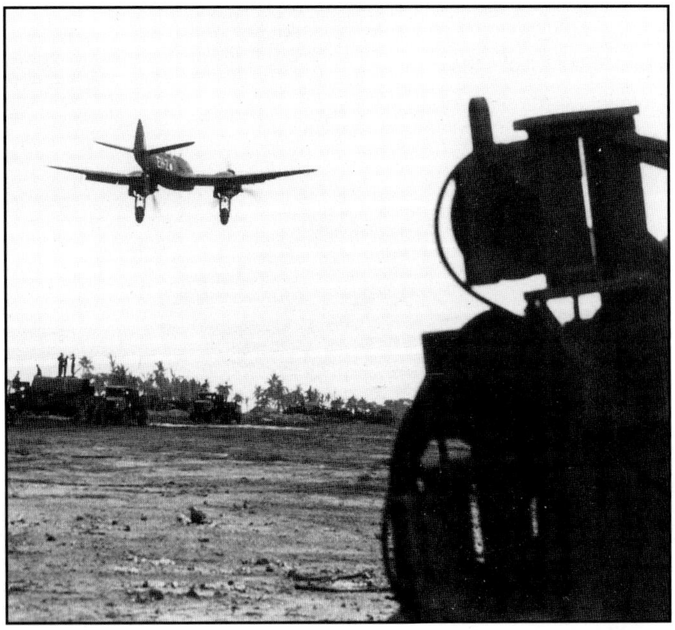

No. 93 Squadron (RAAF)
Code letters - SK
Last of the four RAAF Beaufighter squadrons, it formed at Kingaroy in January1942 under Wing Commander D Gulliver. Operations did not begin until June 1945 by which time the squadron had moved to Labuan. Only two operations were conducted before the end of hostilities and one aircraft lost. The squadron continued to fly its Beaufighters after the war.

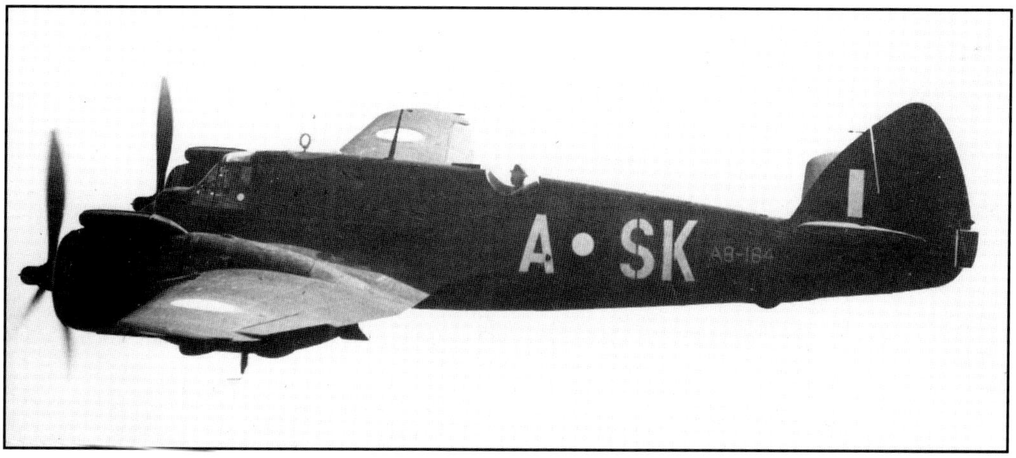

The commanding officer of A Flight, No. 93 Squadron, Squadron Leader McLeod flying the Australian built Mk.21, A8-164.

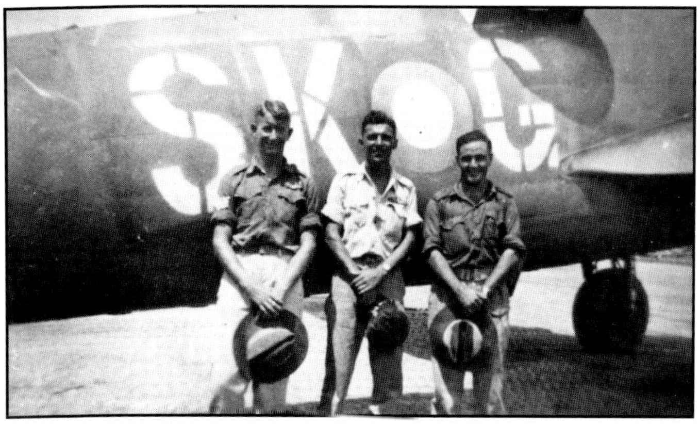

Above: **A8-13, SK-G, of No. 93 Squadron at Tarakan with stencil style codes.**

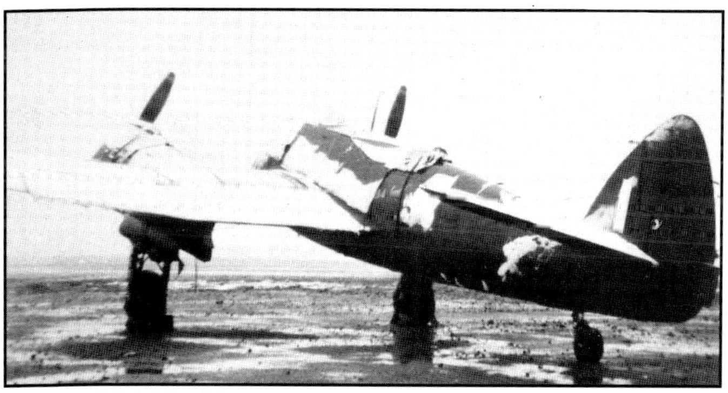

Above: **A8-327 of No. 93 Squadron in the snow at Iwakuni, Japan in March 1946.**

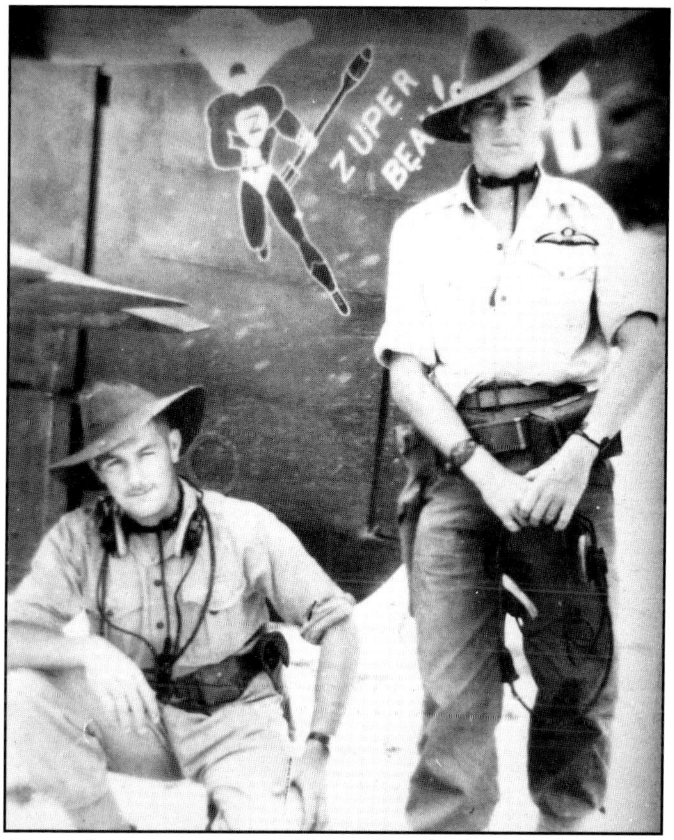

Above: **A new super hero - 'Zuper Beau' otherwise known as A8-133 SK-Z. The aircraft itself was named 'Shirley Faye'.**

Below: **A8-327 showing the bulge for the autopilot.**

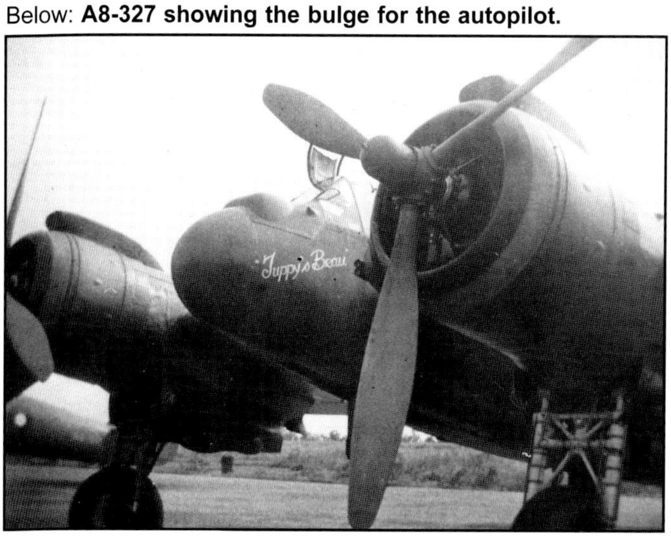

Below: **8-129 at Labuan 16 August 1945. The crew survived.**

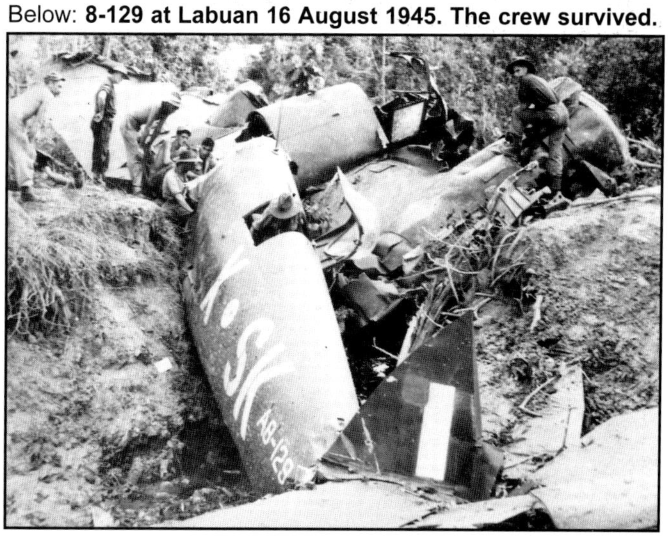

Squadrons / Codes	
5	None
17	None
20	None
22	OA
25	ZK
27	None
29	RO
34	8Q
39	None
42	QM
45	OB
46	None
47	None
68	WM
69	None
84	None
89	None
96	ZJ
125	VA
141	TW
143	HO
144	PL
153	TB
176	None
177	None
211	UQ
217	MW
219	FK
227	None
235	LA
236	MB
248	WR
252	PN & BT
254	QM
255	YD
256	JT
272	None
285	VG
287	KZ
288	RP
307	EW
404 RCAF	EE
406 RCAF	HU
409 RCAF	KP
410 RCAF	RA
455 RAAF	UB
456 RAAF	RX
488 RNZAF	ME
489 RNZAF	P6
515	None
600	BQ
603	XT
604	NG
684	None
695	None

Codes / Squadrons	
BQ	600
BT	252
EE	404 RCAF
EW	307
FK	219
HO	143
HU	406 RCAF
JT	256
KP	409 RCAF
KZ	287
LA	235
MB	236
ME	488 RNZAF
MW	217
NG	604
OA	22
OB	45
PL	144
PN	252
P6	489 RNZAF
QM	254
QM	42
RA	410 RCAF
RO	29
RP	288
RX	456 RAAF
TB	153
TW	141
UB	455 RAAF
UQ	211
VA	125
VG	285
WM	68
WR	248
XT	603
YD	255
ZJ	96
ZK	25
8Q	34

Beaufighter Strike Wings

North Coates
236 Squadron (November 1942 to May 1945)
254 Squadron (November 1942 to May 1945)
143 Squadron (December 1942 to Oct 1945)

Wick
144 Squadron (October 1943 to May 1944)
404 Squadron (October 1943 to May 1944)

Leuchars
455 Squadron (March 1944 to April 1944)
489 Squadron (March 1944 to April 1944)

Langham
455 Squadron (April 1944 to October 1944)
489 Squadron (August 1944 to October 1944)

Davidstow Moor
144 Squadron (May 1944 to July 1944)
404 Squadron (May 1944 to July 1944)

Strubby
144 Squadron (July 1944 to September 1944)
404 Squadron (July 1944 to September 1944)

Banff
144 Squadron (September 1944 to October 1944)
404 Squadron (September 1944 to October 1944)
Nos. 143, 235, and 248 Squadrons made up the Banff Wing with Mosquitos.

Dallachy
144 Squadron (October 1944 to May 1945)
404 Squadron (October 1944 to March 1945)
455 Squadron (October 1944 to May 1945)
489 Squadron (October 1944 to May 1945)

Coastal Command and its single number codes.

In August 1943 Coastal Command broke away from the standard two letter codes and adopted a single number system. The rational of this is difficult to understand. The idea was to identify a squadron on a particular station rather than the squadron itself. This is particularly relevant for Strike Wings where several Beaufighter squadron might operate together. The first squadron of Beaufighters on a station would not carry a code number at all, but if a second Beaufighter squadron arrived at the same station it would carry the number 2, and the original squadron the letter 1. The third Beaufighter squadron would carry the number 3 and so on. If, however, a squadron was operating a different type, lets say Beauforts, at the same station, the system would begin again for that type. Confusing enough for a single airfield, but each had its own squadrons carrying the letters 1, 2, 3 and so on, and when the squadrons moved the numbers were juggled as they arrived and departed. Confusion reigned, not just to the enemy, but to everyone involved. The system was scrapped in July 1944 and the standard two digit codes issued to the squadrons.